THE
ADVANCED
GRAMMAR
BOOK

THE ADVANCED GRAMMAR BOOK

Jocelyn Steer
American Language Institute
San Diego State University

Karen Carlisi
American Language Institute
San Diego State University

Heinle & Heinle Publishers
A Division of Wadsworth, Inc.
Boston, Massachusetts 02116 U.S.A.

For permission to use copyrighted material, grateful acknowledgment is made to copyright holders on page v, which are hereby made part of this copyright page.

Director: Laurie E. Likoff
Full-Service Manager: Michael Weinstein
Production Coordinator: Cynthia Funkhouser
Text Design: Book Builders Incorporated
Cover Design: Caliber Design Planning
Photo Research: Book Builders Incorporated
Text Illustration: Book Builders Incorporated
Production: Book Builders Incorporated
Compositor: Bookworks
Printer and Binder: Malloy Lithographing

The Advanced Grammar Book

Library of Congress Cataloging-in-Publication Data

Steer, Jocelyn.
    The advanced grammar book / Jocelyn Steer, Karen Carlisi.
        p.   cm.
    Includes index.
    1. English language—Grammar—1950–   2. English language—
Textbooks for foreign speakers.   I. Carlisi, Karen.   II. Title.
PE1112.S73   1991
428.2′4—dc20   91-10669
                                                                                      CIP

ISBN 0-8384-2666-2

94 93   9 8 7 5 4 3

TEXT CREDITS

p. 2: Excerpt from "The Business of a Cadillac in America" by Linda Ellerbee. Copyright © 1989 and reprinted by permission of the author. **p. 124:** "Author Votes for Nature Over Nurture" by Lee Dembart. © 1989 by Lee Dembart and reprinted from the *Los Angeles Times*. **p. 211:** "Fast Food and Nutrition" by Connie Roberts, M.D., excerpted from material originally appearing in NEW ENGLAND JOURNAL OF MEDICINE, 1989, v. 32, no. 11, p. 30. **p. 225:** "Small Talk—Conversation or Giant Bore?" by Andy Rooney, Copyright © 1990. Reprinted by permission: Tribune Media Services. **p. 229:** Excerpts from "Happy New Year" by Ellen Goodman, © 1989 The Boston Globe Newspaper Company/Washington Post Writers Group. Reprinted with permission. **p. 231:** "U.S. Visitors Tripping on Our Way of Tipping" by Sehyon Joh. © 1989 and reprinted with permission of Associated Press. **p. 239:** Excerpted from "I Have a Dream" speech by Martin Luther King, Jr. Reprinted by permission of Joan Daves. Copyright © 1963 by Martin Luther King, Jr. **p. 288:** From *Linda Goodman's Sun Signs*, © 1968 by Linda Goodman. Reprinted by permission of Taplinger Publishing Co., Inc. **p. 319:** Excerpted from "Country Music" by Ellen Goodman. Copyright © 1986, The Boston Globe Newspaper Company/Washington Post Writers Group. Reprinted with permission. **p. 342:** Excerpted from "Elixirs of Youth" by Ann Guidici Fettner and Pamela Weintraub in OMNI, v. 9, Oct. 1986, p. 60. **p. 350:** Excerpted from "In the Battle Against Aging, We Forsake Grace for a Larger Arsenal of Weapons" by Ellen Goodman. Copyright © 1988, The Boston Globe Newspaper Company/Washington Post Writers Group. Reprinted with permission. **p. 357:** Excerpted from "Voluntary Simplicity" by Duane Elgin in WHOLISTIC LIVING NEWS, Dec. 1989, p. 7. **p. 383:** Excerpted from "A Union for Peace and Survival" by Dawna Nolan in WHOLISTIC LIVING NEWS, Dec. 1989, pp. 8-9.

ART CREDITS

pp. 19, 47, 60, 76, 161, 250, 333, 371, 374: Alexander Bloch. **p. 23:** © Michael Philip Manheim/Photo Researchers, Inc. **p. 34:** "Mister Boffo" by Joe Martin. Reprinted by permission of Tribune Media Services. **p. 42:** © The Photo Works/Photo Researchers, Inc. **p. 55:** © Bob Fitch/Black Star **p. 69:** "Peanuts" by Charles Schultz. Copyright © 1988. Reprinted by permission of UFS, Inc. **p. 73:** "Dennis the Menace" ® used by permission of Hank Ketcham and © by North America Syndicate. **pp. 82, 290:** UPI/BETTMANN. **p. 87:** © Laimute E. Druskis/Photo Researchers, Inc. **pp. 92, 204, 208:** Art Glazer. **p. 96:** "The Neighborhood" by Jerry Van Amerongen, © 1988, King Features. Reprinted by permission. **p. 99:** "Ramirez," 1989. Reprinted with permission of Copley News Service. **p. 106:** Mimi Forsyth/MONKMEYER. **p. 135:** © Robert Goldstein 1982/Photo Researchers, Inc. **pp. 138, 147:** UPI/BETTMANN NEWSPHOTOS. **p. 149:** Photo Researchers, Inc. **p. 186:** © 1990 Larry Molvehill/Photo Researchers, Inc. **p. 198:** © Spencer Grant/Photo Researchers, Inc. **214:** Vivienne della Grotta/Photo Researchers, Inc. **p. 231:** Lew Merrin/ MONKMEYER. **pp. 238, 273, 303:** © Beryl Goldberg. **p. 247:** © Sam C. Pierson, Jr. **p. 260:** Vivienne della Grotta/Photo Researchers, Inc. and © Moore & Moore Publishing/ Superstock. **p. 274:** "FOX TROT" COPYRIGHT 1989, UNIVERSAL PRESS SYNDI-CATE. Reprinted with permission. All rights reserved. **pp. 306, 380:** © Tom McHugh/Photo Researchers, Inc. **p. 310:** "Punch" by Nay. Reprinted with permission of the New York Times Syndications Sales Corporation. **p. 321:** "Andy Capp" reprinted with special permission of North America Syndicate, Inc. **p. 322:** © C. Capa/Magnum. **p. 356:** © Bill Bachman 1990/Photo Researchers, Inc. **p. 373:** "Marmaduke" by Brad Anderson. Copyright 1989. United Media, reprinted by permission of UFS, Inc.

CONTENTS

Chapter 3: HAVING MORE FUN   42

Chapter 4: MAKING IT!   55

Chapter 7: MAKING A DIFFERENCE   138

Chapter 8: MAKING CHOICES   161

Chapter 9: HEALTH AND FITNESS II   198

Chapter 10: AMERICAN CULTURE II   214

Chapter 11: THE SPIRIT OF AMERICA   238

Chapter 12: DATING AND MARRIAGE   260

PREFACE

TO THE TEACHER

The Advanced Grammar Book is intended for the high level ESL student who has a solid foundation in the fundamentals of English grammar. This text provides the student with a sophisticated analysis of the grammatical structures of English and ample opportunity to practice using them, with the objective of increasing the student's competence in both conversational and written English. The text is designed for both pre-university and non-academic students and as such includes a variety of exercises to develop oral and written competence, allowing the instructor to select those exercises that best suit the needs of a particular class.

The features that contribute to the text's effectiveness are: theme-based grammatical presentation and practice; inductive exercises; well-organized, thorough charts for presentation of the grammatical structures; special notes which focus on exceptions and related structures; a special problems section in each chapter to focus on common errors produced when using the target structure; and the use of cartoons and authentic material.

FORMAT AND CONTENT OF CHAPTERS

The book is divided into fifteen chapters that are self-contained yet ordered with some consideration of grammatical sequence; for example, the verb section precedes the passives. Nevertheless, an instructor could teach the chapters in the order that would best satisfy the needs of the students being taught.

THEME Each chapter of the book is based on a theme to capture the interest of the student and provide a "hook" for the grammatical structure being practiced. The theme is introduced at the outset of the chapter through discussion questions and continues to appear throughout the chapter in the written and spoken exercises in order to motivate the student to practice grammar in a meaningful way.

PREVIEW Following the introduction to the theme of the chapter is the preview section, which consists of a dialogue, letter, article, or interview to further develop the theme while introducing the student to the target structure. Vocabulary from the reading is isolated with definitions, and a cultural note addresses an aspect of American culture related to the theme and depicted in the reading. An inductive exercise based on the reading requires the student to discover and make generalizations about the form and function of the grammatical point of the chapter.

GRAMMATICAL PATTERNS The grammatical patterns sections present the grammatical structures of the chapter. The structures covered in the book are those that the advanced student may have studied previously; however, every effort has been made to focus each chapter on uses that the student perhaps has not yet encountered or mastered. For this reason, most chapters are divided into two sections: the first, "Grammatical Patterns One," is usually a more basic presentation, and the second, "Grammatical Patterns Two," is a more complex treatment. Presentation of the grammatical structure is usually done in chart or list form, which can be assigned for homework and reviewed during class after the students have studied and are prepared to raise questions. A variety of spoken and written exercises that encourage meaningful practice help the advanced student to master and use the grammatical patterns rather than manipulate them artificially. These exercise types include rapid drill, paired oral practice, oral and written paraphrase, interviews, and roleplay.

FEATURES Each chapter contains several special features that provide focus and variety. The "special notes," which are highlighted in boxes throughout the text, contain exceptions to rules and special reminders about the target structure. These can be brought to students' attention during presentation and practice and used as study aids later. The "special problems" sections list common errors that students can make with the grammatical structure. In some chapters there is an excerpt from "authentic materials" written by well-known and respected writers such as the newspaper columnist Ellen Goodman. Each excerpt expands on the theme of the chapter and provides the student with further real-life context for the grammatical structure. At the end of each chapter, students are given a choice of "composition topics" related to the theme of the chapter. These may be assigned by the teacher as homework or journal writing, activities especially useful for classes that combine writing and grammar. Finally, in response to the increasing concern students have about the TOEFL, this text has targetted those structures and types of exercises that may be of assistance to students preparing to take this test. A symbol—■—identifies those explanations and exercises that are "TOEFL-relevant."

HOW TO USE THIS BOOK

The preview section is an inductive exercise that can be used by the instructor as a diagnostic tool to determine what the students already know. The students can benefit from the exercises as a pretest. If the instructor is uncomfortable with an inductive approach, the preview section can be used as a review after the chapter is completed.

The charts can be studied at home, and students can come to class with specific questions. If used in class, the charts can become an inductive tool. Have students cover the section in the chart identifying the rule, and ask them to generate the rule by examining the sentences. In many cases, the chapter has been divided into basic and more complex treatment of the grammatical structure. The "Grammatical Patterns One" section can be skimmed if it is a review.

The readings can be assigned as homework or read in class. Especially when the reading is a dialogue or interview, assigning roles and reading aloud in class can be beneficial.

Encourage students to cooperate on written activities as well as speaking activities. Even fill-in-the-blank exercises can be completed in pairs to encourage interaction. Very often the student is required to write a response after a short discussion, an activity that also lends itself to paired work.

ACKNOWLEDGMENTS

We would both like to give our special thanks to Laurie Likoff for her patience and understanding. We are extremely grateful to Book Builders, and especially to Lauren Fedorko, Jill Wood, and Diane Schadoff, for their excellent work on the design and production of the book. We'd like to thank our many ESL students at the American Language Institute who willingly and enthusiastically suffered through draft after draft of these chapters. We'd also like to express our gratitude to the readers of the manuscript—Sally Cummings, Dawn Schmid, and Patty Anderson—and to the anonymous reviewers for their helpful comments.

I'd like to thank the ALI/PD-02 support group for listening patiently to my grammatical monologues—especially on the progressive. Special thanks, too, to Dick Yorkey for getting me started on writing materials. Finally, the greatest thanks go to my husband, Jo, for his unending patience, support, and understanding.

Jocelyn Steer

I'd like to thank all of my colleagues at the ALI who supported me through the completion of this project, especially Cindy Hofbauer. To my son, Nathan, I would like to express my deep gratitude for being the light at the end of the tunnel.

Karen Carlisi

TO THE STUDENT

As an advanced student of English, you have undoubtedly been studying English grammar for some time and have the feeling that there is nothing left to learn. However, this textbook has been written specifically to address those areas of English grammar that you have not yet mastered or perhaps have never encountered. Therefore, by continuing your study of English grammar with this book, you will build on what you already know and become more fluent in English by being able to use more sophisticated grammatical structures.

This textbook contains fifteen chapters, each centered around a specific grammatical structure and a theme to make your study of the grammar more interesting. Each chapter contains the following parts:

THE READINGS Although this is not a reading book, you may be surprised to find an interview, article, letter, or dialogue with vocabulary highlighted in the text. In this way, you can see how the structure functions in a sentence.

CULTURAL NOTES You will find short explanations of cultural aspects of the United States after most Preview sections in each chapter. These notes are designed to introduce you to the cultural information referred to in the Preview readings.

INDUCTIVE EXERCISES These exercises encourage you to discover and make generalizations about the grammar yourself. Some questions may be more difficult than others, so you will know which structures you need to work on.

CHARTS The grammar is usually presented in chart form so that you can study at home and bring questions to your teacher. Each chart can also serve as a study aid when preparing for tests. Toward the end of each chapter, you will find a special problems section that lists the errors that students often make with the particular structure being studied.

SPEAKING AND WRITING ACTIVITIES Each chapter contains a variety of speaking and writing exercises. Because you are often expected to communicate your ideas about the theme of the chapter rather than simply manipulate the structure, these exercises may seem at times quite challenging to you.

COMPOSITION TOPICS At the end of the chapter, you are given a choice of topics based on the theme so that you can practice using the grammar in your own writing.

TOEFL GUIDES This book is not a TOEFL book; however, because many of you may be required to take the TOEFL, you can identify those explanations and exercises that may be helpful in preparing for the TOEFL by looking for this symbol—■.

AMERICAN CULTURE I

- ▤ Count and noncount nouns
- ▤ Quantifiers

"AMERICA: LOVE IT OR LEAVE IT"
(Bumper sticker popular during the 1960s)

DISCUSSION QUESTIONS

1. Based on what you have read or directly experienced of U.S. culture, what aspect of life in the United States is most different from your own culture?
2. What has your culture "borrowed" from American culture? What has the United States borrowed from your culture?
3. If you were asked to choose one object symbolizing American culture to put in a time capsule, what would that object be?

OBJECTIVES

In this chapter, you will learn:

1. To form regular and irregular plurals
2. To distinguish between count and noncount nouns
3. To use appropriate quantifiers

PREVIEW

DIRECTIONS: Read the following excerpt from an article by the journalist Linda Ellerbee to find out what the title of this column means. Then answer the questions that follow.

THE BUSINESS OF A CADILLAC IN AMERICA
by Linda Ellerbee

1. Mom believed in her country, her husband, her daughter, the Democratic Party, the Methodist church, **the Texas Aggies** and Cadillac cars. And I remember a day, sometime in the last year of her life, when she looked up from a television show she was not watching and said to my dog that at least she'd been right about Cadillacs.

2. The Cadillac thing began before I was born. Mom didn't know **a gasket** from **a casket**, but it didn't matter, because to her, a Cadillac wasn't merely a bigger, **flashier**, better car, it was the biggest, the flashiest, best car in the whole world. The real American Dream Machine.

3. Owning a Cadillac, like being president, was to Mom an inalienable possibility. It said so in the Constitution. More or less.

4. Mom **kept her end of the bargain**. She went to school, went to church, read newspapers, voted, cleaned house, cooked, wifed, mothered and drove Fords, Chevys and then—ta - dah!—an Oldsmobile, a clear sign things were moving in the right direction.

5. In 1970, she got her wish. It was dollar-bill green with an interior more luxurious than our house and a **dashboard** with more buttons, switches and dials than a 747. She was a little sorry she was too late for those wonderful, old curvy fish tails, but at least it still had **fins**. Big, streamlined chrome-tipped go-faster fins. Predator fins.

6. It was her first Cadillac. And it was her last Cadillac. In 1974, my father died. In 1980, my mother had **a stroke**. I flew to Houston to sell the house that she could no longer manage and the car she could no longer drive. Mom felt bad about the house and terrible about the car but was comforted by the thought that her Cadillac would **fetch a pretty penny**. When I told her we got $700 for it, she said I was **an imbecile**. Actually, that was the nicest thing she said.

7. And now, here's **Ralph Nader** telling everybody the Cadillac isn't what it used to be. He says the quality of the Cadillac has been steadily slipping since the early 70s. And bad management is to blame. According to Ralph Nader, General Motors **did in** the American Dream Machine all by itself.

8. . . . In Detroit these days, the real product is profit, not automobiles. In fact, all over America, the new **bottom line** is: If it sells, it's good. Not the other way 'round.

9. . . . This whole Cadillac business has reminded me of what's wrong with living in what they tell me is the Information Age. The trouble is not the technology; it's the information it keeps giving me about the age I'm living in.

10. And so it goes.

VOCABULARY

the Texas Aggies: a football team from an agricultural university in Texas
a gasket: a seal around pipe joints which prevents leakage
a casket: a wooden box in which a dead person is buried
flashy: showy, ostentatious
keep her end of the bargain: to do what one says one will
dashboard: the instrument panel of a car
fins: the triangular chrome appendage over the taillights of a car, like a shark fin
a stroke: a blockage or hemorrhage of a blood vessel to the brain
fetch a pretty penny: command a high price
an imbecile: a stupid person
Ralph Nader: a consumer advocate quite active in the United States
did in: destroyed, ruined
the bottom line: the final conclusion

CULTURAL NOTE / DISCUSSION

Owning a Cadillac in the United States has always symbolized status; that is, if you can buy a Cadillac, then you have somehow realized the American Dream. Recently, however, the Cadillac as status symbol has been replaced by expensive imported cars such as the BMW or Mercedes Benz. Which cars carry status in your country? Why do you suppose cars are so important to an individual's image?

What does Ellerbee mean when she says, "If it sells, it's good. Not the other way 'round"? What is "the other way 'round"? Is this situation found only in the United States?

GRAMMAR CONSIDERATIONS: FOCUS

The following questions are based on the preview text and are designed to help you find out what you already know about the structures in this chapter. Some of the questions may be hard and some of them may be easy. Answer as many of the questions as you can. Work with a partner if your teacher tells you to do so.

1. Can you explain why the author uses no article before the **bold** nouns in the following sentences?
   (a) "And bad **management** is to blame." (paragraph 7)

   _____

   (b) "In Detroit these days, the real product is **profit**, not **automobiles**." (paragraph 8)

   _____

2. "Owning **a** Cadillac, like being president, was to Mom **an** inalienable possibility." Can you explain why *a* is used before *Cadillac* and *an* is used before *inalienable*?

   _____

3. "The trouble is not **the technology**; it's **the information** it keeps giving me about the age I'm living in."

Could the nouns in bold be made plural? If not, why not?

_____

Would you use **much** or **many** in the following blanks? Explain your choice.

Is there _____ technology? _____

Is there _____ information? _____

══════════ GRAMMATICAL PATTERNS ONE ══════════

I. COUNT NOUNS

In general, nouns in English are either count or noncount. Some nouns can have both forms depending on the meaning. Count nouns have both singular and plural forms.

	Singular	**Plural**
COUNT NOUNS	a table	tables
	a book	books
NONCOUNT NOUNS	milk	XXXXX
	love	XXXXX

A. Singular Count Nouns: *A* or *An*?

Singular count nouns are preceded by **a** or **an** depending on the sound of the first letter of the noun, as follows.

USE *a* BEFORE:	USE *an* BEFORE:
1. Nouns or adjectives beginning with a **consonant** sound: ▪ **a** fire ▪ **a** book	Nouns or adjectives beginning with a **vowel** sound: ▪ **an** American ▪ **an** edge
2. Nouns or adjectives beginning with the **vowel U**, when it sounds like **you**: ▪ **a** united front ▪ **a** university	Nouns or adjectives beginning with the **vowel U** when it **doesn't** sound like **you**: ▪ **an** uptight businessman ▪ **an** underfed child
3. Nouns or adjectives beginning with the consonant **H** when it is aspirated: ▪ **a** helper ▪ **a** hostage	Nouns or adjectives beginning with **H** when it is silent: ▪ **an** hour ▪ **an** honest politician

---

SPECIAL NOTE

1. These nouns can be preceded by either *a* or *an:*
   an hotel / **a** hotel, **an** historian / **a** historian.
2. Use *a* before letters with a consonant sound: **a** B.S. degree.
3. Use *an* before letters with a vowel sound:
   an I.Q. test, **an** M.A. degree.

1.1   RAPID DRILL: *A or An?*

DIRECTIONS: Supply *a* or *an* as appropriate. If both are possible, indicate this.

1. _____ A is considered _____ excellent grade in _____ high school in the United States.

2. On the other hand, _____ F is a failing grade.

3. Many private schools require students to wear _____ uniform.

4. I just ate _____ horrible American meal!

5. It's customary to tip _____ hotel porter.

6. It is advisable to leave a small tip for _____ unpleasant waitress in a restaurant.

7. Freedom of religion is considered to be _____ inalienable right of _____ U.S. citizen.

8. Some college students consider _____ M.B.A. degree _____ easy ticket to instant wealth.

9. It is not uncommon to find _____ American who drives _____ European car.

B. Formation of Plural Count Nouns

1. Regular Plural

SINGULAR	PLURAL	PLURAL FORMATION RULE
value tradition Cadillac	values traditions Cadillacs	Add **-s**
tomato mass box church dish	tomatoes masses boxes churches dishes	Add **-es** to nouns ending in **o, s, x, ch, sh.** (See exception below—2, irregular plurals.)
mystery	mysteries	Change (**consonant + y**) to **i** and add **-es.**
toy	toys	Add **-s** to (**vowel + y**).

2. Irregular Plural

The following list includes some of the most common **exceptions** to plural formation, arranged by category. Note that this is **not** a complete list.

SINGULAR	PLURAL	PLURAL FORMATION PATTERN
1. shelf knife wife	shelves knives wives	Change **-f** or **-fe** to **-ves.** **Exceptions:** ■ proof—proofs ■ chief—chiefs ■ belief—beliefs (**believes** is the verb)
2. zoo video radio piano solo Eskimo	zoos videos radios pianos solos Eskimos	Add **-s (not -es)** to: ■ nouns ending in **vowel + o;** ■ foreign words ending in **o;** ■ proper nouns ending in **o.**
3. man foot goose tooth mouse	men feet geese teeth mice	These are some examples of nouns that form their plural by changing the middle vowel(s).
4. sheep deer species series fish	sheep deer species series fish	The singular and plural forms are the same.
5. analysis crisis basis hypothesis oasis (syn)thesis	analyses crises bases hypotheses oases (syn)theses	These are some examples of nouns that form their plural by changing **-is** to **-es.**
6. phenomenon criterion	phenomena criteria	Change **-on** to **-a.**
7. nucleus radius stimulus syllabus cactus	nuclei radii stimuli syllabi cacti	Change **-us** to **-i.** **Syllabuses** is also acceptable as a plural form.

8. curriculum memorandum datum	curricula memoranda data	Change **-um** to **-a**.
9. ox child index	oxen children indices / indexes	These nouns do not follow a pattern.

1.2 WRITTEN EXERCISE: *Plural Formation*

DIRECTIONS: Make these singular nouns plural.

1. odyssey _____
2. Filipino _____
3. phenomenon _____
4. potato _____
5. fish _____

6. goose _____
7. mouse _____
8. belief _____
9. scarf _____
10. syllabus _____

Make these plural nouns singular.

1. hypotheses _____
2. indices _____
3. criteria _____
4. series _____
5. species _____

■ II. NONCOUNT NOUNS

There are two types of noncount nouns.

MASS NOUNS These cannot easily be counted or divided.	■ Please pass the **milk**. ■ Buffalo had two feet of **snow**.	Mass nouns are **always** singular.
ABSTRACT NOUNS These refer to general concepts and ideas.	■ It took **courage** to be so honest. ■ Sometimes I believe that **happiness** is an illusion.	Abstract nouns are **always** singular.

A. Mass Nouns

There are many types of mass nouns. Here are some common examples.

CATEGORY	NOUNS	EXAMPLE SENTENCE
1. LIQUIDS	wine, beer, milk, water, coffee, tea, etc.	▪ I bought some **milk** for breakfast.
2. FOOD These can be solid or granular.	sugar, salt, pepper, rice, flour, etc. cheese, meat, butter, bread, yogurt, etc.	▪ Pass the **salt,** please. ▪ I'd like to buy some **bread**.
3. NATURAL ELEMENTS These include terms relating to the weather and also to natural resources.	weather, rain, snow, hail, ice, wind, heat, etc. wood, oil, gold, iron, petroleum, copper, uranium, etc.	▪ We didn't have much **snow** or **rain** this year. ▪ The **fog** is beautiful in San Francisco. ▪ A lot of **wood** for construction comes from Canada. ▪ **Uranium** is a valuable resource.
4. PROBLEM NONCOUNTS These noncounts often cause problems for students. Study them carefully!!	advice, information, news, luggage, equipment, slang, vocabulary, mail, clothing, furniture, hair, travel, work	▪ Can you give me more **advice** about marriage? ▪ I bought a lot of new **furniture** yesterday. ▪ Have you learned any new **slang**? ▪ I've learned a lot of **vocabulary** this week. ▪ The factory sold its outdated **equipment.** ▪ I just washed my **hair**.

1.3   RAPID DRILL: *Noncount Nouns*

DIRECTIONS: First, identify the following nouns as count (C) or noncount (NC) orally or in writing, as you are instructed by your teacher.

advice	mouse	news	knowledge
luggage	information	furniture	suitcase
slang	mail	assignment	smog
toy	medicine	hypothesis	bottle
people	sheep	traffic	fog
homework	deer	vocabulary	rice
work			

Now choose two nouns from each column and write one sentence for each using *some* + (plural) noun.

EXAMPLE

(advice) The consulate gave the new immigrant **some advice** about becoming a citizen.

1.4 FILL IN THE BLANKS: *Count or Noncount?*

DIRECTIONS: Read the following sentences and make the nouns in parentheses plural whenever it is possible. Remember that **noncount** nouns can **never be plural!**

(soap)   **1.** I need to buy some _____ for the bathroom.

(homework)   **2.** Do we have any _____ for tomorrow?

(sunshine)   **3.** Can we expect some _____ in Hawaii in April?

(postcard)   **4.** Please send me some _____ from your trip.

(stimulus)   **5.** The rats responded to all the _____ in the experiment.

(information)   **6.** If you need _____ about your research topic, you can consult the

(index)   _____ in the library.

(furniture)   **7.** Jack purchased a lot of _____ on credit, and now he can't pay

(bill)   his _____ .

(criterion)   **8.** What _____ did you use in hiring the new receptionist?

(belief)   **9.** The students in this class have differing _____ on the use of nuclear energy.

(mouse)   **10.** The young child laughed when she saw the _____ scamper across the floor.

(hair)   **11.** What did you do to your _____? It looks awful!

(mystery)   **12.** The Bermuda Triangle still remains a _____ .

(traffic)   **13.** I'm sorry I missed the opening ceremonies, but the _____ was horrible on the freeway.

(lightning)   **14.** There was a lot of _____ during last night's storm.

(housework)   **15.** Bill did a lot of _____ over the weekend.

1.5 PAIRED DRILL: *Count and Noncount Nouns*

DIRECTIONS: Student A will formulate a question using the count noun provided. Student B will answer using a noncount synonym or example.

EXAMPLE

CUE: a suitcase
STUDENT A: Do you have a leather **suitcase?** (count)
STUDENT B: Yes, all my **luggage** is leather. (noncount)

1. a letter
2. a chair
3. an assignment
4. an idiom

   5. a job
   6. a dollar
   7. a dress
   8. a possible answer to a problem
   9. a bracelet
   10. an editorial

B. Abstract Nouns

These nouns are noncount when they refer to the general concept. Here are some examples.

CATEGORY	NOUNS	EXAMPLE SENTENCE
1. CONCEPTS AND IDEAS	democracy freedom socialism, etc.	▪ Most Americans believe in **democracy.** ▪ Some Americans take **freedom** for granted.
2. EMOTIONS	anger, fear, sadness, joy, happiness, love, hate, etc.	▪ His **anger** caused her **fear.** ▪ Both **sadness** and **joy** can cause a person to cry.
3. QUALITIES AND TRAITS	wealth, poverty, beauty, luck, intelligence, trust, patience, etc.	▪ **Wealth** is often considered a sign of success. ▪ **Beauty** is in the eye of the beholder.

1.6   PAIRED ACTIVITY: *The Typical American*

DIRECTIONS: How does your culture perceive the typical American? Which traits would most often be associated with an American? Which traits would not? Discuss these questions with a partner from your country or continent and then complete the following sentences using abstract nouns based on your conversation. Add your own sentence for 6.

1. The traits that are **most often** associated with an American are _____ and

   _____ .

2. The traits that are **least often** associated with an American are _____ and

   _____ .

3. My culture perceives the typical American worker as having _____ .

4. The Americans' most likable traits are their _____ and _____ .

5. The Americans' least likable traits are their _____ and _____ .

6. _____

   _____ .

1.7 WRITTEN ACTIVITY: *A Person from Your Country*

DIRECTIONS: Write a short paragraph describing a typical person from your country. Use at least five noncount abstract nouns and underline them. Be sure to capitalize the first letter of any nationality, whether it is used as a noun or as an adjective. (See below.)

SPECIAL NOTE

The names of countries, nationalities, races, and religions are **always capitalized**, whether they are used as nouns or adjectives:

- My best friend is **M**exican.
- He comes from **M**exico.
- He went to a **C**atholic school.
- His father works in a **F**rench restaurant in **M**exico City.

III. NOUNS THAT ARE *BOTH* COUNT AND NONCOUNT

Some nouns can be both count and noncount. Compare the following examples and note how the meaning changes when the noncount noun becomes a count noun.

NONCOUNT MEANING	COUNT MEANING
1. IN GENERAL Americans are drinking more **juice** these days.	KIND OR TYPE Have you been to that new health food restaurant? They serve **15 different juices.**
2. IN GENERAL **Coffee** is the preferred breakfast beverage in the United States.	A SERVING I'd like **two large coffees** to go, please.
3. A SUBSTANCE Many families eat **turkey** only at Thanksgiving.	A DEFINED ITEM He cooked **two turkeys** for Thanksgiving.
4. GENERAL CONCEPT **Education** is the most important issue in the local elections.	AN INSTANCE OF THE GENERAL Every American child is entitled to **a free education.**
5. A SUBSTANCE / MATERIAL **Glass** is used in building many skyscrapers.	AN OBJECT MADE FROM THAT SUBSTANCE The baby broke **a glass.**

SPECIAL NOTE

English often has distinct words to refer to an animal and the meat from that animal. Note these distinctions below. Note also that the animal is always a count noun, but the meat is usually noncount.

THE ANIMAL (count)	THE MEAT (noncount)
a cow	beef, steak, hamburger
a calf	veal
a pig	pork, bacon
a sheep	mutton
a lamb	lamb
a chicken	chicken
a turkey	turkey

1.8   WRITTEN ACTIVITY: *Noncount* or *Count?*

DIRECTIONS: Read the following sentences and indicate whether the **bold** noun is count **(C)** or noncount **(NC).** Then explain the meaning of the noun by referring to the five cases listed above.

EXAMPLE

             C
I'd like to order **two teas,** please.
Meaning: <u>two servings</u>

1. My aunt bought me an **iron** for Christmas.

   Meaning: _____

2. His two children are the **joys** of his life.

   Meaning: _____

3. The cafe down the street is now offering a new **coffee.**

   Meaning: _____

4. **Poverty** is a fact of life in many cities in the United States.

   Meaning: _____

5. The Rockefellers have **a wealth** that most people can't even imagine.

   Meaning: _____

6. Many Americans go into **business** for themselves.

   Meaning: _____

1.9   WRITTEN ACTIVITY: *Noncount* to *Count* Changes

DIRECTIONS: Write two sentences for each of the following, clearly demonstrating the change in meaning when there is a noncount to count shift.

EXAMPLE

democracy: <u>Democracy is based on the will of the majority.</u>

a democracy: <u>The United States is a democracy.</u>

1. beer: _____

   a beer: _____

2. life: _____

   a life: _____

3. business: _____

   a business: _____

4. noise: _____

   a noise: _____

5. love: _____

   a love: _____

GRAMMATICAL PATTERNS TWO

■ I. COUNT AND NONCOUNT EXPRESSIONS OF QUANTITY

Note the different expressions of quantity used with count and noncount nouns.

COUNT NOUN QUANTIFIERS	NONCOUNT NOUN QUANTIFIERS	NOTES
1. These are **the same** for count and noncount nouns:		
■ **some** ideas ■ **a lot of** ideas ■ **lots of** ideas ■ **plenty of** ideas ■ **a lack of** ideas	■ **some** information ■ **a lot of** information ■ **lots of** information ■ **plenty of** information ■ **a lack of** information	**Some, a lot of, lots of, plenty of,** and **a lack of** can be used with both count and noncount nouns.
2. These are **different** for count and noncount nouns:		
■ **several** ideas ■ **many** ideas ■ **a couple of** ideas	■ **(not) much** information	Use **much** only in questions and negative statements. (for example, *Do you have much money? No, I don't have much money.*)

<ul><li>**a few** ideas</li><li>**(very) few** ideas</li></ul>	<ul><li>**a little** information</li><li>**(very) little** information</li></ul>	These expressions are explained in more detail below.
<ul><li>**a great number of** ideas</li><li>**a large number of** ideas</li><li>**a great many** ideas</li></ul>	<ul><li>**a great amount of** information</li><li>**a great deal of** information</li></ul>	These expressions are quite **formal.**

■

SPECIAL NOTE
UNITS OF MEASUREMENT

Many noncount mass items are measured in terms of count units. Study the following examples. See if you can think of any other units of measurement.

- **a quart / gallon / carton / bottle** of liquid
- **a loaf of** bread
- **a pound of** cheese / meat, etc.
- **a dozen** eggs (note that *of* does not precede **eggs**)
- **a stick of** butter
- **a can of** soup
- **a tube of** toothpaste
- **a head of** lettuce

1.10   CHAIN DRILL: *Expressions of Quantity*

DIRECTIONS: Potluck dinners, parties to which each guest brings a dish or beverage, are becoming more popular in the United States as families have less time to prepare an elaborate dinner for a large group. Imagine that your English class is planning a potluck dinner for the end-of-the-term party. How much or many of the following items will be needed for your class?

Have a chain drill to decide what to bring. Student A begins by asking Student B a "how much or how many" question about the item listed. Student B responds by using a more exact unit of measurement. (See special note above.) Note that count nouns must be made plural.

EXAMPLE

STUDENT A: How much bread will you bring?
STUDENT B: I'll bring **a loaf of** bread.
STUDENT C: How much soda do we need?
STUDENT D: We need . . . etc.

1. bread
2. soda
3. coffee
4. chicken
5. cupcake
6. butter
7. potato
8. salad
9. napkin
10. flower
11. egg
12. paper plate
13. sushi
14. ?
15. ?

SPECIAL NOTE
MOST

Be especially careful when using **most**. Note how this quantifier is used.

- **Most of the** early settlers were from Europe. **(most of the)**
- **Most** settlers were from Europe. **(most)**

[INCORRECT: **Most of** settlers were from Europe.]

1.11 PAIRED ACTIVITY: *Expressions of Quantity*

DIRECTIONS: Create a recipe with your partner for the following ingredients. Use exact measurements. You do not need to use all the ingredients. You can add some of your own if you wish. Be ready to write the recipe down or roleplay preparing it for your class.

cheese	tomato sauce	eggs	flour
yeast	mushrooms	pepper	salt

II. (A) *FEW* / (A) *LITTLE*

DIRECTIONS: Read the following story about Carlos and Maria and then study the chart that follows.

Students coming to the U.S. to study often respond to "culture shock" in different ways. Maria is an example of a student who adjusted quickly to life in the U.S. She has been in the U.S. for three months but already she has made three very nice American friends. They often spend their weekends together going to the movies or to the beach. She has even taken on a few babysitting jobs to supplement her income so that she can pay for her leisure activities.

Carlos, on the other hand, is not very satisfied with his American experience. He doesn't have many friends, and the ones he does have don't live with him in the dormitory. He feels lonely and sad, so he spends his weekends writing letters to his family in South America. He also stays in on the weekends because he's on a tight budget. Since life in the U.S. is much more expensive than he imagined, he doesn't have enough money to pay for a dinner out or even an evening at the theater.

QUANTIFIER		EXAMPLE	MEANING
COUNT NOUNS	a few	Maria has **a few** friends.	• **a few = a small number of** friends; a sufficient number
	(very) few	Carlos has **few** friends. Carlos has **very few** friends.	• **few = not many** friends • **Very** adds emphasis.
NONCOUNT NOUNS	a little	Maria babysits, so she has **a little** money.	• **a little = a small amount of** money
	(very) little	Carlos has **(very) little** money for weekend fun.	• **little = hardly any** money at all; an insufficient amount

Here is a summary of the uses of *(a) little* and *(a) few*:

Carlos has **few friends.**	Maria has **a few friends.**
− − *NEGATIVE*	*POSITIVE* + +
Carlos has **little money** for fun.	Maria has **a little money.**

1.12   RAPID DRILL: *Few* and *Little*

DIRECTIONS: Choose five of the following phrases and make sentences using **a few / (very) few** or **a little / (very) little.** Be honest in your answers and be prepared to disagree with your classmates!

EXAMPLE

CUE: snow in Florida
ANSWER: There is very little snow in Florida.

1. money in your pocket
2. friends in this city
3. problems with count and noncount nouns
4. free time in the evening
5. great leaders in the world
6. cold days in August in Tokyo
7. cheap housing in New York City
8. American cars in Seoul

9. tests in this class
10. teachers like this one
11. love in the world
12. intelligent students in this class
13. honest politicians
14. ways to make a lot of money
15. chance for peace in the world
16. delicious food in a school cafeteria

1.13   WRITTEN ACTIVITY: *(A) Few / (A) Little*

DIRECTIONS: Los Angeles and New York are the two biggest cities in the United States. Because of this, they are often competing with each other in areas such as architecture, food, the arts, and overall quality of life. Read the following information about these rival cities. Then describe each one using the nouns provided and one of the following expressions.

(VERY) LITTLE: not much (noncount nouns)	**(VERY) FEW:** not many (count nouns)
QUITE A FEW: a lot (count nouns)	**QUITE A BIT:** a lot (noncount nouns)

EXAMPLE

CUE: Los Angeles doesn't have much greenery in the downtown area.

ANSWER: greenery: Los Angeles has very little greenery in the downtown area.

LOS ANGELES

- The weather is warm throughout the year. It very rarely snows.
- Most people have cars because the public transportation is so poor.
- Los Angelenos go to the many beautiful beaches and the mountains on the weekends because they like to avoid the heavy smog.
- The majority of people in L.A. live in single family homes. The city is spread out because there are so many houses.

NEW YORK

- The weather is quite variable. It's hot and humid in the summer, gray, cold, and snowy in the winter.
- New York has excellent public transportation. Most people don't drive their cars because the traffic is so heavy.
- There are many cultural events in N.Y.—theater, opera, ballet—but residents don't have much open space in which to practice sports.
- Most New Yorkers live in apartments because the population is quite heavy and the land area is quite limited.

LOS ANGELES

1. snow _____

2. public transportation _____

3. beaches _____

4. single family homes _____

5. smog _____

NEW YORK

1. sunshine in the winter _____

2. cars _____

3. open space _____

4. cultural events _____

5. people who live in apartments _____

1.14   WRITTEN ACTIVITY: *All Expressions of Quantity*

DIRECTIONS: Read the following sentences about American universities. Paraphrase these sentences using any appropriate expression of quantity from the list above (for example, **a great deal of**, **plenty of**, **few**, etc.).

EXAMPLE

CUE: An American university professor may give 50–100 pages of reading per night.

ANSWER: An American university professor may give a great deal of reading per night.

1. A foreign student is likely to find all types of entertainment on campus—movies, concerts, plays, and even bowling.

_____

_____

2. In large state universities many students live at home with their families and commute to school.

_____

3. In small private colleges, however, you will find more students living in dorms on campus.

_____

4. A foreign student might be surprised at the amount of "partying" that goes on in the campus dorms, especially on the weekends.

_____

5. At the end of the semester, however, most students have a lot of work, and the noise level is substantially reduced in the dorms.

_____

■ 1.15 CHAPTER REVIEW: *Settling the New World*

DIRECTIONS: Choose any appropriate answer to complete the following sentences about settling the New World. **There may be more than one correct answer.**

1. _____ Pilgrims came to Massachusetts in the seventeenth century.
   - **a.** Many
   - **b.** Much
   - **c.** A great number
   - **d.** A number of

2. About the same time, _____ noblemen from England were settling in Virginia.
   - **a.** some
   - **b.** much
   - **c.** quite a few
   - **d.** a great deal of

3. Unfortunately, _____ settlers from the first permanent English settlement in Jamestown, Virginia, survived.
   - **a.** little
   - **b.** few
   - **c.** not many
   - **d.** not much

4. In Virginia, the land was rich. As a result, _____ colonists were able to prosper from the land and build luxurious homes.
   - **a.** many of the
   - **b.** many
   - **c.** many of
   - **d.** a good many

5. Life was hard in Massachusetts for the early settlers. _____ of their land was as fertile as that in Virginia.
   - **a.** Very little
   - **b.** Very few
   - **c.** Not much
   - **d.** Not many

III. SPECIAL PROBLEMS

Pay special attention to these very common mistakes.

PROBLEM	EXPLANATION
1. Use of **much** in statements: [INCORRECT: A doctor makes **much** money.] CORRECT: A doctor makes **a great deal of** money.	Use **much** only in questions and negative statements. Use another quantifier instead.
2. No plural after - *of* phrases: [INCORRECT: There are a great number **of car**.] CORRECT: There are a great number of **cars**.	A plural count noun **must** follow - *of* phrases like *a great number of*.
3. Count and noncount problems: [INCORRECT: We bought some **furnitures**.] CORRECT: We bought some **furniture**.	Study count and noncount nouns carefully. Remember noncount nouns can never be plural.
4. Plural spelling problems: [INCORRECT: How many **countrys** are there?] CORRECT: How many **countries** are there?	Watch out for the spelling of irregular plural nouns.

■ 1.16   ERROR ANALYSIS: *Count* and *Noncount Nouns*

DIRECTIONS: The following sentences were written by students. Correct any errors in count and noncount noun use, a / an use, and quantifiers. There may be one or more errors in each sentence.

1. In small private colleges, you will find a great amount of students living in dorms.
2. At the end of the semester, however, most students have a larger number of work.
3. At the end of the semester, a great deal of student have a lot of work.
4. A foreign student might be surprised at a great deal of partying that goes on.
5. At the end, most students have plenty work.
6. At the end of the semester, you have very few noise in the dorms.
7. In small private colleges, you'll find a great many of students living in dorms on campus.
8. Bettina would like to take a class in American slangs so she can improve her conversational vocabularies.
9. She bought three pianos for her rental studios.
10. You can get much informations from your advisor about applying to an U.S. university.
11. The automobile factorys in the midwest of United States still have some equipments that are not operated by robots.

COMPOSITION TOPICS

1. Imagine that an American friend of your family is coming to your country to study. Write a letter to him or her describing the aspects of life in your country that you think would be most surprising or difficult for him or her to understand.
2. The United States has often been called the land of freedom. Beginning with the Pilgrims in the seventeenth century, many groups have fled oppression in their own country and come to the United States looking for freedom. In a well-developed composition, explore the concept of freedom and decide if the United States is truly a land of freedom.

INTRODUCTION
TO
VERB TENSES

- Chapter 2: Present, past, and future verbs
- Chapter 3: Perfect verbs
- Chapter 4: Progressive verbs

OBJECTIVES

In this unit you will be working on verb tenses. Much of it may be a review for you, and other sections may be new and challenging. First you will look at each verb tense individually. Then you will have a chance to put everything you have learned together. The sequence of the unit is as follows:

Introduction
Chapter 2: The simple present and past tenses; the future tense
Chapter 3: The perfect tenses
Chapter 4: The progressive tenses; integration of **all** verb tenses

In this unit you will study all the verb tenses and their uses. At the end of the unit you will have a chance to integrate what you know and to practice using many of the verb tenses together.

Note how verb tenses in English are formed. There are three basic times or tenses: **present, past,** and **future**. These combine with the aspects: **simple, perfect,** and **progressive**. The chapters that follow will explain these aspects in detail.

To read the chart, choose the tense (at the top) and combine it with the aspect (on the sides). For example, the past progressive tense is *I was eating*.

ASPECT	TENSE		
	Present	**Past**	**Future**
Simple	I eat.	I ate.	I will eat.
Perfect	I have eaten.	I had eaten.	I will have eaten.
Progressive	I am eating.	I was eating.	I will be eating.
Perfect Progressive	I have been eating.	I had been eating.	I will have been eating.

2.1 IDENTIFICATION EXERCISE

DIRECTIONS: In order to learn the maximum from the verb chapters that follow, it is very important that you know the **names** of all the verb forms. Use the above chart to help you to identify all the verb forms in the following passage written by an Indonesian student living in the United States. Underline the verbs and label them clearly as follows:

simple present	simple past	simple future
present perfect	past perfect	future perfect
present progressive	past progressive	future progressive
present perfect progressive	past perfect progressive	future perfect progressive

present perfect

People <u>have always told</u> me that I am an adaptable person. However, when I came to the United States to study, I found out that I am not as adaptable as I seem. I had already studied six years of English before I left my country of Indonesia. I had been studying conversational English with an American teacher for about a year before I left. So I really didn't expect to have any problems communicating with Americans. I thought to myself, "I will just go to my classes and learn everything I can. Then by the time the TOEFL test arrives, I will have learned everything I need to get 550 on the TOEFL. I'll enter the local university for my M.B.A."

Well, I really wasn't ready for my first months there. At the first orientation meeting at the English school, the Americans were talking to me so fast that all I did was smile and nod. I still don't know what they said to me! I had more surprises—my accent was hard to understand, I didn't like the American food at the cafeteria, the pace in the city was too fast. But the biggest surprise was my progress in English. I didn't get into that university right away.

I'm still studying English. In fact, I've been studying for two semesters now. If all goes as planned, I'll be entering the M.B.A. program next semester. I'll have been living in the United States for an entire year by then. I am able to understand just about everything, and most people understand me. But guess what? I'm still not used to American food!

2

HAVING FUN

▭ Present, past, and future verbs

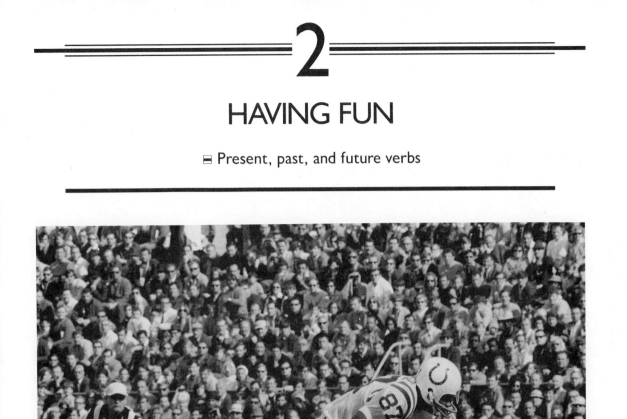

TIME FLIES WHEN YOU'RE HAVING FUN

DISCUSSION QUESTIONS

1. What is your idea of the perfect evening out? Where would you go? What would you do?
2. How do people entertain their friends in your country? What makes a successful party?
3. Which sports do you enjoy watching? Which ones **don't** you like? Why?

OBJECTIVES

In this section, you will learn:

1. To form the simple present, past, and future tenses
2. To use time words with these tenses
3. To spell past forms of the irregular verbs
4. To spell regular past and present verbs

══════ PREVIEW ══════

DIRECTIONS: Read the following conversation between two friends making plans for the evening. Then answer the questions that follow.

JOAN: Where were you last night? We missed you at Tony's surprise birthday party.

MARY: I had **a splitting headache,** so I **stayed in.** Was it fun?

JOAN: I had a good time and Tony was really surprised when he **walked in on** a house full of his friends. But it **broke up** early when the neighbors complained about the loud music. Hey, what're you doing tonight?

MARY: You know I'm home on Wednesday nights. I have my economics class on Thursdays, and tonight I'm going to get ready for tomorrow's test. What about you?

JOAN: I'm taking my sister to that new jazz club downtown. Why don't you join us? The music starts at 9:00 tonight, so you can get some work done before that.

MARY: OK, maybe I'll meet you there. But you know, Joan, if I listen to music, I really prefer hard rock.

JOAN: If we go to the Hard Rock Cafe, then I'll be the one with the splitting headache, Mary. **Besides,** we'll be able to talk if we go to the jazz club. Come on!

MARY: We'll see. I'll call you later. Bye.

VOCABULARY

a splitting headache: a very severe headache
to stay in: stay at home, not go out
walk in on: to enter a situation or place, unaware of what is going on
break up: disband, disperse, finish
besides: an additional reason is . . .

CULTURAL NOTE / DISCUSSION

The Hard Rock Cafe is a chain of restaurant/music clubs located in major cities in the United States and other countries. Have you ever been to a Hard Rock Cafe? Where do you go to listen to music? What type of music do you prefer?

GRAMMAR CONSIDERATIONS: FOCUS

The following questions are based on the preview text and are designed to help you find out what you already know about the structures in this chapter. Some of the questions may be hard and some of them may be easy. Answer as many of the questions as you can. Work with a partner if your teacher tells you to do so.

1. Find a sentence from the dialogue which uses the simple present tense to talk about an activity that occurs regularly. What indicates that this is habitual activity?

   _____

2. Which part of the conversation deals with future plans? Write four different ways that express future plans or actions.

   _____

   _____

   _____

   _____

   Based on the examples, can you explain any differences in the use of each type?

3. List all the past tense verbs from the dialogue. Which are regular? What is the rule for the spelling of regular past tense verbs?

   _____

   _____

   _____

   _____

4. "...I am home on Wednesday nights." If you wanted to insert the following time words, where would you place them in the sentence? At the beginning? Before the verb? After the verb? At the end of the sentence? More than one place?

   always_____

   often_____

   usually_____

   normally_____

GRAMMATICAL PATTERNS ONE

I. OVERVIEW OF THE SIMPLE PRESENT AND SIMPLE PAST TENSES

The information in this section is probably not new for you. Review the following chart and then move on to the sections that follow. They will highlight some of the persistent problems that even advanced learners of English may still have with the simple present and past tenses.

TENSE	EXAMPLE	FUNCTION
PRESENT	1. I **have** my economics class every Thursday. 2. She really **prefers** hard rock music. 3. Water **freezes** at 32° F. 4. A bird **watches** over its nest. 5. A dog **buries** its bones. 6. A dollar **buys** less today than in 1950.	▪ Habitual action ▪ Opinions / preferences ▪ Permanent truths / facts
PAST	7. The neighbors **complained.** 8. She **carried** the bag to the car. 9. The band **played** until dark. 10. The robbery **occurred** at midnight. 11. I **spoke** French when I was young. 12. I **used to speak** French when I was young. 13. I **would** always get in trouble when I was young.	▪ Completed action ▪ Habitual past action ▪ *used to* and *would* refer to past actions. (See modals chapter for an explanation of the difference.)

■ II. SPECIAL PROBLEM 1: TIME WORDS AND THE SIMPLE PRESENT

Time words that answer the question "How often?" (adverbs of frequency) are a problem because of their placement in the sentence. They can have three positions in a sentence: initial, middle, or final. The chart below outlines some of the common positions of time words.

POSITION	TIME WORDS	EXAMPLES
INITIAL Beginning of the sentence with no change in word order	every day (week, etc.) on Mondays (Tuesdays, etc.) sometimes usually often	**Every week** I get a massage. **On Tuesdays,** we eat out. **Sometimes** we get Chinese takeout. **Usually** if I cook, he does the dishes. **Often** I pay by credit card.
MIDDLE Before the verb or after *be*	regularly, habitually, normally, etc.	COMPARE: He **regularly** goes to the gym. He is **regularly** late.

	always often usually sometimes never, rarely, seldom	She **always** arrives before him. She is **always** on time. He **usually** quits before her. He is **usually** the first one out the door. She **rarely** leaves before him. She is **rarely** the first to leave.
FINAL At the end of the sentence	regularly, habitually, normally, sometimes usually every day, week, etc. never, rarely, seldom	He goes to the gym **regularly**. She accompanies him **sometimes**. He quits before her **usually**. She doesn't go **every day**. He misses **rarely**.
CAUTION	**NEVER, NEVER separate the verb from its object with a time word!!**	CORRECT: He lifts weights **regularly**. [INCORRECT: He lifts **regularly** weights.]

2.2   ORAL DRILL: *Placement of Time Words*

DIRECTIONS: Answer the following questions by selecting an appropriate time word from the chart beginning on page 26 for the position indicated in parentheses.

EXAMPLE

CUE: play an instrument (final)
ANSWER: I play the piano **regularly.**

How often do / does . . .

1. You go to a gym to work out? (initial)
2. You speak English outside of class? (final)
3. You make dinner for your friends? (middle)
4. Your father take a vacation? (initial)
5. Your friend attend a symphony concert? (middle)
6. Your mother listen to hard rock music? (final)
7. You go out dancing on Saturday night? (initial)
8. You have parties in your home? (final)
9. You go shopping? (middle)

2.3   PAIRED DISCUSSION: *Time Words*

DIRECTIONS: Work with a partner and discuss how you act in social situations. Describe yourself and your actions using the following time words: **usually, rarely, sometimes, often.**

EXAMPLE

ANSWER: I am **rarely** quiet at a party. I **always** talk to people.

■

SPECIAL NOTE

NEGATIVE ADVERBS IN INITIAL POSITION

Negative adverbs (never, rarely, seldom, barely, scarcely) can occur in initial position in a sentence, although such a position is not common. When they do, you must use **question word order,** as in the examples below.

     Rarely does my sister go out on Saturday night.
     Never does my brother stay home.
     Seldom is the grocery store closed on Sunday.

2.4   ORAL DRILL: *Negative Adverbs in Initial Position*

DIRECTIONS: Restate the following sentences beginning each with the negative adverb found in the sentence.

EXAMPLE

SENTENCE: John rarely goes out on Saturday night.
ANSWER: **Rarely** does John go out on Saturday night.

1. Guillermo rarely goes to the cinema anymore since the tickets are so expensive.
2. I never entertain in my home—I just don't have the time!
3. Loretta seldom goes to a disco since the music is so loud.
4. My parents never go to a rock concert; they prefer the symphony.
5. Jose's grandparents rarely sit through an entire concert without falling asleep.
6. Gladys never rents videos because she prefers to go to the movie theater.
7. Mr. and Mrs. Dupont hardly ever attend the Hollywood parties which they are invited to.
8. Construct your own sentences using *rarely, seldom, never.*

■ 2.5   ERROR ANALYSIS: *Time Words*

DIRECTIONS: Find any errors in the use of adverbs in the following sentences. Correct the error clearly above the sentence.

1. Usually do I drink a beer.

2. We often organize at night barbecues around the swimming pool.

3. Never I stay at home to do my homework when I can go out with my friends.

4. My boyfriend is every day at my house.

5. Rarely the recreational facilities at this institution are fully utilized.

2.6   WRITTEN ACTIVITY: *Simple Present*

DIRECTIONS: Write a short paragraph describing what you do in your leisure time or imagine what a famous person or fictional character (such as Superman) does in his or her leisure time. Say what is **usually, sometimes,** and **rarely** done. Use a variety of time words in a variety of positions in the sentences.

III. SPECIAL PROBLEM 2: SPELLING

Below are a few trouble spots you should be especially careful of in spelling the present and past tense verbs.

TROUBLE SPOT	PRESENT	PAST
1. When the verb ends in *y:* (a) **Change y to i and add -es or -ed** (b) **EXCEPT** when *y* is preceded by a vowel; then **just add -s.**	• carry-carries • bury-buries • play-plays • stay-stays	• carry-carried • bury-buried • play-played • stay-stayed
2. When the verb ends in -s, -z, -ch, -sh: Always **add -es or -ed**	• wash-washes • kiss-kisses • watch-watches	• wash-washed • kiss-kissed • watch-watched

3. Past tense—One-syllable verb
 (a) **Double the consonant:**
  (Vowel + consonant)
 (b) **Don't double the consonant:**
  (2 vowels + consonant)
	——
	
	——
		• hop-hopped
		• pat-patted
		• help-helped
		• rain-rained

4. Past tense—Two-syllable verb
 (a) **Double the consonant:**
  ▪ Stress on **second** syllable
  ▪ One final vowel + consonant
 (b) **Don't double the consonant:**
  ▪ Stress on **first** syllable
  ▪ One final vowel + consonant
 (c) **Don't double the consonant:**
  ▪ Two final vowels + consonant
  ▪ Stress can be on either syllable
		• ad**mit**-admitted
		• pre**fer**-preferred
		
		• **mas**ter-mastered
		• **sof**ten-softened
		
		• refrain-refrained
		• succeed-succeeded

2.7 SPELLING TROUBLE SPOTS

DIRECTIONS: Give the correct present or past form as indicated.

Add -s, -es, or -ies:

1. fish   _____

2. catch   _____

3. hope   _____

4. die   _____

5. cry   _____

6. say   _____

Provide the past form:

7. intensify   _____

8. happen   _____

9. control   _____

10. repeat   _____

11. study   _____

12. commit   _____

■ 2.8   EDITING ACTIVITY: *Simple Present*

DIRECTIONS: Edit the following paragraph for spelling, subject-verb agreement, and time-word placement. **Don't forget the -*s* on third person singular!**

Mrs. John Dupont III will be hosting her annual Charity Ball on Friday. She organize every year this event to benefit the Children's Hospital. Usually the ball is held in the Ballroom of the Hilton Hotel. Rarely 400 people attends the event since it is considered to be **the** social event of the season. Last year, Mrs. Dupont postponned the event due to the untimely death of the mayor. Let's all hope it happen this year.

IV. SPECIAL PROBLEM 3: IRREGULAR VERBS

Some verbs are not regular in their past and past participle forms. Refer to the list of these verbs in the appendix at the end of this chapter. Make a note of the verbs you still don't know and practice them regularly until you do.

A. Possible Spelling Patterns

Although these verbs are irregular, some of them follow patterns of formation, outlined below. Keep these patterns in mind when you are studying the verbs.

POSSIBLE SPELLING PATTERNS FOR IRREGULAR VERBS	EXAMPLES		
	BASE	PAST	PAST PARTICIPLE
1. NO CHANGE	cut burst let	cut burst let	cut burst let, etc.

2. SAME PAST AND PAST PARTICIPLE	bend	bent	bent
	build	built	built
	mean	meant	meant, etc.
3. -EEP, -EPT, -EPT	creep	crept	crept
	sleep	slept	slept
	keep	kept	kept, etc.
4. -IN-, -AN-, -UN-	drink	drank	drunk
	sing	sang	sung
	ring	rang	rung, etc.
5. VOWEL CHANGE IN PAST Add **-n** to base for past participle	grow	grew	grown
	draw	drew	drawn
	drive	drove	driven
	forgive	forgave	forgiven
	forsake	forsook	forsaken
	give	gave	given, etc.

2.9 PAIRED DRILL: *Irregular Verbs*

DIRECTIONS: Work in pairs. Have your partner cover up the past and past participle columns of the list of irregular verbs in the appendix to this chapter, pages 37–41. Choose any 15 verbs and test your partner's knowledge of the irregular forms. Then switch roles. Keep a list of the verbs your partner needs to study and then test him or her again in the next class.

■ B. Troublesome Verbs

The following verbs are often confusing for speakers of English. Study them carefully.

VERB + OBJECT (Transitive verbs)	VERB ONLY (Intransitive verbs)
LAY, LAID, LAID to put or place • He **lays** his keys there every day. • She **laid** the book on the table.	LIE, LAY, LAIN to assume a horizontal position • Cats often **lie** on warm cars. • He **lay** down on the couch.
HANG, HUNG, HUNG to suspend • The proud owner of the painting **hung** it on the wall.	HANG, HANGED, HANGED to kill by hanging • The spy **was hanged** at dawn.
RAISE, RAISED, RAISED to lift, to grow, to bring up • The student **raised** her hand.	RISE, ROSE, RISEN to increase • Prices **rose** 10% last month.

2.10   TROUBLESOME VERBS: *Rapid Drill*

DIRECTIONS: Answer the following questions using one of the six verbs listed in the chart on page 31.

1. Your mother was extremely tired yesterday afternoon. What did she do?
2. What does your teacher do with his / her books when he / she comes into the classroom?
3. What happens to the level of water in a river after a flood?
4. Country X is in an inflationary period. What do you suppose happened to food prices?
5. What did the father do with his baby after she fell asleep?
6. Where did you put your coat after you walked into the house?
7. Where do you go when you want to take a nap?
8. What did the soldiers do after they captured the enemy?

2.11   ORAL EXERCISE: *Small Group Activity*

DIRECTIONS: You were invited to a party for the employees of your company by your boss. After you had accepted the invitation, your best friend offered you free tickets to the most exciting ball game of the year. You decided to go to the game and skip the party, but now you have to come up with an excuse for your boss. In small groups, create an imaginative story to explain why you were unable to attend the party. Use the past tense of **two verbs from each group** below. Be ready to report the excuse either orally or in writing.

Group 1	Group 2	Group 3
cling	flee	shrink
bleed	grind	spin
dive	lay	weave
creep	freeze	wind
bear	fling	spread

2.12   WRITTEN EXERCISE: *A Disastrous Evening*

DIRECTIONS: In a well-written paragraph, describe a particularly bad evening that you have had in your life. Include several irregular verbs from the three groups above and underline them.

EXAMPLE

The worst evening of my life <u>was</u> the first time I <u>went</u> out with my wife. We were eating at a very nice restaurant and she was wearing a white silk dress. I went to drink my coffee and it <u>fell</u> out of my hands and spilled all over her dress. . . .

2.13   CROSSWORD PUZZLE: *All Irregular Verbs*

DIRECTIONS: Complete the crossword puzzle by using the appropriate irregular verbs from the list in the appendix.

ACROSS CLUES

1. Ronald Reagan _____ he would never run for president again.
3. The small wound _____ profusely.
4. Maria was excited because she had been _____ for the "Student of the Year" award.
6. The hurricane _____ through Miami and knocked down all the trees.
9. Will the baseball game be _____ on national television?
11. I was _____ three aces in my poker game yesterday.
13. The criminal was _____ in the public square for all to see.
14. The car went over the bridge and _____ into the river.
16. The telephone rang before John _____ up his coat.
17. The car slid on the ice and _____ around three times.
18. The waiter _____ the woman's cigarette.

DOWN CLUES

2. Have you ever _____ a camel?
4. The soldier _____ carefully through the forest to avoid being seen by the enemy.
5. Have you _____ the dog yet? He must be hungry.
7. Someone had _____ a caricature of the disliked teacher on the board.
8. To make flatbread you need to _____ the wheat berries into a fine powder.
10. David _____ out of his chair when he saw his old girlfriend.
12. The baseball had been _____ so hard, it went into the outfield.
15. Daniel _____ the cake into two pieces and offered one to his mother.

GRAMMATICAL PATTERNS TWO

I. FUTURE FORMS

Note the different ways in which the future may be formed and used. Many of these sentences are taken from the Preview section.

FORM	EXAMPLE	USE / EXPLANATION
WILL + MAIN VERB	<ul><li>It **will rain** tomorrow.</li><li>The music **will start** at 9:00.</li><li>I **will meet** you there.*</li><li>I'll **pick** you up if you need a ride.</li></ul>	Predictions Scheduled events Promises Offers
BE GOING TO + VERB	<ul><li>I'm **going to take** my sister to the new jazz club.</li><li>I'm **going to get** ready for my economics class.</li></ul>	The use of **be going to + verb** expresses future events, often planned or thought about before the moment of speaking. This form expresses more sureness about the future.
SIMPLE PRESENT	<ul><li>The music **starts** at 9:00.</li><li>The plane **leaves** at 4:00.</li></ul>	Use this form to express future, scheduled events, with verbs such as: *start, begin, finish, etc.* and *leave, depart, arrive, etc*.
PRESENT PROGRESSIVE	<ul><li>I'm **having** dinner at John's tomorrow night.</li></ul>	Use this form for most future events, except predictions and offers, when it is clear to the listener through the context or from the time expressions that the event is in the future.

*Shall can replace *will* here, but this is more common in British English. (I shall meet you there.) In American English, *shall* is usually used as an invitation or suggestion, as in, "Shall we dance?"

Reprinted by permission of Tribune Media Services.

Question: Why did the speaker use *will* for the future tense in this comic?

2.14 ORAL PRACTICE: *Future Forms*

DIRECTIONS: Choose two or three of the following that you would like to respond to by using an appropriate form of the future. Be ready to respond orally when asked by your teacher.

1. Make a prediction about your life in ten years.
2. Tell the class about your weekend plans.
3. Offer to help your teacher with some aspect of the class.
4. Make a prediction about the next music trend in your country.
5. Inquire of your neighbor about his or her plans for this evening.
6. Answer that inquiry.
7. Try to guess about the activities and content of your next English class.
8. Offer to take your teacher out to a nice restaurant.
9. Make a promise about coming to class on time and doing all the homework.
10. Make a promise to the class about a future party.

2.15 FILL IN THE BLANKS: *Be Going To* or *Will*?

DIRECTIONS: Fill in the blanks with *be going to* + *verb* or *will* + *verb*, depending on the meaning of the sentence. In some cases, both forms are possible.

1. MOTHER: The phone's ringing, John.

   JOHN: I (get) _____ it.

2. Gloria, you mean so much to me. I (be / always) _____ there for you.

3. A: What are your plans for Saturday afternoon?

   B: I (take) _____ my mother shopping.

   A: Hey, (pick up) _____ some tennis balls for me if you stop by a sporting shop?

   B: I'd love to, but I just don't think I (have) _____ the time.

4. Northtown's population is increasing daily. Soon, there (be) _____ more than half a million people living there.

5. Some teachers believe that every student (have) _____ his or her own computer one day.

2.16 WRITTEN ACTIVITY: *Future Forms*

DIRECTIONS: Fill in the blanks with an appropriate form of the future. **Do not use *will*** in every blank. **Use all four types** of future forms depending on the context.

MICHAEL: Guess what! My father (retire) _____ on Friday.

GEORGE: Really? Do you think he (be) _____ happy?

MICHAEL: I don't know. As long as he's healthy, he (be) _____ satisfied.

GEORGE: Well, let's take him out to celebrate tonight.

MICHAEL: Unfortunately, I can't. I (go) _____ out of town on business

tonight and my flight (leave) _____ at 6:00 P.M.

2.17   FILL IN THE BLANKS: *All Forms*

DIRECTIONS: Circle **any** correct answer. There may be one, two, three, or four correct answers.

1. It _____ tomorrow.
   - **(a)** will rain
   - **(b)** is going to rain
   - **(c)** is raining
   - **(d)** rains

2. "Mr. Williams _____ up his wife at 3:00 later this afternoon. He won't be back in the office after that. Shall I have him call you tomorrow?'' the secretary told the caller.
   - **(a)** will pick
   - **(b)** is going to pick
   - **(c)** is picking
   - **(d)** picks

3. I'm sorry that I can't stay longer at this meeting, but my child's play _____ in one hour. I can't miss that!
   - **(a)** will start
   - **(b)** is going to start
   - **(c)** is starting
   - **(d)** starts

4. "I _____ your exams tomorrow,'' the teacher said. "I promise!''
   - **(a)** will return
   - **(b)** am going to return
   - **(c)** am returning
   - **(d)** return

5. "Do you have any toothpaste left?'' asked John.
   "No, but I _____ some for you when I go downtown,'' Jack said.
   - **(a)** will get
   - **(b)** am going to get
   - **(c)** am getting
   - **(d)** get

═══════ COMPOSITION TOPICS ═══════

1. Describe a visit you have had from an out-of-town friend. What places in your city did you visit? Where did you go to eat?
2. In the United States, sports fans eagerly await the biggest football event of the year—the Super Bowl. People have parties or go to restaurants with big-screen T.V. to watch the game. Does your country have a similar sporting event? Describe the event and why it is so important to people in your country. If you prefer, describe a cultural or national event that takes place in your country with a great deal of celebration.

APPENDIX: IRREGULAR VERBS

A. Group One Verbs (A–D)

SIMPLE FORM	PAST	PAST PARTICIPLE
arise	arose	arisen
awake	awoke	awoken
be (is / are)	was / were	been
bear	bore	borne; born
become	became	become
begin	began	begun
bend	bent	bent
bind	bound	bound
bite	bit	bit / bitten
bleed	bled	bled
blow	blew	blown
break	broke	broken
bring	brought	brought
broadcast	broadcast	broadcast
build	built	built
burst	burst	burst
cast	cast	cast
catch	caught	caught
choose	chose	chosen
cling	clung	clung
come	came	come
cost	cost	cost
creep	crept	crept
cut	cut	cut
deal	dealt	dealt
dig	dug	dug
dive	dived / dove	dived
do	did	done
draw	drew	drawn
drink	drank	drunk
drive	drove	driven

B. Group Two Verbs (E–Q)

SIMPLE FORM	PAST	PAST PARTICIPLE
eat	ate	eaten
fall	fell	fallen
feed	fed	fed
feel	felt	felt
fight	fought	fought
find	found	found
flee	fled	fled
fling	flung	flung
fly	flew	flown
forget	forgot	forgotten
forgive	forgave	forgiven
forsake	forsook	forsaken
freeze	froze	frozen
get	got	got / gotten
give	gave	given
go	went	gone
grind	ground	ground
grow	grew	grown
hang	hung	hung
have	had	had
hear	heard	heard
hide	hid	hidden
hit	hit	hit
hold	held	held
hurt	hurt	hurt
keep	kept	kept
kneel	knelt	knelt
know	knew	known
lay	laid	laid
lead	led	led
leave	left	left
lend	lent	lent
let	let	let
lie	lay	lain
light	lit / lighted	lit / lighted
lose	lost	lost
make	made	made
mean	meant	meant
meet	met	met
pay	paid	paid
prove	proved	proven / proved
put	put	put
quit	quit	quit

C. Group Three Verbs (R–W)

SIMPLE FORM	PAST	PAST PARTICIPLE
read	read	read
ride	rode	ridden
ring	rang	rung
rise	rose	risen
run	ran	run
say	said	said
see	saw	seen
seek	sought	sought
sell	sold	sold
send	sent	sent
set	set	set
shake	shook	shaken
shoot	shot	shot
show	showed	showed / shown
shrink	shrank	shrunk
shut	shut	shut
sing	sang	sung
sink	sank	sunk
sit	sat	sat
sleep	slept	slept
speak	spoke	spoken
spend	spent	spent
spin	spun	spun
split	split	split
spread	spread	spread
spring	sprang	sprung
stand	stood	stood
steal	stole	stolen
stick	stuck	stuck
strike	struck	struck / stricken
swear	swore	sworn
sweep	swept	swept
take	took	taken
teach	taught	taught
tear	tore	torn
tell	told	told
think	thought	thought
throw	threw	thrown
understand	understood	understood
wear	wore	worn
weave	wove	woven
wind	wound	wound
write	wrote	written

D. Meanings of Selected Verbs

VERB	MEANING	EXAMPLE
TO BEAR	▪ to bring forth, as a child ▪ to tolerate, to withstand	▪ Some women **bear** children under very severe conditions. ▪ She **bore** the pain stoically.
TO BLEED	▪ to lose blood	▪ He **bled** after he cut himself with a knife.
TO BURST	▪ to fly apart in pieces, to explode ▪ to interrupt, to intrude	▪ The balloon **burst** instantly when the child pricked it with a pin. ▪ The angry employee **burst** into her boss's office.
TO CAST	▪ to throw, to fling ▪ to put a magic spell on someone	▪ He **cast** the fishing line into the water. ▪ The bad witch **cast** a spell on the innocent boy and turned him into a frog.
TO CLING	▪ to stick to, often something soft ▪ to hold onto, especially an idea	▪ The tight dress **clung** to her body. ▪ The vice-president **clung** to his original ideas for expansion.
TO CREEP	▪ to move slowly, usually on all fours	▪ The fugitives **crept** stealthily through the tunnel.
TO DEAL	▪ to distribute ▪ to have concern with	▪ She shuffled and **dealt** the cards to all the players. ▪ The social worker **dealt** with the problems of the poor.
TO FLEE	▪ to escape	▪ The prisoner **fled** from the jail.
TO FLING	▪ to throw, to send suddenly	▪ The angry child **flung** his toys across the room.
TO FORSAKE	▪ to give up, to quit, to abandon	▪ He had not **forsaken** his principles in spite of his poverty.
TO GRIND	▪ to reduce to small particles, usually using a rigid instrument	▪ The cook **ground** the pepper. Kim **ground** her coffee in the Moulinex.
Compare TO HANG TO HANG	▪ to suspend (hang, hung, hung) ▪ to kill by hanging (hang, hanged, hanged)	▪ The proud owner of the van Gogh painting **hung** it on the wall. ▪ The spy was **hanged** at dawn. (This is a **regular** verb.)

Compare TO LIE	• to assume a horizontal position (lie, lay, lain)	• He **lay** down on the couch.

TO LAY	• to put or place
	  (lay, laid, laid)
		• She **laid** the book on the table.
		  (This is a **transitive verb;** it must have
		  a direct object.)

TO SINK	• to descend lower and lower
	
	• to degenerate
		• The fishing boat **had sunk** to the bottom
		  of the sea before the Coast Guard
		  arrived.
		• The young widower's morale **has sunk**
		  rapidly due to his wife's sudden death.

TO SPIN	• to move quickly in a circular motion	• The student's head **spun** from all the new vocabulary words.
TO SPLIT	• to divide in half	• Bobby **split** the wood and put it in a neat pile.

TO SPRING	• to move suddenly upward or forward	• On Christmas morning the young child
		  sprang out of bed and ran downstairs to
		  open his presents.

TO STRIKE	• to hit	• The car lost control and **struck** a tree.

TO SWEAR	• to make a vow or promise
	
	• to use profane language
		• John threw out his cigarettes and **swore**
		  he would never smoke again.
		• When the young boy **swore,** his mother
		  washed his mouth out with soap.

TO SWEEP	• to remove dirt with a brush or broom
	
	• to move over with speed or force
		• The housekeeper **swept** the dirt under
		  the rug.
		• The tornado **swept** through the Texas
		  town and killed many people.

TO WEAVE	• to form by interlacing strands of material
	
	• to unite into a coherent whole
		• The peasant woman made her living by
		  selling the baskets she **had woven.**
		• The accounts of the politician's
		  childhood are **woven** into the biography.

TO WIND	• to have a curving course
	
	• to tighten the spring (as in a watch)
		• The river **wound** through the valleys of
		  the country.
		• The little boy **had wound** the watch so
		  tightly that it broke.

3

HAVING MORE FUN

■ Perfect verbs

HAVING MORE FUN

DISCUSSION QUESTIONS

1. Can you explain the expression "Born to shop"? Do you enjoy shopping? Why or why not?
2. If you won a free trip around the world, where you would go? What would you do?

OBJECTIVES

In this chapter you will learn:

1. To form the present perfect, the past perfect, and the future perfect tenses
2. To recognize differences in uses between the simple and perfect tenses
3. To use appropriate time words with each perfect tense

PREVIEW

DIRECTIONS: Read the following conversation between Cheryl and Patty, who work in the same office. They are talking about where they went on their honeymoons. Find out why Patty can't join Cheryl on her vacation.

PATTY: Where did you go on your honeymoon?

CHERYL: We went to Las Vegas. Can you believe it?

PATTY: *Las Vegas!* What was it like? I've never been there before.

CHERYL: I hadn't been there either and I really hated it! It's not exactly the most romantic place to spend your honeymoon. How about you? Where did you go?

PATTY: We went to Hawaii. Now **that** was romantic! Have you been there?

CHERYL: Oh, I love Hawaii. I've been there three times so far. In fact, we will be there for Christmas this year. Have you ever gone back?

PATTY: No. John and I haven't taken a vacation since our honeymoon three years ago.

CHERYL: Then why don't you and John join us for Christmas? By then, we'll have gotten the bonus the company promised us. Think about it. You deserve a vacation.

PATTY: Oh, Cheryl, we can't. We've just bought a new car. Maybe next year...

GRAMMAR CONSIDERATIONS: FOCUS

The following questions are based on the preview text and are designed to help you find out what you already know about the structures in this chapter. Some of the questions may be hard and some of them may be easy. Answer as many of the questions as you can. Work with a partner if your teacher tells you to do so.

1. Cheryl says, "We went to Las Vegas" in line 2. Could she also say, "We have gone to Las Vegas"? Why or why not?

   _____

2. What time word indicates that an action was repeated and will probably be repeated in the future?

   _____

3. Find the one sentence with the past perfect tense (**had** + past participle). Write that here. Can you explain why this was used instead of a simple past?

   _____

4. Find the one sentence with the future perfect tense (**will have** + past participle). Could you use a simple **future** tense here? Why or why not?

   _____

GRAMMATICAL PATTERNS ONE

I. PERFECT TENSES

A. Forms

To form a perfect tense, use an appropriate form of the auxiliary *have* and the past participle of the main verb.

TENSE	FORM	EXAMPLE
PRESENT PERFECT	**have / has + past participle**	I **haven't taken** a vacation since our honeymoon.
PAST PERFECT	**had + past participle**	I **hadn't been** there either.
FUTURE PERFECT	**will have + past participle**	We **will have gotten** our bonus by then.

B. A Comparison: Simple vs. Perfect Tenses

SIMPLE TENSES	PERFECT TENSES
Use any of the **simple tenses** to talk about one single event in the past, present, or future, without relating that to another event or state in time.	Use a **perfect tense** to relate one event or state that occurs **before** another event or state in the past, present, or future. A point of reference is always stated or implied.
<div align="center">———————X——————— event 1</div>	<div align="center">———————X———————X——————— event 1 event 2</div>
▪ I went to Las Vegas in 1971. ▪ I will go there again in ten years.	▪ I had never been to Las Vegas before I went there on my honeymoon. ▪ I had never been to Las Vegas before.

■ C. Uses: The Present Perfect

Note how the present perfect and simple past tenses differ in use.

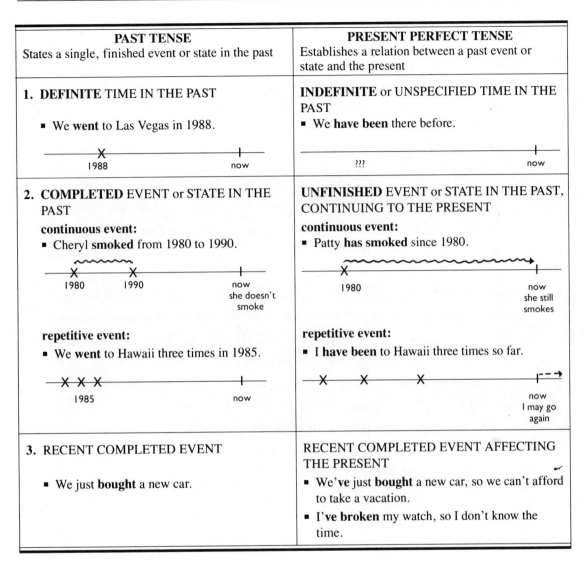

PAST TENSE States a single, finished event or state in the past	PRESENT PERFECT TENSE Establishes a relation between a past event or state and the present
1. DEFINITE TIME IN THE PAST - We **went** to Las Vegas in 1988.	**INDEFINITE** or UNSPECIFIED TIME IN THE PAST - We **have been** there before.
2. COMPLETED EVENT or STATE IN THE PAST **continuous event:** - Cheryl **smoked** from 1980 to 1990. **repetitive event:** - We **went** to Hawaii three times in 1985.	**UNFINISHED** EVENT or STATE IN THE PAST, CONTINUING TO THE PRESENT **continuous event:** - Patty **has smoked** since 1980. **repetitive event:** - I **have been** to Hawaii three times so far.
3. RECENT COMPLETED EVENT - We just **bought** a new car.	RECENT COMPLETED EVENT AFFECTING THE PRESENT - We've just **bought** a new car, so we can't afford to take a vacation. - I've **broken** my watch, so I don't know the time.

3.1 FILL IN THE BLANKS: *Past* or *Present Perfect?*

DIRECTIONS: Fill in the blanks with the appropriate tense—**past** or **present perfect.** If both tenses are possible, indicate this.

1. A: _____ you ever _____ (go) to Yellowstone Park before?

   B: Yes, I _____ (go) there three years ago.

2. Jill _____ (be) to Disneyland five times before.

Last year, Jill _____ (take) her parents there when they _____ (come) to visit her.

3. Jennifer is quite excited about going to the Rolling Stones concert since she _____ (never / see) them in concert before.

4. A: Can you give me a ride downtown?

B: Sorry, I can't. I _____ (just / have) an accident and I'm a nervous wreck.

5. Dear Mom,

Sorry that I _____ (not / write) you last week, but I _____ (be) so busy lately at the hospital. Three of the doctors _____ (be) sick and so I _____ (have to) fill in for them all last week.

Daniel and I finally _____ (go) to see the Bolshoi Ballet. I _____ (never / see) such a crowd at our local theater! Our seats _____ (be) quite good, and we could see the dancers very well. We _____ (be) all surprised, though, when the prima donna _____ (slip) and _____ (fall) during the first act. She _____ (break) her leg and they _____ (take) her to the hospital immediately.

I _____ (not / make) airplane reservations for Thanksgiving yet, but I promise I will very soon. I can't wait to see all of you again. Write soon.
Love, Jack

D. Time Words: Present Perfect

The following time words are often used with the present perfect tense.

USE	TIME WORDS	EXAMPLES
INDEFINITE TIME IN THE PAST	• before • in the past • ever • yet • already	• I have been to Paris **before.** • I've studied this **in the past.** • Have you **ever** seen a UFO? • I haven't seen a UFO **yet.** • I've **already** taken Spanish 101.

UNFINISHED ACTION	• **for** + period of time • **since** + specific date • **until now** • **up to now** • **so far** • **thus far**	• He's been sick **for a month.** • He's been sick **since June.** • We haven't had snow **until now.** • We've had good weather **up to now.** • We've had three storms **so far.** • They've had six children **thus far.**
RECENT COMPLETED ACTIVITY	• **just** • **recently** • **barely**	• I've **just** finished my test. • George has **recently** moved. • The show has **barely** begun.

3.2 WRITTEN ACTIVITY: *Time Expressions*

DIRECTIONS: Provide a time word to justify the use of the tenses in the following dialogue.
Refer to the above chart for present perfect time words.

EXAMPLE

My sister has visited Paris <u>before</u>.

MIKE: Have you ever been skydiving _____?
1

KATHY: Funny you should ask me that. I tried it for the first time _____, and it was
2

great. I can't believe that I've lived _____ without ever trying it before.
3

MIKE: I've done it six times _____, and you know, it still scares me to death! I keep
4

doing it, though, because I love the thrill. Hey, I'm going tomorrow. Why don't you

join me?

KATHY: I'm sorry, I can't. I've _____ made plans to have lunch with Nancy. Well . . .
5

maybe I can talk her into trying it!

SPECIAL NOTE

SINCE AND FOR

Be careful of the difference in use between **since** and **for**:

SINCE + SPECIFIC DATE OR TIME:
- I have been here **since June.**
- I haven't smoked **since I was a teenager.**

FOR + A PERIOD OF TIME:
- I have been here **for five months.**
- Dave worked on this house **for the whole vacation.**

3.3   FILL IN THE BLANKS: *Since* or *For*?

DIRECTIONS: Fill in the blanks with **since** or **for,** as appropriate.

I haven't seen him . . .

1. _____ the whole vacation.

2. _____ the 4th of August.

3. _____ his entire youth.

4. _____ the beginning of winter semester.

5. _____ many years.

6. _____ he got married.

7. _____ the whole month of October.

8. _____ October 4.

9. _____ two hours.

10. _____ he was a baby.

3.4   ORAL DRILL: *Since* and *For*

DIRECTIONS: Choose three of the following cues to respond to, using **since** or **for,** as indicated. Your answer will be made with the negative form of the verb.

EXAMPLE

CUE: gone to a movie / since
ANSWER: I haven't gone to a movie since 1988.

1. got a haircut / for
2. read a novel / since
3. spoken my native language / for
4. written to my family / since
5. told a joke / since
6. had an argument with my mother or father / for
7. gone to the beach / for
8. done the dishes / since
9. taken a test / for
10. gone to the dentist / since

3.5 PAIRED DRILL: From *Indefinite* to *Specific Time*

DIRECTIONS: It is quite common to begin a conversation with the present perfect as an opener for a longer conversation. Often the speaker moves from the present perfect (indefinite time) to a past tense to discuss a specific time. Note how this happens in the following dialogue.

A: **Have** you ever **been** to France?
B: Yes, once.
A: When **were** you there?
B: I **went** in 1989 for the bicentennial celebration.

Practice this technique with a partner. Find out about your partner's likes and leisure activities by choosing a verb and time word from the lists below. Begin with the present perfect and follow up with a specific question using the simple past. Take turns and try not to use the same verb or time word twice.

EXAMPLE

A: Have you ever tried octopus before?
B: Yes, I have.
A: Oh, really, when did you eat it?
B: When I was in Japan.

Verbs	Time Words	
food (eat, try, taste)	so far	up to now
sports (play, practice)	until now	for X years
music (listen to, play)	before	since
books (read, buy)	when	recently
travel (visit, go, see)	in the past	last year, month, etc.

GRAMMATICAL PATTERNS TWO

I. PAST PERFECT TENSE

Note how the past perfect is different from the past.

PAST TENSE	PAST PERFECT TENSE
ONE EVENT OR STATE IN THE PAST	**TWO** EVENTS OR STATES IN THE PAST, ONE OCCURRING BEFORE THE OTHER*
▪ I **went** to Las Vegas in 1988.	▪ I **had graduated** from college when I **got** married.
	▪ I **had graduated** from college before I **got** married.

Timeline (left): X at 1988 ——— now

Timeline (right): X^1 (had graduated) ——— X^2 (married) ——— now

*Event 1 is in the past perfect.

3.6 SENTENCE COMPLETION: *Past Perfect*

DIRECTIONS: Complete the following sentences with a true statement. Note that **before** is followed by the *second* (most recent) event and **after** is followed by the *first event*.

EXAMPLE

CUE: **Before** I came to class today, . . .
ANSWER: Before I came to class today, I had already eaten breakfast.
CUE: I came to class **after** . . .
ANSWER: I came to class **after** I had eaten breakfast.

1. Before I graduated from high school, . . .
2. I learned English after . . .
3. Before I met my current boyfriend / girlfriend / husband or wife, . . .
4. I learned to talk after . . .
5. Before we studied this unit in the book, . . .

Now state what happened in the world before these events.

6. Anwar Sadat was assassinated after . . .
7. After the Iranian revolution occurred, . . .
8. Before World War II broke out, . . .
9. Columbus sailed to America after . . .
10. Before Elvis Presley played music, . . .

II. TIME WORDS: PAST PERFECT

The following time words are often used with the past perfect tense.

TIME WORDS	EXAMPLES	NOTE
▪ BEFORE ▪ AFTER ▪ ALREADY	▪ I (had) graduated from college **before** I got married. ▪ I got married **after** I (had) graduated from college. ▪ I had **already** graduated from college.	▪ In conversation, the simple past is often used with **before** and **after**.
BY THE TIME	I had graduated from college **by the time** I got married.	Use past perfect before **by the time** and the simple past after this time word.
UNTIL	He (had) never skiied **until** he moved to Colorado.	The use of the past perfect is optional here.

Compare:
 ▪ WHEN =
   BEFORE
 	
 ▪ WHEN =
   RIGHT AFTER
 	
 ▪ WHEN =
   WHILE
	1. The president **had already been assassinated when** the revolution started.
	
	 2. The military general **was assassinated when** the revolution started.
	
	 3. Lightning struck the man **when** he was walking across the golf course.
		▪ You must use the past perfect in 1. Otherwise, it could have the same meaning as 2.
		 ▪ Use the simple past in **both** clauses.

▪

SPECIAL NOTE

AFTER VS. AFTERWARD

After and **afterward** are not used the same way. Note the difference in sentence structure and in punctuation in the sentences below.

AFTER: Jack will do the dishes **after** he watches the news.
AFTERWARD: Jack will watch the news. **Afterward,** he will do the dishes.

3.7 SCRAMBLED STORY: *Using Past Perfect Time Words*

DIRECTIONS: Here is a jumbled series of events recounting how Tim and Jean met, fell in love, and got married. In pairs or small groups, reconstruct this story in the correct order. Combine events by using one of the time words on page 50. Have each sentence include a past and a past perfect verb, if possible. There may be several correct versions.

Tim asked Jean to meet his parents.
Jean said she had to think about it.
Tim asked Jean her name.   .
Tim talked to Jean.
Tim watched Jean come into his store every day for several weeks.

Jean got a good job offer in another city.
Jean made him her favorite lasagna dinner.
Tim asked Jean out on a date to a movie.
Tim came over for dinner every night.
Tim asked Jean to marry him.
They fell in love.

3.8   FILL IN THE BLANKS: *Past, Present Perfect,* or *Past Perfect?*

DIRECTIONS: Fill in the blanks using a **simple past, present perfect,** or **past perfect tense.**

Carla and Maria are two students at St. Michael's College.

They (be) ＿＿＿＿＿＿ at St. Michael's since June. They (be) ＿＿＿＿＿＿ at St. Michael's
           1   2
for two months when they (decide) ＿＿＿＿＿＿ to go to Florida.
                                     3

They (rent) ＿＿＿＿＿＿ a car and (drive) ＿＿＿＿＿＿ to Florida. They (be) ＿＿＿＿＿
            4   5   6
on the road for two hours when they (have) ＿＿＿＿＿＿ a flat tire.
                                         7

They (wait) ＿＿＿＿＿＿ four hours before a police officer (arrive) ＿＿＿＿＿＿.
             8   9
"Can I help you?" the officer said.

Maria was tired and she barked at the officer, "We (be) ＿＿＿＿＿＿ here for four hours. It's
                                            10
about time somebody (show up) ＿＿＿＿＿＿ to help us!"
                               11
The police officer was apologetic. He (change) ＿＿＿＿＿＿ the tire for them. The two
                                          12
women (thank) ＿＿＿＿＿＿ the officer and (drive) ＿＿＿＿＿＿ off to Florida.
             13   14

III. FUTURE PERFECT TENSE

Note how the future perfect is different from the future.

FUTURE	FUTURE PERFECT
ONE EVENT OR STATE IN THE FUTURE	**TWO** EVENTS IN THE FUTURE, ONE OCCURRING BEFORE THE OTHER*
▪ We **will get** our bonus on December 15.	▪ By the time Christmas arrives, we **will have gotten** our bonus.

├———————————————X————
 now   December 15
                        bonus
	├————————X^1————————X^2———
	 now December 15 December 25
	             bonus Christmas
	
	 *Event 1 is in the future perfect.

THE FUTURE EXPRESSES A **STATE**	THE FUTURE PERFECT EXPRESSES **ONLY** AN EVENT OR POINT IN TIME.
▪ I **will be** 48 years old by Christmas. (The state = being 48 years old)	▪ I **will have celebrated** my 48th birthday by Christmas.

3.9 FUTURE PERFECT: *A Three-Year Plan*

DIRECTIONS: The chart below represents the three-year plans of Sarah and Clark, who are neighbors and friends. Read the chart, and in the section entitled YOU, fill in events and accomplishments that might happen to you. Then complete the sentences that follow. Be ready to compare your answers with your classmates'.

	IN 1 YEAR	IN 2 YEARS	IN 3 YEARS
Sarah	xxxxxxxxxxx	Gets married	Writes her first novel
Clark	Has his first grandchild	Retires from work	Moves to Florida
You			

1. By the time Sarah gets married, Clark _____.
2. By the time Sarah finishes her novel, Clark _____.
3. By the time Clark moves to Florida, I _____.
4. By the time I _____, Clark _____.
5. By the time I _____, Sarah _____.

3.10   FILL IN THE BLANKS: *Future* or *Future Perfect?*

DIRECTIONS: Fill in the blanks with an appropriate form of the future or future perfect.

1. Tomorrow is an important day for Colette. She (go) _____ to the high school prom, an annual formal dance for high school seniors.

2. She (wear) _____ a long dress, and her date, Jason, (wear) _____ a tuxedo.

3. Today she is quite busy getting ready for tomorrow's event. Hopefully, by tomorrow at 6, she (go) _____ to the hairdresser and her mother (pick) _____ up her dress from the store. Her father (buy) _____ her the pearl earrings he promised.

4. Jason is busy too. This afternoon, he (rent) _____ his tuxedo and (get) _____ his hair cut. By the time he picks Colette up, he (wash) _____ the car and (buy) _____ her the corsage he ordered.

5. Today Colette looks like an ordinary teenager in jeans and a T-shirt. By tomorrow, she (be) _____ an elegant woman in formal attire.

IV. SPECIAL PROBLEMS WITH SIMPLE AND PERFECT TENSES

Pay special attention to these very common mistakes.

PROBLEM	EXPLANATION
1. USE OF THE PRESENT PERFECT WITH *AGO* [INCORRECT: I have arrived here 3 months ago.] CORRECT: I arrived here 3 months ago.	You must use the **past** tense with *ago*.
2. USE OF THE PRESENT TENSE WITH *SINCE* AND *FOR* [INCORRECT: I am here for 3 months.] CORRECT: I have been here for 3 months.	Use the **present perfect** with *since* and *for*.
3. INCORRECT USE OF *SINCE* AND *FOR* [INCORRECT: I have been here since 3 months.] CORRECT: I have been here **since January**. I have been here **for 3 months**.	*SINCE* + SPECIFIC TIME / DATE *FOR* + PERIOD OF TIME

■ 3.11 ERROR ANALYSIS: *Simple* and *Perfect Tenses*

DIRECTIONS: Correct any errors in the uses of simple and perfect verb tenses in the following sentences. Do not change anything that is already correct. Some sentences may not have any errors.

1. When I came to the United States for the first time, I have had difficulty understanding the sales clerks in the stores.
2. Ronald Reagan has been president for eight years before he retired.
3. The band plays since three hours. Do you think the players will take a break soon?
4. The movie starts at 9:00. It's 9:10 now, so by the time we get there, we will have missed the first 30 minutes.
5. Have you choosen your china pattern yet? I'd like to buy you a place setting for your wedding present.
6. Pete is getting married next year. By then, he will know his fiancee for five years.
7. I hope I can use verbs correctly in English when I will finish this course!
8. My family and I are in Alaska since five years, and we still aren't used to the long, dark winters.
9. I am here for six months, and I still can't speak English.

══════════════ COMPOSITION TOPICS ══════════════

1. The twenty-first century is right around the corner. What do you think will have happened to you or your country by then? Write a short paragraph in which you predict events in your life. Discuss events in your personal and professional life. Include possible events in your country, if you like. Begin your paragraph as follows:
   The twenty-first century will begin in just a few years. By then, I will have _____
2. Do you think that teenagers (aged 14–18) should be allowed to go out with friends or on dates without adult supervision? Why or why not?

4

MAKING IT!

▤ Progressive verbs

TO MAKE IT: **To achieve fame or financial success through hard work or talent**

SUCCESS

To laugh often and love much,
to win the respect of intelligent people and the affection of children,
to earn the appreciation of honest critics and endure the betrayal of false friends,
to appreciate beauty,
to find the best in others,
to give of one's self,
to leave the world a little better, whether by a healthy child,
a garden patch,
or a redeemed social condition,
to have played and laughed with enthusiasm and sung with exultation,
to know even one life has breathed easier,
this is to have succeeded.

Ralph Waldo Emerson

DISCUSSION QUESTIONS

1. How is success measured in your country? (for example, money, fame, intelligence, achievements, etc.) Do you personally agree with this standard of success? Why or why not?
2. Describe a person whom you consider to be successful. What is his or her "secret to success"?
3. Rate how important the following elements are in achieving success—hard work, intelligence, luck, personality, connections, ambition, education, and honesty.

OBJECTIVES

In this chapter you will learn:

1. To form the progressive in all tenses
2. To know when to use the progressive form
3. To recognize verbs that cannot be used with the progressive
4. To use time expressions with the progressive

════ PREVIEW ════

DIRECTIONS: Read the following letter that Mitsy wrote to her boyfriend, Randall. Randall and Mitsy live in San Diego, California. Mitsy is in New York City now interviewing for an important marketing position with a very large company. Then answer the questions that follow.

Dear Randall,

1 I really miss you! This afternoon while you were probably **basking** in the San Diego sun, I was having my interview with the vice-president of marketing of Smith Corporation. Wow, is he ever a **hard nut to crack!** I've met with him three times so far and I'm having a hard time convincing him that I'm the **top-notch** candidate for the job. He's forever reminding me that I'm too young and inexperienced for this high-stress position. I'll be seeing him tomorrow at 7:00 A.M. to **go over** my **portfolio**. (They sure do start their days earlier here on the east coast.) **Keep your fingers crossed**.

2 That's enough about my situation out here. What about you? Have you been feeding the dog? Have you been getting my mail for me? I hope you haven't been seeing your **ex-girlfriend**.

3 Randall, I've been thinking pretty seriously about your marriage proposal. Don't you think that twenty-four is a bit young **to go to the altar**? Besides, neither of us has a decent job yet and we should really be off to a good start professionally and financially before we **tie the knot**. I'm not saying no, but I guess we just need a little more time.

4 See you on Friday. Let's hope that I'm the new international marketing director for Smith Corporation by then.

Love and kisses,

Mitsy

Mitsy

VOCABULARY

basking: lying
hard nut to crack: a person who is difficult to convince of something (informal)
top notch: of superior quality
to go over: to review
portfolio: a sampling of a person's artistic or professional work
to keep your fingers crossed: to hope for a good outcome (informal)
ex-girlfriend: former girlfriend
to go to the altar: to get married (figurative)
to tie the knot: to get married (informal; slang)

CULTURAL NOTE / DISCUSSION

The term *yuppie* comes from the abbreviation for **Y**oung **U**rban **P**rofessional and refers to the stereotyped young successful professional, living in an urban setting. Yuppies place a great deal of value on material wealth. The archetypal yuppie earns a high salary, drives an expensive imported car, and prefers the finer (expensive) things in life.

What evidence do you have from this letter that Mitsy is or might want to become a yuppie?

GRAMMAR CONSIDERATIONS: FOCUS

The following questions are based on the preview text and are designed to help you find out what you already know about the structures in this chapter. Some of the questions may be hard and some of them may be easy. Answer as many of the questions as you can. Work with a partner if your teacher tells you to do so.

1. Mitsy uses the **present progressive tense (is / are + verb-ing)** to describe her present, ongoing activity.

2. Mitsy uses the **present progressive** to express her frustration with the vice-president who is interviewing her.

3. Mitsy uses the **past progressive (was / were + verb-ing)** to relate ongoing activities that she and Randall were doing **at the same time** in the past.

4. Mitsy uses the **present perfect progressive (have / has been + verb-ing)** to talk about a repetitive activity that Randall (she hopes) did and will continue to do until she returns home.

5. Mitsy uses the **future progressive (will be + verb-ing)** to talk about a continuous activity in the future.

GRAMMATICAL PATTERNS ONE

1. SIMPLE PROGRESSIVES

A. Forms

To form the simple progressive, use an appropriate form of the auxiliary *be* and a *verb-ing* as follows:

TENSE	FORM	EXAMPLE
PRESENT PROGRESSIVE	**is / are + verb-ing**	I **am having** a hard time convincing him I'm the top-notch candidate.
PAST PROGRESSIVE	**was / were + verb-ing**	I **was having** my interview with the vice-president of Smith Corporation when you called.
FUTURE PROGRESSIVE	**will be + verb-ing**	**I'll be seeing** him tomorrow at 7:00 A.M.

■ B. Uses of Simple vs. Simple Progressive: A Comparison

Note how the simple progressive tenses differ in use from the simple tenses.

SIMPLE PROGRESSIVE TENSES (Past, Present, and Future)	SIMPLE TENSES (Past, Present, and Future)
1. **CONTINUOUS** ACTIVITY To emphasize the **continuous** nature of an activity in the past, present, or future. ■ I **was swimming** between 6:00 and 7:00. ■ Mitsy **is having** an interview right now. ■ She**'ll be swimming** in tomorrow's meet.	1. **HABITUAL** ACTIVITY To talk about **regular, habitual** activity in the past, present, or future. ■ I **swam** regularly as a child. ■ I **swim** every day. ■ **I'll swim** a mile a day for a month.
2. ACTIVITY IN PROGRESS **INTERSECTED** BY A NON-CONTINUOUS ACTIVITY ■ I **was eating** breakfast when the earthquake hit.* eating earthquake now *The activity in progress is in the progressive.	2. **NON-CONTINUOUS** ACTIVITY ■ The earthquake **hit** at 10:00 A.M. yesterday. earthquake now

3. TWO **CONTINUOUS** ACTIVITIES OCCURRING AT THE SAME TIME	3. TWO **HABITUAL** EVENTS
■ While you **were basking** in the sun, I **was having** an interview.	■ He **cooked** and she **served** the food in their first restaurant.

SPECIAL NOTE

THE PROGRESSIVE TO EXPRESS ANNOYANCE

In conversation, the simple progressive tense can be used to express **annoyance, insult,** or **frustration.** In this case, a time expression such as **always, forever, etc.** must be inserted between the auxiliary and the verb-ing.

■ Randall **is always leaving** the door open, and it drives me crazy!

■ Mitsy **was forever complaining** about my old car until I finally bought a new one.

4.1 WRITTEN EXERCISE: *Uses of the Simple Progressives*

DIRECTIONS: Fill in the blanks with a correct simple progressive form (past, present, or future) of the verb in parentheses. Insert the time word when appropriate. Label the use of the progressive in the sentence (continuous action, intersected action, or annoyance).

EXAMPLE

When you get in at the airport tonight, I <u>will probably be having</u> dinner with a client.

(probably / have)

USE: intersected action

1. He _____ in front of the television. I'm not surprised he failed

(always / sit)

his courses.

   USE: _____

2. When you get back from the movies tonight, I'll _____ .

(sleep)

   USE: _____

3. At this very moment, the TOEFL grading committee _____ your

(score)

test.

   USE: _____

4. President Kennedy was shot while a spectator _____ movies of the

(take)

presidential visit.

   USE: _____

5. The young girl decided not to marry her fiance because he _____

(forever / gamble)

away his money in Las Vegas.

   USE: _____

4.2   PAIRED ACTIVITY: *Expressing Annoyance*

DIRECTIONS: Work in pairs. Choose one of the following situations to roleplay.

1. Imagine that you and your partner are two very successful executives living together (a husband and wife or two friends). You have had a lot of stress at work lately and are in the middle of a big fight about each other's living habits. Express annoyance and frustration about your partner's bad habits at home. Use the present progressive and an appropriate adverb (always, forever, every day, etc.).
2. Imagine that you and your partner work for the same company. Both of you dislike your boss. You are having a conversation about all the things your boss does that really irritate you. Express your annoyance and frustration about your boss by using the progressive tense with an appropriate adverb (always, forever, every day, etc.).

EXAMPLE

STUDENT A: I can't stand the way you do the dishes! You**'re always leaving** pots and pans in the sink.

STUDENT B: Well, my dishwashing is a lot better than your cleaning! You**'re forever sweeping** the dust under the rug!

4.3   ORAL DRILL: *Present* or *Present Progressive?*

DIRECTIONS: Add a response to the following statements to demonstrate the difference between using **always** to express **habitual activity** and **annoyance**. Add your own statements and responses for 9 and 10.

EXAMPLE

CUE: He always goes to church on Sunday morning. (habitual activity)
ANSWER: So he can't take you to the airport then.

CUE: He's always going out with his friends on Sundays. (annoyance)
ANSWER: And I wish he would spend time with me instead.

1. He always buys me chocolates.
2. He's always buying me chocolates.
3. My mother always calls me.
4. My mother's always calling me.
5. The teacher always reviews the important information.
6. The teacher is always repeating information.
7. My boss always talks to me in the morning.
8. My boss is always asking me to get him coffee in the morning.

9. _____

10. _____

4.4   FILL IN THE BLANKS: *Simple Present* or *Progressive*?

DIRECTIONS: Fill in the blanks with either a simple present or present progressive form, as appropriate. (Be especially careful with the adverb **always**, which, when not used to express annoyance, must be followed by the simple present tense.)

1. Jack _____ out the garbage on Thursday mornings.
   (always / take)
2. In fact, if you look out the window, you will see that he _____
   (do)

   that now.

3. After he _____ out the trash, he _____ in his
   (take)   (hop)

   car and _____ off to work.
   (speed)
4. His wife _____ about him on the road because he _____
   (always / worry)
   _____ over the speed limit.
   (always / go)
5. Today, Jack is late and the chairman of the board of his corporation _____

   _____ for him impatiently.
   (wait)
6. What the chairman of the board doesn't know is that a police officer _____

   _____ Jack a ticket for speeding.
   (give)

II. PERFECT PROGRESSIVES

A. Forms

To form the perfect progressive, use an appropriate tense of the auxiliary *be* and *verb-ing* as follows.

TENSE	FORM	EXAMPLE
PRESENT PERFECT PROGRESSIVE	**HAVE / HAS + BEEN + VERB-ING**	I hope you **have been feeding** the dog.

| PAST PERFECT PROGRESSIVE | **HAD BEEN + VERB-ING** | Randall **had been waiting** for Mitsy's answer to his marriage proposal for three weeks when her letter finally arrived. |
| FUTURE PERFECT PROGRESSIVE | **WILL HAVE BEEN + VERB-ING** | By the time Randall and Mitsy get married, they **will have been dating** for three years. |

B. Uses

Use the perfect progressive in the following two cases.

TENSE	USE
PRESENT PERFECT PROGRESSIVE PAST PERFECT PROGRESSIVE FUTURE PERFECT PROGRESSIVE	**1.** TO TALK ABOUT AN ACTIVITY THAT BEGAN BEFORE AND CONTINUES UP TO: a. the moment of speaking ▪ I **have been** thinking about your marriage proposal. *(continuous)* ▪ I hope you **have been feeding** the dog. *(repetitive)* b. another action in the past ▪ I **had been thinking** about you when your letter arrived. c. another action (or time) in the future ▪ By the time Mitsy gets home from New York at 2:00 A.M., Randall **will have been sleeping** for two hours.* *The continuous activity is in the progressive.
PRESENT PERFECT PROGRESSIVE PAST PERFECT PROGRESSIVE	**2.** TO TALK ABOUT A CONTINUOUS ACTIVITY WITH TEMPORARY EFFECTS WHICH: a. are still apparent ▪ He **has been eating** onions—I can smell it! b. were still apparent ▪ I could tell she **had been crying** because her eyes were red and puffy.

4.5   WRITTEN EXERCISE: *Use of Perfect Progressives*

DIRECTIONS: Fill in the blanks with the correct form of a perfect progressive verb (present perfect, past perfect, or future perfect). Label the use of the progressive: Previous continuous action (**PCA**), Repetitive action (**RA**), or Temporary effects (**TE**).

1. I could tell that Johanna (play) _____ with her mother's cosmetics. She had lipstick and mascara all over her face.

   USE: _____

2. We (get up) _____ at the same time every day of our married life. Why should we change now?

   USE: _____

3. My date had better show up soon. By the time he finally arrives, I (wait) _____ at this restaurant for a long time.

   USE: _____

4. It smells delicious in here! (bake) _____ you _____ _____?

   USE: _____

5. We (get) _____ free cable T.V. for almost a year when the cable T.V. company discovered the error and disconnected it.

   USE: _____

4.6 RAPID DRILL: *Temporary Effects*

DIRECTIONS: Using the cue provided by your partner or your teacher, form a sentence using a perfect progressive form to indicate the recent activities of the person.

EXAMPLE

STUDENT A: Her eyes are red.
STUDENT B: She's been crying.

STUDENT A: His eyes were red.
STUDENT B: He had been crying.

1. Her shoes are full of mud.
2. The toys are all over the floor.
3. The kitchen was full of dirty pots and pans.
4. His voice is hoarse.
5. She has ketchup on her face.
6. His nose was red.
7. His face is sunburned.
8. She's out of breath.
9. He smells like tobacco.

C. Uses of Present Perfect vs. Present Perfect Progressive: A Comparison

You know that a progressive tense emphasizes the continuous nature of an activity. Note how the present perfect tense differs specifically in use from the present perfect progressive tenses.

PRESENT PERFECT PROGRESSIVE	PRESENT PERFECT
1. RECENT ACTIVITY Emphasis is on the **recency** of the past activity. A time word like **lately** or **recently** emphasizes this, but is not necessary to convey recency. ■ I've been writing a lot of songs (lately). ■ We've been eating at this restaurant a lot (lately). ■ Randall has been feeding Mitsy's dog.	1. INDEFINITE TIME IN THE PAST Emphasis is on the completed action, occurring at an **indefinite time** in the past. The tense does not indicate how long ago the action happened. ■ I've written a lot of songs (in the past). ■ We have eaten at that place before. ■ Mitsy has taken care of Randall's dog in the past.
2. EMPHASIS ON THE LENGTH AND DURATION ■ Mitsy has been writing **for six hours**. ■ Jack has been singing in the choir **for many years**.	2. EMPHASIS ON THE QUANTITY ■ Randall has written **six pages**. ■ June has sung **in six operas**.
3. NO DIFFERENCE IN MEANING With certain verbs (for example, verbs of living, occupation, and vocation) there is no difference in meaning between a present perfect and present perfect progressive tense. ■ **I have been living** here for five years. ■ The secretary **has been working** at this site for a week.	 ■ **I have lived** here for five years. ■ The secretary **has worked** at this site for a week.

4.7   ORAL DRILL: *Present Perfect* or *Present Perfect Progressive?*

DIRECTIONS: Complete these statements with a phrase of **quantity** or **length of time** or a time expression to justify the verb tense used.

EXAMPLE

CUE: I've written . . .

ANSWER: I've written six letters to my parents.

CUE: I've been writing . . .

ANSWER: I've been writing for three hours and my hand is tired.

1. My friend has been talking . . .
2. My friend has talked to me about her problems with her boyfriend . . .
3. Our teacher has taught us . . .
4. Our teacher has been teaching us . . .
5. My government has been working on . . .
6. The news has covered . . .
7. I have talked . . .
8. You have been talking . . .
9. I've never written . . .
10. He's been watching . . .

SPECIAL NOTE

THE PROGRESSIVE FOR A TONE OF COMPLAINT

The present perfect progressive often expresses a tone of complaint more strongly than the present perfect.

- Someone's been eating my chocolate! (And I'm not happy.)
- I've been waiting for you for two hours! (I'm angry.)

4.8 FILL IN THE BLANKS: *Present Perfect* vs. *Present Perfect Progressive*

DIRECTIONS: Use a **present perfect** or **present perfect progressive tense.** Be ready to explain your choices. In some cases, both might be correct.

1. I (read) _____ the book you lent me, but I'm not finished yet.

2. I (read) _____ the book you lent me. In fact, I stayed up until 3 A.M. last night to finish it!

3. Who (take) _____ money out of my purse? This is the second time this week that this (happen) _____ .

4. The professor (explain) _____ this math problem five times and the class still can't understand it.

5. The professor (explain) _____ this math problem for one hour and the students still can't understand it.

6. I'm really very sorry I'm late. (wait) _____ you _____ _____ long? I got stuck in traffic.

7. Where have you been?!! I (wait) _____ for two hours. I already finished lunch.

8. The FBI (investigate) _____ many financial brokers recently for trading violations. I wonder if they (arrest) _____ my stockbroker?

9. My sister (live) _____ in Iowa, Ohio, and Wisconsin. Recently her family (live) _____ in Dublin, Ireland.

10. Lately, some big companies (test) _____ their employees for drugs. My roommate said they (test) _____ her twice so far this year.

4.9 LATE AGAIN!: *Present Perfect* or *Present Perfect Progressive?*

DIRECTIONS: Read the following situations and decide what the person would probably say. Choose a present perfect or a present progressive tense depending on the context and feelings of the speakers. Be ready to roleplay the situation with a partner if instructed by your teacher.

1. You are in a restaurant. Your brother is late again, so you aren't really surprised or angry. While you were waiting, you ate three pieces of cake. What do you say when your brother finally arrives?

   BROTHER: I'm sorry I'm late.

   YOU: That's okay _____

2. Your friend is late again. She was supposed to pick you up at 7:30 for the 8:00 show. She asked you to wait for her outside in front of your apartment building so she wouldn't have to find a place to park. It's raining quite a bit. She arrives at 7:55. What do you say?

   _____

3. You are the owner of a small restaurant. It's Friday night and you are expecting a large crowd for dinner. Your head waitress is late again. Ten minutes after you open the restaurant, the mayor of the city walks in. Your head waitress doesn't show up until one hour later. What do you say to her?

   _____

4. Make up your own situation for the class to respond to.

   _____

D. A Comparison: Future Perfect Progressive vs. Future Perfect

FUTURE PERFECT PROGRESSIVE	FUTURE PERFECT
1. CONTINUOUS FUTURE ACTIVITY To emphasize the **length of time** or **duration** of a future event occurring before and up to another future event. ■ By the time John retires, Jane **will have been practicing** for 10 years. 10 years X¹ —————— X² now retires	COMPLETED FUTURE ACTIVITY To refer to a future event **completed** before another future event or time. ■ By the time John retires from the hospital, Jane **will have graduated** from medical school. X¹ X² now graduates retires
2. NO DIFFERENCE IN MEANING The future perfect progressive emphasizes the **duration** of the activity. ■ By the time John retires, Jane **will have been practicing** medicine for 10 years.	The future perfect does not emphasize **how long**; it emphasizes the **completed activity**. ■ By the time John retires, Jane **will have practiced** medicine for 10 years.

4.10   FILL IN THE BLANKS: *Future Perfect* vs. *Future Perfect Progressive*

DIRECTIONS: Use a **future, future perfect,** or **future perfect progressive.** Note when more than one tense is possible.

1. A: How much longer (be) _____ in the United States?

   B: About another year.

   A: By the time you leave, how long (study) _____ English altogether?

   B: Eighteen months. I hope I (master) _____ the English language by then!

2. A: Is your sister older or younger?
   B: She's 12 years older. It's hard to believe this, but by the time I graduate next year, she

   (direct) _____ her own dance company for 10 years.

   A: That's like me. By the time I graduate from high school, my brother (complete)

   _____ his Ph.D. in biophysics.

III. TIME EXPRESSIONS

The following chart presents the most common time expressions used with the progressive tenses.

TENSE / TIME EXPRESSION	EXAMPLES
1. PRESENT PROGRESSIVE ▪ **This semester** ▪ **Today** ▪ **Right now** ▪ **At this moment** ▪ **At this time** ▪ **While / when / as** ▪ **In + time word**	▪ **This semester** I am studying English in California. ▪ **Today** women are having fewer children. ▪ I am reading this chart **right now.** ▪ My brother isn't working **at this moment.** ▪ We aren't accepting any reservations **at this time.** ▪ **While** you are studying, I'll go shopping. ▪ People are buying more houses **in this decade.**
2. PAST PROGRESSIVE ▪ **During** ▪ **At that time / moment** ▪ **By then / by that time** ▪ **While / when / as** ▪ **In + time word**	▪ The teenager was throwing popcorn **during** the film. ▪ I was selling insurance **at that time** in my life. ▪ Jim got married in 1960. **By then** I was working. ▪ Van's mother arrived **while** he was teaching. ▪ Houses were selling quickly **in the 1960s.**
3. PRESENT PERFECT PROGRESSIVE ▪ **By now** ▪ **So far** ▪ **Up to now** ▪ **This + time word** ▪ **Today** ▪ **All + time word** ▪ **Since + specific time** ▪ **For + duration**	▪ The soup has been boiling for an hour **by now.** ▪ It has been raining for three hours **so far.** ▪ **Up to now** I've never been skiing. ▪ I have been getting all A's **this semester.** ▪ I've been cleaning house **today.** ▪ I've been thinking about you **all week.** ▪ I've been writing **since** 9:00. ▪ I've been reading **for** 3 hours.

4. PAST PERFECT PROGRESSIVE ■ **By then** ■ **At that time** 　**At that moment** 　**By that time** ■ **For / since**	■ Sue had been running 3 hours **by then.** ■ Jack and Jill were divorced in 1966. **At that time** they had already been seeing a marriage counselor **for** 3 years.
5. FUTURE PERFECT PROGRESSIVE ■ **By then** ■ **By that time** ■ **By the time*** ■ **For**	■ My store will celebrate its anniversary next year. **By then,** I will have been operating the store **for** 10 years. ■ **By the time** I leave the United States, I will have been studying English **for** 10 months.

*See also the adverb clause chapter for a detailed discussion of ''by the time.''

4.11   PAIRED CONVERSATION: *Time Expressions*

DIRECTIONS: Work in pairs. Talk about your habitual, past, current, and future activities by choosing a verb from the list on the right and a time word from the list on the left. Student A asks Student B a question using any appropriate tense. Student B will answer the question. Then students reverse roles. Some time words necessitate the progressive tense; others do not. **Pay careful attention to verb tenses. Try not to use the same verb or time word twice.**

EXAMPLE

CUE: right now / do
STUDENT A: What is your father probably doing right now?
STUDENT B: He's probably having breakfast.

Time Words	**Verbs**
right now	do
in this decade	eat
at this moment	think
yesterday	read
while	travel
every afternoon	play
this semester	live
in the 1990s	cook
throughout the class	earn
in your younger days	write
by the time	study
always	work
regularly	prepare
at this time	complain

4.12   FILL IN THE BLANKS: *Time Expressions*

DIRECTIONS: Do you think how you dress at work can affect your success? How do people "dress for success" in your country? Fill in the blanks in the following sentences using one of the time expressions listed below.

right now	in the 1960s
always	currently
in the next century	at that time / moment
this + time word	today

1. In 1975, John T. Molloy wrote his famous book, *Dress for Success*, about the importance of attire and a person's success in the working world. Dark suits and ties have

   _____ been the uniform of male executives.

2. Although the majority of corporate presidents and vice-presidents are still not female,

   _____ we are seeing more and more women assuming middle management positions.

3. Women's office fashion has changed since the 1960s. _____ many women were sporting mini-skirts, high heels, and bright jewelry.

4. However, _____ women are wearing conservative suits with discreet accessories.

5. Are women copying men? Or are they simply aware that a more serious approach to fashion results in being taken more seriously? What will the future bring? What will women be

   wearing _____?

4.13   WRITTEN EXERCISE: *Changes*

DIRECTIONS: Using the above exercise as a model, write about one aspect of life at the workplace or in school that is changing in your country. Use time expressions as appropriate.

4.14   WRITTEN EXERCISE: *Milestones*

DIRECTIONS: Write about the milestones, or important events, in your life. Use at least one time expression from each of the progressive tenses listed on pages 67–68.

Reprinted by permission of UFS, Inc.

Questions:

1. What did the form letter really want to know?
2. What did she think the letter wanted to know?

═══════ GRAMMATICAL PATTERNS TWO ═══════

═══════ PREVIEW ═══════

DIRECTIONS: Read the following interview between a wealthy American businessman and a newspaper journalist. Then answer the questions that follow.

INTERVIEWER: Mr. McDougall, what do you consider to be your secret to success?

MCDOUGALL: That's not an easy question to answer since each person perceives success in a different way. For me, I believe that my success was a result of hard work.

INTERVIEWER: I see. Didn't luck **enter into the picture**?

MCDOUGALL: Well, yes, I'd have to say that it did. Good old-fashioned luck. You know, after my first million, I thought my luck had **run out**. But it hadn't. My fortune is growing every day, and I'm having a great time watching that happen.

INTERVIEWER: Did you always want to be rich?

MCDOUGALL: I'll tell you. I have **a strong drive**. I've always had it. I had been wanting to be a millionaire long before I even opened my first fast food restaurant, and I never **lost sight of** my goal. And for me success means money. Who ever heard of a successful businessman who is poor?

INTERVIEWER: Thank you, Mr. McDougall. One last question. Is money all there is? I mean, don't you ever think about the people around you, the homeless, the environment?

MCDOUGALL: Look here. I'm doing **my share**. I'm providing jobs for people. I'm paying for their health care. If somebody wants a job and is willing to work, send them to me. They don't need to be on the street.

     To answer your question—no, money can't buy everything, **as the saying goes**. There's your health, your family, your friends. I've got all three and I can say I'm happy and I'm loving my life.

VOCABULARY

to enter into the picture: to have something to do with it
to run out: to end, to disappear
a strong drive: a strong motivation to pursue and achieve a specific goal
to lose sight of: to forget
my share: my part
as the saying goes: according to the common statement or proverb

DISCUSSION

How do this businessman's values compare with yours? Is he really "doing his share"? How does his viewpoint compare with the idea of success expressed in the poem on page 55.

4.15 GRAMMAR CONSIDERATIONS: *FOCUS*

DIRECTIONS: The following questions are based on the preview text and are designed to help you find out what you already know about the structures in this section. Some of the questions may be hard and some of them may be easy. Answer as many of the questions as you can. Work with a partner if your teacher tells you to do so.

1. Compare the use of *have* in the following sentences. Is there any difference in meaning?
(a) I'm having a great time watching that happen.
(b) I have a strong drive.

Can you explain why (a) uses a progressive form and (b) does not? _____

_____

2. There are several verbs of **mental processes** (for example, *think*) in the interview. Write those verbs here.

_____

What tense is used with each?

3. *Love* is not usually used in the progressive. For example, we say "I love you." Can you guess why the businessman says "I'm loving my life"? _____

_____

I. VERBS NOT USED IN THE PROGRESSIVE

Some verbs cannot be used in a progressive form. The following chart lists these by category.

A. Voluntary and Involuntary Verbs

Verbs of sensory perception can be divided into two groups. Note the differences below.

CATEGORY	NO PROGRESSIVE	MAY USE PROGRESSIVE
SENSORY PERCEPTION	**Involuntary verbs** These refer to passive, unconscious activities. **Do not use these in the progressive form.**	**Voluntary verbs** These refer to active, conscious activities. **These verbs can be used in the progressive form.**
Sound	*Hear* ■ I was unable to sleep because I **heard** the neighbors quarreling.	*Listen to* ■ I **was listening** to Beethoven's Ninth Symphony when the electricity went off.

Smell	*Smell* ■ Your hair **smells** great!	*Smell* ■ Why **was** your dog **smelling** my couch?
Taste	*Taste* ■ This cake is delicious! It **tastes** just like my mother's!	*Taste* ■ I burned myself while I **was tasting** the soup.
Sight	*See* ■ Judy **saw** the photographers as she walked down the runway. (See the special note below for an exception to this verb.)	*Look at / Watch* ■ Judy **was looking at** the dress in the window. (for stationary objects) ■ The audience **was watching** Judy as she twirled around in her dress. (for moving objects)
Touch	*Feel* ■ She **felt** a cold draft in the old house.	*Feel / Touch* ■ The man **was feeling** his stubbly beard.

4.16   FILL IN THE BLANKS: *Voluntary* and *Involuntary Verbs*

DIRECTIONS: Read the following sentences and fill in the blanks with an appropriate form of the verb in parentheses. In several cases you will need to choose between an involuntary or voluntary verb, depending on the context of the sentence.

EXAMPLE

What kind of music (listen to / hear) <u>are you listening to</u> right now? (voluntary verb)

1. Shh! Could you please turn down that music? I (listen to / hear) _____

   the president's State of the Union address and I can't (listen to / hear) _____
   a word of what he's saying.

2. Mrs. Jones is considered by many to be a poor mother, because her children always (watch

   / see) _____ T.V. programs of little educational value.

3. After the seance yesterday evening, Mary and Bob (feel) _____ the
   presence of an unfriendly ghost in their living room.

4. The blind man (feel) _____ the cat's soft fur when she suddenly
   scratched his arm.

5. Quick! Call the fire department! I (smell) _____ something burning.

DENNIS THE MENACE

"HOW DO YOU EXPECT ME TO HEAR YOU WHEN I WASN'T EVEN *LISTENING* ?"

Used by permission of Hank Ketcham and © by North America Syndicate.

4.17   WRITTEN EXERCISE: *Voluntary* and *Involuntary Verbs*

DIRECTIONS: Note Dennis' use of both a voluntary (**listen**) and involuntary (**hear**) verb in the above comic. Demonstrate your understanding of the difference between the voluntary and involuntary use of sensory verbs. Write one sentence for each verb listed below.

1. a) listen to
   b) hear
2. a) watch
   b) see
3. a) touch
   b) feel
4. a) smell (voluntary)
   b) smell (involuntary)
5. a) taste (voluntary)
   b) taste (involuntary)

SPECIAL NOTE
SEE = VISIT or DATE

Sometimes SEE = VISIT or DATE, as in the following examples. You can use the progressive in these cases:

(1) **I'm seeing** Gary now; we might get married soon. (He's my boyfriend. We go out on dates.)

(2) I'll **be seeing** the doctor at 4:00 P.M. (I have a visit with the doctor.)

B. Other Verbs Not Used in the Progressive

CATEGORY	NO PROGRESSIVE	MAY USE PROGRESSIVE (Exceptions)
POSSESSION AND RELATION	<ul><li>I **have** three cars now.</li><li>She **possesses** many good traits.</li><li>How many houses do you **own?**</li><li>He **belongs** to a health club.</li><li>This milk **contains** vitamin D.</li></ul>	1. *to have = to experience*<ul><li>**I'm having** a great time watching that happen.</li><li>Paula's **having** a difficult time learning French.</li></ul>
EMOTION AND ATTITUDE	<ul><li>I **love** to play tennis!</li><li>He **hates** mayonnaise.</li><li>I **prefer** to live in a city now.</li><li>She **cares** about her TOEFL score.</li><li>He **hopes** she will marry him.</li></ul> <ul><li>I **want** to be a writer.</li></ul>	2. *love/hate:* Occasionally, *love* and *hate* can be used in the progressive in conversation for **very strong emphasis:**<ul><li>How do you like your new job? **I'm loving** it. (something new)</li><li>**I'm loving** my life. (emphasis—I **do** love my life.)</li></ul>3. *Want* can be used in the progressive in the **perfect tenses only:**<ul><li>I **had been wanting** to be my own boss for a long time.</li></ul>
MENTAL ACTIVITY AND PERCEPTION	<ul><li>He **thinks** abortion is immoral.</li><li>She **considers** cheating to be a serious offense.</li><li>He **believes** in reincarnation.</li></ul> <ul><li>I **don't mean** to insult you.</li></ul> <ul><li>I **remember** you from the party!</li><li>I'm sorry, but **I've forgotten** your name.</li><li>I **didn't recognize** you with your new haircut.</li></ul>	4. If *think about / consider* ≠ believe, you **may** use a progressive form:<ul><li>I **am considering** taking a trip.</li><li>He **has been thinking** about changing careers.</li></ul>5. *mean = have the intention*<ul><li>**I've been meaning** to call the doctor, but I've been so busy.</li></ul>6. *cumulative effects* Use a progressive with verbs of mental activity and an expression like *more and more* to emphasize the incompleted, step-by-step process:<ul><li>More and more, **I'm recognizing** the need for regular exercise.</li><li>It's so sad. My grandmother **is** slowly **forgetting** everything.</li></ul>
STATIVE VERBS	<ul><li>Laura **is** a teacher.</li><li>You **look** like a million bucks!</li><li>It **appears** much easier than it is.</li><li>You **seem** depressed.</li></ul>	7. *be = behave unusually*<ul><li>Our professor **is being** really unreasonable; she's asked us to write three papers this semester.</li></ul>

4.18 RECOGNITION EXERCISE: *Verbs Not Used in the Progressive*

DIRECTIONS: Reread the preview interview. Circle and identify the verbs in the speech that belong to any of the following categories: Possession and Relation (**P&R**), Sensory Perception (**SP**), Emotion and Attitude (**E&A**), Mental Activity and Perception (**MA&P**), and Stative verbs (**S**). If any of these verbs are progressive, be ready to explain why.

4.19 WRITTEN EXERCISE: *Verbs of Emotion* and *Mental Activity*

DIRECTIONS: Read the following pairs of sentences and decide if the progressive verb form is grammatically correct. Mark **I** next to the incorrect sentences and **C** next to the correct ones. Then write a short explanation why in the space provided.

EXAMPLE

I	I am wanting to travel around the world now.
	Do not use a progressive with **want** in the simple tenses.

C	I have been wanting to see the movie "Back to the Future" for a long time.
	You can use a progressive with **want** in the perfect tenses.

1. _____ The President is considering the economy to be an important issue in this year's election.

_____ The President is considering visiting South America next year.

2. _____ Since Jeannette hasn't spoken Chinese in two years, she is slowly forgetting everything she learned.

_____ What did you say your name was? I'm forgetting it now.

3. _____ Robert has been meaning to visit his elderly aunt in the hospital for some time now, but he has been quite busy at his new job.

_____ You'd better go to your room right now, Kathy. I am meaning it when I say it!

4. _____ How do you like your new house? Oh, I'm just loving it more every day.

_____ I'm just loving roses!

4.20 PAIRED ACTIVITY: *Verbs Not Used in the Progressive*

DIRECTIONS: Read the following dialogue aloud with a partner. Then decide if it is possible to change the verbs in bold to a progressive form. Refer to the chart for assistance. Then read the dialogue again, changing to a progressive whenever possible. Be ready to give reasons for changing these verbs.

Situation: Ms. Kelley is the vice-president of marketing for Peoria Paper Products. Aaron, her marketing assistant, has been with the company for five years. In this dialogue, Aaron is asking Ms. Kelley for his first salary increase.

KELLEY: Good morning, Aaron. **Do you want** to talk to me about something?

AARON: Well, yes, Ms. Kelley. **I've thought** carefully about my situation here at Peoria Paper Products. As you know, I've been here for five years and I've contributed a great deal during that time. I **don't feel** that my present salary level reflects my contributions.

KELLEY: I see. What makes you think that you deserve such a raise?

AARON: For one thing, as my familiarity with our markets increases, I **understand** more and more about the needs of our customers. This helps us design more effective and profitable marketing campaigns.

KELLEY: Mmm, hmmm. . . .

AARON: And our sales have increased 10% since I arrived.

KELLEY: Uh huh. . . .

AARON: And other marketing assistants with my track record earn twice my salary.

KELLEY: Well, Aaron, as I **listen to** you describe your accomplishments, your request for a raise **seems** more and more reasonable. I **believe** a raise is in order, so I'll be in touch with the Personnel Department immediately to do the necessary paperwork.

AARON: Thank you, Ms. Kelley. I **have wanted** this for quite a while.

4.21 PAIRED ACTIVITY: *A Small Success*

DIRECTIONS: Think about an experience you had that represents a small success for you (for example, performing well on a job interview, performing in a school play, etc.) Describe this experience to your partner, explaining what happened, what you were feeling and thinking at the time. Be ready to recount the experience in written form, if your teacher asks you to do so.

II. SPECIAL PROBLEMS WITH THE PROGRESSIVE

PROBLEM	EXPLANATION
1. USE OF SIMPLE PRESENT FOR CURRENT ONGOING ACTIVITY [INCORRECT: I read my economics book now.] CORRECT: I am reading my economics book right now.	Use the progressive for ongoing activity.
2. USE OF PROGRESSIVE TO EXPRESS HABITUAL ACTIVITY [INCORRECT: What are you doing for a living?] CORRECT: What do you do for a living?	Use the simple present for habitual activity.
3. USE OF PRESENT WITH *THIS + TIME WORDS* [INCORRECT: I take 3 courses this semester.] CORRECT: I am taking 3 courses this semester.	Use a progressive tense with *this + time words*
4. NO PROGRESSIVE TO CONTRAST AN ONGOING ACTIVITY WITH A SUDDEN ACTION [INCORRECT: I ironed my shirt when the electricity went off.] CORRECT: I was ironing my shirt when the electricity went off.	When one ongoing activity is intersected by another, more sudden action, use the progressive to show this contrast.

■ 4.22 PROGRESSIVE REVIEW

DIRECTIONS: Circle any correct answer. **There may be one, two, or three correct answers.**

1. I could tell by the hoarseness of his voice that he _____ at the soccer game.
   (a) was screaming
   (b) had been screaming
   (c) had screamed

2. By this time tomorrow, she _____ to Hawaii.
   (a) is flying
   (b) will be flying
   (c) flies

3. At this time in his life, John _____ a better job.
   (a) seeks
   (b) is seeking
   (c) has been seeking

4. Every month the bank _____ me a statement of my transactions.
   (a) will have been sending
   (b) sends
   (c) has been sending

5. I _____ that your advice about writing a letter to the company was very helpful.
   (a) have been thinking
   (b) think
   (c) am thinking

6. By the time the ship arrives, we _____ for two hours.
   (a) will have been waiting
   (b) will be waiting
   (c) are waiting

7. I _____ to send this package of books, but I just haven't had time.
   (a) meant
   (b) have been meaning
   (c) will be meaning

8. The children _____ to go to the circus for a long time before their grandparents finally took them.
   (a) were wanting
   (b) had wanted
   (c) had been wanting

9. The Johnsons are so rich that they _____ three houses.
   (a) own
   (b) have been owning
   (c) are owning

10. Based on the evidence the defense has prepared, it _____ that they will win the case.
   (a) has been seeming
   (b) is seeming
   (c) seems

■ 4.23 ERROR ANALYSIS: *The Progressive*

DIRECTIONS: Some of the following sentences have errors in verb form. Make the necessary changes clearly. **Do not change anything that is already correct. Be ready to explain the mistakes and your corrections.**

1. I wonder what that exotic spice in this sauce is. I am tasting tumeric and coriander, but there is another spice that I can't identify.
2. By the time her husband was awakened by the smoke, she had already been smelling the fire downstairs and called the fire department.
3. I touched the expensive vase when it suddenly fell to the floor and smashed into many pieces. I felt very embarrassed when I told my grandmother about it.
4. Lisa, did you forget everything I taught you about setting a table? You put the fork on the wrong side of the plate!

5. Jim studied in his room when his sister arrived, so he didn't hear the door open.
6. As the elderly man crossed Main Street last night, he was assaulted and robbed by two armed boys.
7. My sister and I take the same classes this semester.
8. During the entire party, I wasn't recognizing the girl in the red dress until she began to laugh.
9. This year, the university works hard to recruit students from Malaysia.
10. Go call the fire department. I am smelling smoke.
11. In spite of many arguments against the idea, John is still believing that men are superior to women.
12. I'm not understanding what you are trying to say right now.
13. My baby sister is being a real brat today, so I am going to the beach.
14. Have you cried? Your face is red and blotchy.
15. These days, American parents are having fewer children than ever before.
16. I'm not agreeing with any of my professor's theories this semester.
17. Lorenzo told Maria that he was thinking that they were seeing too much of each other.
18. I crossed Skyline Drive when I suddenly heard the loud screech of tires. I turned around and there was a huge moving van just a few feet from me. I'm lucky I didn't get run over.
19. Have you drunk whiskey tonight? I am smelling it on your breath.

COMPOSITON TOPICS

1. Compare your personal idea of success with the philosophy expressed in the poem at the beginning of the chapter.
2. Describe a successful person you currently know. Explain what he or she is presently doing and how he or she managed to achieve success.
3. "Time is money." "Money talks." "A penny saved is a penny earned." These are some very popular expressions that many Americans use to express their attitude about the value of money. Many Americans believe that money will bring them a certain amount of happiness, and the typical American would like to earn enough money to live comfortably. Buying on credit has become popular in the United States as more consumers wish to have their material possessions now and pay for them later. In a well-written composition, discuss your own attitudes, emotions, and perceptions of money, indicating how they might be different from those conveyed by the expressions above.

━━━━━ VERB INTEGRATION EXERCISES ━━━━━

DIRECTIONS: The exercises in this section practice all the verb tenses and forms—simple, progressive, and perfect. They require you to compare and contrast the use of verbs in many different contexts.

■ **1.** The following is the passage from the introduction to this unit without the verb tenses. See if you can complete the passage correctly. All 12 verb forms are included.

People (always / tell) _____ me that I (be) _____ an adaptable person. However, when I (come) _____ to the United States to study, I (find) _____ out that I (be) _____ not as adaptable as I (seem) _____ . I (already / study) _____ six years of English before I (leave) _____ my country of Indonesia. I (study) _____ conversational English with an American teacher for about a year before I (leave) _____ . So I really (not / expect) _____ to have any problems communicating with Americans. I (think) _____ to myself, "I (just / go) _____ to my classes and learn everything I can. Then by the time the TOEFL test (arrive) _____ , I (learn) _____ everything I need to get 550 on the TOEFL. I (enter) _____ the local university for my M.B.A."

Well, I really wasn't ready for my first months there. At the first orientation meeting at the English school, the Americans (talk) _____ to me so fast that all I did was smile and nod. I still (not / know) _____ what they (say) _____ to me! I (have) _____ more surprises—my accent (be) _____ hard to understand, I (not / like) _____ the American food at the cafeteria, the pace in the city (be) _____ too fast. But the biggest surprise (be) _____ _____ my progress in English. I (not / get) _____ into that university right away.

I'm still studying English. In fact, I've been studying for two semesters now. If all goes as planned, I (enter) _____ the M.B.A. program next semester. I (live) _____ in the United States for an entire year by then. I can understand just about everything, and most people can understand me. But guess what? I'm still not used to American food!

2. Write your own story about going to a foreign country or new city based on the above text. Try to use all 12 verb forms if at all possible. Underline all the verbs.

3. The following chart appeared on page 21. Note that these sentences have little meaning without additional information such as time expressions, additional clauses, or explanation. Complete these sentences to justify the verb tense used.

I eat cornflakes for breakfast.	I ate	I will eat
I have eaten	I had eaten	I will have eaten
I am eating	I was eating	I will be eating
I have been eating	I had been eating	I will have been eating

4. Storytelling is often difficult in a foreign language because of the many verb tenses required to describe the action in the story. Choose a popular fairytale or children's bedtime story from your country. Recreate that story in English, in writing. Use as many verb tenses as is naturally possible and underline them. Be ready to share your story with the class orally.

5. Below are three brief biographies of well-known people. Choose one and write a summary of his life in well-composed complete sentences. If you prefer, you can go to the library to research a different individual not represented here. Use the most appropriate verb tenses to express time relationships. Add time expressions.

Thomas Paine
- born in 1737 in England
- emigrated to America in 1774
- appearance of his pamphlet *Common Sense* in 1776, urging American colonists to declare independence
- writer and radical
- wrote *The Crisis* during the war
- returned to England in 1791
- wrote *The Rights of Man* in 1791–92, defending the French Revolution
- as a result, he left England for France
- returned to United States in 1802 and died there

Pele
- full name is Edson Arantes do Nascimento
- born in 1940 in Brazil
- considered the best soccer player of all time
- led the Brazilian national soccer team to victory in 1958, 1962, and 1970
- joined the New York Cosmos in 1975
- played with them until 1977
- North American Soccer League gained credibility
- scored 1,281 goals during his career as a soccer player

Malcolm X
- born Malcolm Little in 1925
- U.S. African-American radical
- in prison 1946–52
- converted to Black Muslims during this time
- became their leader in 1963
- founded Organization of Afro-American Unity (OAAU) in 1964
- OAAU supported "brotherhood," not separation
- assassinated in 1965 at an OAAU meeting

6. First fill in the section YOU below with the story of your life. Pair up with another student and compare the events of your lives, asking questions and making comparisons. Then fill in the section YOUR PARTNER. Be ready to share with your class orally.

EXAMPLE

A: What kind of work were you doing in 1985?
B: I was working for an insurance company. And you?
A: While you were working for the insurance company, I was in school.

	YOU	**YOUR PARTNER**
DURING THE PAST FIVE YEARS:		
• Professional activities		
• Educational activities		
• Family activities		
• Leisure activities		

THIS YEAR ■ Professional activities ■ Educational activities ■ Social activities		
FUTURE ■ Briefly describe what you think your life will be like in the future.		

7. Use any appropriate verb tense. If more than one is possible, indicate this.

    A. (A postcard from Janine to her sister Jocelyn)

Greetings from London! We (have) _____ a blast here! The weather (be) _____ unbelievable and the city (be) _____ full of charm. We (visit) _____ all the sites for kids in London and the kid in me (have) _____ a good time. We (have) _____ a chance to see "Phantom of the Opera." When you come in August, I (get) _____ you tickets.

Hope you (be) _____ well.

Jocelyn Jones
423 Brown St.
Kensico, NY 12345
U.S.A.

B. (A letter to an English teacher from a former student)

> I (just / finish) _____ my first quarter here. It (be) _____ such a nightmare that I (be) _____ so happy when I (finish) _____ my final exams. This business school (be) _____ very tough—at least for me with my average skills. In fact, four courses at four credit hours (take) _____ almost every hour of my day.
>
> According to the most recent survey from Business Week, this school (rate) _____ among the 20 best schools!
>
> I (have) _____ a nice holiday with a two-day visit to Toronto and the rest in Rochester with –5°F. How about you? (you / still / teach) _____ that writing class?
>
> Please give my regards to your husband.

C. (A letter from a friend after the birth of her baby)

> Life (change) _____ tremendously since Matthew's arrival and for the most part we (love) _____ it. He (be) _____ almost 10 months old and he (be) _____ already quite a character! He almost (walk) _____ and he (say) _____ "DaDa" for the first time tonight when Mickey (come) _____ home. I would love to spend more time with him and I (propose) _____ a part-time job to my boss. I (not / know) _____ what will come of it. If he doesn't agree, I may just quit for the time being. I can always go back to work, but never back to Matthew's childhood.
>
> Mickey (work) _____ hard at being a lawyer as well as a father these days. He (do) _____ a great job at both.

> How are you? We would love to see you. Any chance that you (be) _____ on the east coast next year? Please write or call when you can. I (want) _____ to know how you are.

D. (A thank you letter)

> Thanks so much for the beautiful sterling silver earrings. They (win) _____ the approval of my whole family. I can think of several outfits that they (complement) _____.
>
> The weather here (be) _____ gorgeous and I (go) _____ to the beach every day for three to four hours. Now I (have) _____ that attractive rosey glow to replace the usually pasty white of winter.
>
> I hope you (feel) _____ better. Thanks again for your gift.

8. Compare the following sets of sentences. Decide if the sentences have the same meaning. If not, indicate the difference in the space provided.

EXAMPLE

A: I read few books.
B: I am reading a book.
_____ Same meaning
___X___ Different meaning: (a) describes regular activity; (b) describes what that person is doing now

1. **(a)** My son eats my leftovers every day.
   (b) My son is always eating the leftovers in the fridge.
   _____ Same meaning
   _____ Different meaning: _____

2. **(a)** Just a few people in this class have been doing all the talking.
   (b) Just a few people have talked so far. Does anyone want to add anything?
   _____ Same meaning
   _____ Different meaning: _____

3. **(a)** I'll be 60 on Friday.
   (b) I will have turned 60 by Friday.
   _____ Same meaning
   _____ Different meaning: _____

4. **(a)** I'm in a pretty good mood.
   (b) I've been in a pretty good mood.
   _____ Same meaning
   _____ Different meaning: _____

5. **(a)** I've been living in this old house for six years.
   (b) I've lived in this old house for six years.
   _____ Same meaning
   _____ Different meaning: _____

6. **(a)** Eloise has never seen snow.
   (b) Eloise never saw snow.
   _____ Same meaning
   _____ Different meaning: _____

7. **(a)** Jack left when Judy arrived.
   (b) Jack had left when Judy arrived.
   _____ Same meaning
   _____ Different meaning: _____

8. **(a)** Cynthia cleaned the house before her mother came to visit.
   (b) Cynthia had cleaned the house before her mother came to visit.
   _____ Same meaning
   _____ Different meaning: _____

9. **(a)** I've been meaning to do it.
   (b) I meant to do it.
   _____ Same meaning
   _____ Different meaning: _____

10. **(a)** He's being a difficult child.
    (b) He is a difficult child.
    _____ Same meaning
    _____ Different meaning: _____

9. Work in pairs. Choose three of the pairs of sentences above. Incorporate each sentence into a three to four line conversation between two people to make the exact meaning of the sentence clear. (You will have six conversations.) Write these down and be ready to present them to the class.

EXAMPLE

CUE: I read few books.
A: What do you do in your spare time?
B: I like to ride my bicycle and do stuff outdoors.
A: Don't you like to read?
B: No, I'm not that type. I read few books in my spare time.

5

HEALTH AND FITNESS I

▤ The sentence: Introduction

DISCUSSION QUESTIONS

1. Do you consider yourself a healthy individual? What aspects of your lifestyle help you to maintain your health? What bad habits do you have that are threatening to your health?
2. Are you involved in a sports or exercise program? Is there any sport that you've never tried that you're curious about?
3. What kind of medical system do you have in your country? Is medical care expensive? Do you have medical insurance?

OBJECTIVES

In this chapter you will learn:

1. To understand the distinction between phrases and clauses
2. To understand the components of English sentences in a variety of forms
3. To recognize and correct faulty sentences

PREVIEW

DIRECTIONS: Read the following interview between Randy Brown, a leading T.V. journalist, and Joyce Coles, the famous actress who popularized aerobics instruction.

RANDY: Tell me, Joyce. What made you become so seriously involved in **aerobics** instruction?

JOYCE: Well, you know, I've always been kind of a **health nut,** but for 10 years I hadn't been very good about **staying in shape** because of my film career. Two years ago, I attended one of the first aerobics classes here in L.A., and I felt so great afterwards that I signed up for a year of classes. I really **got into it** for a year and then decided to start a class of my own.

RANDY: And now you have your own **fitness center** and a videotape that has sold millions.

JOYCE: Yeah, I took some time off from making movies for awhile to **get** the fitness center **off the ground.** The video was a fairly simple project because I was already running classes at the center in Hollywood.

RANDY: You know, you've been an inspiration to many women who thought there was **no getting around** the **middle-aged spread.** What is your message to these women?

JOYCE: I want them to realize that we can stay fit and beautiful by **working out** regularly. If our bodies are in shape, our minds work better and we feel better about ourselves.

RANDY: Is working out the only answer? What about diet?

JOYCE: Of course, a balanced diet along with a regular program of exercise is the real key to **getting into shape** and maintaining for an extended period of time. There are too many **fad diets** out there that can be very unhealthy and even dangerous.

RANDY: Well, Joyce, I'm sure you know what you're talking about because you are definitely the **picture of health.** Thanks for talking to us today, and we'll look forward to your upcoming video of aerobics for pregnancy.

JOYCE: Thank you, Randy, it was a pleasure speaking with you.

VOCABULARY

aerobics: an exercise routine set to music and designed to increase the heart rate

health nut: a person who is preoccupied with health

get into shape: improve your physical condition so that you are at your ideal weight and your muscles are toned

staying in shape: maintaining a good physical condition through regular exercise and good diet

get into (something): become interested and involved in something

fad diet: a strict diet that promises rapid weight loss and that becomes very popular

fitness center: a place for physical training usually consisting of a running track, swimming pool, weight room, exercise bicycles, and saunas

get (something) off the ground: get a new project started

no getting around: no avoiding

middle-aged spread: heaviness around the middle of the body that can occur during middle age

picture of health: looking perfectly fit and healthy

a balanced diet: eating the proper amount of food from the four major food groups and avoiding unhealthy foods

CULTURAL NOTE / DISCUSSION

In recent years a health craze has swept the United States. Many people are preoccupied with maintaining a healthy diet and a regular program of exercise. Is there much emphasis on health and exercise in your country? What kinds of diets and exercise are popular?

GRAMMAR CONSIDERATIONS: FOCUS

The following questions are based on the preview text and are designed to help you find out what you already know about the structures in this chapter. Some of the questions may be hard and some of them may be easy. Answer as many of the questions as you can. Work with a partner if your teacher tells you to do so.

1. In the following two sentences from the preview, **and** is used as a connector. How is the pattern of the two sentences different based on the function of this connector? How could you change the sentences so that they have the same pattern?
   a. Two years ago, I attended one of the first aerobics classes here in L.A., **and** I felt so great afterwards that I signed up for a year of classes.
   b. I really got into it **and** then decided to start a class of my own.

2. What is the difference between the two underlined groups of words in the sentences below?
   a. The video was a fairly simple project because I was already running classes. . . .
   b. I hadn't been very good about staying in shape because of my film career.

3. Find an example in the preview of an incomplete sentence. How could you make this sentence complete?

GRAMMATICAL PATTERNS

I. PHRASES AND CLAUSES

The following chart demonstrates the difference between phrases and clauses.

DEFINITION	TYPE	EXAMPLE
PHRASE: Two or more words that serve a particular function in a sentence. A phrase doesn't have one or more components (for example, subject, verb) which would make it a sentence.	1. NOUN PHRASE 2. VERB PHRASE 3. PREPOSITIONAL PHRASE 4. GERUND PHRASE[a] 5. INFINITIVE PHRASE[a] 6. PARTICIPIAL PHRASE	1. **Many fad diets** are unhealthy. 2. Vegetarians **often need to take** vitamins. 3. You should eat breakfast **in the morning.** 4. **Swimming, cycling, and playing tennis** are her favorite ways to exercise. 5. She really likes **to swim, to ride her bicycle, and to play tennis.** 6. **Knowing the harmful effects of fats,** health conscious people limit their intake. (Present participle of a verb, used in a phrase that serves as an adjective.)
CLAUSE: A clause contains a subject and a verb. An **independent clause** can stand alone as a sentence. A **dependent clause** cannot stand alone as a sentence. It must be joined to an independent clause.	1. INDEPENDENT CLAUSE 2. DEPENDENT CLAUSE ▪ Adjective[b] ▪ Adverb[b] ▪ Noun[b]	1. **Sarah maintains a very balanced diet.** 2. **Because John has a heart problem,** he is on a low-cholesterol diet. ▪ You must choose a diet **which you can live with.** ▪ **Although Richard is overweight,** he doesn't exercise. ▪ Sharon thought **that she would lose 40 pounds on her new diet.**

[a]See Chapter 14 for more explanation about gerund and infinitive phrases.
[b]See the chapters that follow for more explanation about adjective, adverb, and noun clauses.

5.1 RAPID DRILL: *Phrase* or *Clause?*

DIRECTIONS: State whether each underlined group of words is a phrase or a clause.

EXAMPLE

Due to the growing interest in better health, many people are joining fitness clubs. (Phrase)

1. Because of the latest trend in health and exercise, health clubs are opening everywhere.

2. My favorite time to exercise is in the morning after getting up and before eating breakfast.

3. A leading expert in the field of nutrition has stated that calories play a more important role in weight gain than anything else.

4. Despite her repeated efforts to lose weight, she has had no success.

5. Getting enough sleep and eating well are essential in order to stay healthy.

6. I go to the health club every day to work out although it is very often an effort to get myself there.

7. Alicia likes any kind of exercise; however, she has never tried windsurfing or kayaking on the ocean.

5.2   WRITTEN EXERCISE: *How Healthy Are You?*

DIRECTIONS: How healthy do you think you are? Use each pair of phrases below to write a sentence that describes your lifestyle and health. Use a variety of phrase and clause types in your sentences and be prepared to distinguish the phrases from the clauses.

EXAMPLE

get up early / stay up late: I always get up early in the morning and stay up late at night.
(One independent clause with two verb phrases)

OR

Because I always get up early in the morning, I can't stay up late.
(One dependent clause and one independent clause)

1. a healthy diet / plenty of exercise

_____

2. get enough sleep / feel tired

_____

3. drink alcohol / smoke cigarettes

_____

4. my health / every day of my life

_____

II. THE PARTS OF A SENTENCE

A. The Subject

The subject of a sentence can have a variety of forms as demonstrated in the chart below.

FORM	EXAMPLE
NOUN PRONOUN NOUN PHRASE GERUND PHRASE INFINITIVE PHRASE NOUN CLAUSE	▪ **Joyce** has her own fitness center. ▪ **She** teaches aerobics classes at the center. ▪ **The aerobics classes** are very demanding. ▪ **Staying in shape** requires exercise and a balanced diet. ▪ **To avoid the middle-aged spread** is his primary goal. ▪ **What form of exercise you choose** affects the kind of results you get.

See the chapters on noun clauses, gerunds, and infinitives for more explanation.

5.3   ORAL PRACTICE

DIRECTIONS: You are a health expert and you must create a set of guidelines for optimal health. Create your guidelines using each given word or phrase as the subject of a sentence.

EXAMPLE

Good health . . .
Good health is a product of balanced nutrition and a regular program of exercise.

1. A regular program of exercise . . .
2. Taking aerobics classes . . .
3. What you eat . . .
4. Junk food, coffee, cigarettes, and alcohol . . .
5. Fad diets . . .
6. Staying healthy and fit . . .
7. The best way to avoid getting sick . . .
8. You . . .

B. The Verb

English verbs are either transitive or intransitive. If a verb is **transitive,** the action of the verb is received by a **direct object.** If the verb is **intransitive,** the action of the verb remains in the verb and there is **no direct object.** The chart below classifies some of these verbs.

VERBS	EXAMPLE	NOTES

TRANSITIVE VERBS *ALWAYS TRANSITIVE* *Verb + Direct Object* **have, use, do, want, need, say, hold, hit, choose, watch, spend, wear, keep, attend, raise, lay, bring up**	1. Jim **had** <u>a cold</u> last week.
	      D.O.
	 2. We **make** <u>dinner</u> at 5:00.
	      D.O.
	 3. She **wanted** <u>a better grade</u>.
	      D.O.
	 4. I'm **using** <u>the weight room</u>.
	      D.O.
	 5. She's **bringing up** <u>three sons</u>.
	      D.O.
		These verbs are always followed by a direct object.

Verb + (Indirect) Object + Direct Object **give, buy, tell, take, sell, make, send, bring, get, pay**	6. He **gave** <u>me</u> <u>some advice</u>.
	     I.O. D.O.
	 7. She **sold** <u>me</u> <u>a bicycle</u>.
	     I.O. D.O.
	 8. She **sold** <u>a bicycle</u> <u>to me.</u>
	     D.O. I.O.
	 (NOT: She **sold to me** a bicycle.)
	 9. He **made** <u>her</u> <u>a cake</u>.
	     I.O. D.O.
	 10. He **made** <u>a cake</u> <u>for her</u>.
	      D.O. I.O.
	 (NOT: He **made for her** a cake.)
		Some verbs can be followed by an indirect object before the direct object to indicate the receiver of the direct object.
		
		 When *to* or *for* are used with the indirect object, they come after the direct object.

TRANSITIVE OR INTRANSITIVE *Verb + Direct Object* **eat, play, begin, finish, practice, leave, ring, sing, teach, learn, see, hear, break, read, write, taste, smell**	1. I **began** <u>the project</u>.
	     D.O.
	 2. The class **is beginning** now.
	 3. I **eat** <u>breakfast</u> every morning.
	     D.O.
	 4. Yesterday I **didn't eat** all day.
	 5. Stop and **smell** <u>the roses!</u>
	      D.O.
	 6. The roses **smell** lovely.
		Some verbs can be either transitive or intransitive, depending on the context and meaning.

| INTRANSITIVE VERBS
LINKING VERBS
be, seem, appear, become | 1. A regular program of exercise
     _{subj.}
 is the real key to staying in shape.
       _{comp.}
 2. Kathy **seems** very healthy.
   _{subj.}   _{comp.} | Linking verbs are followed by a *complement,* which completes the verb and is equal to the subject of the sentence. |
| *ACTION VERBS*
walk, run, work, live, sleep, work out, come, go, arrive, listen, speak, rise, lie, talk, get dressed, laugh, grow up | 3. In the afternoons, Bruce **works out.**
 4. Bruce **works out** every day.
 5. Susan **gets dressed** after breakfast.
 6. Mark **grew up** on rice and fish. | Action verbs can stand alone with no object or complement. These verbs are usually followed by a phrase. |

5.4   ERROR CORRECTION: *Transitive* or *Intransitive?*

DIRECTIONS: Correct the error in each of the sentences below based on whether the verb is transitive or intransitive.

EXAMPLE

[INCORRECT: I love to **run** the park in the morning before work.]
CORRECT: I love to **run in the park** in the morning before work.

1. When parents are growing up their kids, they should teach them about good nutrition.
2. If I want to ask my teacher a question, I always rise my hand.
3. In the morning I get dressed my clothes.
4. My aerobics instructor said me about the new music she will use.
5. The dinner was so delicious last night. I never tasted before.
6. I arrive the gym very early in the morning.
7. When my mother was raising, she always emphasized the benefits of fresh fruits.

5.5   ORAL PRACTICE: *Transitive* and *Intransitive Verbs*

DIRECTIONS: Your partner or teacher will ask you a question. Answer the question using the verb provided in parentheses. If the verb can be either transitive or intransitive, use it in both ways in your answer.

EXAMPLE

What are your eating habits? (eat)
TRANSITIVE: I try to eat three balanced meals every day.
INTRANSITIVE: I always read the newspaper while I'm eating.

1. Are you a good cook? (cook)
2. What are your sleeping habits? (sleep)
3. Did your mother teach you about good nutrition? (grow up)
4. Which skills are your strongest in English? (read / write / speak / listen)

5. What do you usually do when you have a headache? (lie)
6. What is your routine before you go to work or school in the morning? (leave)
7. Where do you sit when you go to the movies? (see)
8. What do you think about aerobics? (seem)

5.6 ORAL PRACTICE: *The Picture of Health*

DIRECTIONS: Describe someone you know who is the "picture of health"—in very good health and physically fit. Use a variety of transitive and intransitive verbs from the chart on pages 93–94.

C. Direct Object and Complements

As you have already seen, a direct object receives the action of a transitive verb, and a complement completes the idea of an intransitive verb. The chart below lists the various forms that direct objects and complements can take.

FORM	EXAMPLE
DIRECT OBJECT 1. Noun 2. Pronoun 3. Noun phrase 4. Gerund phrase 5. Infinitive phrase 6. Noun clause	1. Joyce teaches **aerobics** every day. 2. She enjoys **it.** 3. Joyce has **her own fitness center and a videotape.** 4. Her students like **exercising to music.** 5. Joyce hopes **to open another fitness center** soon. 6. She knows **how to make this business successful.**
COMPLEMENT 1. Adjective 2. Noun phrase 3. Infinitive phrase 4. Noun clause	1. Joyce seems **happy.** 2. Joyce is **an aerobics instructor.** 3. Her dream is **to have two fitness centers.** 4. Fitness is **what she really believes in.**

5.7 RECOGNITION EXERCISE: *Identifying Sentence Parts*

DIRECTIONS: For each sentence below, underline the subject once, circle the verb, and underline the direct object or complement twice. Be prepared to describe each of those sentence parts.

EXAMPLE

Jim and his wife (eat) three balanced meals every day.

Jim and *wife* are nouns. *Eat* is a transitive verb. *Three balanced meals* is a direct object.

1. What Rachel really enjoys is taking long walks in the evening.
2. Due to the growing number of people at this fitness center, we are expanding.
3. Taking too many vitamins can be harmful to your body.
4. The secret to avoiding stress is managing your time wisely and exercising regularly.
5. Many avid joggers, cyclists, and swimmers have recently begun competing in the triathalon.

6. To be in excellent physical condition is what Grace has always strived for.

7. Michelle and her friends follow a strict vegetarian diet.

5.8 EXERCISE: *Verbs at Work*

DIRECTIONS: Identify the parts of the sentence in the following cartoon. Then replace the verb in the cartoon with *exercises*. What other changes do you have to make when you do that?

Mr. Carlisle probes the very frontier of fitness technique.

5.9 RAPID DRILL: *Scrambled Sentence Parts*

DIRECTIONS: Unscramble the following sentences and add the part of the sentence that is missing. Identify the missing part.

EXAMPLE

SCRAMBLED: Walking to work / every day / my only exercise / for the past month

UNSCRAMBLED: My only exercise for the past month <u>has been</u> walking to work. (Missing part: verb)

1. are / although / I / don't have / much time to do them / my favorite activities
2. and / are / a very difficult workout / my aerobics instructor / sore / this morning / gave / my muscles
3. through the park / when the dew is still on the grass / to walk / is / early in the morning
4. last week / that I would feel better / when I saw her / if I got more sleep / my doctor / me
5. grow / because of the pesticide use / in their back yards / many people / instead of buying them in the stores
6. get dressed / I take a shower / the sun / and / I / after

III. SENTENCE TYPES

A. Sentence Types According to Function

The chart below demonstrates the different types of English sentences according to their function.

TYPE	EXAMPLE	NOTES
DECLARATIVE subj. + verb + (obj.)	Headaches can sometimes be attributed to diet.	Makes a statement Ends in a period

INTERROGATIVE
wh + aux. + subj.
   + verb **OR**
wh + be + subj.
 	
   OR
aux. + subj. + verb
   OR
aux. + **not** + subj. +
verb
   OR
aux. + **not** + subj. +
adj.
 	
   OR
subj. + verb + obj.
	1. How does diet affect health?
	2. Who is the president?
	3. How many calories can you have?
	4. What time is it?
	   [INCORRECT: What time it is?]
	5. Is the new diet working?
	6. Have you started it yet?
	7. Haven't you worked out today?
	
	8. Aren't you tired?
	9. Don't you want to run with me?
	
	10. You ate onions for breakfast?
	11. You don't like ice cream?
		▪ A **wh**-question asks for information. (**who, what, why, when, where, how**)
		▪ Sometimes a quantifier or noun follows the **wh**-word. (3, 4)
		▪ A **yes / no** question asks for **yes** or **no** as an answer. (5, 6)
		▪ A **negative** question asks for confirmation or expresses disbelief. (8, 9)
		
		▪ A declarative sentence can be used as a question to express surprise. (10, 11)

IMPERATIVE simple verb + (obj.)	1. Drink plenty of fluids. 2. Don't forget to take your vitamins. 3. Be careful of drafts.	▪ Used as a command (1), reminder (2), or warning (3).

EXCLAMATORY
subj. + verb + (obj.)
   OR
what + noun
   OR
what + noun + subj.
   + verb
   OR
how + adj.
   OR
how + adj. + subj.
   + verb
	1. I lost 5 pounds!
	
	2. What a great workout!
	3. What difficult exercises!
	4. What a great teacher she was!
	
	5. How fascinating!
	
	6. How interesting that class was!
		▪ Used to express strong feelings such as surprise, pleasure, excitement, etc.
		▪ An exclamatory sentence ends with an exclamation point.
		▪ Errors are often made in word order, e.g., [INCORRECT: How interesting was that class!]

5.10   RAPID DRILL: *Exclamatory Sentences*

DIRECTIONS: Use an exclamatory statement to respond to each of the following situations.

EXAMPLE

CUE: You just heard some great news.
RESPONSE: What great news I just heard!

1. Your workout was exhilarating.
2. Your doctor has a very abrupt manner.
3. Your day at work was very stressful.
4. You feel sick.
5. You have found a great running path in the forest.
6. It's 105° F. today.
7. You just saw a beautiful sunset.

5.11   PAIRED PRACTICE: *Asking Questions*

DIRECTIONS: On the lines below, write five statements of fact about health and fitness. Take turns with your partner relating to each other the facts you have written. After one of you has made a statement, the other should ask a question about the information, using a different type of question each time.

EXAMPLE

STATEMENT: Some people suffer from environmental illness.
QUESTION: What exactly is environmental illness?

STATEMENTS:

1. _____
2. _____
3. _____
4. _____
5. _____
6. _____

5.12   ERROR CORRECTION: *Question Formation*

DIRECTIONS: Correct the errors in the following questions.

1. How many times you ran around the track?
2. What kind of running shoes they are?
3. Who you talked to about your sore arm?
4. What kind of doctor you have?
5. When you are going to the clinic?
6. How often you take these vitamins?
7. How many people you asked about the new equipment?

5.13   ORAL PRACTICE: *Sentence Types*

DIRECTIONS: Use a variety of sentence types to ask questions, give commands, make comments, and express surprise about the situations below.

EXAMPLE

Your friend is extremely thin. ("Are you sick?" "How thin you are!")

1. You sit down for your lunch break at work, and your office partner pulls out potato chips and a candy bar.
2. During a party, a friend of yours who never smokes is chain smoking.
3. You are walking up the stairs with a friend, and your friend is experiencing shortness of breath.
4. A friend of yours whom you haven't seen in six months looks extremely tired.
5. Your mother is putting six teaspoons of sugar into her coffee.
6. Your father, who experienced a heart attack a year ago, just ran two miles.
7. You are working out with your friend, and she just lifted two 100-pound weights.

5.14   EXERCISE: *What's Funny?*

DIRECTIONS: Read the following cartoon and discuss why it's funny. On the lines below, write the man's statement as a question and then as an exclamatory sentence with a different structure from the original.

Reprinted with permission of Copley News Service.

QUESTION: _____

EXCLAMATORY: _____

5.15   PAIRED PRACTICE: *Your Diet*

DIRECTIONS: After recording your diet for three days in the chart, show your partner and discuss how healthy your diet is.   As you discuss your diet with your partner, respond to the instructions below the chart on the next page.

MY DIET			
DAY 1 BREAKFAST	LUNCH	DINNER	SNACKS
DAY 2 BREAKFAST	LUNCH	DINNER	SNACKS
DAY 3 BREAKFAST	LUNCH	DINNER	SNACKS

1. Show surprise at two of the things your partner ate.

   a. _____

   b. _____

2. Make two observations or conclusions about your partner's diet.

   a. _____

   b. _____

3. Ask your partner two questions about the diet.

   a. _____

   b. _____

4. Tell your partner to make two important changes in his / her diet.

   a. _____

   b. _____

5.16   ORAL AND WRITTEN PRACTICE: *Weight Watchers*

DIRECTIONS: Weight Watchers is a well-known organization that is devoted to helping people reduce their weight. They have a strict diet that their members follow, regular meetings that their members attend, and their own food available in supermarkets. Write down at least five questions that you would like answered to better understand how the Weight Watchers program works. Then, if possible, make a telephone call to get the answers to your questions. If it is not possible for you to call, write your questions in a letter to the organization.

B. Sentence Types According to Structure

The chart below demonstrates different types of English sentences according to their structure.

TYPE	STRUCTURE	EXAMPLE
SIMPLE	one independent clause	▪ Scientists have developed artificial fat.
COMPOUND	two independent clauses joined by a **coordinating conjunction**	▪ You can eat all the fatty foods you want, **and** your body won't absorb the fat.
COMPLEX	one dependent clause joined to an independent clause by a **subordinating conjunction**	▪ **Although** you will be ingesting fatty foods, your body won't absorb the fat.
COMPOUND-COMPLEX	at least one independent clause and one dependent clause plus one additional clause	▪ Although you will be able to enjoy a variety of your favorite desserts and you will be ingesting all that fat, your body won't absorb the fat.

5.17   WRITTEN EXERCISE: *Sentence Types*

DIRECTIONS: For each of the illnesses or injuries below, write four sentences (one of each type from the above chart) describing your own experience. If you have no experience with the illness yourself, write what you know about it or substitute it with an illness that you have experienced. Label each sentence as is shown in the example.

EXAMPLE

ILLNESS: Common Cold
(simple) I come down with a cold once a year.
(compound) I usually get a sore throat, a stuffy nose, and I feel very tired and rundown.
(complex) Although I feel pretty miserable, I'm happy that it only lasts a few days.
(compound-complex) When I get a cold, I drink a lot of juice and rest in bed, but I never go to the doctor.

1. ILLNESS: Headaches

_____

_____

_____

_____

2. ILLNESS: Flu

_____

_____

_____

_____

3. INJURY: Broken bones

_____

_____

_____

_____

IV. FAULTY SENTENCES

A. Sentence Fragments

A sentence fragment is an incomplete sentence that is written as if it were a sentence. A sentence fragment is missing one or more sentence parts such as a subject, a verb, or an object. Read the following passage and notice the sentence fragments that are underlined. Discuss what component of the sentence is missing.

A vegetarian is a person who doesn't eat meat. For several reasons. Some vegetarians are opposed to the killing of animals. And being a vegetarian is a form of protest. These vegetarians don't eat any red meat or poultry. Or use any animal products such as leather or fur. Other vegetarians don't eat red meat for health reasons. Because red meat contains a lot of fat.

5.18 WRITTEN EXERCISE: _Correcting Sentence Fragments_

DIRECTIONS: In the passage below about macrobiotic diet, underline the sentence fragments. Then, on the lines below the passage, rewrite the passage so that there are no fragments. You may have to add some words.

A macrobiotic diet is based on the concept of yin and yang in Eastern philosophy and the natural balance of nature. An example. There is no meat in a macrobiotic diet. The small number of teeth in our mouth used for chewing meat compared to the other kind of teeth. Macrobiotics believe that we are not designed to have meat in our diet. Sugar also. Brown rice, which requires a lot of chewing, is the primary food in the macrobiotic diet. When we chew the rice, natural sugar is produced in the mouth. So we don't need any sugar from other sources. Of course, vegetables along with brown rice. Because they are such a rich source of vitamins and other essential nutrients.

_____

_____

_____

_____

_____

B. Run-On Sentences

There are two types of run-on sentences as shown in the chart below.

TYPE	RUN-ON SENTENCES	CORRECT SENTENCES
1. Two or more clauses incorrectly joined	I used to be a very healthy person, but recently my lifestyle has changed and I have developed some bad **habits they** include smoking cigarettes, drinking coffee, staying up late, and eating junk food.	I used to be a very healthy person, but recently my lifestyle has changed and I have developed some bad **habits that** include smoking cigarettes, drinking coffee, staying up late, and eating junk food.
2. Too many clauses in one sentence	I used to be a very healthy person, but recently my lifestyle has changed, and I have developed some bad habits, and they include smoking cigarettes, drinking coffee, and I stay up late and I eat too much junk food because I really can't resist it.	I used to be a very healthy person, but recently my lifestyle has changed, and I have developed some bad **habits. They** include smoking cigarettes **and** drinking coffee**; I also** stay up late and eat too much junk food because I really can't resist it.

5.19   WRITTEN EXERCISE: *Run-on Recognition*

DIRECTIONS: Determine whether each sentence below is a run-on sentence and justify your answer. Then, if necessary, make corrections so that it is not a run-on sentence.

1. Because Grace is a vegetarian, she must pay special attention to the amount of protein in the food she eats, so she eats a lot of beans, she also eats eggs.
2. When Grace first became a vegetarian, she missed eating meat since she had always liked the food she eats, so she eats a lot of beans, she also eats eggs.
3. When Grace first became a vegetarian, she missed eating meat since she had always liked the taste of it, but now she can't imagine eating meat because she has grown to appreciate the pure taste of meatless cuisine, and meat tastes very strange to her, and so she is happy to be a vegetarian.
4. Sometimes it's very difficult to eat out in restaurants due to the limited meatless choices on menus although that is changing now with the increase in vegetarian restaurants.

5. Grace is opposed to the killing of animals, so not only is she a vegetarian but she is also very disturbed by the use of animal fur for clothing.
6. She feels better now that she doesn't eat meat anymore, she feels more humane and she feels healthier.
7. Being a vegetarian and feeling that she is doing her share to protect animals, Grace becomes irritated when people question her motives for being a vegetarian although she tries to be patient with such people, and she tries to make them understand the value of saving animals, but often people just don't understand.

V. SPECIAL PROBLEMS

PROBLEM	EXPLANATION
INSERTING AN OBJECT AFTER AN INTRANSITIVE VERB [INCORRECT: I get up **the morning.**] CORRECT: I get up in the morning.	If the verb is intransitive, there is no direct object.
DOUBLE SUBJECT [INCORRECT: My **sister she** is healthy.] CORRECT: My **sister** is healthy. **OR My sister and brother** are happy.	A sentence can have a compound subject but not a double subject.
SENTENCE FRAGMENT [INCORRECT: Taking care of your health.] CORRECT: Taking care of your health is very important.	A sentence must have a subject, a verb, and usually a direct object or complement.
RUN-ON SENTENCE [INCORRECT: The mind affects the body in many ways for example we can become ill as a result of stress.] CORRECT: The mind affects the body in many ways; for example, we can become ill as a result of stress. [INCORRECT: One way that the mind affects the body can be seen when depression or stress results in illness, which proves that the mental state is causing the illness and doctors are now treating these illnesses by treating the psychological problem.] CORRECT: One way that the mind affects the body can be seen when depression or stress results in illness, which proves that the mental state is causing the illness. Doctors are now treating these illnesses by treating the psychological problem.	One sentence cannot contain two independent clauses unless joined by the proper punctuation and/or sentence connector. Do not include too many clauses in one sentence.

5.20   ERROR ANALYSIS

DIRECTIONS: Correct the errors in the sentences below. Do not change anything that is already correct.

1. To play soccer, baseball, and hockey.
2. Because this is such an important meeting, I'm wearing nice.
3. The professor told about the experiments in cardiovascular improvement.
4. This new method of losing weight seems.
5. How many times you ran around the track?
6. How that concert was enjoyable!
7. After the game, the crowd left the parking lot in a very orderly fashion there were no problems.
8. Doctors they make me nervous.
9. Although many people haven't read this book.
10. After the lecture was over, where you went?

═══ COMPOSITION TOPICS ═══

1. Describe your diet and physical activities, and explain how they help you to stay healthy and fit.
2. Write a persuasive essay about the advantages and disadvantages of certain diets.
3. Describe a recent breakthrough or discovery in medicine, and discuss its implications.

6

EXPERIENCE IS
THE BEST TEACHER

⊟ Noun clauses

EXPERIENCE IS THE BEST TEACHER   (Or is it?)

DISCUSSION QUESTIONS

1. Is it possible to learn as much from experience as it is from school? How do you learn best—from books or from direct experience?
2. What are some of the events or experiences in a person's life that may mark the transition from childhood to adulthood? What are some other important transitions in a person's life?
3. How did you learn English? What do you think is the ideal way to learn a second language? Why?

OBJECTIVES

In this chapter you will learn:

1. To identify the function of noun clauses
2. To use proper punctuation and capitalization for direct speech
3. To report statements, questions, and imperatives using indirect speech
4. To use a variety of introductory noun clause verbs
5. To use the subjunctive form in noun clauses

══════════ PREVIEW ══════════

DIRECTIONS: Read the following letter that Jack writes to his parents after his first week at the university to find out if he is homesick. Then answer the questions that follow.

Dear Mom and Dad,

1. The first week of college is over and I can tell you it really wasn't easy. I never thought that it would be so difficult to live away from my family. I miss you all so much. What I miss the most are our family dinners—Dad's barbeque chicken and Mom's chocolate cake. You can imagine how awful the food is here.

2. The **campus** is really beautiful, but the dorm is quite basic. In fact, it's exactly how I **pictured it**—linoleum floors, **bunk beds**, and pale green walls. The people in my dorm are **pretty friendly**. There was a party for new students this weekend and my roommate introduced me to many of his friends. "Jack was the star player on his basketball team in high school," he said to all the women he knew. I told him later that he had embarrassed me.

3. I got into all the classes I wanted. The fact that I had **preregistered** last spring made all the difference. Some of the other freshmen in my dorm didn't do that and now they're **stuck with dud** classes.

4. Well, I'd better do some studying now. I hope that I can come home in two weeks for **homecoming weekend** at Wilson High. It all depends on how much work I have.

I miss you a lot! I'm sure the second week will be better. Don't worry!!

Love,

Jack

Jack

VOCABULARY

campus: the land and buildings of a school
bunk beds: two beds, one placed over the other
to picture it: to imagine how something looks
pretty friendly: very friendly (informal)
to preregister: to sign up for classes ahead of time
to be stuck with something: to end up with something that is less than desirable
dud: not exciting (informal)
homecoming weekend: a high school or college weekend for former students who come back
     for the occasion

CULTURAL NOTE / DISCUSSION

Students in the United States often attend a university in a town far from where their parents live, or, if they attend a school in their hometown, they often choose to live in a dormitory or in an apartment with other students. When students move away, the event is often dramatic for both the parents and the children because it symbolizes the beginning of the child's independence and adult life. In your country, at what age do people leave their parents' home to live on their own? Why do they leave?

GRAMMAR CONSIDERATIONS: FOCUS

The following questions are based on the preview text and are designed to help you find out what you already know about the structures in this chapter. Some of the questions may be hard and some of them may be easy. Answer as many of the questions as you can. Work with a partner if your teacher tells you to do so.

1. Find the example of an exact record of what someone has said (that is, **direct speech**) in the letter. Write that here. Note the punctuation.

_____

2. Jack uses **indirect speech** to tell his parents how he felt about what his roommate said. Find that statement and rewrite it in quotation marks, paying careful attention to the punctuation.

_____

3. What is the direct object in the second sentence of paragraph 1?

_____

4. What is the subject of sentence 4 in paragraph 1?

_____

GRAMMATICAL PATTERNS ONE

I. FORMS OF NOUN CLAUSES

A. Description

A noun clause is a clause (subject and verb group) that functions as a noun in a sentence; that is, it stands for **something**:

> I never thought **(something)**.
> I never thought **(that it could be so difficult)**.

A noun clause consists of a connecting word **(CW)**, a subject **(S)**, and a verb **(V)** as follows:

$$\text{CW} \quad \text{S} \qquad \text{V}$$

I never thought **that it could be so difficult**.

B. Connecting Words

There are two types of connecting words.

CONNECTING WORDS	EXAMPLE
1. THAT CONNECTORS If **that** appears after the verb, it can be deleted.	▪ I never thought **(that) it could be so difficult**.
2. WH- CONNECTORS You **cannot delete WH-** connecting words. WHAT HOW WHEN WHETHER / IF WHERE WHY	▪ **What I miss the most** are our family dinners. ▪ You can imagine **how awful the food is here**. ▪ I don't know **when I can come home**. ▪ I'm not sure **whether I'll have a lot of work**. ▪ I don't know **where I should begin**. ▪ I can't understand **why he didn't go to Yale**.

II. FUNCTIONS OF NOUN CLAUSES

A noun clause can function in five ways in a sentence.

FUNCTION OF THE CLAUSE	EXAMPLE
SUBJECT OF THE SENTENCE	*(subject)* ▪ **What I miss the most** are our family dinners. ▪ **That he liked school** surprised his parents. ▪ **Whether or not he'll pass his classes** is another question. ▪ **Whoever misses the test** will fail.
COMPLEMENT OF THE SENTENCE A complement comes after the verb **be** and other linking verbs (**seem, look, appear,** etc.)	*(complement)* ▪ It is exactly **how I pictured it**. ▪ It seems **that he likes his school**.
OBJECT OF THE VERB	*(object of the verb)* ▪ I never thought **that it could be so difficult**. ▪ You can imagine **how awful the food is**.
OBJECT OF A PREPOSITION	*(object of a preposition)* ▪ It all depends on **how much work I have**.
AN APPOSITIVE Here, the clause completes the noun, ***the fact***. Such appositives occur after nouns like **fact, belief, idea, doubt,** etc.	*(appositive)* ▪ The fact **that I preregistered** made all the difference. ▪ The idea **that I would graduate soon** frightened me.

6.1   TYPES OF NOUN CLAUSES: *Breaking Away*

DIRECTIONS: Read the following statements made by parents and children about the difficulty of breaking away. Underline the noun clauses and indicate their function in the sentence: **S** (subject), **C** (complement), **OV** (object of the verb), **OP** (object of a preposition), or **A** (appositive).

EXAMPLE

CUE: I told my mother that I was moving out.

ANSWER: I told my mother that I was moving out.

         Function: OV

1. The most difficult thing about living away from my parents is that I have to do my own cooking and cleaning! (Kathy)

 Function: _____

2. What I like the best is the freedom I have to make my own decisions. (Sara)

 Function: _____

3. My mother told me that I would miss her and she was absolutely right! (Jeremy)

 Function: _____

4. The age at which children leave home depends on how mature they are. (Arnold)

 Function: _____

5. The fact that my children want to live with me during their college years doesn't mean that they are weak or immature. (a mother)

 Function: _____

 Function: _____

6. I want whatever is best for my kids. If they are ready to leave, then they should have the freedom to do so. (a father)

 Function: _____

6.2   DISCUSS AND WRITE: *Leaving Home*

DIRECTIONS: Do you think that young adults (ages 18–22) should be encouraged to leave home and live on their own? Do you think that they will grow up faster and be stronger individuals if they do? If they choose to stay with their parents, should they pay for room and board or should everything be given to them? At what age should a parent suggest his or her child break away and live independently?

Discuss these questions in pairs or small groups. Then write several sentences based on your discussion, using the five types of clauses listed on page 109. Underline the clauses and identify their functions in the sentence.

III. DIRECT SPEECH

When repeating a person's words exactly, use **direct** (or quoted) **speech**. Note the punctuation, capitalization, and use of quotation marks (" ") in the following examples of direct speech, which are taken from some people's ideas about breaking away.

TYPE OF QUOTATION	EXAMPLE
STATEMENT The period (.) comes at the end of the entire sentence, not the quote.	■ "What I like the best is having the freedom to make my own decisions," Sara said. OR ■ Sara said, "What I like the best is having the freedom to make my own decisions."
QUESTION / EXCLAMATION The (?) and (!) come at the end of the quote, not the sentence. Put a period (.) at the end of the sentence.	■ "My mother told me I would miss her and she was absolutely right!" Jeremy exclaimed. ■ "Didn't you think you would miss your family?" her sister asked. ■ His sister asked, "Didn't you think you would miss your family?"
ONE SENTENCE, SEPARATED Insert commas before and after *Kathy said* and do not capitalize the second part of the sentence.	■ "The most difficult thing about living away from my parents," Kathy said, "is that I have to do my own cooking and cleaning."
TWO SENTENCES, SEPARATED Place the period after *one father said*. Capitalize the first word of the second sentence.	■ "I want to do whatever is best for my kids," one father said. "If they are ready to leave, then they should have the freedom to do so."

6.3 WRITTEN EXERCISE: *Punctuating Quotations*

DIRECTIONS: Read the following well-known quotations and rewrite them using proper punctuation, capitalization, and quotation marks.

1. To be or not to be   Hamlet stated   that is the question.

_____

2. Those who lack belief   Lao Tzu said   will not in turn be believed.

_____

3. I think therefore I am   wrote Descartes.

_____

4. The great question that has never been answered   Sigmund Freud is noted as saying   and which I have not yet been able to answer despite my thirty years of research into the feminine soul is: What does a woman want?

_____

_____

_____

5. Mankind must put an end to war   John F. Kennedy once said   or war will put an end to mankind.

_____

_____

6.4   WRITTEN EXERCISE: *A Memorable Conversation*

DIRECTIONS: What was the most important or interesting conversation you have ever had? Write down that conversation using direct speech and the appropriate punctuation. Indent the first line of each new speaker as follows:

"What are you doing tonight?" Steve asked Patricia.

"I'm planning on studying for my final exam tomorrow. I'll be in the library all night," she answered. "Why? Did you want to do something special?"

"I thought you might like to go see a movie with me," John said.

■ IV. INDIRECT SPEECH: LATER REPORTING

To report speech after a certain time has passed, use **indirect speech** and follow these guidelines:

1. Do not use quotation marks.
2. Change the verb to a past form, if possible.
3. Change the pronouns and adverbs to show that it is reported, not quoted, speech.
4. Use an appropriate introductory clause verb (say, tell, answer, ask, etc.).

A. Reporting Statements

DIRECT SPEECH	INDIRECT SPEECH
The verb tense **changes** to a past form in these statements, except for sentences 6 and 8.	
1. "I **want** to attend a U.S. university," John said.	John said that he **wanted** to attend a U.S. university.
2. "I **am looking** for a program in computer science," John said.	John said that he **was looking** for a program in computer science.
3. "I **sent** away for the program description," John said.	John said that he **had sent** away for the program description.

4. "I **was thinking** about starting this September," John said.	John said that he **had been thinking** about starting that September.
5. "I **haven't filled out** the application form yet," John said.	John said that he **hadn't filled out** the application form by that time.
6. "I **had written** the statement of purpose before," John said.	John said that he **had written** the statement of purpose before.
7. "I **will apply** for my visa tomorrow," John said.	John said that he **would apply** for his visa the following day.
8. "I **had been writing** for two hours when the electricity went out," John said.	John said that he **had been writing** for two hours when the electricity had gone out.

The **modals** in the following statements change their form in indirect speech.

1. "My academic counselor **can help** me with the paperwork," John said.	John said that the academic counselor **could help** him with the paperwork.
2. "The Consul **may be** available now," the receptionist said. *(possibility)*	The receptionist said that the consul **might be** available then. *(possibility)*
3. "You **may go** in now," the receptionist said. *(permission)*	The receptionist said that he **could go** in at that time. *(permission)*
4. "You **must bring** 3 photographs," the receptionist said.	The receptionist said that he **had to bring** 3 photographs.

The following modals **do not change their form**.

1. "I **couldn't come** yesterday because of my work schedule," John said.	John said he **couldn't come** the day before because of his work schedule.
2. "I **should ask** my bank for the financial statement," John said.	John said that he **should ask** his bank for the financial statement.
3. "The bank **couldn't have sent** the documents yet," John said.	John said that the bank **couldn't have sent** the documents by that time.
4. "I **shouldn't have waited** so long," John said.	John said that he **shouldn't have waited** so long.

SPECIAL NOTE
ADVERB AND PRONOUN CHANGES

Pronouns and adverbs of time and place must also be changed when you report direct speech. Here are some of the most common changes.

DIRECT SPEECH	**INDIRECT SPEECH**
ADVERB CHANGES:	
yet	by that time
today	that day
tomorrow	the next day, the following day, a day later

yesterday	the day before, the previous day
last week / month, etc.	the previous week, the week before
this week / month, etc.	that week
next week / month, etc.	the following week, the next week, a week later
now	then, at that time
this	that
these	those

PRONOUN CHANGES:

"I will write **my** mother," John said.	John said that **he** would write **his** mother.
"**You** can always call **me** collect," Sarah told John.	Sarah told John that **he** could always call **her** collect.
"**We** will miss **you**!" John's sisters told him.	John's sisters told him that **they** would miss **him**.

6.5 ORAL DRILL: *Reporting Statements*

DIRECTIONS: A group of students in an English class were talking about the difficulties of learning a second language. Report their statements using the sequence of tenses just listed.

EXAMPLE

CUE: "I feel like a baby every time I come into my English class," Lise said.
ANSWER: Lise said that she felt like a baby everytime she went into her English class.

1. "I've been studying English for six years and I still can't get the tenses right!" Paolo said.
2. "When I'm writing, I can get the grammar right. But when I'm speaking, it's impossible," said Mariko.
3. "Yesterday, I was talking to the airlines on the phone and I understood nothing!" said Pietro.
4. "Even though the classes in this school are terrific, we really need contact with Americans," said Fattaneh.
5. "Tomorrow I'll take the TOEFL exam. I wonder if I can get the score I need," Ali said.
6. "Pronunciation is the problem for me. I tried to order lunch today at the restaurant and the waiter couldn't understand me. I was really embarrassed," said Than.
7. "I love learning English grammar. It's so logical!" said Heidi.
8. "All I know is that I must study harder," said Takashi.
9. "Last week I had trouble with verb tenses. This week I'm having trouble with pronouns!" said Françoise.
10. "I just can't spell in English. I should take a course in spelling," said Ibrahim.
11. What are your problems in learning English? Share them with a partner and then report your partner's problems to the class.

■ **B. Reporting Questions**

Follow these guidelines when reporting questions:

1. Use statement, not question, word order in the indirect speech.
2. For *yes / no* questions, use **if** or **whether** as the connecting word.
3. For *wh*-questions, retain the appropriate *wh*-word (what, where, etc.).
4. Use an appropriate introductory clause verb (ask, inquired, etc.).

	DIRECT SPEECH	INDIRECT SPEECH
Yes / No questions	"**Do** you **have** your passport with you?" the receptionist asked John.	The receptionist asked John **if** he **had** his passport with him. OR The receptionist asked John **whether** he **had** his passport with him.
Wh- questions	"**Where should I pay** for my visa?" John asked the receptionist. "**Where is** the cashier's desk?" John asked the receptionist. "**How can I apply?**" John asked. "**When did** you **send** us the form?" the receptionist asked John.	John asked the receptionist **where** he **should pay** for his visa. John asked the receptionist **where the cashier's desk was**. John asked **how he could apply**. The receptionist asked John **when he sent in the form**.
CAUTION	Use question word order in direct speech: (auxiliary - subj. - verb?) "**How much does** the visa **cost**?" John asked.	Use **statement word order** in indirect speech: (subject - verb) John asked **how much** the visa **cost**.

6.6 REPORTING QUESTIONS: *What Should I Do with My Life?*

DIRECTIONS: Making decisions about your life can be difficult, so some people go to career counselors to help them. Here are some questions people ask career counselors. Imagine that you are the career counselor, and report the following questions using indirect speech and the sequence of tenses outlined above. Then offer an answer to the question.

EXAMPLE

CUE: "Do I need a college education to get a good job?" (Gloria)
ANSWER: Gloria asked me if she needed a college education to get a good job, and I told her that it wasn't necessary but it was recommended.

1. "What's the best age to get married?" (Bob)
2. "Can I have a successful career and a family too?" (Sally)
3. "Where are the best jobs?" (Candy)
4. "How can I write a good resumé?" (George)
5. "What will be the fastest growing jobs in the future?" (Linda)
6. "How should I ask my boss for a raise?" (Gary)
7. "How can I find out what my skills are?" (Kim)
8. "Do I need a degree in business to start my own business?" (Fred)
9. "Did I make a mistake by leaving my first job after one year?" (Louise)
10. "Is it possible to work in the same office as my spouse?" (Teresa)

■ C. Indirect Questions

Note how questions change when they become object noun clauses in a sentence. Note that statement word order is used and no change of tense is required since this is **not** reported speech.

QUESTION: What is the population of China?
             What does *vendetta* mean?

ANSWER: I don't know
             I don't remember
             I wonder   what the population of China is.
             I'm not sure   what *vendetta* means.
             I'd like to know

6.7   PAIRED ACTIVITY: *How Much Do You Know?*

DIRECTIONS: Work in pairs. Take turns formulating questions about the following information. Begin your question with the **wh-**word in parentheses. Use *I don't know* if you can't answer your partner's question. Do not shift to a past tense.

EXAMPLE

CUE: the fifth president of the United States (who)
STUDENT A: Who was the fifth president of the United States?
STUDENT B: I don't know who the fifth president of the United States was.

STUDENT A:

1. the author of *The Old Man and the Sea* (who)
2. The president of Thailand (who)
3. [the meaning of] *leap year* (what does)
4. Universal Studios (where)

STUDENT B:

1. the winner of the Nobel Peace Prize in 1989 (who)
2. the population of the world (what)

3. [the meaning of] *get off my back* (what does)
4. Flagstaff (where)

D. Reporting Imperatives

You can report imperative statements in two ways.

DIRECT SPEECH	INDIRECT SPEECH / INFINITIVE	INDIRECT SPEECH / NOUN CLAUSE + MODAL
"Complete this assignment for homework," the teacher told the students.	▪ The teacher told the students **to complete** the assignment for homework.	The teacher told the students **that they should complete the assignment for homework.** (Use the modals **should, had to, ought to, had better.**)
NEGATIVE IMPERATIVES: "Don't do exercise 12," she added.	▪ The teacher told the students **not to do** exercise 12.	The teacher told the students **that they shouldn't do exercise 12.**

6.8 ORAL DRILL: *Reporting Imperatives*

DIRECTIONS: Report the following imperative statements in the two ways just outlined. Use **told** when you report and imagine who might have given that imperative.

EXAMPLE

CUE: "Be quiet!"
ANSWER: The librarian told the students to be quiet.
The librarian told the students that they should be quiet.

1. "Clean up your room!"
2. "Type up this report!"
3. "Don't come late anymore!"
4. "Stand up straight!"
5. "Don't forget my birthday!"
6. "Take out your passport!"
7. "Stop smoking!"
8. "Get me the newspaper!"
9. "Get in line!"
10. "Don't turn away when I'm talking to you!"
11. Practice giving and reporting commands with your classmates.

SPECIAL NOTE

SAY and **TELL** are used differently.

1. **Say** is followed by a *that* clause. (To + indirect object can follow **say**, but it is not common:)
   - She said (to me) that she was leaving.
2. **Tell** is always followed by an indirect object and a *noun* clause.
   - She told **me** (that) she was leaving.
3. **Tell** is usually used with imperatives and is followed by an indirect object + infinitive.
   - She told me to go.

6.9   PAIRED ACTIVITY: *Reporting Imperatives*

DIRECTIONS: Choose one of the following situations to discuss with your partner.

Situation A: You and your partner are living in a foreign country. You are having difficulty adjusting to this new culture and are not at all happy. Take turns with your partner stating your problems and offering solutions. Be ready to write down or report your conversation orally in the following two ways.

EXAMPLE

Jack told me that he hated American food and I told him to learn to cook.
Jack told me that he hated American food and I told him he should learn to cook.

Situation B: John is a 42-year-old American businessman. He is currently going through a midlife crisis. His work, which was once fulfilling, is now monotonous and meaningless to him. He has lost interest in his wife and finds himself looking at younger women. He is depressed and feels trapped in his life. With your partner, decide on five things John should do to get out of his depression and start living a full life again. Be ready to write down or report your conversation orally in the following two ways.

EXAMPLE

We would tell John to take a vacation.
We would tell John that he should take a vacation.

V. REPORTING CONNECTED DISCOURSE

6.10   DISCUSSION: *Nature* vs. *Nurture*

DIRECTIONS: Discuss the following questions with your partner or in small groups. Take notes during your discussion because you will be asked to report your discussion in a later exercise.

1. What does it mean to be intelligent?
2. Are you born with intelligence or is it something that you learn? Explain your answer.

3. An I.Q. test is often used to measure a person's intelligence. What do you think about these tests? Does a high I.Q. ensure academic or professional success?

4. Is there any difference in the type or amount of intelligence between men and women? If so, what is it?

A. Introductory Clause Verbs

The following is a list of common verbs used to introduce noun clauses that report speech or express ideas. These verbs have been grouped according to their function. Note that this list is not complete. (Anything enclosed within parentheses is optional.) Add your own verbs to this list as you come across them.

FUNCTION	NOTES	VERBS
TO REPORT ALMOST ANY STATEMENTS	■ Use these verbs to report objective information. They do not convey the speaker's feelings.	He **said** (to me) that he would go. He **reported** (to me) that . . . She **stated** (to me) that . . . He **mentioned** (to me) that . . . He **told me** that . . . (*An indirect object must follow* **told.**)
TO GIVE ADDITIONAL INFORMATION	■ Use these verbs to report several bits of information given by the same speaker.	He **further stated** (to me) that he would stay an hour. He **continued to say** (to me) that . . . She **added** (to me) that . . . He **later mentioned** (to me) that . . .
TO PRESENT FACTUAL INFORMATION	■ Use these verbs to report a brief announcement. ■ You **must** use a pronoun after each.	She **informed us** that the class was cancelled. He **notified us** that . . . She **advised us** that . . .
TO PRESENT A STRONG ARGUMENT OR OPINION	■ Use these verbs to report an opinion or argument. ■ They are arranged from weak to strong.	He **believed** that the death penalty was wrong. She **maintained** that . . . She **claimed** that . . . He **asserted** that . . . She **argued** that . . . He **declared** that . . .
TO RESPOND	■ Use these verbs to report a response to a statement or question.	He **replied** that it was a social issue. She **responded** (to me) that . . . He **answered** (me) that . . . She **agreed** (with me) that . . . She **concurred** (with him) that . . . He **disputed** (the fact) that . . . He **disagreed** (with him) that . . .
TO CONCLUDE		She **concluded** that her boss was right. He **realized** that . . .

6.11   WRITTEN EXERCISE: *Introductory Clause Verbs*

DIRECTIONS: Each of the following sentences uses *said* to introduce the noun clause. Substitute a more precise introductory clause verb from the list on page 119 and write it in the space provided.

1. Christine **said** that women are more intelligent than men because they are more open-minded.

   _____

2. John **said** that the size of the brain does not affect the intelligence of a person or animal.

   _____

   And Christine **said** that the size of the brain does affect one's intelligence. She **said** that the human brain is larger now than it was thousands of years ago.

   _____

   _____

3. The proctor **said** that the I.Q. test would be held in Room 414.

   _____

4. Cheryl **said** that there was no question in her mind that intelligence was learned and not instinctive.

   _____

   But John **said** that a person was born with intelligence and did not acquire it through experience.

   _____

5. Martha **said** that we were all born with a certain amount of intelligence. However, she also **said** that we can increase that amount by discipline and education.

   _____

   _____

6.12   WRITTEN EXERCISE: *Nature* vs. *Nurture*

DIRECTIONS: Write a summary of your conversation about the nature / nurture controversy from the Preview Discussion, Exercise 6.10. Do not use the verb **said** in your summary; use a variety of introductory clause verbs from the list on page 119 instead. Be ready to report your summary to the class orally.

B. Reporting Phrases and Exclamations

Note how the following phrases and exclamations are reported in indirect speech.

DIRECT SPEECH	INDIRECT SPEECH
"Hello!"	She greeted him.
"What a nice day!"	She exclaimed that it was a nice day.
"No."	She refused. She disagreed.
"Yes."	She accepted. She agreed.
"Sure."	She agreed (enthusiastically, hesitantly, etc.)
"I'd love to go with you!"	She accepted the invitation.
"Thank you."	She thanked him.

C. Reporting Several Statements by One Speaker

When you are telling a story or reporting extended discourse, it is important to link the many ideas or statements logically and concisely. Note how this has been done below.

DIRECT SPEECH	INDIRECT SPEECH
1. "We would love to send Martha to Harvard. We just can't afford it," Mrs. White said.	Mrs. White said that they would love to send Martha to Harvard **but that** they just couldn't afford it.
2. "Is it possible for Martha to get a scholarship for the tuition? Then we could afford the room and board," Mrs. White told the college counselor.	She asked if it was possible for Martha to get a scholarship for the tuition **because in that case** they could afford the room and board.
3. "Yes, it is possible to get a scholarship. There are many possible sources of funding," the college counselor said.	The college counselor told Mrs. White that it was possible to get a scholarship **and that** there were many possible sources of funding.

6.13   A JOB INTERVIEW: *Reporting Connected Discourse*

DIRECTIONS: Read the following dialogue between an employer (E) and a job applicant (JA). Then report the interview by completing the paragraph that follows with indirect speech.

E: Please sit down. Do you smoke?

JA: I do occasionally, but I don't like to when I'm working.

E: Where have you worked before?

JA: I spent six years as a receptionist in a doctor's office.

E: Can you use a computer?

JA: Of course I can.

E: Then I'd like you to take this test.
   (After the test)

E: You did well on the test. I'd like to offer you the job.

JA: Thank you. When do you want me to start working?

E: As soon as you like.

JA: I'll be here on Monday morning.

Some time ago, Louise applied for a job in a dental office and last Thursday she went for an interview. When she was shown into the office manager's office, he told her _____ and asked her _____. She told him that _____ but _____. Then he asked her _____ and she told him _____. He wanted to know _____ and she replied that _____. He gave her a test and then said _____. She _____ him and asked _____. He replied _____ and she _____.

6.14   EAVESDROPPING: *Reporting Connected Discourse*

DIRECTIONS: Imagine that you overheard the following conversations last week. How would you report them to your classmates? First complete the dialogues. Then be ready to report the conversations, orally or in writing, using connected discourse.

1. Imagine that you were eating your lunch in a park near your home. A young couple was sitting on the bench next to yours, within earshot. You couldn't help listening to their conversation. Supply an appropriate ending. Then report the conversation in indirect speech.

   MAN: Marry me!
   WOMAN: I can't. I'm too young. I have a lot to do before I settle down.
   MAN: Promise me you'll marry me in five years then.
   WOMAN: I'd better not make that kind of promise today. I might break your heart later.
   MAN: It's already broken.

   WOMAN: _____

2. You're sitting in a local coffee shop. A middle-aged couple is sitting in the booth behind you. They don't realize that you can hear every word they say. Supply an appropriate ending. Then report the conversation in indirect speech.

   MAN: Well, did you do it?
   WOMAN: Yes, I did it.
   MAN: Where?

WOMAN: In a deserted alley, not too far from my house.

MAN: When?

WOMAN: It must have been around 3 A.M. yesterday. No one was around. I don't think anyone saw me.

MAN: Was it noisy? I mean, do you think anyone heard you?

WOMAN: Yeah, there was some noise; there always is. But it was fast. I don't think anyone heard. No one came around. Then I took off.

MAN: Where'd you put it?

WOMAN: _____

MAN: _____

6.15 A MEMORABLE CONVERSATION: *Reported*

DIRECTIONS: Report the memorable conversation that you wrote in direct speech on page 112 earlier in the chapter. Use indirect speech and a variety of introductory clause verbs.

6.16 PAIRED ORAL ACTIVITY: *Roleplay*

DIRECTIONS: Create a short dialogue based on one of the following situations. Then present it to the class. Have your classmates reconstruct the dialogue using connected discourse.

1. A teacher catches her student cheating on a final exam.
2. Two men have asked a woman for a date on Saturday night. She asks her friend for advice.
3. A worker asks the boss for a raise.
4. Create your own situation.

6.17 A DISCUSSION: *Reporting Connected Discourse*

DIRECTIONS: Work with a partner and another pair of students. Each pair will choose one of the following questions to discuss for five to ten minutes. Pair A will listen and take notes of Pair B's discussion. Then you will switch roles. After you have finished discussing your topics, report the discussion in writing or orally, as instructed by your teacher.

1. Should young children (ages 3–6) be enrolled in a school and be taught skills to prepare them for elementary school, or should they simply be allowed to play without structure?
2. Should adolescents (ages 12–16) be allowed to choose their school and leisure activities (for example, music, sports, etc.), or should they follow their parents' desires?
3. Should high school students who are planning on studying science at a university be required to study language and literature? Should language and literature students be required to study science?
4. Should international students be required to have a 550 TOEFL score in order to be admitted to a U.S. university, or should each school have its own entrance exam?

═══════ ANALYSIS OF AN AUTHENTIC TEXT ═══════

DIRECTIONS: The following text is a review of *Why Humans Vary in Intelligence* by Seymour Itzkoff, a book that examines the question of intelligence. Note the reviewer's extensive use of noun clauses to report Itzkoff's ideas.

AUTHOR VOTES FOR NATURE OVER NURTURE
A Book Review by Lee Dembart

Why Humans Vary in Intelligence by Seymour Itzkoff

1. Today we take up a book that asserts flatly and **unflinchingly** that intelligence is hereditary and that significant differences in native intelligence exist and can be measured between the sexes and between the races. It further says that these biological differences in intelligence are completely explainable by mankind's evolutionary history.

2. The author, Seymour W. Itzkoff of Smith College, argues that the **perennial** question of **nature** vs. **nurture** "has been resolved . . . on the side of nature," and he supplies much evidence in support of that view.

3. What's more, he says, **social niceties** and political necessities make it impossible for society to face these facts. Instead, reformers invent "an endless progression of 'bourgeois,' 'racist,' 'sexist' **demons** that **ostensibly** stand in the way of **their ever-receding Utopia.**

4. . . . Scholars continue to debate what, if anything, I.Q. tests measure and whether intelligence is one **trait** or many. Not Itzkoff. "I.Q. is in some measure predictive of intellectual achievement in school and in life," he said "and I.Q. variance between one person and another is about 70% heredity and 30% environment."

5. Nor does he have any doubt that there is a male intelligence and a female intelligence and that the reason that men do much better than women in activities like mathematics and chess is that men have a "spatial / visual gene" that women do not. He dismisses the explanation that women from birth are socialized away from these activities, and he recounts experimental evidence to support his claim that there is a basic biological trait at work, independent of what girls are taught.

6. The key event in the eventual success of Homo sapiens, he says, was the development of a large brain which, in addition to **bestowing** intelligence, also made men aggressive and predatory with an instinct to subjugate and control.

7. . . . The fact that women do well in tasks that require **fine** motor visual and manipulating skills, such as sewing, typing, and putting together tiny computer elements shows, Itzkoff said, "that women are more **placid,** patient, and careful, whereas males, often more impatient and irritable, can **be corralled** less easily into this kind of careful, precise, mostly monotonous labor."

8. Itzkoff said his conclusions represent the consensus of knowledgeable researchers, that the debate is over, and that these findings "have **punctured** the hopes of those who dreamed that an **egalitarian** world of uniformly intelligent and cultured persons could be created by waving **a magic wand** of philanthropic social, economic, and educational policies."

Not so fast. The other side isn't willing to give up yet.

VOCABULARY

unflinchingly: without a doubt
perennial: neverending
nature: in this case, resulting from the genes
nurture: in this case, resulting from social learning
social niceties: propriety
demons: devils
ostensibly: shown outwardly
their ever-receding Utopia: a disappearing ideal world
trait: characteristic
bestowing: creating
fine: detailed and precise
placid: calm
to be corralled: to be held in
punctured: destroyed
egalitarian: equal
a magic wand: a magic stick

DISCUSSION

Based on your conversation with your partner in Exercise 6.10, Preview Discussion, on which points do you agree and disagree with the author, Itzkoff? Did any of Itzkoff's statements surprise you?

GRAMMAR CONSIDERATIONS: FOCUS

1. Underline all the noun clauses in the book review, and identify them according to their function in the sentence (subject, object of the verb, object of the preposition, complement, or appositive).
2. Circle all the introductory clause verbs. Refer to the list of such verbs and identify the functions of the verbs in the article. Note any verbs in the text that are not on the list.

GRAMMATICAL PATTERNS TWO

PREVIEW

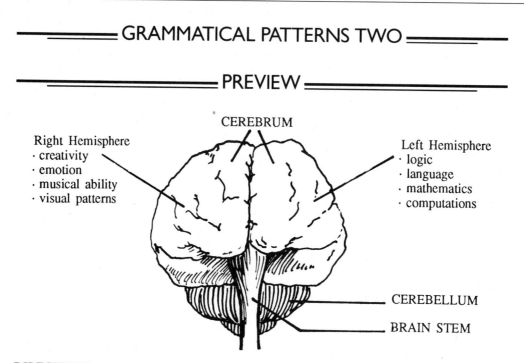

CEREBRUM

Right Hemisphere
· creativity
· emotion
· musical ability
· visual patterns

Left Hemisphere
· logic
· language
· mathematics
· computations

CEREBELLUM

BRAIN STEM

DIRECTIONS: Do you know the difference between the right and left brain? Read the following lecture on this distinction, given in a university psychology class. Then answer the questions that follow.

1 "In our last meeting, I told you that two facts regarding the brain have recently become apparent. **2** First, the brain has two parts which function independently. **3** Second, each hemisphere interprets the world through distinctly different processes. **4** Today we will look at how each hemisphere functions.

5 "That the left brain processes information in a linear and logical way is one of the most basic differences. **6** The left brain draws on rules. **7** Thus, yesterday when I prepared my lecture, I made an outline of the talk. **8** I used my left brain to organize the information in a clear and logical way.

9 "The right brain, on the other hand, is the creative hemisphere. **10** It processes information simultaneously and is able to relate that information. **11** My daughter used her right brain last week when she painted a picture of our house.

12 "Tomorrow we'll see how the two hemispheres talk to each other. **13** Why don't you review chapter 6 in the textbook before class? **14** There'll probably be some difficult terminology. **15** It's essential that you be very familiar with the technical terminology. OK. See you next week. Have a good weekend!''

GRAMMAR CONSIDERATIONS: FOCUS

The following questions are based on the preview text and are designed to help you find out what you already know about the structures in this chapter. Some of the questions may be hard and some of them may be easy. Answer as many of the questions as you can. Work with a partner if your teacher tells you to do so.

1. What is the subject of sentence 5? _____

   Rewrite sentence 5 beginning your sentence with "One of the most basic..."

   One of the most basic differences _____

   _____

   Which of the two sentences would you most likely find in a textbook? In a conversation?

2. What is unusual about one of the verbs in sentence 15?

   _____

   Can you explain why a special form of the verb is used in this sentence?

   _____

3. Imagine that one of your classmates was sick and asked you to report what the professor said.

   For sentence 9, which verb tense would you use in indirect speech? _____

   _____

   Why? _____

   In sentence 13, what is the meaning of "Why don't you...?" _____

   How would you report that statement?

   _____

I. SPECIAL CONSIDERATIONS IN INDIRECT SPEECH

Native speakers do not always follow the sequence of tenses listed above. There are many factors to consider that influence this choice. They are listed below. In some cases, a change is optional. In others, a specific change is **not possible.**

A. Optional Cases

It is not necessary to change the verb tense in the following cases. However, it is always grammatically correct to do so.

FACTORS TO CONSIDER	EXAMPLE
1. THE MOMENT OF REPORTING It is not necessary to change the verb when the speech is reported **immediately.**	▪ A: I hate this professor's voice. B: What did you say? A: I said that I **hate** this professor's voice. **(hated)**
2. THE INFORMATION REPORTED ▪ If the information is **factual** or **generally accepted,** you may use the present tense in the reported speech.	▪ The professor said that water **freezes** at 32° F. **(froze)**

■ If the information is related to **habitual action,** and is still true at the moment of reporting, you may use the present tense in the reported speech.	■ She said she **writes** to her boyfriend daily. **(wrote)**
3. FORMAL VS. INFORMAL SPEECH ■ In **informal** conversation, speakers often do not change the past to a past perfect form. ■ In **formal** English, it is best to change a past verb to a past perfect form.	■ ''I had a great time at the party,'' Corinne said. Corinne said she **had** a great time at the party. **(had had)** ■ The lecturer stated that there **had been** many causes of the economic recession.

6.18   ORAL DRILL: *Optional Cases*

DIRECTIONS: Match the quote with the probable speaker. Then report the speech. Indicate when it is necessary to change the verb tense.

1. Intelligence is 70% genetically determined and 30% environmentally determined.''

2. ''I can't come to the phone right now because I'm in the shower.''

3. ''Did you have a hard day at work?''

4. ''You must learn how to control your eating habits.''

5. ''I've been working out at the gym about once a week.''

6. ''We've been to Tokyo three times.''

7. ''The 1980s were a decade of unprecedented buying.''

■ Maria told her roommate to tell her friend on the phone
■ The newscaster claimed

■ The doctor told the patient
■ The husband asked his wife
■ The neighbor boasted

■ The patient told the doctor
■ The psychology teacher stated

B. Other Cases

FACTORS TO CONSIDER	EXAMPLE
1. THE INTENTION OF THE SPEAKER If the direct speech is a **request** or **suggestion,** the reported speech must express that.[a]	''Why don't you take me to a nice restaurant?'' the woman asked the man. ■ The woman asked the man if **he would** take her to a nice restaurant. ■ The woman suggested that the man take her to a nice restaurant. ''I want order in this courtroom!'' the judge said. ■ The judge **insisted that there be order** in the courtroom.[b]

2. THE REAL TIME, NOT THE VERB FORM If a simple present or present progressive verb form is used to express future time, report the speech using *would*.	"The train leaves at 6:00 P.M. tomorrow," the man said. ▪ The man said that the train **would leave** at 6:00 P.M. the next day.
3. THE INTRODUCTORY CLAUSE VERB If the verb introducing the noun clause is in the present tense, do not change the verb tense in reported speech. A present tense is often used to report statements which a person makes regularly.	▪ The president **says** he will increase funds for education. ▪ Gloria **says** she **loves** her husband.

ªSee Section II on The Subjunctive Form After Expressions of Urgency for more explanation.
ᵇSee the detailed list of these verbs on page 131.

6.19 PAIRED DRILL: *Optional* and *Other Cases*

DIRECTIONS: Work in pairs. Cover your partner's side of the page. Student B asks Student A the questions and Student A finds the appropriate quote and reports the speech. Then switch roles. Change to a past form **only when necessary.**

STUDENT A

1. "You need to buy some new clothes."

2. "Why don't you make dinner tonight, dear."

3. "I'll be 40 years old in two more months!"

4. "I want everyone to be on time for class tomorrow!"

5. "I'm never getting married."

Now switch roles

6. What did George's mother relate to her neighbor?

7. What do presidents always say before getting elected?

8. What did Jackie's Japanese roommate say?

9. What did the doctor suggest to his patient?

10. What did the student ask her teacher?

STUDENT B

▪ What did the angry teacher say to her students?

▪ What did Jack say to his best friend?

▪ What did Bob say to his mother?

▪ What does Sandra's mother say to her every time she sees her?

▪ What did the wife suggest to her husband?

▪ "When does the TOEFL exam start?"

▪ "George got a 4.0 grade point average after his first semester at Yale."

▪ "I promise to reduce taxes this year."

▪ "I always take my shoes off before going into someone's home."

▪ "How about losing 20 pounds?"

■ II. THE SUBJUNCTIVE FORM AFTER EXPRESSIONS OF URGENCY

Compare the following sentences, which have the same meaning but different uses.

(a) It is important for her to take science classes. (informal, conversational—for example, parents talking to each other about their daughter)
(b) It is important that she take science classes. (more formal, written—for example, the principal talking to the parents about their daughter)

To form the more formal expression, use the simple form of a verb (the infinitive without *to*) in a noun clause after these expressions of urgency.

FORM	EXAMPLE
■ Use the simple form of a verb (the infinitive form without **to**) after these expressions of urgency. ■ Pay careful attention to the form of the third person singular (he, she, it)—**no third person singular -s!!**	It is **essential that** she **go** to an ivy league school. **important that** **crucial that** **desirable that** **imperative that** **necessary that** **urgent that** **vital that** **best that** **recommended**
■ When forming a negative with these expressions, place **not** before the simple form of the verb.	It is **essential** that she **not** fail any courses.

6.20   RAPID DRILL: *Expressions of Urgency*

DIRECTIONS: Choose three of the following questions to answer using an expression of urgency and a noun clause. Choose the expression of urgency that seems most appropriate. Be ready to answer when your teacher calls on you.

EXAMPLE

CUE: Your sister wants to get into a good university. What must she do?
ANSWER: It is essential that she have a good academic record.

1. Jane is having problems adjusting to life in a big city. What should she do?
2. Robert is worried because he can't seem to make friends in his office. What can he do?
3. Terry just found out that one of his colleagues has been stealing from the shop. What would you tell him?
4. If you want to have a successful party, what must you do?
5. If you want to have a successful job interview, what should you **not** do?
6. What should you do (or not do) to be healthy?

7. Bob is 40 years old and still single. He'd like to get married. Give him some advice.

8. What should be done to save the environment?

6.21 PAIRED ACTIVITY I: *A Happy Marriage*

DIRECTIONS: You and your partner are planning on getting married. You are discussing how to develop and maintain a happy marriage. Take turns making statements using the expressions of urgency on page 130. When you have finished discussing the topic, write your sentences in the space provided.

EXAMPLE

It is advisable that my wife work outside the home.
It is imperative that my husband be rich.
It is best that we take vacations together.

1. _____

2. _____

3. _____

■ III. THE SUBJUNCTIVE FORM AFTER VERBS OF REQUEST

Use the following verbs to make a strong request. Note the use of the simple form of the verb in the noun clause.

FORM	EXAMPLE		
■ Use the simple form of a verb (the infinitive without **to**) after these verbs of request. ■ Pay special attention to the form of the third person singular (he, she, it)	WEAK The psychologist STRONG	**suggested** **advised** **proposed** **asked** **requested** **desired** **urged** **insisted** **demanded** **commanded**	that he **set** specific goals.
■ When forming the negative with these verbs, place **not** before the simple form of the verb.	He requested that she **not** say a word.		
■ Do not change the subjunctive verb in **indirect speech.**	"It is best that my wife have her own career." (direct) The husband said it was best that his wife **have** her own career. (indirect)		

| Note the position of **not** in the indirect speech. | "It is important that she not give up her career." (direct)
 He said that it was important that she **not give up** her own career. (indirect) |

6.22   PAIRED ACTIVITY II: *A Happy Family*

DIRECTIONS: It is now 15 years later and you and your partner have enjoyed a happy and successful marriage. Now you have a teenage child. Unfortunately, your child is not doing very well in his or her schoolwork and also has some serious behavior problems at home. Discuss the problem with your partner (your spouse) and find some solutions. Then report the strong requests you will make to your child, using the verbs listed on page 131. Write down your requests in the space provided.

EXAMPLE

We suggest that our son stay home on the weekends and study.

1. _____

2. _____

3. _____

4. _____

6.23   WRITTEN EXERCISE: *The Subjunctive Form*

DIRECTIONS: Choose one of the following situations and write a letter outlining the problem and making recommendations. Use sentences with verbs of request and expressions of urgency.

1. You are the manager of a small store. Recently, one of your employees has been quite negligent in her work and even rude to the customers. You would like to terminate her, but she is a friend of the store owner. Write a letter to the boss, explaining your situation and making some recommendations.
2. You are a junior high school teacher. One of your students, Mark, has been acting up in class and exhibiting quite disruptive behavior. You know that Mark is a very smart student and capable of doing excellent work. You think he is under the influence of some irresponsible students at school. Write a letter to the guidance counselor of the school, describing the problem and making some recommendations.

IV. REDUCTION OF NOUN CLAUSES

Note how the following noun clauses can be reduced to phrases. (See Chapter 14 for more detail on this topic.)

REDUCTION	EXPLANATION
▪ It is best ⎰ **that she change her job.** ⎱ for her **to change her job.**	▪ Noun clauses after verbs of request and urgency can be reduced to infinitive phrases.

▪ The psychologist suggested { **that she quit.** / **to her to quit.**		
▪ I don't understand { **what I have to do.** / **what to do.**		▪ The subjects of each clause are the same. Reduce to an infinitive phrase but keep the **wh-** word.
▪ I don't know { **when I should go.** / **when to go.**		
▪ He told me { **what I had to do.** / **what to do.**		▪ The subject of each clause is different. Reduce to an infinitive phrase.
▪ He told me what **not** to do.		▪ Note the position of **not** in the reduced clause.

6.24 ORAL DRILL: *Reduction of Noun Clauses*

DIRECTIONS: Read the following situations and make a statement about them by using a reduced noun clause.

EXAMPLE

CUE: John is in the middle of a busy intersection in a foreign city. He is looking at all the street names. He has a confused look on his face.
ANSWER: He's lost and he doesn't know **where to go.**

1. Suzanne is in her room looking at all her clothes strewn on her bed. Her date is arriving in ten minutes but she still hasn't gotten dressed.
2. Joe has gained a lot of weight. He went to the doctor to get some advice.
3. Kyoko has six brochures on her desk about English-speaking schools in the United States. She must make a decision, but she is not sure which school is the best.
4. Kim and Blake want to adopt a child. They don't know a lot about the procedure, so they went to a lawyer.
5. Benny is failing his economics class. He went to talk to the professor.
6. Emory forgot the time of his dental appointment.
7. Jane is new in town. She's not sure about the stores. She needs to buy a new dress.
8. My dog has fleas. Help!!
9. I can't stop smoking. Please give me some advice.
10. Turn to your partner and share a problem you have. Then offer advice to each other.

V. NOUN CLAUSES IN SUBJECT POSITION

Note the following uses of noun clauses in subject position.

USE	EXAMPLE
STALLING FOR TIME ▪ If you wish to gain a little time before answering a difficult question, rephrase it as a noun clause and place it at the beginning of the answer.	▪ Mother: What did you do while I was gone? Son: **What I did while you were gone** is a long story!

Use **whether** for **yes** / **no** questions.	▪ Did you pay a lot of money for your house? **Whether I paid a lot of money for my house** is not important.
WRITING FORMAL SENTENCES ▪ Placing the noun clause at the beginning of the sentence creates a more formal, academic sentence.	Informal: It is obvious that mental well-being is linked to physical health. Formal: **That mental well-being is linked to physical health** is obvious.

6.25   RAPID DRILL: *Avoiding Personal Questions*

DIRECTIONS: The following questions are very personal and would probably cause embarrassment to any American. To avoid answering such nosey questions, transform each question into a noun clause and place it in subject position. Use the following expressions to help you avoid answering the questions.

EXAMPLE

Question: How old are you?

Possible Response:

How old I am is . . .
- none of your business.
- not important.
- confidential.
- not an issue.
- not your problem.
- etc.

1. How much money does your father make?
2. How much do you weigh?
3. Are your parents divorced?
4. What's your I.Q.?
5. How many friends do you have?
6. When was your first kiss?
7. What did you get on the last grammar test?
8. Are you religious?
9. Are you planning on getting married?
10. Did you take a shower this morning?

Now *you* ask your teacher some personal questions.

11. _____

12. _____

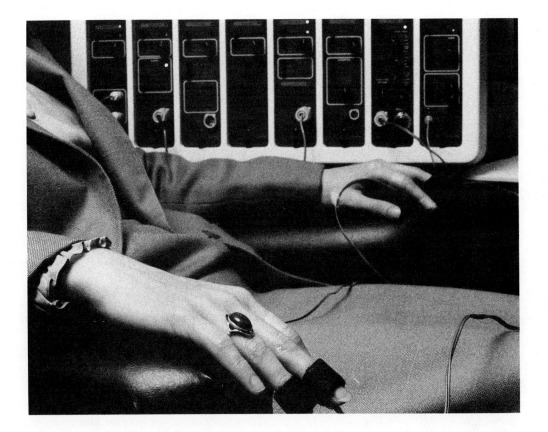

6.26 WRITTEN EXERCISE: *Noun Clause in Subject Position*

DIRECTIONS: Read the following text on the human potential movement in the United States to find out what a mind gym is. Then answer the questions that follow.

THE HUMAN POTENTIAL MOVEMENT

The human potential movement was an important trend in the United States that started over a quarter of a century ago and still plays an important role in the lives of many Americans today. This movement focused on the spiritual and creative development of the individual. Groups formed to explore their inner feelings communally. New approaches to treating the emotional and psychological problems of individuals emerged. Americans were caught up in a desire to achieve complete happiness and fulfillment. Encounter groups, T-sessions, Gestalt therapy, Past Life therapy—these are only a few of the types of activities that flourished during this time. Today, we see vestiges of the movement in the latest innovation, the mind gym. A mind gym is exactly what it sounds like: a place to go to relax and exercise your mind using the latest equipment in biofeedback and flotation tanks. It is not surprising that the number of mind gyms is increasing steadily as our lives become hectic and stressful. What a curious thought: in the future we won't be taking exotic vacations to Hawaii to get away from it all; we'll be taking out a membership in the nearest mind gym!

Now answer each of the questions based on the text. Begin each of your answers with a noun clause in subject position.

EXAMPLE

CUE: What is one reason why the Human Potential Movement flourished?

ANSWER: **That Americans were caught up in a desire to achieve complete happiness and fulfillment** provides one explanation.

1. Why did the human potential movement flourish in the United States?
2. What is not surprising to the author?
3. What is a curious thought to the author?
4. In your opinion, what is one explanation for the stress in modern life?
5. What might be one disadvantage of going to a mind gym?

VI. SPECIAL PROBLEMS WITH NOUN CLAUSES

Pay careful attention to these special problems.

PROBLEM POINT	EXPLANATION
1. NO **TO** AFTER **SAID + OBJECT** She said me that she would go.	Don't confuse these constructions: ■ She **said to me** that . . . ■ She **told me** that . . .
2. USING *THAT* TO REPORT A **YES / NO** QUESTION He asked me that I had any sisters.	Use **if** or **whether** to report **yes / no** questions.
3. USING INCORRECT WORD ORDER TO REPORT A **WH-** QUESTION I don't know what time is it.	Use **statement** word order to report a **Wh-** question.
4. USING THE AUXILIARY *DON'T* IN REPORTING IMPERATIVES She told us to don't go.	Use **not** in front of the infinitive.
5. USING INCORRECT PRONOUNS OR ADVERBS IN THE INDIRECT SPEECH She told me that I didn't want to go here.	Change the pronouns and adverbs to indicate that it is indirect and not direct speech.
6. USING AN INCORRECT FORM OF THE VERB AFTER VERBS OF URGENCY AND REQUEST He insisted that she sees a doctor.	Use the simple form of the verb in these cases.

■ 6.27 ERROR ANALYSIS: *Noun Clauses*

DIRECTIONS: Find any errors in noun clause construction and tense. Correct the errors clearly above the sentence.

1. A few students asked the teacher why was there going to be a final exam.
2. The teacher told to the students that it is crucial that they learn to take tests.
3. According to the students, however, it was more important that they were given more class time.
4. The president told to the United States to don't worry about the recent stock market problems because the economy was strong and healthy.
5. What is my father's annual income is none of your business.
6. This is exactly that I noticed at my age.
7. What are we in such a situation is only an example for our children.
8. That at what age a parent should suggest her child break away and live independently is that a parent should consider.

=========== COMPOSITION TOPICS ===========

In this chapter, you have had the chance to read about and discuss the question of intelligence, human experience, and learning. Choose one of the following topics and write a composition in which you clearly formulate your own ideas.

1. Write an extended definition of *intelligence* in which you discuss the question of nature vs. nurture. Draw on the sources presented in the chapter to support your own ideas.
2. "Men and women can never have the same type or amount of intelligence." Agree or disagree with this statement and give strong reasons to support your position.
3. A turning point is an event in your life that seriously changed the direction of your life. A new career, a marriage, a baby, a divorce, a death—these are events that often change one's life dramatically. Write a composition in which you describe such an event that you have experienced. Explain why it was so meaningful and important to you.

7

MAKING A DIFFERENCE

▭ Adjective clauses

TO MAKE A DIFFERENCE:
To have an influence or impact on the people around you or your environment

DISCUSSION QUESTIONS

1. What is the difference between a celebrity and a hero? Name a living person who is a hero for you and explain why.
2. How are you presently making or how do you hope to make a difference in the future?
3. How would you like to be remembered after you die?

OBJECTIVES

In this chapter you will learn:

1. To combine sentences using adjective clauses
2. To distinguish and punctuate restrictive and nonrestrictive adjective clauses
3. To reduce adjective clauses

=== PREVIEW ===

DIRECTIONS: Read the following text on the Live-Aid Concert to find out more about Bob Geldof. Then answer the questions that follow.

1. On July 13, 1985, more than a billion people from all over the world were witness to a rock concert *which hosted over sixty rock acts on two continents simultaneously.* The person *who was responsible for the Live-Aid Concert,* as it was called, was Bob Geldof, an **abrasive** rock singer with the Boomtown Rats. Geldof had one objective in **pulling off** the largest rock concert ever—he wanted to raise money for the **famine** relief effort. Geldof gave tirelessly to a project *for which he did not receive even a penny.*

2. It all began on a quiet evening when Bob and his girlfriend decided to **stay in** and watch a **documentary** on Ethiopia on T.V. It was a program *that Geldof is not likely to ever forget.* He watched as a **relief worker** had to choose 300 starving people out of 10,000 to receive a small ration of butter oil. Greatly moved by that experience, Geldof decided to do something for the hungry of the world. He wrote and recorded **the single** "Do They Know It's Christmas," *which raised $11 million.* The U.S. equivalent, "We are the World," quickly followed, *which raised even more money.* Soon **donations** started pouring into the Live-Aid Foundation set up by Geldof from people *whose conscience had been rattled by this rock singer's dedication and commitment.*

3. However, the single act which *Geldof will always be remembered for* was, of course, the Live-Aid Concert. Such well-known musicians as Bob Dylan, Mick Jagger, Phil Collins, U-2, Tina Turner, and Madonna performed in the JFK Stadium in Philadelphia and Wembly Stadium in London. The concert brought in over $60 million for famine relief. It also brought the reality of starvation into the homes of viewers in 90 countries.

4. Geldof often wonders what would have happened if he hadn't stayed home that night.

VOCABULARY

abrasive: unrefined, irritating in manner
to pull off: to achieve, to organize successfully
famine: a severe shortage of food
to stay in: to spend the time at home, not go out
documentary: a film or T.V. program based on factual information
relief worker: a person working for a social project
the single: a 45 rpm record
a donation: a gift of money or objects given to an organization

CULTURAL NOTE / DISCUSSION

The Live-Aid Concert of 1985 started a trend in which rock stars in the United States began to host benefit concerts to raise money for various social concerns, such as the situation of the farmer in the midwest of the United States, the spread of AIDS, and human rights. Have you ever attended such a concert? What do you think of rock stars hosting such concerts?

GRAMMAR CONSIDERATIONS: FOCUS

The following questions are based on the preview text and are designed to help you find out what you already know about the structures in this chapter. Some of the questions may be hard and some of them may be easy. Answer as many of the questions as you can. Work with a partner if your teacher tells you to do so.

1. The clauses in italics in the preview are all adjective clauses; that is, they modify nouns. Circle the noun being modified by each clause.

2. Compare the following clauses from paragraph 1.
    (a) "...a rock concert **which** hosted over 60 rock acts..." and
    (b) "The person **who** was responsible for the Live-Aid Concert..."

Why is **which** used to introduce clause (a) and **who** used to introduce clause (b)?

_____

3. Now look at the following clause from paragraph 2:
"...a program **that** Geldof is not likely to ever forget."

Does **that** refer to a person or thing? Could it also refer to a person, for example, in place of **who** in clause (b) in question 2? Now, make a rule for the use of **which, who,** and **that.**

_____

_____

4. Compare the following clauses:
    (a) "...a project **for which** he did not receive even a penny." (paragraph 1)
    (b) "...the single act **which** Geldof will always be remembered **for**..." (paragraph 3)

Note the position of the preposition **for** in both clauses. Could **for** be moved to the end of the clause in (a)? Could it be placed before **which** in (b)?

_____

_____

GRAMMATICAL PATTERNS ONE

I. ADJECTIVE CLAUSE: FORM

An adjective clause is a group of words (relative word, subject, and verb) that follows a noun and modifies and/or restricts that noun. Note how the second sentence in the following examples becomes the adjective clause. (**A** = antecedent; **RW** = relative word, **S** = subject, and **V** = verb)

- The person was Bob Geldof. He was responsible for the concert.

clause
The person **who was responsible for the concert** was Bob Geldof.
   ↓   ↓ ↓
   A   **RW** **V**

- It was a program. Geldof is not likely to forget the program.

clause
It was a program **that Geldof is not likely to forget.**
      ↓   ↓   ↓ ↓
      A   **RW** **S** **V**

II. TYPES OF ADJECTIVE CLAUSES

There are two types of adjective clauses.

Restrictive:	The single act **which Geldof will be remembered for** was the Live-Aid Concert.	A restrictive adjective clause limits the antecedent.
Nonrestrictive:	He recorded "Do They Know It's Christmas," **which eventually raised $11 million.**	A nonrestrictive adjective clause gives additional information, not necessary to identify the noun being modified.

Grammatical Patterns One will examine restrictive adjective clauses. Grammatical Patterns Two will look at nonrestrictive adjective clauses.

III. RESTRICTIVE CLAUSES: RELATIVE WORDS

A relative word connects the adjective clause to its antecedent. Note the different functions of these relative words as outlined on page 142.

FUNCTION OF THE RELATIVE WORD	EXAMPLE	NOTES
SUBJECT OF THE CLAUSE	**(subject) (verb)** ▪ The person **who / that** *was responsible for the concert* was Geldof. ▪ More than a billion people witnessed a concert **that / which** *hosted over 60 rock acts.*	▪ Use **who** or **that** for people. ▪ Use **that** (or **which**) for things.
OBJECT OF THE CLAUSE	**(object) (subject)** ▪ It was a program **that** *Geldof is not likely to forget.* ▪ Some of the performers saw musicians **who(m)** *they hadn't seen in years.* ▪ Some of the performers saw musicians ~~whom~~ *they hadn't seen in years.*	▪ Here, **that** is the object of the clause and **Geldof** is the subject. ▪ Use **who** or **whom** for people in object position. ▪ The relative word as object can be deleted.
OBJECT OF A PREPOSITION	▪ Geldof gave tirelessly to a project **for which** *he did not receive a penny.* ▪ Geldof gave tirelessly to a project **that** *he did not receive a penny* **for**. ▪ Geldof gave tirelessly to a project ~~that~~ *he did not receive a penny* **for**.	▪ An adjective clause can follow most prepositions. ▪ The preposition can be placed at the end of the clause. This is informal. ▪ The relative word can be deleted if the preposition is at the end.
POSSESSIVE	Donations poured in from people **whose** *conscience was rattled by Geldof's commitment and dedication.* (It was the people's conscience that was rattled.)	▪ **Whose** shows possession and usually refers to persons.

7.1   WRITTEN EXERCISE: *Restrictive Adjective Clauses*

DIRECTIONS: Read the following sentences. Put parentheses ( ) around the adjective clauses. Underline the antecedents. Circle the relative words. Then identify the relative words as follows: subject **(S)**, object **(O)**, object of a preposition **(OP)**, or possessive **(P)**. Refer to the above chart when you need help.

EXAMPLE

___O___   It was a <u>program</u> ((that) Geldof is not likely to forget).

_____ **1.**   This is a story that I have told many times.

_____ 2. It's the story of a very wealthy and successful man who worked in a large corporation in New York City.

_____ 3. Here was a man whose main goal in life was to make money and gain prestige. One day he woke up and asked himself the question, "Why?"

_____ 4. So he walked into the same building that he had walked into for the previous 15 years and marched into his boss's office.

_____ 5. "I quit!" he exclaimed. Then he went to the bank that he had his money in and took out a million dollars.

_____ 6. He then started a nonprofit organization that raised money for children afflicted with leukemia.

_____ 7. A great deal of the money came from a wealthy donor whose son had died of leukemia.

7.2   FILL IN THE BLANKS: *Amnesty International*

DIRECTIONS: What do you know about the organization, Amnesty International? Read the following sentences to find out more. Fill in the blanks with any appropriate relative words (**that, which, who, whom, whose,** or **∅**). Show all possibilities.

Amnesty International is a human rights organization _____ was founded in
                                                              1

London. Its work centers on the rights of "prisoners of conscience," men and women

_____ governments have imprisoned them for their beliefs, ethnic origin, language, or
       2

religion. A program _____ Amnesty International has been well known for is its adop-
                        3

tion program. This involves a group of concerned citizens _____ select a prisoner of
                                                                  4

conscience and write to the government _____ has imprisoned him or her, asking for
                                            5

the prisoner's release.

Amnesty International has done a great deal to defend human rights, for _____ it
                                                                            6

was awarded the Nobel Peace Prize in 1977.

■ A. Whose

Note how the two sentences below can be combined using **whose:**

I have a friend. His father works for Amnesty International.

I have a friend **whose** father works for Amnesty International.

7.3   RAPID DRILL: *Whose*

DIRECTIONS: You are the director of a relief organization that sends workers to third world countries. Decide if you would or would not hire the following people to go to Africa to develop their food supply and explain why. Use **whose** in your response.

EXAMPLE

CUE: His health is poor.

ANSWER: I wouldn't hire a man whose health is poor, because he needs to be strong in order to do his job effectively.

CUE: Her degree is in anthropology.

ANSWER: I would hire a person whose degree is in anthropology because she would be familiar with foreign cultures.

1. His father is dying.
2. Her mother is a famous movie star.
3. His cross-cultural experience is limited.
4. Her husband can't accompany her.
5. His university major was philosophy.
6. Her work experience is on a farm.
7. His age is 50.
8. Her appearance is sloppy.
9. His application was illegible and late.
10. Her skin is sensitive to the sun.

7.4 PAIRED DRILL: *Whose*

DIRECTIONS: Discuss the following questions with a partner, using **whose** in your response. Be honest!! Be prepared to share (and defend if necessary) one or two of your answers with the class.

1. What kind of person do you dislike?
2. What kind of man or woman will you (or did you) marry?
3. What kind of people do you like?
4. What kind of leader does your country need?
5. What type of person would you never do business with?
6. Say something about the kind of mother you have.
7. Say something about the kind of father you have.
8. What kind of boss do you prefer?
9. What kind of friend do you need?
10. What type of government do you think is the best?

B. Object of Prepositions

Note how these two sentences can be combined using an adjective clause. Note also the degree of formality.

---

1. Amnesty International is the organization. I told you **about it.**

Informal: Amnesty International is the organization

          $\emptyset$ **I told you about.**
          that I told you **about.**
          which I told you **about.**
          about which I told you.

Formal:

2. The prisoner was released. Amnesty International wrote to the prisoner.

Informal: The prisoner
{
∅ Amnesty International wrote **to** was released.
who(m) Amnesty International wrote **to** was released.
that Amnesty International wrote **to** was released.
Formal:
to whom Amnesty International wrote was released.
}

7.5 ORAL DRILL: *Objects of Prepositions*

DIRECTIONS: Combine these sentences in as many ways as possible. **Use the second sentence as an adjective clause.**

EXAMPLE

CUE: Money is a commodity. We can't live without it.
ANSWER: Money is a commodity that/which we can't live without.
∅ we can't live without.
without which we can't live.

1. I went to an island in the Pacific for vacation. My travel agent had told me about it.
2. My brother has a pen pal. He has been writing to him for 20 years.
3. Danielle Steele wrote many novels. She has received a good deal of money for them.
4. Martin Luther King, Jr., organized the Montgomery bus boycott. He was jailed for this.
5. King believed in Christian principles. He combined nonviolent passive resistance with them.
6. King gave his "I've Got a Dream" speech in 1963 to 250,000 people. He was famous for it.

C. Relative Words of Place and Time

Adjective clauses can modify places and time in the following ways.

1. Place

The prisons are filthy. Many prisoners of conscience were sent to the prisons.

Informal: The prisons
{
∅ | many prisoners of conscience were sent **to** are filthy.
where | many prisoners of conscience were sent are filthy.
that | many prisoners of conscience were sent **to** are filthy.
which | many prisoners of conscience were sent **to** are filthy.
Formal:
to which | many prisoners of conscience were sent are filthy.
}

2. Time

1980 is the year. Amnesty International won the Nobel Peace Prize then.

Informal: 1980 is the year
{
∅ | Amnesty International won the Nobel Peace Prize.
that | Amnesty International won the Nobel Peace Prize.
when | Amnesty International won the Nobel Peace Prize.
}

| *Formal:* | { **in which** | Amnesty International won the Nobel Peace Prize. |
| | { **during which** | Amnesty International won the Nobel Peace Prize. |

SPECIAL NOTE
RELATIVE WORDS OF TIME

Use these prepositions with the following units of time:
    YEAR during which, in which
    DAY: on which
    MONTH: during which, in which

7.5   PAIRED ACTIVITY: *Time and Place*

DIRECTIONS: Test your knowledge of dates and places. See if you can identify more than your partner. Take turns identifying these times and places by using an appropriate preposition and relative word. **Do not use *when* or *where*.**

EXAMPLE

December 25
December 25 is the day on which Christians celebrate Christmas.

Student A	Student B
1. February 14	**1.** Halloween
2. July 4	**2.** April 15
3. the ninth month of the Muslim calendar	**3.** 1492
4. 1776	**4.** The fourth Thursday in November
5. A nursing home	**5.** The Forbidden City
6. 10 Downing Street	**6.** A kennel
7. Epcot Center	**7.** The Alamo

7.6   WRITTEN ACTIVITY: *Using All Types of Adjective Clauses*

DIRECTIONS: Combine the following sentences using the second sentence as an adjective clause. Write as a unified paragraph.

1. Mother Theresa was born into a family in Albania. Her family was very wealthy.
2. Her mother often took her daughter to visit the poor. Their miserable living conditions left a lasting impression on Mother Theresa.
3. She left the convent and started her own congregation. She had to obtain approval from the Vatican for it.
4. In 1954 Mother Theresa set up a home for the dying with 26 volunteers. The volunteers' life was austere: no possessions and a 16-hour work day.

5. In 1979 she received the Nobel Peace Prize. She was criticized by some people for this. These people believed she had helped the poor but had not contributed to world peace. The Nobel Prize was intended for world peace.

6. She has also received criticism in the United States. There, some feminists disagree with her anti-abortion stance.

D. Special Uses of Restrictive Adjective Clauses

1. TO DEFINE

Restrictive adjective clauses are often used to define or describe as in the following examples. Note the use of the expressions:

one who or **a person who** (for persons)
a (time) in which (for periods of time or events)

- A philanthropist is **one who gives large amounts of money to charitable causes.**
- The 1950s was a decade **in which conformity was very important.**
- Capitalism is an economic system **which believes in free enterprise.**

2. TO EMPHASIZE

The following construction is used when speakers or writers want to emphasize a certain point. Compare the following two sentences and note how **(b)** underscores the writer's point:

(a) Karl Benz first developed the automobile, but Henry Ford is remembered for making it affordable to the public.

(b) Karl Benz first developed the automobile, but **it is really Henry Ford who is remembered for making it affordable to the public.**

7.7 PAIRED ACTIVITY: *Defining*

DIRECTIONS: Work with a partner to develop clear definitions or descriptions of the following terms and events. Use a dictionary for any difficult terms. Write a definition for each one, using an adjective clause. Then compare and discuss these with another pair of students.

Define these terms:

1. an altruist
2. a misogynist
3. democracy
4. culture shock
5. charity
6. a volunteer
7. a donation
8. a benefactor

Characterize these times:

1. the 1980s
2. middle age
3. motherhood
4. adolescence

7.8 ORAL ACTIVITY: *Emphasizing*

DIRECTIONS: Your teacher will identify the following famous people or organizations by what they have done or invented. Some of the statements will be true and others will be false. See if you can identify the errors and correct them. Use the following constructions in your responses:

"Are you sure? I believe it was really _____ who / when / where / that, etc."
OR
"Oh, I think it was _____

EXAMPLE

CUE: Thomas Edison
TEACHER: Thomas Edison invented the telephone.
STUDENT: No, I believe it was really Alexander Graham Bell who invented the telephone.

- Marie Curie
- Charles Darwin
- Florence Nightingale
- Babe Ruth
- Pele
- Sigmund Freud
- Neil Armstrong
- The League of Nations

GRAMMATICAL PATTERNS TWO

PREVIEW

DIRECTIONS: How would you feel today if you had been somewhat responsible for the development of the atomic bomb? Read the following text on J. Robert Oppenheimer and answer the questions that follow.

THE FATHER OF THE ATOMIC BOMB

1. J. Robert Oppenheimer, who was perhaps the most brilliant nuclear physicist of our century, is often referred to as "the father of the atomic bomb." After receiving a bachelor and master's degree at Harvard University in only three years, Oppenheimer went abroad for his doctorate in

the "new" nuclear physics in Cambridge, England and at the University of Gottingen, where he met other brilliant scientists. These scientists, who would later **figure** prominently in his life, included Edward Teller and Leo Szilard. After that, he taught in Holland, where he was affectionately given the name "Oppie," which **stuck** for life.

2. In 1942 he was made director of the Manhattan District, a project for the development of the atomic bomb, which had not yet been produced by any country. Oppie gathered **a coterie** of brilliant scientists around him who eagerly and willingly worked at finding a way to build this bomb. Oppie had a powerful effect on the people who worked for him. They were amazed at his diverse interests and talents—physics, poetry, gourmet foods, and spiritual matters.

3. It is almost hard to believe that it was this brilliant lover of poetry and fine wine who inspired capable scientists to create the most destructive weapon on earth. In fact, after the bomb had been dropped on Hiroshima and Nagasaki, Japan in August of 1945, Oppie himself was disturbed by the power of his own creation. He then tried to establish a formal agreement between the United States and the Soviet Union which would forbid the production of such weapons. The United States and the Soviet Union, which by that time had begun making its own bombs, were unable **to strike** any such cooperative agreement. And so, the arms race had begun.

VOCABULARY

to figure: to appear, to have a place
stuck: stayed
a coterie: a group of people
to strike: to make

GRAMMAR CONSIDERATIONS: FOCUS

The following questions are based on the preview text. Answer as many of the questions as you can. Work with a partner if your teacher tells you to do so.

1. Underline all the adjective clauses in the text. (There are 11.) Circle the noun that each clause modifies.
2. Compare the punctuation of these two clauses:
   (a) J. Robert Oppenheimer, **who was perhaps the most brilliant nuclear physicist of our century,** is often referred to as "the father of the atomic bomb." (paragraph 1)
   (b) Oppie had a powerful effect on the people **who worked for him.** (paragraph 2)

   Can you explain why the punctuation is different? Could you delete the adjective clause in sentence (a) and still have a meaningful sentence? Could you do that for sentence (b) and keep the same meaning?

3. Rewrite the following sentence, changing the phrase in bold to an adjective clause.

   In 1942 he was made director of the Manhattan District, **a project for the development of the atomic bomb.**

■ I. NONRESTRICTIVE ADJECTIVE CLAUSES

Nonrestrictive adjective clauses provide additional information that is not necessary to identify the noun being modified. These clauses, unlike restrictive clauses, are set off by commas in writing and pauses in speech. Often the nonrestrictive clause can be deleted from the sentence without causing undue confusion in meaning.

Note how the meaning of a sentence can be completely changed by a restrictive or nonrestrictive clause.

TYPE	EXAMPLE	NOTES
NONRESTRICTIVE ADJECTIVE CLAUSES	• The scientists, who adored Oppie, stayed until the end of the project. (ALL ADORED OPPIE, ALL STAYED)	• Do not use the relative word **that** in a nonrestrictive clause. Use **who(m)** for people and **which** for things. • Always set off the nonrestrictive clauses by commas. • This sentence implies that **all** the scientists adored Oppie and **all** stayed until the end of the project.
	• Oppenheimer met Edward Teller, **whom** he would never forget.	• The relative word can **never** be deleted in a nonrestrictive clause, even if it is the object of the clause or of the preposition.
RESTRICTIVE ADJECTIVE CLAUSES	The scientists **who / that** adored Oppie stayed until the end of the project. (ADORED OPPIE & STAYED) (DIDN'T ADORE OPPIE & DIDN'T STAY)	• The relative word **that** can always replace **who** or **which** in a restrictive clause. • Do not use commas with restrictive clauses. • This sentence implies that there were **two** groups of scientists: those who adored and those that did not. Those that did **not** adore Oppie did not stay.
	Oppenheimer made friends **(that)** he would never forget.	• The relative word **can** be deleted if it is the object of the clause or a preposition.

7.9 RAPID DRILL: *Pronunciation of Clauses*

DIRECTIONS: Your teacher will read a series of sentences. If there is a pause before and after the adjective clause, you will know that it is a nonrestrictive clause. If there is no pause, then it is restrictive. Circle the sentence you hear your teacher say. Note the different pronunciation patterns on page 152. Then answer the comprehension questions that follow.

The book, which I lent you, is on the table.

The book which I lent you is on the table.

1. (a) My friends, who are rich, will be at the party.
   (b) My friends who are rich will be at the party.
   In which sentence are **all** his friends rich?
2. (a) The students, who were attentive in class, passed the test.
   (b) The students who were attentive in class passed the test.
   Which sentence states that only **some** of the students were attentive?
3. (a) The tennis players, who were women, won the tournament.
   (b) The tennis players who were women won the tournament.
   Which sentence states that **all** of the players were women?
4. (a) My boyfriend, who is from France, is sitting over there.
   (b) My boyfriend who is from France is sitting over there.
   Which sentence implies that she has more than one boyfriend?
5. In pairs, practice your own pronunciation. See if your partner can distinguish between the two types of intonation patterns.

■ II. WHEN TO USE NONRESTRICTIVE ADJECTIVE CLAUSES

Use nonrestrictive clauses in the following cases.

CASE	EXAMPLE
1. WHEN THE ANTECEDENT HAS BEEN PREVIOUSLY IDENTIFIED	• Oppie met some brilliant scientists in Germany and England. **These scientists, who would later figure prominently in his life,** included Edward Teller and Leo Szilard.
2. WHEN THE ANTECEDENT IS A PROPER NOUN	• **J. Robert Oppenheimer, who was perhaps the most brilliant nuclear physicist of our century,** is often referred to as the father of the atomic bomb.
3. WHEN THE ANTECEDENT IS A ONE-OF-A-KIND NOUN	• The goal of the project was to develop **the atomic bomb, which had not yet been done by any country.**

7.10 ADJECTIVE CLAUSE IDENTIFICATION

DIRECTIONS: Read the following sentences and underline all adjective clauses. Label the clauses as restrictive **(R)** or nonrestrictive **(NR)** and be ready to explain why. Insert commas before and after the nonrestrictive clauses.

EXAMPLE

_NR_   Sophon and Srey, <u>who were from Cambodia,</u> arrived at the Burlington Airport on a wintry day in Vermont.

_____ **1.** A large group of people some of whom included members of Sophon's family as well as Americans were anxiously waiting for these refugees to arrive.

_____ **2.** The American volunteers who had organized this reunion included English teachers, retired physicians, politicians, and homemakers.

_____ **3.** As Srey and Sophon walked through the gate, Channel 3 which was the local T.V. station quickly moved in to film and interview them.

_____ **4.** Afterwards, everyone went to the apartment which had been rented for them. The apartment which was located in the middle of town was very small.

_____ **5.** Sophon and his family were only one of many Indochinese refugee families who were resettled in Vermont.

7.11 WRITTEN EXERCISE: *MADD*

DIRECTIONS: What are the penalties in your country for driving while under the influence of alcohol? The following sentences are about Candy Lightner and the organization that she founded, Mothers Against Drunk Driving (MADD). Incorporate the information in parentheses into the sentence by changing it to an adjective clause. Decide if the clause is **restrictive** or **nonrestrictive.** Then insert commas where necessary.

EXAMPLE

CUE: On May 3, 1980, Cari Lightner (Cari was 13 years old) was walking to a church carnival.
ANSWER: On May 3, 1980, Cari Lightner, **who was 13 years old**, was walking to a church carnival.

1. Cari was suddenly hit by a drunk man. (the man's car swerved out of control)
2. The man was Clarence Busch. (Busch was a cannery worker) (he had been arrested many times for drunk driving)
3. Cari's mother Candy (Candy had two other children) was at a cocktail lounge with some friends when she decided to do something about the danger of drunk drivers.
4. She decided to start an organization. (her friend named it MADD)
5. She went to see the Governor of California, Jerry Brown. (she tried to convince him to start this organization)
6. Even though he refused her request, Candy went to his office every day. (she talked to anyone at the office about her idea)
7. Brown finally relented and now Candy's organization (it has 600,000 volunteers) has 320 chapters.
8. MADD was largely responsible for getting a law passed in California. (the law imposes a minimum $375 fine and imprisonment for drunk drivers with many offenses)

7.12 ADJECTIVE CLAUSE REVIEW

DIRECTIONS: Change each of the following sentences in parentheses into a relative clause and write it in the space provided. Insert commas when necessary.

Clara, _____who works at the university_____ and David _____ went
         (Clara works at the university.)   (David is her husband.)

on a drive to the desert _____ The road _____
               (They had never been to the desert before.)

_____ went up into the mountains _____
        (They travelled on the road.)   (The mountains had snow.)

and then down the mountains into a flat area _____. The wind
                           (The area was very dry.)

was blowing very hard and David _____ was a little worried
                   (His car is small.)

worried about keeping his car on the road.

III. ADJECTIVE CLAUSES THAT MODIFY SENTENCES

Compare the following sentences and note how an adjective clause can modify an entire sentence and not just a noun.

COMPARE: ■ I don't like our *uniform,* **which the principal picked out this year.** ■ *This year students are required to wear uniforms,* **which I completely agree with.**	This is a nonrestrictive clause that modifies the **noun,** *uniform.* This is a nonrestrictive clause that comments on the **previous statement,** "students are required to wear uniforms."
PUNCTUATION	■ A comma always precedes a sentence clause, just as in any nonrestrictive clause.

7.12   ORAL DRILL: *Sentence Clauses*

DIRECTIONS: Respond to the following statements with an adjective clause that comments on the statement and expresses your thoughts and feelings.

EXAMPLE

CUE: Many workers in the United States don't have health insurance, . . .
ANSWER: . . . which has become a serious problem.

1. The Berlin Wall was torn down quickly, . . .
2. Nelson Mandela, a political prisoner in South Africa, was freed in 1990, . . .
3. The environment has become a very serious political issue, . . .
4. Mikhael Gorbachev was named the "man of the decade" in 1990, . . .
5. The United States allows the death penalty, . . .
6. Most U.S. universities require a score of 550 on the TOEFL, . . .
7. The greenhouse effect is making summers warmer in the midwest of the United States, . . .
8. Teachers earn low salaries in many states, . . .
9. There are many more fax machines in the world, . . .
10. Practically everyone in the United States has a T.V. now, . . .

IV. NONRESTRICTIVE CLAUSES AFTER EXPRESSIONS OF QUANTITY

Note how these sentences can be combined using an adjective clause after an expression of quantity (for example, both, many, much, etc.)

TWO SENTENCES	ONE SENTENCE + ADJECTIVE CLAUSE	NOTES
I have many friends. All of **them** are from foreign countries.	I have many friends, **all of whom are from foreign countries.**	▪ Replace the pronoun with **whom** for people.
I couldn't decide between two universities. Both of **them** were reputable.	I couldn't decide between two universities, **both of which were reputable.**	▪ Use **which**—not **that**—for objects.
I have many friends. Many of their spouses work at home.	I have many friends, **many of whose spouses** work at home.	▪ Use **whose** for possession. ▪ Always insert commas before and after the clause.

7.13   WHY DO PEOPLE DO WHAT THEY DO? *Clauses After Expressions of Quantity*

DIRECTIONS: Read the following sentences about motivations and explanations for human behavior. Combine the sentences using an expression of quantity.

EXAMPLE

CUE: There are many theories about why people do what they do. The majority of them have some validity.

ANSWER: There are many theories about why people do what they do, **the majority of which** have some validity.

1. Sigmund Freud believed that people were driven by very basic drives of the pleasure principle and the death wish. Both of these drives originate in the unconscious.
2. B. F. Skinner maintained that the environment shapes our behavior. Any aspect of our behavior can be both learned and unlearned.
3. Carl Rogers firmly held the belief that humans are innately good. All people are motivated by a self-actualizing principle.
4. Abraham Maslow described several stages of human development. The highest stage is self-actualization.
5. There are many other psychologists. Many of their theories about motivation, however, are not well known.

7.14 SENTENCE COMPLETION: *Adjective Clauses After Expressions of Quantity*

DIRECTIONS: Complete the following sentences using the expression of quantity given and an adjective clause.

EXAMPLE

I have many interests, <u>most of which are not intellectual</u>.

1. In my room there are many objects, the most expensive _____

2. There are many restaurants in this city, the majority _____

3. In this class there are many students, few _____

4. I have known many admirable people, the most _____

7.15 WRITTEN ACTIVITY: *Combining Sentences*

DIRECTIONS: Write a short paragraph about the organization International Physicians for the Prevention of Nuclear War. Use the information listed below, and feel free to include some of your own thoughts about the existence of nuclear weapons in our world. In your paragraph **use at least five different types of adjective clauses,** including both restrictive and nonrestrictive, and underline them. Refer to the chart at the beginning of the chapter for a comprehensive list of all types of clauses.

International Physicians for the Prevention of Nuclear War (IPPONW)
- a worldwide federation of medical doctors and health professionals
- founded in 1980 by two U.S. citizens and two Soviet citizens
- the objective of the organization is to consolidate medical opinion against the danger of nuclear arms
- has organized programs to warn the public of these dangers
- supports the following efforts:
  - stopping nuclear testing
  - putting a freeze on the development of atomic weapons
  - not taking funding away from social programs to develop nuclear arms
- won the Nobel Peace Prize in 1985

V. ADJECTIVE CLAUSE REDUCTION

Note how adjective clauses can be reduced (shortened). Sentence (1) of each pair has a **full adjective** clause, and sentence (2) has a **reduced** adjective clause.

	REDUCTION	NOTES
BE + *ADJECTIVE*	1. The person **who was responsible for the concert** was Bob Geldof. 2. The person **responsible for the concert** was Bob Geldof.	- Delete subject relative word and delete the **BE** verb.

PASSIVE	1. Amnesty International is an organization **which was founded in London.**	▪ Delete the **BE** verb and keep the past participle.
	2. Amnesty International is an organization **founded in London.**	
PROGRESSIVE	1. Oppenheimer had the best scientists **who were working with him.**	▪ Delete the auxiliary **BE** and keep the verb-ing.
	2. Oppenheimer had the best scientists **working with him.**	
VERBS OTHER THAN **BE**	1. More than a billion people witnessed a concert **which hosted over 60 acts.**	▪ When there is no **BE** verb, change the verb to an -ing form as in (2)—hosting.
	2. More than a billion people witnessed a concert **hosting over 60 acts.**	
NON-RESTRICTIVE CLAUSES	1. J. Robert Oppenheimer, **who was perhaps the most brilliant physicist of our time,** is often called the father of the atomic bomb.	▪ The same rules as above apply to nonrestrictive clauses.
	2. J. Robert Oppenheimer, **perhaps the most brilliant physicist of our time,** is often called the father of the atomic bomb.	▪ Be sure to keep the commas in the resulting reduced clause.

7.16 CLAUSE REDUCTION: *Important American Women*

DIRECTIONS: Reduce the adjective clauses in the following sentences to phrases.

1. Betty Friedan, who was the founder of the National Organization for Women, was one of the first women to recognize the need for a women's organization.
2. Gloria Steinem, who has been a key player in the women's movement, has a number of talents, which consist of brains, comic perception, and extremely good looks.
3. The woman who was given the first license to fly in the United States was Amelia Earhart.
4. Geraldine Ferraro, who is now living in New York City with her family, was the first female to run for vice-president of the United States.
5. At 19 months Helen Keller had a disease that was never diagnosed and that left her deaf, dumb, and blind.

7.17 MAKING CHOICES: *Reduction of Adjective Clauses*

DIRECTIONS: Each of the following situations requires you to make a choice. Answer the question posed in each by using a reduced relative clause. Then discuss your decisions in groups or pairs.

1. You are a senator in a small democratic country with a large number of poor people. Recently, two pieces of legislation (bills) have been proposed regarding the problems with the poor. The first bill suggests providing moderate housing for the poor at no cost to them. The other bill proposes giving food regularly to the poor. Which bill would you vote for?

2. You have just inherited one million dollars. Since you are a widow and all of your children are grown, you would like to donate this money to a good cause. But you are having a difficult time deciding which cause is the most worthy. You have narrowed down your choices to three: AIDS research, Harvard University (your alma mater), and the local symphony orchestra, which has had financial problems. What will your final choice be?

3. Your nephew, who is 18 years old, is about to enter the university. He has come to you for some advice concerning his future plans. He is not certain which area of study would be the best for his future. These are his choices: (a) Business: He could get a good job and be financially secure. (b) Science: He is worried about the environment. (c) Education: He loves kids and believes that education is the key to a country's future. What discipline would you advise him to study at the university?

4. Imagine that you could choose a specialist to go to who could change your life completely. One could improve your physical appearance, another could increase your intelligence. A third could provide you with endless wealth. The fourth would make you a very friendly and popular person. Which specialist would you visit?

VI. SPECIAL PROBLEMS WITH ADJECTIVE CLAUSE USE

PROBLEM	EXPLANATION
1. REPETITION OF THE PRONOUN IN THE CLAUSE [INCORRECT: I really enjoyed the Vietnamese food that I had it yesterday.] CORRECT: I really enjoyed the Vietnamese food that I had yesterday.	■ The relative word replaces the noun in the adjective clause.
2. AGREEMENT [INCORRECT: I met some people who was from my country.] CORRECT: I met some people who were from my country.	■ Make sure the antecedent agrees with the verb in the clause.
3. LOCATION OF THE CLAUSE [INCORRECT: We went to a Hawaiian island for our fiftieth wedding anniversary *that was deserted and romantic.*] CORRECT: For our fiftieth wedding anniversary we went to a Hawaiian island *that was deserted and romantic.*	■ Place the clause as close to the antecedent as possible.

4. NO PREPOSITION OR PARTICLE [INCORRECT: The restaurant that she went was crowded and noisy.] CORRECT: The restaurant that she went **to** was noisy and crowded.	▪ Be sure to place the preposition or particle at the end of the clause.
5. USING **THAT** FOR NONRESTRICTIVE CLAUSES [INCORRECT: I like martial arts, that teach balance and strength.] CORRECT: I like martial arts, **which** teach balance and strength.	▪ If the clause is nonrestrictive, you **must** use **which** and not **that** for things.

■ 7.18 ERROR ANALYSIS

DIRECTIONS: Each of the following sentences has an error in adjective clause use. Find the errors and correct them. Refer to the above chart, but note that some errors may not be among the types listed there.

1. You wouldn't believe the test that we had it in our structure class last week!
2. John went to see a friend that his father is the president of his college.
3. My husband adores lumpia that is an Indonesian-style egg roll.
4. There is an old bridge crosses the river in my town.
5. The class schedule that I got it yesterday has many errors on it, which I am going to complain to the administration.
6. My economics professor will let me take my final exam after vacation for that I am very grateful.
7. In my house I have all kinds of paintings, most of them are from the twentieth century.
8. This is the kind of plant that you usually have to fertilize it regularly.
9. I used to have this doctor that I'd never go back to her.
10. 96.5 F.M. is one radio station that I listen a lot.
11. I love Georgia O'Keeffe's paintings that are all on exhibit in Los Angeles now.
12. She left her textbook on the table in the kitchen that she needs for class tomorrow.
13. I had an interesting talk with two students, both of them are from Turkey.
14. For my birthday I got a beautiful piece of crystal, which I love crystal.
15. Montpelier that is the capital city of Vermont has six months of winter.
16. I would never marry a man that his religion is different from mine.
17. The movie that Loretta and Jack went yesterday was *Rain Main,* which they loved.
18. The IPPONW, which was founded in 1980 by two Soviet and two United States citizens.
19. Their objective is to consolidate medical opinion against the danger of nuclear arms which have bad effects on people whose mental and physical are destroyed.

COMPOSITION TOPICS

1. Each year *Time* magazine chooses the Man of the Year, a man or woman who has contributed a great deal to the world during that year. If you were on the staff of *Time* magazine and were asked to submit a recommendation for the year that has just passed, who would you recommend? In a short essay, explain why you think that individual deserves to be called the Man of the Year. Describe the person's accomplishments and why you think he or she has made a difference.

2. Describe a person or an event that has made a difference in your life. Be specific in explaining how that person or event changed you.

3. Who is / was the most important individual in your country? Write a short essay explaining why that person is / was vital for your country and how he or she will change / changed your country's history.

8

MAKING CHOICES

⊟ Adverb clauses

"WHATEVER HAPPENS, HAPPENS"   **Decisions, decisions!**

DISCUSSION QUESTIONS

1. Do you believe in fate (destiny)? Do you believe you have the freedom to shape your life?
2. When you have an important decision to make, whom do you talk to?
3. If a close friend came to you for help in making a difficult decision (for example, a marriage or career choice), would you just listen or would you give him or her specific advice?
4. Is there any danger in giving people advice?

OBJECTIVES

In this chapter, you will learn:

1. To form and use adverb clauses of time, place, reason, result, direct contrast, opposition, purpose, and manner
2. To punctuate these clauses
3. To reduce adverb clauses

PREVIEW

DIRECTIONS: Read the following letter that Joanne wrote to her friend Carole. Then answer the questions that follow.

Dear Carole,

1. At last I've got a moment to write you! I really wish that we lived closer to each other *so that* we could have lunch together once in awhile. *Although* we've only seen each other twice in the past five years, you're still my very best friend.

2. The baby **is due** in two months. Jack and I are truly excited! But, Carole, I'm so undecided about what to do *after* the baby arrives. *Whenever* I try to decide between staying home and continuing my job at the advertising agency, I just get more confused. The **dilemma** has really **come to a head now that** my boss is **putting on the pressure** for a definite answer. Maybe you can help me *since* you were always better at making decisions.

3. I think I know what you would advise me to do: make a list of the advantages and disadvantages and write them down. That's what I did and here's what I came up with. *While* my **heart** tells me to stay home, my **head** tells me to go back to work. One side of me says, "How can you leave your beautiful baby at home *while* you **trudge off** to work and design ad copy all day?" The other side says, "Joanne, *if* you leave your job now, you won't get another one that pays so well and uses your artistic talent." It's true; I like working. I also think I would like being with my baby. You know that my income **is just gravy** *as* Jack's business is quite successful now. *Unless* the economy **softens**, I could take two or three years off.

4. Please write and let me know what you think I should do. And Carole, I hope you're planning a visit soon!

Love,

Joanne

Joanne

VOCABULARY

to be due: will be born
a dilemma: a problem with two equally likely resolutions
to come to a head: to reach a critical point
to put on the pressure: to demand immediately
my heart: my feelings
my head: my rational thinking
to trudge off: to go somewhere slowly and unwillingly
to be just gravy: to be supplementary, extra (informal English)
to soften: in this case, to weaken

CULTURAL NOTE / DISCUSSION

Many mothers in the United States are faced with the choice between staying home with their babies or going back to work. What are the advantages and disadvantages of each alternative? What would you advise Joanne to do?

GRAMMAR CONSIDERATIONS: FOCUS

The following questions are based on the preview text and are designed to help you find out what you already know about the structures in this chapter. Some of the questions may be hard and some of them may be easy. Answer as many of the questions as you can. Work with a partner if your teacher tells you to do so.

1. The words in italics in the preview letter introduce adverb clauses. Which of those words have approximately the same meaning as the words below? Write them in the space provided.

   a) at the same time as _____

   b) each time _____

   c) if not _____

2. What type of relationships do the following words show between the ideas in the sentence? (purpose, time, contrast / opposition, condition)

   a) although (paragraph 1) _____

   b) so that (paragraph 1) _____

   c) after (paragraph 2) _____

3. Locate and underline the two sentences in the letter using the word **while**. Does **while** have the same meaning in each sentence? If not, what is the difference?

   _____

4. Compare the punctuation of these two sentences. How is it different? Can you explain why there is a difference?
   (a) "Although we've seen each other only twice in the past five years, you're still my very best friend."
   (b) "Maybe you can help me since you were always better at making decisions."

   _____

GRAMMATICAL PATTERNS ONE

I. ADVERB CLAUSES: POSITION AND PUNCTUATION

Adverb clauses are **dependent clauses.** The words that introduce these clauses are **subordinating conjunctions.**

	subordinating conjunction
You are still my best friend	↓ **although** we've only seen each other twice in the past five years.
(main clause)	(dependent clause)

Note the position and punctuation of the adverb clauses below (in bold).

EXAMPLE	NOTE
1. **Although we've only seen each other twice in the past five years,** you are still my very best friend.	POSITION OF CLAUSE ■ The adverb clause can occur in initial position as in sentence 1 or after the main clause as in sentence 2.
2. You are still my very best friend **although we've only seen each other twice in the past five years.**	PUNCTUATION OF CLAUSE ■ Place a comma after an adverb clause in initial position as in sentence 1. No comma is necessary in sentence 2.

■ II. SUMMARY CHART OF ADVERB CLAUSE USE

There are many types of adverb clauses, depending on the relationship expressed in the sentence. Below is a list of these clauses and the subordinating conjunctions for each type. Since many of these may not be new for you, test yourself by covering up the left column and trying to identify the type of clause by looking at the example.

TYPE OF CLAUSE AND SUBORDINATING CONJUNCTIONS	EXAMPLE
1. TIME after, before, when, while, as, whenever, since, until / till, as soon as, once, as long as	I'm undecided about what to do **after the baby arrives.**
2. PLACE where, wherever, everywhere, anywhere	**Everywhere I look,** I see mothers with their newborn babies!

3. REASON / RESULT because, since, as, now that, inasmuch as, as long as, so that / such that	Maybe you can help me **since you were always better at making decisions.**
4. DIRECT CONTRAST while, whereas	**While my heart tells me to stay home,** my head tells me to go back to work.
5. OPPOSITION although, even though, though, despite the fact that, in spite of the fact that	**Although we've seen each other only twice in the past five years,** you are still my very best friend.
6. CONDITION if, unless, provided that, only if, whether or not, in case, even if	**Unless the economy softens,** I could take two or three years off. (See the chapter on the conditional for a more complete explanation.)
7. PURPOSE so that, in order that	I wish we lived closer **so that we could have lunch together once in awhile.**
8. MANNER as, as if, as though	You look **as though you are ready to have the baby soon!**

8.1 ADVERB CLAUSE RECOGNITION: *The Pros and Cons of Staying Home*

DIRECTIONS: Here is the list that Joanne made of the advantages and disadvantages of staying home with her baby.

1. Underline the subordinating conjunctions in each of the following sentences and identify them by type (for example, time). Refer to the above chart for a complete list.
2. Put a check next to those sentences that require a comma and then insert one where necessary.

EXAMPLE

✔   time   After her baby is born, a mother's life changes dramatically.

The advantages of staying home:

1. _____   The mother can give her baby a great deal of attention as she will not be gone during the day.

2. _____   Whenever the child is hungry the mother will be able to feed her child.

3. _____   The mother will be the primary caregiver so that the child will feel secure.

4. _____   Although the mother won't have the social contact she is used to at work she won't be completely exhausted at the end of the day by trying to juggle what is in fact two full-time jobs.

The disadvantages of staying home:

1. _____   Despite the fact that she must leave her child at day care the mother will be able to retain her position and salary at work.

2. _____   The mother will lose her job unless she returns to work after the maximum six-week maternity leave.

3. _____   Wherever you live there are many competent and caring daycare workers who need the income.

4. _____   While the baby is at day care there will be social contact with other babies and adults.

III. TIME CLAUSES

SUBORDINATING CONJUNCTION	EXAMPLE	NOTES
1. AFTER / BEFORE **2.** WHEN	▪ **After** I *finish* college, I will work in my father's company. ▪ **Before** I started this job, I *(had) traveled* around the world. ▪ Joe was in college **when** he met Jill. ▪ They *had known* each other two years **when** they got married.	▪ **Never use the future** in a dependent time clause. Use the simple present tense. ▪ The past perfect in sentences with **before** and **after** clauses is optional. ▪ **When** = during / at that time; before ▪ If **when** = **before**, then the past perfect is necessary in the main clause.
3. WHILE / AS	▪ The children are in day care **while** Lou Anne *is working*. ▪ **As** Lou Anne was taking her children to day care, she saw a bus hit a tractor trailer.	▪ A **progressive** tense is usually used in **while** and **as** clauses. ▪ **While** and **as** have the same meaning.
4. BY THE TIME	▪ **By the time** the baby is born, Jack and Linda will have been married for four years.	▪ See the Special Note on page 168 for an explanation.
5. SINCE	▪ Sue *has been working* **since** Johnny was born.	▪ Use any appropriate perfect tense in the independent clause.

6. WHENEVER	• **Whenever** George thinks about getting married, he gets butterflies in his stomach.	• **Whenever** = each time that. • Use a simple present or past tense in a **whenever** clause.
7. ONCE	• **Once** Carole graduates from law school, she will move to New York.	• **Once** = after
8. AS SOON AS	• **As soon as** she moves there, she will rent an apartment.	• **As soon as** = immediately after
9. UNTIL / TILL	• Alex won't get married **until** he can afford a house.	• **Until** = up to that moment
10. AS LONG AS SO LONG AS	• Joan will never leave her hometown **as long as** her mother is alive.	• **as / so long as** = during the entire time that

---

SPECIAL NOTE

Intensifiers can be used for emphasis with the following subordinating conjunctions of time.

- **just as** = at precisely that time
- **just when**

The plane took off **just as / when** we arrived at the airport.

- **shortly before / after**
- **immediately before / after**

He changed his will **shortly / immediately before** he died.

- **long before / after**

She had divorced him **long before** he died.

- **ever since**

She has been afraid to fly **ever since** she was a child.

8.2 RAPID DRILL: *Adverb Clauses of Time*

DIRECTIONS: State what types of decisions you will make or have made before, during or after these events. Use the subordinating conjunction in parentheses. Use the intensifiers listed above when appropriate.

EXAMPLE

CUE: leave home (before)
ANSWER: Before I leave home, I must decide where to live.

1. have a baby (as soon as)
2. buy a house (long before)
3. look for a job (while)

  4. enter the university (once)

  5. change jobs (whenever)

  6. retire (once)

  7. travel to foreign country (immediately after)

  8. get married (before)

  9. get divorced (shortly before)

10. move to another city (whenever)

8.3   FILL IN THE BLANKS: *Verb Tenses with Adverb Clauses*

DIRECTIONS: Fill in the blanks using any appropriate verb. Be careful of the tenses.

EXAMPLE

Right after Bob <u>brushes his teeth</u>, he will go to bed.

  1. Long before he was elected president, Ronald Reagan _____ a movie actor.

  2. Once I _____ 550 on the TOEFL, I can start my master's program.

  3. As soon as an earthquake _____ , you had better run for cover.

  4. As long as she _____ , Mrs. Rose never missed having Sunday dinner with her children.

  5. I _____ when the telephone rang.

  6. As Mr. Jones _____ at Sweetwater's restaurant, his wife was sitting at the Waterworks restaurant.

  7. She _____ since I have known her.

  8. Whenever my teacher _____ , I get really frustrated.

  9. I will study English until I _____ .

10. I will retire from my job after I _____ .

11. We _____ ever since class began.

SPECIAL NOTE

Note the verb tenses used with **by the time.**

- By the time she **leaves, I will have finished** dinner.
     (present)   (future perfect)

- By the time she **left, I had already finished** the test.
     (past)   (past perfect)

(See Chapter 3 for an explanation of the future perfect tense.)

8.4 SENTENCE COMPLETION: *Choosing a Friend*

DIRECTIONS: Complete the following sentences about choosing and keeping friends. The subordinating conjunctions of time are in bold.

1. **Whenever** I meet someone for the first time, I_____.

2. I won't invite someone to my house for dinner **until** _____.

3. I consider a person to be a close friend **once** _____.

4. I **will** trust a friend **as long as** _____.

5. I know that I have a good friend **when** _____.

6. **As soon as** _____, I will help a friend.

7. I will lend a friend money **so long as** _____.

8. By the time _____, I had three good friends.

8.5 WRITTEN EXERCISE: *A Life Story*

DIRECTIONS: Write a composition in which you describe the major events of the life of one of your parents or grandparents. Use at least four adverb clauses of time. Underline the subordinating conjunctions.

IV. PLACE CLAUSES

SUBORDINATING CONJUNCTION	EXAMPLE	NOTES
WHERE ANYWHERE WHEREVER EVERYWHERE	▪ I want to live **where** my children will be safe. ▪ I will not raise my children **anywhere** there is crime. ▪ **Everywhere** there are drugs, you will find violent crimes.	▪ **where** = a specific place ▪ **anywhere / wherever** = any place ▪ **everywhere** = all places

8.6 RAPID DRILL: *Place Clauses*

DIRECTIONS: Complete these statements using a place clause.

1. I like to shop anywhere . . .
2. I love restaurants where . . .
3. I don't go anywhere . . .
4. Everywhere I look, . . .
5. Wherever there are rich people, . . .
6. Anywhere there is political repression, . . .

7. I will always go wherever . . .
8. In a movie theater, I always sit where . . .
9. I will buy a house anywhere . . .
10. Everywhere you go, you can find . . .

V. REASON CLAUSES

SUBORDINATING CONJUNCTION	EXAMPLE	NOTES
BECAUSE AS SINCE AS / SO LONG AS	**Because** her parents divorced when she was small, Marie is reluctant to marry. **As long as** you are in the kitchen, could you get me a glass of water?	▪ All of these words state a cause and have the same meaning as **because**. ▪ **As / so long as** is used more in conversation.
NOW THAT	**Now that** Maria's father has moved far away, she only sees him once a year.	▪ **Now that = because now**
INASMUCH AS IN VIEW OF THE FACT THAT ON ACCOUNT OF THE FACT THAT AS A RESULT OF THE FACT THAT ON THE GROUNDS THAT DUE TO THE FACT THAT	Her parents were granted a divorce **inasmuch as** they had irreconcilable differences.	▪ These all mean **because**. ▪ These words are used in **formal writing and speaking** only.

8.7 PAIRED EXERCISE: *Adverb Clauses of Reason*

DIRECTIONS: First answer yes, no, or maybe to the following questions. Then discuss the **reasons** for your answers with a partner. **Use other subordinating conjunctions than because!**

EXAMPLE

Would you marry someone from a different culture?   Yes.
"Of course I would marry someone from another culture since it is not the person's nationality that counts for me but the personality."

1. Would you marry someone from a different religion than yours?
2. Would you put your parents in a nursing home when they get old?
3. Would you think of donating some of your money to a good cause?
4. If you couldn't have children of your own, would you adopt one?
5. If a family member needed a kidney transplant, would you donate yours?
6. If you saw someone cheating on an important test, would you report that person?

7. If you saw a friend's child shoplifting at a record store, would you report that child?
8. If you inherited a lot of money, would you donate some of it to your school?
9. Would you work in a foreign country if you were offered a job there?
10. Would you ever live on a farm?

8.8 WRITTEN ACTIVITY: *Adverb Clauses of Reason*

DIRECTIONS: Choose one of the questions in exercise 8.7 and write a short paragraph explaining your decision. Use at least **three** adverb clauses of reason. Do not use *because* in your paragraph!

8.9 WRITTEN ACTIVITY: *Formal Adverb Clauses of Reason*

DIRECTIONS: You are the T.V. news producer for a local station, WBBY. Recently one of your anchors, Diane Johnson, has been losing ratings for a number of reasons. You have the unpleasant task of dismissing her. Write Ms. Johnson a letter in which you explain why the T.V. station can no longer employ her. Use a variety of the **formal subordinating conjunctions** listed on page 170. You may use the reasons listed below or create your own.

REASONS FOR DISMISSAL:
- tardiness
- low ratings and loss of advertising dollars
- tired and untidy appearance perhaps due to stress or alcohol abuse
- stiff competition from the new cable news network
- budget cuts by WBBY

■ VI. RESULT CLAUSES

Compare how result can be expressed in the two constructions below. How are they different in terms of their structure? A review of count and noncount nouns (chapter 1) would be helpful at this point.

	SO...THAT	SUCH...THAT
The population is small. The mail carrier knows where everybody lives.	The population is **so** small **that** the mail carrier knows where everybody lives.	This town has **such** a small population **that** the mail carrier knows where everybody lives.

A. Such...that Constructions

SUCH...THAT CONSTRUCTION	EXAMPLE
SUCH A / AN + ADJECTIVE + SINGULAR COUNT NOUN + (THAT)	- This rural town has **such a small population (that)** the mail carrier knows where everybody lives.

SUCH + ADJECTIVE + PLURAL NOUN + (THAT) or SUCH + ADJECTIVE + MASS NOUN + (THAT)	▪ The town sells **such inexpensive antiques (that)** tourists can't resist buying them. ▪ The local restaurant serves **such good food (that)** people go there from miles away.
SUCH + ABSTRACT NOUN + (THAT)	▪ At night there is **such quiet (that)** I don't have any trouble sleeping.

B. So . . . that Constructions

SO . . . THAT CONSTRUCTION	EXAMPLE
SO + ADJECTIVE + THAT	▪ The city is **so polluted that** I often think of moving to the country.
SO + ADVERB + THAT	▪ But my job pays **so well that** I can't afford to give it up.
SO MUCH / LITTLE + (ADJECTIVE) + MASS NOUN + THAT	▪ There is **so much (noisy) traffic on my street that** I have to keep the windows closed. ▪ There is **so little entertainment in the country that** I would probably be bored.
SO MANY / FEW + (ADJECTIVE) + COUNT NOUN + THAT *plural*	▪ I've got **so many friends here that** it would be hard to leave. ▪ American cities have **so few parks that** I often long for open green spaces.

SPECIAL NOTE

If you place **so** or **such** at the beginning of a sentence, then you must use **question (inverted) word order** as in the following examples:

- ▪ **Such good food** does that restaurant serve that people go there from miles away.
- ▪ **So polluted is that city** that many people suffer from respiratory problems.

8.10   FILL IN THE BLANKS: *So or Such?*

DIRECTIONS: Here are a few reasons why people chose to marry their husbands and wives. Fill in the blanks with **so** or **such**, as appropriate.

1. Mark has _____ beautiful eyes that I fell in love with him at first sight.

2. My wife is _____ intelligent that she runs her own business now.

3. Jill and I had _____ stimulating conversations that I was immediately attracted to her.

4. His family was _____ a welcoming group of people that I immediately felt accepted.

5. _____ witty was my husband that I couldn't stop laughing on our first date!

8.11 REVIEW: *Much* or *Many, Few* or *Little?*

DIRECTIONS: Fill in the blanks with **much / little** or **many / few,** as appropriate. Remember: use **much** (or **little**) + noncount nouns and **many** (or **few**) + **count nouns.** Then complete the sentences.

EXAMPLE

CUE: I have so <u>little</u> money that <u>I can't go out to dinner</u>.

1. I have so _____ free time that _____ .

2. This class has so _____ tests that _____ .

3. Japan has so _____ people that _____ .

4. Alaska has so _____ people that _____ .

5. I know so _____ English that _____ .

6. My house has so _____ furniture that _____ .

7. I have so _____ choices in my life that _____ .

8. My city has so _____ entertainment at night that _____ .

9. I go to so _____ movies that _____ .

10. We have so _____ homework that _____ .

8.12 WRITTEN EXERCISE: *Homeschooling*

DIRECTIONS: Read the following paragraph about homeschooling. Then answer the questions using a **so . . . that** or **such . . . that** construction in each answer.

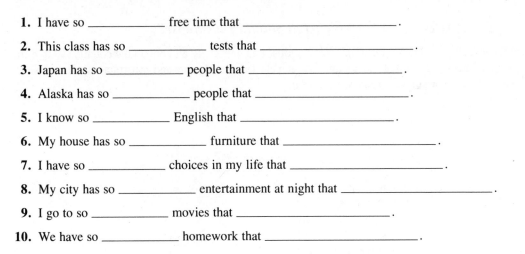

Bill and Laura Gold live in rural Ohio. They have three children. When it was time to send their children to school, Bill and Laura decided that they wanted to teach their children at home, to do "homeschooling." They made this decision because they didn't want their children exposed to some of the negative aspects of public schools such as the poor food in the cafeteria, the possibility of drugs and violence, and the discipline problems in the classroom. In addition, Laura felt that because of the large number of students in each class, the children wouldn't get enough attention. She believed that with more individual attention at home, the children would learn more quickly. She also thought that their children would have more confidence in their ability to learn if they studied at home with her in a nonthreatening atmosphere. In short, Laura felt that their children would get a better education if they were schooled at home. The only possible problem would be a lack of time. If Laura got too busy at home with other activities, she might not devote enough time to teaching.

1. Why did Laura and Bill decide to do homeschooling for their children?

2. In particular, how did Laura feel about the class size in the public schools?

3. What is the one problem Laura thinks she might have?

4. What is your opinion about homeschooling? What are some advantages or disadvantages?

8.13   RAPID DRILL: *Which Job Should He Choose?*

DIRECTIONS: Jay has been offered two jobs, one in the city and one in the country. Help him see the advantages and disadvantages of each choice. Use the cue and construct a sentence using a **so . . . that** or **such . . . that** construction.

EXAMPLE

CUE: The city is noisy.
ANSWER: The city is so noisy that you won't sleep well at night.

1. The city has cultural events.
2. The city has many museums.
3. The country has few shopping malls.
4. The country has poor schools.
5. The city has dirty air and water.
6. The city has a lot of crime.
7. The job in the city pays more.
8. The job in the country is less stressful.
9. There are few good restaurants in the country.
10. The country is a safe place for kids.

8.14   PAIRED ROLEPLAY: *Which Car to Buy?*

DIRECTIONS: You and your partner are trying to decide which car to buy. One wants a practical four-door sedan. The other prefers a flashy expensive sports car. Roleplay the situation and try to persuade your partner. Use the **so . . . that** and **such . . . that** constructions listed on pages 171–172. Be ready to write your statements down afterwards if instructed by your teacher.

EXAMPLE

STUDENT A: The sedan is so inexpensive that I could pay cash.

STUDENT B: Yes, but it's such an ugly car that I wouldn't want to drive it!

SEDAN		SPORTS CAR	
Pro	**Con**	**Pro**	**Con**
▪ inexpensive	▪ ugly	▪ attractive	▪ dangerous
▪ dependable	▪ no status	▪ good pickup	▪ expensive
▪ a lot of room	▪ no power	▪ goes fast	▪ small
▪ inexpensive to fix	▪ no resale value	▪ desirable car	▪ expensive to fix

8.15 ERROR ANALYSIS: *Clauses of Time, Place, Reason, and Result*

DIRECTIONS: Find the errors in the following sentences and correct them clearly. Some sentences may not have any errors.

1. Alaska is such cold state that few people want to live there.
2. Earthquake insurance is such an important in some states that more and more homeowners are buying it.
3. I have so few good friends that I often get lonely.
4. I would really like to go to Egypt. Because I would like to see the pyramids there.
5. As the professor spoke about the causes of the greenhouse effect, he showed many slides.
6. Gloria and Jack will try a six-month separation before they will get divorced.
7. Gerald will move where are clean air and water.
8. Cheryl was talking to her mother during that the earthquake hit.
9. Because an imported car is very expensive, so I will buy a domestic one.

8.16 WRITTEN ACTIVITY: *Adverb Clauses of Time, Place, Reason, and Result*

DIRECTIONS: Choose one of the following situations and write a letter. Use at least **four** adverb clauses of time, place, reason, and result and underline the subordinating conjunctions.

1. You are studying at a university in the United States. Your family expects you to return home at the end of this semester, but your academic department has asked you to stay for at least two years as a teaching assistant. You are torn between pleasing your family and pleasing yourself. You like the United States, you like the people in your department, and you think that you would learn a lot as a teaching assistant. Make a decision whether to stay or return home. Then write a letter to your family or to the department explaining the situation and your decision.

2. While you were in the United States attending a conference in your field, you were asked to stay on for one month to help set up a new office. Your employer in your country completely agreed and encouraged you to take advantage of the opportunity. After one month, your colleagues liked your work so much, they asked you to stay on for another year. You love the challenge of the work and the people you work with. However, you know it would be very hard for your elderly parents and your present employer to have you gone for an additional year. Make a decision and write a polite refusal letter either to your United States company or your employer, explaining your situation and your decision.

VII. DIRECT CONTRAST AND OPPOSITION CLAUSES

SUBORDINATING CONJUNCTION	EXAMPLE	NOTES

Direct contrast:
  WHILE
  WHEREAS
	■ **While** private schools are very expensive, public schools are free in the United States.
	■ Private schools provide a lot of individual attention **whereas** public schools don't have the means to cater to individual students.
	■ Private schools are very expensive, **while** public schools are free in the United States.
		■ Use **while** and **whereas** to show that two things or situations are in direct opposition or contrast.
		■ **While** and **whereas** have the same meaning, but **whereas** is more formal.
		
		■ Unlike other subordinating conjunctions, **while** and **whereas** may occur before either the main or adverb clause with **no change in meaning.**
		■ A comma is sometimes placed after the main clause, but it is not necessary.

Concession:		■ A concession clause shows contrast by placing limits on the ideas in the main clause. The main clause shows surprising or unexpected results.

ALTHOUGH EVEN THOUGH THOUGH	▪ **Although** private schools provide careful supervision, many students still use drugs and alcohol. ▪ Private school students often get accepted into good colleges, **though** some choose to go to work instead.	▪ **Although, even though,** and **though** have basically the same meaning. ▪ A comma is sometimes placed after the main clause but it is not obligatory.
IN SPITE OF THE FACT THAT DESPITE THE FACT THAT	▪ **In spite of the fact that** public schools have bad reputations, there are many qualified and caring teachers who work there.	▪ These phrases have the same meaning as **although.**

8.17 RAPID DRILL: *Contrast Clauses*

DIRECTIONS: Transform the following sentences using an appropriate subordinate conjunction from the list beginning on page 176.

EXAMPLE

CUE: It's hot in Texas, but it's bitter cold in Alaska right now.

ANSWER: While it's hot in Texas, it's bitter cold in Alaska right now.

1. A high school diploma is very important, but many students drop out before they graduate.
2. Many wealthy families can afford to send their kids to private school, but they put them in public school.
3. Private school academic programs are excellent, but public school athletic programs are first-rate.
4. The long-term effects of homeschooling have not been determined, but many families feel that this is the best way to protect their children from negative influences found in public schools.
5. Some students graduate from high school, but they have difficulty reading and writing.

SPECIAL NOTE

The following constructions may be substituted for **although.**

1. AS + ADJECTIVE + AS + SUBJECT + LINKING VERB
   - ▪ **Although** he is intelligent, he couldn't pass the law exam.
   - ▪ **As intelligent as he is,** he couldn't pass the law exam.
2. AS + ADVERB + AS + SUBJECT + VERB
   - ▪ **Although** he cooks well, his dinner last night was a disaster!
   - ▪ **As well as he cooks,** his dinner last night was a disaster!
3. AS + MUCH + AS + SUBJECT + VERB
   - ▪ **Although he studied a lot,** he failed the exam.
   - ▪ **As much as he studied,** he failed the exam.

8.18   RAPID DRILL: *Contrast Clauses*

DIRECTIONS: Gloria was engaged to Mike for one year. Two weeks before the wedding she decided that he was not the right person for her to spend her life with. Below are some of the things that Gloria said to Mike. Transform them using the **as...as construction** from the special note on page 177.

EXAMPLE

CUE: Although I enjoy your company very much, I don't love you.
ANSWER: As much as I enjoy your company, I don't love you.

1. Although you are very wealthy, money isn't the only factor.
2. Although you tried very hard to make me love you, I never fell in love.
3. Although you are good looking, I am not attracted to you.
4. Although you have been very kind to me, your parents never accepted me.
5. Although you love me very much, I don't believe this marriage can work.
6. (Add your own sentence.) _____.

■ VIII. REDUCTION OF TIME-AND-CAUSE CLAUSES TO PREPOSITIONS

Note how the following clauses can be reduced to prepositional phrases.

PREPOSITION	CLAUSE
CONTRAST **despite** **in spite of** } + *noun* **regardless of**	**despite the fact that** **in spite of the fact that** } + *clause* **although**
■ **Despite** *the rain,* we went to the game.	■ **Despite the fact that** *it rained,* we went to the game.
■ **In spite of** *the bad weather,* we held the picnic outdoors.	■ **In spite of the fact that** *the weather was bad,* we held the picnic outdoors.
■ **Regardless of** *his careful planning,* there were still some transportation problems.	■ **Although** *he had planned it carefully,* there were still some transportation problems.
CAUSE **as a result of** **because of** } + *noun* **due to** **in view of**	**because** **since** } + *clause* **etc.**
■ **As a result of** *her hard work,* she got a promotion.	■ **Because** *she worked hard,* she got a promotion.
■ **Because of** *her getting an important account,* she won an award.	■ **Because** *she got an important account,* she won an award.
■ **Due to** *the strong economy,* business was good.	■ **Because** *the economy was strong,* business was good.
■ **In view of** *the strong stock market,* she invested in stocks.	■ **Because** *the stock market was strong,* she invested in stocks.

8.19   FILL IN THE BLANKS: *Despite* or *Despite the Fact That?*

DIRECTIONS: Read the following statements made by public school teachers and fill in the blanks with **despite** or **despite the fact that.**

EXAMPLE

CUE: I enjoy teaching at a public school <u>despite</u> the discipline problems.

1. _____ the media often gives bad reports, many of my students are hardworking and honest kids.

2. _____ the great dropout rate, many of our students go on to college and become professionals.

3. _____ the low pay, I would never change my job.

4. _____ they get an eight-week break in the summer, public school teachers get burned out easily.

5. _____ better working conditions, I would never teach at a private school.

6. Now transform the above sentences using the alternative form. That is, change **despite + noun** to **despite the fact that + clause** and vice versa.

EXAMPLE

CUE: I enjoy working at a public school despite the discipline problems. **(despite + noun)**
ANSWER: I enjoy working at a public school despite the fact that I face discipline problems every day. **(despite the fact that + clause)**

SPECIAL NOTE

Note how the following sentence has been reduced using a possessive before the gerund *donating.*

- Because he donated a kidney, she was able to live.
- **Because of his donating a kidney,** she was able to live.

8.20   USING PREPOSITIONS OF CONTRAST

DIRECTIONS: Return to Exercise 8.17 on page 177. Transform one clause in each of those sentences to a phrase using one of the prepositions listed on page 178.

8.21   USING PREPOSITIONS OF CAUSE AND CONTRAST: *The Death Penalty*

DIRECTIONS: In some countries of the world, the death penalty is legal while in others it is not. In small groups discuss the policy in your country and the possible causes for this death penalty policy. Then take a stand yourself on this issue. After your group discussion, complete the sentences that follow.

1. I believe the death penalty should _____ .

2. Despite _____ , I believe _____

_____ .

3. It is best that _____ in view of _____

_____ .

4. Because of _____ , my country _____

_____ .

8.22   PAIRED DEBATE: Using *Although* to Concede

DIRECTIONS: When you are presenting an argument either in writing or speaking, it is common to concede, or recognize, another point of view and then to point out the problems or flaws with this point of view. For example, if a teenage son wanted to persuade his parents to buy him a car, he might make the following argument.

"Although a car is very expensive, I will be able to do your errands for you and you will have more free time."

Choose one of the following topics to discuss with your partner. Take opposing sides on the issue. Debate the issue, using **although** to concede to your partner's opposing point of view. Be ready to write your ideas in a paragraph if instructed by your teacher.

1. Children should be required to wear uniforms to school.
   Children should be able to choose what to wear to school.

2. A woman would make a fine president of the United States.
   A woman would not be suitable as president of the United States.

3. Handguns should be available for individuals to buy.
   People should not be able to buy handguns.

4. Men and women should sign financial agreements before getting married.
   Men and women should not sign financial agreements before getting married.

IX. PURPOSE CLAUSES

Compare the following sentences.

1. He ate a lot last week, **so** he gained five pounds.	He is **not** happy about this. He did not do it on purpose. This is a result.
2. He ate a lot last week **so that** he could gain some weight.	He **wanted** to gain weight. He did it on purpose.

Sentence 2 expresses **purpose.** It states **why** he ate a lot. Note how this construction is used in the following examples.

SUBORDINATING CONJUNCTION	EXAMPLE	NOTES
SO THAT + MODAL	■ Jim studied business **so (that)** he could work for his father.	■ **So that** is always followed by a modal—will, would, can, could, may, might. ■ **That** is sometimes deleted with no change in meaning.
IN ORDER THAT	■ Ruth studied architecture **in order that** she could design the house of her dreams.	■ **In order that** has the same meaning and use as **so that,** but it is not commonly used.
IN ORDER TO + INFINITIVE	■ Jim studied business **in order to** work for his father. ■ John wore a raincoat **in order not to** get wet.	■ The above clauses can be reduced to infinitive phrases. ■ Note the position of **not.**

A. Modal Choice with *So That* Constructions

The type of modal used in the **so that** clause depends on the verb tense used in the main clause. Note the examples below.

TENSE OF MAIN CLAUSE	EXAMPLE	MODAL USED IN *SO THAT* CLAUSE
PRESENT HABITUAL	■ I **eat** fiber regularly **so that** my cholesterol level **will** not increase. ■ I take the kids to the babysitter **so that** I **can** have some free time.	■ **will** (to be sure) ■ **can** (to be able to)
PAST	■ I **got** a babysitter **so that** I **could** go to the race. ■ I **helped** my brother train **so that** he **would** win the race. ■ I **helped** my brother train **so that** he **might** win the race.	■ **could** (to be able to) ■ **would** (to be sure) ■ **May** and **might** are sometimes used, but are not common.
FUTURE	■ I **will join** a diet center **so that** I **can** lose 20 pounds. ■ I will only shop when I am not hungry **so that** I **won't** buy any junk food.	■ **can** ■ **will**

8.23 FILL IN THE BLANKS: *Can / Could* or *Will / Would?*

DIRECTIONS: Fill in the blanks with **can, could, will,** or **would,** as appropriate.

1. He became a doctor so that he _____ earn money.

2. She became a doctor so that she _____ help people.

3. The government raised taxes so that it _____ pay back its debts.

4. A bird protects its nest so that none of the chicks _____ get hurt.

5. Mark studied hard so that he _____ get an A.

6. The presidential candidate will campaign nonstop so that he _____ win the election.

7. The policeman stopped the drunk driver so that no one _____ get killed on the road.

8.24 RAPID DRILL: *You Are What You Eat*

DIRECTIONS: Read the following sentences about food choices. Transform the **in order to + infinitive** phrase to a **so that + modal** construction.

EXAMPLE

CUE: Jack drinks coffee **in order to** wake up in the morning.
ANSWER: Jack drinks coffee **so that** he can stay awake in the morning.

1. Early settlers in the United States dried fruits and vegetables in order to have something to eat in the winter.
2. Robert will go on a fruit fast in order to clean out his system of toxins.
3. Some people give up dairy products in order to avoid winter colds.
4. Claire ate a box of chocolates this morning in order to feel better after her boyfriend left her.
5. David will eliminate sugar in his diet in order to lose some weight.
6. My mother fed us a lot of dairy products in order to strengthen our bones.
7. My husband eats a lot of leafy green vegetables in order to get enough calcium.
8. Many vegetarians don't eat meat in order to spare animals from a brutal death.

8.25 DISCUSS AND WRITE: *So That* Construction

DIRECTIONS: In pairs or small groups discuss your eating habits and food choices. What do you eat and drink? What do you not eat? Why do you make the choices that you do? Then write four to five sentences using **so that + modal** and **in order that** to summarize both your own food choices and those of your classmates.

X. MANNER CLAUSES

SUBORDINATING CONJUNCTION	EXAMPLE	NOTES
AS IF	▪ This room looks **as if** a tornado hit it.	▪ **As if** and **as though** are used to answer the question "how?"

AS THOUGH	■ My boss treats me **as though** I **were** a secretary, which I definitely am not! ■ You look **as if** you **are** very tired.	■ When the **as though / as if** clause is untrue, as it is in this example, use **were**, not **was**. ■ If the statement is possibly true, as in this example, then the verb **be** takes its usual form.
(LIKE)	■ This room looks **like** a tornado hit it.	■ **Like** is a preposition, so it is followed by a noun, not a clause. It may be followed by a clause in informal conversation, but it is not considered standard English.

8.26 ORAL DRILL: *As If / As Though*

DIRECTIONS: Work with a partner and write the answers to the following questions using **as if** or **as though** in your response.

EXAMPLE

CUE: How does your house look after a party?
ANSWER: It looks as though a hurricane swept through it.

1. How does your teacher look when you don't do your homework?
2. How do you feel after a two-week vacation?
3. How do you look after taking a hard exam?
4. How do you feel after spending two hours in rush hour traffic?
5. How does a person look after falling asleep at the beach in the sun?
6. Jason is giving a presentation to the board of directors of his company. How should he speak to the group?
7. Georgette is singing at her opera debut tonight. How should she sing?
8. Ron is leaving for a year in the army. How should he and his girlfriend spend their last day together?
9. Lydia is going to her first formal dance tonight. How should she dress?
10. Mark is running for mayor of his city and he is going to his first political rally tonight. How should he act there?

8.27 PAIRED ACTIVITY: *All Adverb Clauses*

DIRECTIONS: Roleplay the following situations with a partner. Use the subordinating conjunctions listed. Be ready to present your roleplay to the class if instructed by your teacher.

SITUATION 1: The director of personnel of IBM is interviewing a potential candidate for the position of marketing director.
SUBORDINATING CONJUNCTIONS: **since, so that, whenever**

SITUATION 2: A boss has given his employee too much work. The employee is trying to complain politely but firmly to the boss.
SUBORDINATING CONJUNCTIONS: **as soon as, before, in spite of the fact that, despite**

SITUATION 3:   A police officer has stopped a driver for speeding.
SUBORDINATING CONJUNCTIONS: **while, once, as if**

SITUATION 4:   A tenant is complaining to his landlord about a leaky faucet.
SUBORDINATING CONJUNCTIONS: **such that, everywhere, while**

◼ 8.28   FILL IN THE BLANKS: *Review*

DIRECTIONS: Fill in the blanks with any appropriate answer. **There may be more than one correct answer.**

1. _____ his illness, Jack continued to work.

    (a) In spite of   **(c)** Despite the fact that
    (b) Despite of   **(d)** Inasmuch as

2. _____ David tried, he couldn't remember his first-grade teacher's name.

    (a) As hard as   **(c)** Despite the fact that
    (b) Although   **(d)** Due to the fact that

3. Many people decrease their fat intake so that they _____ control their cholesterol.

    (a) can   **(c)** could
    (b) will   **(d)** would

4. Jack is leaving his job because his boss treats him as if he _____ his personal slave.

    (a) is   **(c)** were
    (b) was   **(d)** had been

5. Frank had _____ on his vacation he didn't want to return.

    (a) a so good·time   **(c)** such a good time
    (b) so much good time   **(d)** so much fun

8.29   SENTENCE COMBINING: *Review*

DIRECTIONS: Combine the following sentences using a subordinate conjunction from the list below:

so . . . that	so that	while	whereas
inasmuch as	now that	once	despite the fact that

1. I tied a string around my finger. I wanted to be sure to remember to mail my Mother's Day card.

   _____

2. There aren't many parking spaces. I had to drive around 15 minutes waiting for one.

   _____

3. This quiz is easy. The last one was extremely difficult.

_____

4. I don't have class on Thursday evenings any more. I can watch my favorite T.V. show.

_____

5. Gladys will get 550 on her TOEFL. After that, she will begin her law studies.

_____

8.30   DISCUSS AND WRITE: *A Moral Dilemma—Kohlberg's Theory*

PART ONE DIRECTIONS: Read the following situation and think about the answers to the questions at the end. In pairs or small groups, discuss your answers. This situation was used for a study, the results of which will be explained below.

A woman was dying of cancer. Only one drug could save her and that drug had just been discovered in the town where she lived. Her husband did not have the money to buy the drug, which cost 10 times as much as it did for the druggist to make. He was able to borrow only half of the money, so he went to the druggist to ask him if he would sell it to him at half price or let him pay for it later. The druggist refused, so the husband broke into the store and stole the drug to save his wife. Should the husband have done that? Why or why not?

PART TWO DIRECTIONS: How did you and your classmates evaluate the husband's action? What made you approve or disapprove of his action? Read the following paragraphs about one psychologist who used this situation to identify several levels of moral reasoning. Then, rewrite the paragraphs and combine sentences whenever it is possible. Use a variety of adverb clauses and subordinators. You may change words, sentence structures, and sentence order.

1. The psychologist Lawrence Kohlberg studied moral behavior. He wanted to examine the moral reasoning of a person faced with a moral dilemma. In his experiment, Kohlberg first told his subjects a story with a moral dilemma. Then he asked his subjects to tell him how the person in the story should act and why. Kohlberg analyzed this data. Then he identified three levels of moral behavior. He found that an individual must pass through stage one. Then that individual can move on to stage two.

2. Level One: Preconventional (Children)

    At this stage, the child is influenced by the **outcome** of his behavior. He does not analyze society's standards. A child is punished, so the action is bad. A child is rewarded. The action is good.

3. Level Two: Conventional (Middle Childhood)

    The child is influenced by the ideals of the social group (the family, peer group, country). The desire for approval is strong. The child obeys society and authority.

4. Level Three: Postconventional (Adolescence to Adulthood)

    The person separates himself from the identity of the group. This is in contrast to what the person does at level two. The individual has his or her own values at this stage but realizes that other values exist. The highest level of moral reasoning is Universal Orientation. The person at this stage has abstract and very broad and complete moral principles.

PREVIEW

DIRECTIONS: Read the following letter written to the advice columnist, Edith. Find out what the writer's problem is. Then answer the questions that follow.

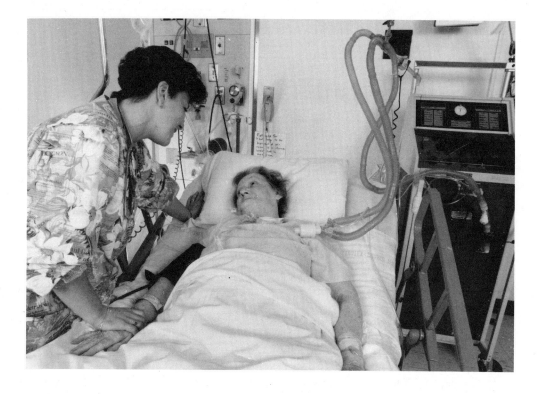

Dear Edith,

I never thought I would find myself writing a Dear Edith letter, but I don't know who else **to turn to**.

Four years ago my brother found out he had **a degenerative disease** for which there was no cure. *Being optimistic*, he lived his life normally. He believed that scientists would surely find some sort of treatment. Well, they haven't. Last year *while visiting friends in California*, he had a serious attack and he had to be hospitalized. *Upon returning to Des Moines*, he came to me and told me how horrible his hospital visit had been. He said he wouldn't want to endure that again. *Having realized that **his prognosis** was not good*, he made me promise that when his condition worsened and he became nonfunctional, that I would have the doctors withdraw all **life-support systems**. *Not really believing that such a situation could ever occur*, I assured him that I wouldn't let him suffer.

Edith, two months ago, he relapsed into **a coma**. The doctors have told me that there is no hope for recovery. They also said that he could go on living with the life-support system for quite a while. I don't know what to do. *Having promised my brother*, I feel that it is my duty to do what he asked. On the other hand, I believe that as long as there is time, there is hope.

I hope that you can help me with this very difficult decision.

Distressed in Des Moines

VOCABULARY

to turn to: to go for advice
a degenerative disease: an illness which gets worse and worse
a prognosis: a prediction about the future state of a disease
life-support systems: devices that perform human functions and allow a person to live
a coma: an extended period of unconsciousness caused by injury or disease.

CULTURAL NOTE / DISCUSSION

There is an increasing number of patients in the United States who choose to refuse life-saving treatment in order to die naturally when all life-support systems are withdrawn. A patient who is still relatively healthy can sign a document (called a **living will**) making this request. What is your reaction to the dilemma stated in the letter? Do you agree that " . . . as long as there is time, there is hope?" What would you do in such a situation?

GRAMMAR CONSIDERATIONS: FOCUS

1. All the phrases in italics in the Dear Edith letter are adverb clauses of time and reason that have been reduced (that is, shortened by omitting words). Work with a partner to transform these phrases into clauses.

EXAMPLE

CUE: *Being optimistic*, he lived his life normally. (reason)
ANSWER: <u>Because he was optimistic</u>, he lived his life normally.

a. *Not really believing that such a situation could ever occur*, I assured him that I wouldn't let him suffer. (reason)

   Since I _____ , I assured him that I wouldn't let him suffer.

b. Last year *while visiting friends in California*, he had a serious attack and he had to be hospitalized. (time)

   Last year _____ he had a serious attack and he had to be hospitalized.

2. How did you change sentence (b) above from a phrase to a clause?

   _____

3. Compare these two sentences:
   (a) While he was visiting friends in California, he had a serious attack.
   (b) While he was visiting friends in California, his illness became worse.

   Sentence (a) can be shortened to *While visiting friends in California*, he had a serious attack. Sentence (b) cannot be shortened this way. Can you guess why?

   _____

4. Compare these sentences from the preview:

(a) Having realized that his prognosis wasn't good, he made me promise that when his condition worsened and he became nonfunctional, I would have the doctors withdraw all life-support systems.

(b) Having promised my brother, I feel that it is my duty to do what he asked.

Which sentence best expresses a time relationship? A cause-effect relationship? Could either sentence express **both** relationships?

══════ GRAMMATICAL PATTERNS TWO ══════

■ I. ADVERB CLAUSE REDUCTION: AN INTRODUCTION

Adverb clauses of **time, reason,** and **opposition** can be reduced to adverb phrases without any change in meaning. (The phrases are in italics in the sentences below.)

TIME:

Clause:	**While she lived in the nursing home,** Mrs. Rose had adequate medical care.
Phrase:	*(While) living in the nursing home,* Mrs. Rose had adequate medical care.

Notes:
- The subjects of both clauses must be the same; otherwise reduction is not possible.
- The subject is deleted.
- The verb form is changed to **verb-ing** form.
- Retaining **while** is optional.

REASON:

Clause:	**Because she was healthy,** she didn't need special care.
Phrase:	*Being healthy,* she didn't need special care.

Notes:
- The subject **and** the subordinator **because** are deleted.
- The verb form is changed to **verb-ing.**
- *Being healthy* = because she was healthy.

OPPOSITION:

Clause:	**Although Mrs. Rose was happy in the nursing home,** she missed her house.
Phrase:	*Although happy in the nursing home,* she missed her house.

Notes:
- The subject and **be** are deleted.
- Retain the subordinator **although** and the adjective.

All three types of reduction will be discussed in detail beginning on page 190.

8.31   RECOGNITION EXERCISE: *Clause Reduction*

DIRECTIONS: As previously stated, you may reduce a clause **only if the subjects in the two clauses are the same.** Read the following story about Mrs. Rose and underline the subjects in each sentence. Then put a check (✔) next to the sentences that can be reduced.

EXAMPLE

CUE: _____ Because <u>Mrs. Rose</u> was alone, <u>her children</u> put her in a nursing home.
(The subjects are different—Mrs. Rose and her children—so this can't be reduced.)
CUE: __✔__ Because <u>they</u> lived far away, <u>Mrs. Rose's children</u> decided to put their mother in
a nursing home. (Here the subjects are the same and so reduction is possible.)

_____ **1.** Before her husband died, Mrs. Rose was happy living in her Victorian house.
_____ **2.** Because her house was so big, Mrs. Rose didn't want to stay there alone after her
husband's death.
_____ **3.** Her children found a very good nursing home for her because they were worried
about her alone in the house.
_____ **4.** While she was well, Mrs. Rose was quite comfortable in the home.

_____ **5.** After she had a heart attack, the doctors advised her to have a pacemaker put in.

_____ **6.** The pacemaker allowed her to lead a normal life while it was functioning well.

_____ **7.** However, after she wore it for two years, she began to have heart problems again.

_____ **8.** The doctors advised her to have a new one put in since the old one was not
working well.
_____ **9.** Mrs. Rose decided not to have a new pacemaker installed because she didn't want
to prolong her life anymore.
_____**10.** Her children were outraged because they felt she should try to live as long as
possible.

8.32 RECOGNITION EXERCISE: *Time or Cause?*

DIRECTIONS: Both time and cause clauses reduce to **verb-ing** phrases. This may be
confusing. Read the following sentences about the right-to-die issue. If the relationship
expressed is time, write **T**. If it is cause, write **C**. If both are expressed, write **B**. Be ready to
discuss your answers.

EXAMPLE

__C__ Being comatose, Karen Ann Quinlan was unable to make her own decisions.

_____**1.** Not wanting to keep their daughter on a respirator, Karen's parents persuaded the
courts to allow them to make decisions for their daughter. This was in 1978.
_____**2.** Treating a 54-year-old woman with Alzheimer's disease in 1990, Dr. Jack
Kevorkian devised what the press called a "suicide machine," which would allow
the patient to end her own life.
_____**3.** Taking a poll on this topic, the National Hemlock Society found that 58% of the
people they polled believed a physician should be allowed by law to end the life of a
terminally ill patient.
_____**4.** Hoping to avoid a long and drawn-out illness that would cause a great deal of
suffering for their family, many people are signing living wills.
_____**5.** Being of sound minds and bodies, the signers of these wills give their physicians
and family members permission to let them die naturally.

■ II. CLAUSE REDUCTION: TIME

	REDUCTION	NOTES
BEFORE	**1. Before she had her heart attack,** Mrs. Rose was happy in the nursing home. **2. Before having her heart attack,** Mrs. Rose was happy in the nursing home. **3. Before her heart attack,** Mrs. Rose was happy in the nursing home.	With **before, after,** and **since:** ■ Delete the subject; ■ Change the verb to a **verb-ing** form (a participial phrase); ■ Keep the subordinator.
AFTER	**4. After she had worn it for two years,** she began to have problems with the pacemaker. **5. After wearing it for two years,** she began to have problems with the pacemaker. **6. After two years,** she began to have problems with the pacemaker.	■ Sometimes the clause can be reduced to a prepositional phrase as in sentences 3 and 6.
SINCE	**7.** Mrs. Rose's children have visited her twice **since they arrived in town.** **8.** Mrs. Rose's children have visited her twice **since arriving in town.**	
WHILE	**1.** Mrs. Rose had a heart attack **while she was visiting with her daughter.** **2. While visiting with her daughter,** Mrs. Rose had a heart attack. **3. Visiting with her daughter,** Mrs. Rose had a heart attack.	With **while:** ■ Delete the subject; ■ Change the verb to an **-ing** form; ■ **While** may be deleted when the meaning is "at the same time."
AS	**1.** Mrs. Rose had a heart attack **as she was visiting with her daughter.** **2. Visiting with her daughter,** Mrs. Rose had a heart attack.	With **as:** ■ **As** must be deleted; ■ The phrase must come at the beginning of the sentence.
AS SOON AS	**1. As soon as the children heard about their mother's heart attack,** they rushed to the hospital. **2. Upon hearing about their mother's heart attack,** the children rushed to the hospital. **3. On hearing about their mother's heart attack,** the children rushed to the hospital.	With **as soon as:** ■ Replace **as soon as** with **upon;** ■ Change the verb to an **-ing** form; ■ **On** can also replace **as soon as.**

8.33   ORAL DRILL: *Reduction of Time Clauses*

DIRECTIONS: Read the following pairs of sentences. Combine the sentences using an adverb clause of time. Reduce the clause **whenever possible.**

EXAMPLE

CUE: Mrs. Rose had a heart attack. She was visiting with her daugher.

ANSWER: Mrs. Rose had a heart attack while visiting with her daughter.

1. Lila heard that she won the lottery. She immediately called her mother.
2. She was talking to her mother. A van from the T.V. station pulled up to her house.
3. The T.V. crew set up the equipment. They knocked on Lila's door. She hadn't finished talking to her mother.
4. They asked her what she was going to do with the million dollars. Lila said she didn't know.
5. She closed the door. She immediately heard the telephone ring.
6. She was talking to the newspaper on the telephone. She heard the doorbell ring.
7. Lila talked to 14 reporters that day. She decided she never wanted to win the lottery again.

■ III. CLAUSE REDUCTION: REASON

	REDUCTION	**NOTES**
BECAUSE SINCE AS	1. **Because she lived all alone,** Mrs. Rose was happy to move to a nursing home. 2. **Since she lived all alone,** Mrs. Rose was happy to move to a nursing home. 3. **As she lived all alone,** Mrs. Rose was happy to move to nursing home. 4. **Living all alone,** Mrs. Rose was happy to move to a nursing home.	Sentences 1, 2, 3, and 4 have the same meaning. To reduce clauses of reason: ▪ Delete the subject and the subordinator; ▪ Change the verb to an **-ing** form.
VERB BE	1. **Because she was all alone,** Mrs. Rose was happy to move to a nursing home. 2. **Being all alone,** Mrs. Rose was happy to move to a nursing home.	If the verb is **be,** change to **being.** This expresses reason.
NEGATIVE	1. **Because she didn't want to prolong her life any longer,** Mrs. Rose refused a new pacemaker. 2. **Not wanting to prolong her life any longer,** Mrs. Rose refused a new pacemaker.	If the adverb clause is negative, as in sentence 1, place **not** in front of the **-ing** verb, as in sentence 2.
BECAUSE OF	1. **Because of her loneliness,** Mrs. Rose was happy to move to a nursing home.	**Because of** is a reduction of a reason clause. (See Grammatical Patterns One of this chapter for more explanation.)

8.34   RAPID DRILL: *Reduction of Reason Clauses*

DIRECTIONS: Below are some for and against statements about the right to refuse life-saving treatments in cases of terminal or severe illnesses. Reduce these clauses of reason to participial phrases **whenever possible.** (Remember that the subjects in both clauses must be the same to reduce adverb clauses.)

EXAMPLE

CUE: Many people refuse such treatment because they don't have the money to pay for it.
ANSWER: Not having the money to pay for it, many people refuse such treatment.

FOR

1. Since some patients are octogenerians, they feel that they have lived long enough.
2. Many patients don't want to be a burden to their children.
3. Other patients choose to die because the pain is intolerable.

AGAINST

5. Many people disagree with a person's right to die because they believe there is always hope for a cure.
6. Some doctors disagree with a person's right to die since it can create serious legal complications for the hospital.
7. Because many people believe that only God can make such decisions, they oppose the right-to-die decision.

■ IV. CLAUSE REDUCTION: OPPOSITION

	REDUCTION	NOTES
ALTHOUGH	1. **Although she was lonely,** Mrs. Rose tried to have a positive attitude.	▪ Adverb clauses with **although, though,** and **while** (of opposition) can be reduced to phrases.
	2. **Although lonely,** Mrs. Rose tried to have a positive attitude.	▪ Note how sentence 2 reduces to **subordinator + adjective;**
THOUGH	3. **Though she is an old person,** Mrs. Rose still feels young.	
	4. **Though an old person,** Mrs. Rose still feels young.	▪ Sentence 4 reduces to **subordinator + noun**
WHILE	5. **While she felt lonely,** she still tried to remain positive.	
	6. **While feeling lonely,** she still tried to remain positive.	▪ Sentence 6 reduces to **subordinator + verb-ing.**

8.35   WRITTEN ACTIVITY: *Reduced Clauses of Opposition*

DIRECTIONS: Read the following statements. Choose five that you do not completely agree with. Write a sentence for each one and present your ideas by using a reduced clause of opposition.

EXAMPLE

CUE: The only way to learn English is by going to an English-speaking country.
ANSWER: Although extremely beneficial, going to an English-speaking country can be very expensive for students; they can also learn by taking classes in their town.

1. The English make the best cars.

    _____

2. Money is the root of all evil.

    _____

3. Mothers should stay home with their children.

    _____

4. Husbands should share equally in the housework and child care.

    _____

5. When people have problems, they should go to a psychologist.

    _____

6. Teenagers should not be allowed to own their own cars.

    _____

7. Capitalism is the best economic system in the world today.

    _____

8. The United Nations should have an army.

    _____

9. Large corporations should be obliged to donate 1% of their profits to charity.

    _____

10. One day the world will solve its conflicts in ways other than war.

    _____

8.36 SENTENCE COMPLETION: *Reduced Clauses of Time, Reason, and Opposition*

DIRECTIONS: Complete the following sentences.

1. Being a student of English, _____

2. Upon coming to this class, _____

3. After teaching for two hours, _____

4. While this is an excellent school, _____

5. Not wanting to _____

6. Being _____

7. Though _____

8. Since coming to _____

8.37   WRITTEN ACTIVITY: *Reduced Clauses of Time, Reason, and Opposition*

DIRECTIONS: Answer the letter to Edith found on page 186. Use at least four reduced clauses. Underline them.

◼ V. CLAUSE REDUCTION: HAVING + PAST PARTICIPLE

Having + past participle can express **time** or **reason,** or both.

	REDUCTION	**NOTES**
TIME after	1. **After the patient (had) refused the life-saving treatment,** he was released from the hospital. 2. **After refusing the life-saving treatment,** the patient was released from the hospital. 3. **(After) having refused the life-saving treatment,** the patient was released from the hospital.	▪ Sentences 1, 2, and 3 have the same meaning. ▪ Retain **after** in sentence 2. ▪ You may delete **after** in sentence 3, but doing so may express a cause-effect relationship. (See below.)
REASON because since as	**Because he had lost his close relatives,** the patient didn't want to live any longer. **Having lost his close relatives,** the patient didn't want to live any longer.	▪ The patient lost his relatives **before** his decision. A time and reason relationship is expressed. ▪ Use **having + past participle** to express that time-reason relationship. ▪ Delete **because, as,** or **since.**

8.38   SENTENCE COMPLETION: *Having + Past Participle*

DIRECTIONS: Complete the following sentences using **(after) having + past participle,** as appropriate.

1. After having lost the game, _____

2. Having lost the game, _____

3. The Berlin Wall came down _____

4. The United States and the Soviet Union signed an arms agreement _____

5. Having realized _____

■ **VI. CLAUSE REDUCTION: THE PASSIVE**

Note how passive adverb clauses can be reduced to phrases in the following sentences.

	REDUCTION	NOTES
BEING + PAST PARTICIPLE	**Before the patient was released,** he had to sign a hospital form. **Before being released,** the patient had to sign a hospital form.	▪ If the action in the adverb clause occurs after or at the same time, use **being + past participle** of the verb in the adverb clause.
HAVING BEEN + PAST PARTICIPLE	**Because he had been given his last treatment,** the patient was able to go home. **Having been given his last treatment,** the patient was able to go home.	▪ If the action in the adverb clause occurs before, use **having + been + past participle** of the verb in the adverb clause.

8.39   LIVING WILLS: *Clause Reduction*

DIRECTIONS: Rewrite the statements in parentheses as reduced adverb clauses if it is possible. If it is not possible, simply write the full clause. Add subordinators when necessary. Pay special attention to punctuation.

I have had this battle with my parents about euthanasia and living wills. _____,
                                                                     (Because they are Catholic)

it is against their religion to do anything to end a person's life. _____, I do
                                                                    (Since I am not a practicing Catholic)

not have any religious problems with this behavior; in fact, there are many reasons why I may

choose to sign a living will. For example, _____, my uncle became
                                            (after he had spent 6 months in the hospital)

extremely ill and depressed. In fact, he often talked about wishing he would die, but he said that

he wanted to see me married _____. _____, I
                             (before he died). (Because I have seen my uncle suffer with a terminal illness)

prefer to have all life-support devices withheld for myself. It can also be a great expense for the

family. My uncle was in great debt from his medical bills _____.
                                                          (before he was operated on for the last time)

VII. SPECIAL PROBLEMS WITH ADVERB CLAUSE USE ═══════

PROBLEM	EXPLANATION
1. SENTENCE FRAGMENT [INCORRECT: He wasn't accepted at the university. Because his grades were low.] CORRECT: He wasn't accepted at the university because his grades were low.	An adverb clause is a dependent clause. Make sure you have **two** subject-verb groups.

2. PUNCTUATION [INCORRECT: Because his grades were low he wasn't accepted at the university.] CORRECT: Because his grades were low, he wasn't accepted at the university.	If you begin your sentence with the adverb clause, it must be followed by a comma.
3. DANGLING PARTICIPIALS [INCORRECT: While painting the house, the telephone rang.] CORRECT: While painting the house, I heard the telephone ring.	You can only reduce the adverb clause when the subjects are the same in both clauses. The incorrect sentence indicates that the telephone painted the house. This, of course, is impossible. The correct sentence expresses the speaker's intended meaning.
4. BECAUSE OF + NOUN CLAUSE [INCORRECT: Because of he had low grades, he wasn't accepted at a university.] CORRECT: Because of his low grades, he wasn't accepted at the university.	Don't use a clause after **because of.** Use a noun.
5. USING SO INSTEAD OF SUCH [INCORRECT: She has so big feet that she can't find shoes.] CORRECT: She has such big feet that she can't find shoes.	**So** is followed by an adjective only. **Such** is followed by an adjective + noun.
6. USING DOUBLE CONNECTORS IN THE SAME SENTENCE [INCORRECT: Although it was raining, but we went swimming anyway.] CORRECT: Although it was raining, we went swimming anyway. [INCORRECT: Because it was cold, so we built a fire.] CORRECT: Because it was cold, we built a fire.	Do not use **but** and **although / because** and **so** in the same sentence.

■ 8.40 ERROR ANALYSIS: *Adverb Clauses*

DIRECTIONS: Find any errors in the following sentences and correct them clearly. Do not change anything that is already correct.

1. Because coming from a very conservative family, Carlos was shocked at coeducational dormitories in the United States.
2. While painting the house, the thunder struck.
3. She slipped as walking to school.
4. Having been being an English teacher, Cheryl can explain grammar very well.

5. Before coming to the United States, Ali studied statistics.
6. Although schools on the east coast are prestigious and well-respected, but schools on the west coast are less expensive.
7. I know that I have a good friend when I was lonely.
8. As soon as I will fix my bike, I'll ride over to your house.
9. I will trust a friend as long as that friend will be honest with me.
10. I must tell you that one condition of my scholarship is that once I graduated, I must return to my country.
11. I wish we could live together in the United States so that you should come to this country.
12. While my rational side tells me to go back, on the other hand, my mind tells me to stay here.
13. If I go back, I will have no job at home so I have to live far from you, so that I prefer to live in Toledo than at home.
14. Even though I tried my best, but I didn't pass the final examination.
15. Many people choose to die because of a lack of money or the medicine to cure them has not been found.

COMPOSITION TOPICS

1. Describe the most difficult decision that you have ever had to make.
2. All people have experienced **procrastination** at some point in their lives. Why do people procrastinate? What are some techniques for avoiding procrastination?
3. The text that follows is a living will. Read it and decide if you would or could sign such a document. Then write a composition in which you argue for or against such legal documents.

TO MY FAMILY, MY DOCTOR, MY LAWYER, AND ALL OTHERS CONCERNED

Death is as real as birth, growing up, and getting old. In fact, it is the only certainty we have in this life. If the moment should arise when I am not able to make decisions about my future, let this document be an expression of my desires and directions while I am still of sound mind and body.

If there arises a time when no reasonable expectation of recovery exists for me, either from a physical or mental disability, then I direct that I be allowed to die and not be kept alive by medication or by heroic measures. I do wish that medication be given to me to relieve the intense suffering, even if this should shorten my life.

I have carefully considered everything before signing this document. It is in agreement with my convictions and beliefs. I wish that these instructions be carried out to the extent allowed by the law.

9

HEALTH AND FITNESS II

■ The sentence: Integration

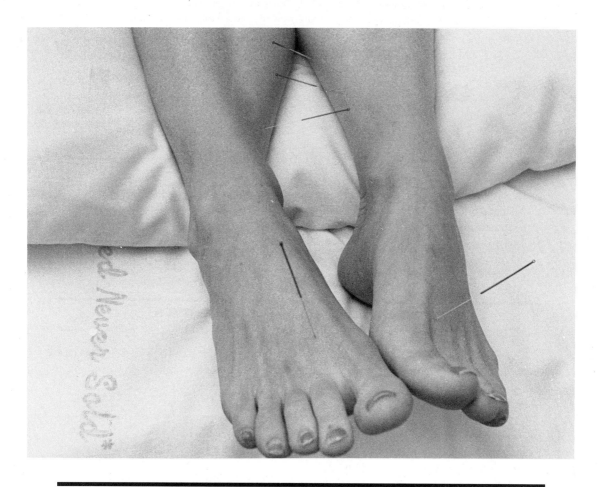

DISCUSSION QUESTIONS

1. Do you know people who suffer from migraine headaches? How do they describe these headaches?
2. In your country, is there a newspaper column where you can write to a doctor?
3. What kind of alternative medical treatment, such as relaxation therapy or biofeedback is practiced in your country?

OBJECTIVES

In this chapter you will learn:

1. To understand a variety of sentence connectors and sentence types to express relationships between ideas
2. To write more sophisticated sentences through sentence combining
3. To recognize faulty parallelism and to use correct parallel structures in sentences

---

PREVIEW

DIRECTIONS: Read the following letter from a newspaper column entitled "Doctor Jones" in which a medical doctor answers health-related questions submitted by readers.

DEAR DOCTOR JONES:

1. I have suffered from migraine headaches for years now, and time and again I am shocked at the attitude people have about migraines. Many people have no understanding of the pain and suffering that accompanies a migraine; consequently, they think that I am exaggerating when I describe the experience. Could you please educate your readers about this illness?

MISUNDERSTOOD MIGRAINE SUFFERER

DEAR MISUNDERSTOOD:

2. I fully sympathize with your frustration since I am a migraine sufferer myself. The pain is **indescribable** although in my case it usually feels like someone is **driving a chisel into** the side of my head. Not only are migraine headaches painful, but they also cause **nausea.** I usually have to lie completely still in a dark room if I **feel a migraine coming on.** Because of the **debilitating** effects of migraines, a migraine sufferer can miss several days of work with one headache.

3. As a result of research done on these headaches, there is now medication which can treat migraines, but it is not always effective. Although medication is ineffective for some migraines, patients can learn how to deal with them through **relaxation therapy** and **biofeedback.**

4. Cluster headaches, a related illness, cause the same kind of **excruciating pain** as migraines but to an extreme degree. Whereas a migraine is one continuous headache, cluster headaches repeatedly start and stop over a period of time. I had a patient who once had an attack of cluster headaches which lasted one week. Every six hours a new headache would start and would last from three to four hours. Like migraines, cluster headaches usually attack the left side of the head.

5. I hope that as we learn more about this serious affliction, we will be able to relieve the pain more efficiently. In the meantime, let's hope that anyone who has never suffered from a migraine will be a little more compassionate and understanding now that they are informed.

VOCABULARY

indescribable: something unable to be described because it is so extreme

driving (something) into (something): hitting or pounding one object so that it is forced into another, for example, driving a nail into a piece of wood

nausea: the sick feeling in the stomach which often precedes vomiting
to feel (an illness) coming on: to have the feeling that an illness is approaching
debilitating: weakening or harming usually to the point of making it difficult to function
relaxation therapy: a form of treatment which relieves pain through relaxation
biofeedback: using audio or visual display of brain waves to control one's bodily functions
excruciating pain: severe, unbearable pain

GRAMMAR CONSIDERATIONS: FOCUS

The following questions are based on the preview text and are designed to help you find out what you already know about the structures in this chapter. Some of the questions may be hard and some of them may be easy. Answer as many of the questions as you can. Work with a partner if your teacher tells you to do so.

1. Read through the preview and try to find sentences of as many different types as you can.
2. Find a sentence expressing **direct** opposition. What word tells you this is opposition? Can you think of a synonym for that word?
3. Find three sentences expressing **cause** and **effect.** What words are used to express cause and/ or effect? What is the difference between these words?
4. What is the difference in meaning between the following two sentences?

   Every six hours a migraine headache would start and would last from three to four hours.

   Every six hours a migraine headache would start and last from three to four hours.

   Which sentence is better?

═══════ GRAMMATICAL PATTERNS ═══════

◼ I. SENTENCE VARIETY

By using a variety of sentence connectors and sentence types, one idea can be expressed in different ways. The following chart reviews the variety of possible sentences to express one idea.

FUNCTION: ADDITION	
CONNECTORS	*EXAMPLES*
COORDINATING CONJUNCTION **and**	▪ Migraine headaches are painful, **and** they cause nausea.
CONJUNCTIVE ADVERBS **in addition, additionally, furthermore, moreover, also**	▪ Migraine headaches are painful; **in addition,** they cause nausea.

CORRELATIVE CONJUNCTIONS **not only . . . but also**	■ **Not only** are migraine headaches painful, **but** they **also** cause nausea. (Question order follows **not only,** and the subject of the following clause is usually placed between **but** and **also**.)
PREPOSITIONAL PHRASES **in addition to, along with, as well as**	■ **In addition to** being painful, migraine headaches cause nausea.

FUNCTION: OPPOSITION

CONNECTORS COORDINATING CONJUNCTION **but**	*EXAMPLES* ■ Medication is ineffective for some migraines, **but** patients can learn how to deal with them.
SUBORDINATING CONJUNCTIONS **although, despite the fact that**	■ **Although** medication is ineffective for some migraines, patients can learn how to deal with them.
CONJUNCTIVE ADVERBS **however, nevertheless**	■ Medication is ineffective for some migraines; **however,** patients can learn how to deal with them.
PREPOSITIONAL PHRASES **despite, in spite of**	■ **Despite** the ineffectiveness of medication for some migraines, patients can learn how to deal with them.

FUNCTION: CAUSE / EFFECT

COORDINATING CONJUNCTIONS **for** (cause), **so** (effect)	■ A migraine sufferer can miss several days of work during one migraine, **for** migraines are debilitating. ■ Migraines are debilitating, **so** a migraine sufferer can miss several days of work with one headache.
SUBORDINATING CONJUNCTIONS **because, since**	■ **Because** migraines are debilitating, a migraine sufferer can miss several days of work with one headache.
CONJUNCTIVE ADVERBS **therefore, as a result, consequently**	■ Migraines are debilitating; **therefore,** a migraine sufferer can miss several days of work with one headache.
PREPOSITIONS **because of, due to, as a result of**	■ **Because of** the debilitating effects of migraines, a migraine sufferer can miss several days of work with one headache.

FUNCTION: COMPARISON

COORDINATING CONJUNCTION
and ... too

- Migraines are felt on one side of the head, **and** cluster headaches usually attack one side **too.**

SUBORDINATING CONJUNCTION
just as

- **Just as** migraines are felt on one side of the head, cluster headaches usually attack the left side of the head.

CONJUNCTIVE ADVERBS
similarly, in comparison

- Migraines are felt on one side of the head; **similarly,** cluster headaches usually attack the left side.

PREPOSITIONS
like, similar to

- **Like** migraines, cluster headaches usually attack the left side of the head.

FUNCTION: CONTRAST

COORDINATING CONJUNCTION
but

- A migraine is one continuous headache, **but** cluster headaches repeatedly start and stop over a period of time.

SUBORDINATING CONJUNCTIONS
whereas, while

- **Whereas** a migraine is one continuous headache, cluster headaches repeatedly start and stop over a period of time.

CONJUNCTIVE ADVERBS
in contrast, on the other hand

- A migraine is one continuous headache; **in contrast,** cluster headaches repeatedly start and stop over a period of time.

PREPOSITIONS
unlike

- **Unlike** a migraine, which is one continuous headache, cluster headaches repeatedly start and stop over a period of time.

FUNCTION: CONDITION

SUBORDINATING CONJUNCTIONS
if, unless, only if, even if

- **If** you don't lie still in a dark room when you have a migraine, you will become nauseous.

CONJUNCTIVE ADVERB
otherwise (See the chapter on conditionals for more explanation.)

- You should lie still in a dark room when you have a migraine; **otherwise,** you will become nauseated.

9.1   WRITTEN EXERCISE: *Sentence Combining*

DIRECTIONS: For each of the following pairs of sentences, decide what the relationship between the two sentences is. Then, combine each pair of sentences into one sentence, using one of the connectors from the preceding chart. Write the new sentence on the line.

EXAMPLE

Most fitness centers provide a variety of exercise equipment for their members. A running track, a sauna, and a pool are available too.

RELATIONSHIP: Addition

In addition to a running track, a sauna, and a pool, most fitness centers provide a variety of exercise equipment for their members.

1. Some members come to the fitness center to work out daily. Other members can only fit it into their schedule once or twice a week.
   RELATIONSHIP:

   _____

2. The membership is supposed to be limited. My fitness center is often too crowded.
   RELATIONSHIP:

   _____

3. Sometimes my fitness center is full of people. Sometimes I can't even use the equipment.
   RELATIONSHIP:

   _____

4. I never buy any snacks at the juice bar. The prices are very high.
   RELATIONSHIP:

   _____

5. Most fitness centers have a membership fee that members must pay on an annual basis. My fitness center does too.
   RELATIONSHIP:

   _____

9.2   WRITTEN EXERCISE: *Sentence Variety*

DIRECTIONS: Read the paragraph below about Jennifer's decision to improve her health. For each function given below the paragraph, write three sentences using different connectors to express the same idea from the paragraph. As the example shows, identify the connector and circle the connector in the sentence.

One year ago, Jennifer decided that she was going to change her lifestyle and start taking better care of her health. She was overweight from a diet high in fat and sugar. She was out of shape from a lack of exercise. She also felt tired most of the time with hardly enough energy to climb the stairs to her apartment at the end of the day. She smoked a pack of cigarettes a day and frequently drank beer. When she decided to change her ways, she started by changing her diet so that grains, legumes, vegetables, and fruits took the place of the fat and sugar. She quit smoking, signed up for an aerobics class, and started cycling on weekends. Since then, she has lost 25 pounds, and is now in excellent shape. Only one problem remains. She still gets tired climbing the stairs to her tenth-floor apartment.

EXAMPLE

FUNCTION: cause / effect

COORDINATING CONJUNCTION: Her diet was very high in fat and sugar, (so) she was overweight.

SUBORDINATING CONJUNCTION: (Because) her diet was very high in fat and sugar, she was overweight.

CONJUNCTIVE ADVERB: Her diet was very high in fat and sugar; (therefore,) she was overweight.

1. FUNCTION: ADDITION

_____

_____

_____

2. FUNCTION: CONTRAST

_____

_____

_____

3. FUNCTION: OPPOSITION

_____

_____

_____

4. FUNCTION: CAUSE / EFFECT

_____

_____

_____

■ II. PARALLELISM

In English, any time two similar structures are joined, they must be parallel. Notice how the first sentence below contains two parallel structures, whereas the second sentence does not and is, therefore, incorrect.

a. In addition to **playing tennis** and **hiking in the mountains,** I also enjoy surfing.
b. In addition to **playing tennis** and **I hike** in the mountains, I also enjoy surfing.

The following chart demonstrates the variety of parallel structures that are possible.

PARALLEL STRUCTURES	
SINGLE WORDS	
NOUNS	▪ John writes **poetry** and **novels**.
VERBS	▪ Coleen **runs** and **works out**.
ADJECTIVES	▪ This diet is not only **difficult** but also **effective**.
ADVERBS	▪ Bill started his new diet **reluctantly** yet **aggressively**.
PHRASES	
NOUN PHRASES	▪ **A balanced diet** is as important as **a regular program of exercise**.
VERB PHRASES	▪ When Jack gets a cold, he **takes a lot of vitamins** and **drinks a lot of fluids**.
ADVERBIAL PHRASES	▪ Linda and Dan walk a mile to work and back **in the morning** and **at night**.
GERUND PHRASES	▪ Jim's doctor recommended **cooking healthier meals** and **getting more rest**.
INFINITIVE PHRASES	▪ Ruth wanted to lose ten pounds, so she tried to **eat less** and **exercise more**.
PARTICIPIAL PHRASES	▪ **Hoping to reduce the stress in her life** and **not having to worry about money**, Joyce quit her job.

CLAUSES

NOUN CLAUSES	▪ Gary realized **that he was losing weight** but not **that he was becoming anemic**.
ADJECTIVE CLAUSES	▪ This is the diet **that promises instant results** and at the same time **that can cause malnutrition**.
ADVERB CLAUSES	▪ **Because she couldn't swallow** and **since she had good medical insurance,** she decided to have her tonsils out.

■ 9.3 WRITTEN EXERCISE: *Faulty Parallelism*

DIRECTIONS: Find the faulty parallelism in each of the following sentences and correct it.

1. What great shape she's in and she looks healthy!
2. The doctor wanted to find out why Linda was underweight and about her blood sugar level.
3. Following a regular program of exercise is more beneficial for me than to be on a fad diet.
4. What I like best about my fitness center are the modern lifecycle machines and they have such a beautiful Olympic size swimming pool.
5. Not only is Jim healthy but how athletic he is.
6. Due to his son's persistence and because he wanted to lose 10 pounds, Frank decided to join a fitness center.
7. When Richard realized that his eating habits were the cause of his illness, he began to plan his meals more conscientiously and in a careful way.

9.4 WRITTEN EXERCISE: *Parallel Structures*

DIRECTIONS: To each sentence below, add a structure that is parallel to the one that is underlined. Use the information provided in parentheses for the additional structure.

EXAMPLE

CUE: Kathy knows that she has too much stress in her life. (As a result, Kathy's health is not very good.)

NEW SENTENCE: Kathy knows that she has too much stress in her life and that she is unhealthy as a result.

1. Because she has two jobs, Kathy leads a very stressful life. (She is a single mother.)

2. In order to reduce the level of stress in her life, Kathy has quit one of her jobs. (She now has a live-in housekeeper.)

3. Kathy is not happy with her present physician's attitude about stress. (She doesn't like the way he treats the problem.)

4. Despite the fact that she gets a lot of exercise, which supposedly reduces stress, she still feels stressed out. (She's taking special vitamins designed to lower stress.)

_____

5. Joining a stress-management program has helped her. (She learned how to meditate.)

_____

6. The program has taught her how to prioritize her responsibilities. (She is also finding out what she can do in stressful situations.)

_____

III. REVIEW EXERCISES

9.5 RECOGNITION EXERCISE: *Identifying Phrases* and *Clauses*

DIRECTIONS: In each sentence below, determine whether the underlined item is a phrase or a clause. On the line provided, write the type of phrase or clause that it is.

EXAMPLE

Despite her busy schedule, Rhonda works out at the gym every morning.   Adverbial phrase

1. Cholesterol and all of its harmful effects has been the topic of every major conference on health recently. _____

2. Many Americans have recently reduced the amount of red meat in their diet since red meat is a major source of cholesterol. _____

3. Some people have to be very careful of their cholesterol intake because of the existing high level of cholesterol in their body. _____

4. Being so concerned about their health, many middle-aged Americans have also reduced their intake of dairy products, which are a source of cholesterol. _____

5. Nutritionists have pointed to the low cholesterol level of populations in Asia where very little red meat is consumed. _____

6. Since the beginning of these findings on cholesterol, meat producers have increased their advertising, emphasizing the benefits of red meat. _____

7. Limiting consumption of red meat and cutting down on dairy products are two ways of maintaining a healthy cholesterol level. _____

■ 9.6   FILL IN THE BLANKS: *Sentence Connectors*

DIRECTIONS: Fill in the blank in each sentence below with an appropriate connector from the choices offered after each sentence. There may be more than one correct answer.

1. In recent years, health food stores have become very popular in America _____

   _____ the increased knowledge about foods that can benefit health. (due to, because, for, because of)

2. _____ there has been an increase in the use of pesticides, more and more people are buying organic fruits and vegetables, which can be found in health food stores. (because, therefore, because of, since)

3. Many people want to take a variety of vitamins and food supplements daily;

   _____, health food stores provide a full supply of such products. (so, therefore, as a result of, as a result)

4. _____ the prices are higher at health food stores, the health conscious customers are plentiful. (although, despite, but)

5. These stores sell _____ food and vitamins, _____

   _____ beauty products. (and . . . or, not only . . . but also, in addition to . . . and)

6. Some health food stores provide a number of free publications about holistic living and

   environmental concerns _____ their other products. (additionally, in addition to, also, as well as)

7. Health food stores usually sell a wide variety of organic and commercial fruits and

   vegetables _____ the big chain grocery stores, which usually only provide commercial produce. (whereas, but, unlike)

8. These grocery store chains may start offering some organic produce, _____

   _____ the competition of the health food stores is starting to have an effect. (for, because of, nevertheless)

◼ 9.7 WRITTEN EXERCISE: *Changing Phrases* and *Clauses*

DIRECTIONS: In each of the following sentences, a phrase or clause is underlined. If a phrase is underlined, change the phrase to a clause and write it on the line provided in the new sentence. If a clause is underlined, change it to a phrase and write it on the line provided in the new sentence. As long as the meaning is unchanged, any corresponding clause or phrase may be used.

EXAMPLE

Because the brain and the immune system are so closely related, our mental state can affect our health.

Because of the close relationship between the brain and the immune system, our mental state can affect our health.

1. Although many people are skeptical about the relationship between mental state and health, a number of scientists are providing unquestionable evidence that there is indeed a very strong relationship.

   _____,

   a number of scientists are providing unquestionable evidence that there is indeed a very strong relationship.

2. Despite the separation of mind and body by traditional Western medicine, it is obvious that these two entities function as one.

   _____,

   it is obvious that these two entities function as one.

3. Due to the changes in the immune system produced by certain emotional states, it is now thought that stress, for example, can result in greater susceptibility to illness.

   _____,

   it is now thought that stress, for example, can result in greater susceptibility to illness.

4. Whereas Western physicians have been reluctant to accept these new theories, witch doctors, faith healers, and Eastern mystics have held these beliefs since ancient times.

   _____,

   witch doctors, faith healers, and Eastern mystics have held these beliefs since ancient times.

9.8 ORAL INTERVIEW: *Mind* and *Body*

DIRECTIONS: Interview at least two people (either your classmates or English speakers outside of class) using the following questions about the relationship between mind and body. Take notes on the lines provided.

1. Have you ever become ill as a result of emotional or psychological trauma? Explain.

   _____

   _____

   _____

2. What medical treatments do you know about that are based on the relationship between the mind and the body? How do they work?

_____

_____

_____

9.9   WRITTEN FEEDBACK

DIRECTIONS: What do **you** think about the relationship between mind and body? Can you remember times in your life when you became ill as a result of an emotional crisis or extreme stress? Write one or two paragraphs about this topic, stating your opinion and giving examples from your own life. Compare this with the information you gathered from the above interview. Use a variety of clauses and sentence connectors for sentence variety.

IV. SPECIAL PROBLEMS WITH SENTENCES

PROBLEM	EXPLANATION
DOUBLE CONNECTOR [INCORRECT: **Because** people have become so health conscious, **so** the life span of the average American has increased.] CORRECT: **Because** people have become so health conscious, the life span of the average American has increased.	■ Two clauses can be joined by **one** connector that expresses the logical relationship between the ideas in the two clauses.
ILLOGICAL PLACEMENT OF CONNECTOR [INCORRECT: I smoke cigarettes **although** my lungs are healthy.] CORRECT: **Although** I smoke cigarettes, my lungs are healthy.	■ Be sure that the sentence connector **logically** relates one idea to another.
FAULTY PARALLELISM [INCORRECT: My doctor told me **that I should take an iron supplement** and **I should eat more iron-rich foods**.] CORRECT: My doctor told me **that I should take an iron supplement** and **that I should eat more iron-rich foods**.	■ Include all the necessary components for parallel structures.

■ 9.10 ERROR ANALYSIS

DIRECTIONS: Find and correct the error in each of the following sentences. Some of the sentences may be correct as they are.

1. Because a very good diet, Sandra is always healthy.
2. How that aerobics class was exciting!
3. The common cold can make you feel very miserable; therefore, staying at home in bed.
4. What you can do to improve your health?
5. Although I've been maintaining a very healthy diet, but I've been sick.
6. She is in very good shape; consequently, she exercises regularly.
7. With excellent nutrition, a generous supply of vitamins, a lot of rest, and plenty of exercise.
8. Not only is medicine important when you're sick, but take care of yourself too.
9. But the relationship between body and mind is very interesting.
10. Many doctors charge very expensive rates for example my doctor.
11. What month it is?
12. The magazine that I read, it is about how to increase longevity through better health.
13. Shari really enjoys ocean kayaking and to go hiking in the desert.
14. The sun shines my window, so I have my plants in the window box.
15. I heard about an acupuncture clinic it also has a specialist on herbal medicine.
16. This is a combination of vitamins that build up the immune system and they prevent infection from spreading.

═══════ ANALYSIS OF AN AUTHENTIC TEXT ═══════

DIRECTIONS: Read the following text about fast food, referring to the vocabulary below.

FAST FOOD FARE AND NUTRITION
by Connie Roberts, M.S., R.D.

1. Every second, an estimated 200 people in the United States order one or more hamburgers. The U.S. National Restaurant Association estimates that on a typical day 45.8 million people—a fifth of the American population—are served at fast-food restaurants. The fast-food industry boasts phenomenal growth. From 1970 to 1980, the number of fast-food outlets increased from 30,000 to 140,000, and fast-food sales increased 300%. Fast-food chains have expanded to college campuses, military bases, and other countries. The menus have become more varied, and hours of operation have expanded to include breakfasts.

2. The trend toward increased consumption of fast foods by Americans has been attributed to the growing employment of women outside the home, the increasing number of people living alone, smaller families, the **prevalence** of less formal lifestyles, the increase in **disposable income,** and consumers' desire and demand for convenience. These trends suggest a growing reliance on fast foods for more than one meal a day, beginning at young ages. Because such foods serve a need in a fast-paced society, they are probably a permanent part of the lifestyle of many Americans. We must, therefore, be concerned about the effect of fast foods on our health and nutritional status.

3. . . . Fast-food dining has been so well accepted that recommendations to reduce or eliminate it are likely to meet with little or no success. The more **efficacious** approach is to improve the nutritional quality of fast foods and the eating practices of its consumers.

4. Fast-food chains should be regarded as one of many possible food sources, with advantages and limitations that must be considered within the context of one's total diet. For such considerations, consumers need to be educated about how to choose foods, especially when eating out. Health professionals should be able to provide some advice, but much more could be done by the fast-food establishments themselves. First, in addition to **disclosing** the protein and vitamin contents of their foods, fast-food restaurants should provide information on the number of calories and the levels of important minerals and fats (quantity and type), so that consumers can make informed choices. Second, they should provide printed menus for consumers wishing to restrict their intake of sodium, calories, or fats, indicating the best choices for such a meal. Third, they should expand their efforts to identify the nutrient contents of foods—for example, at salad bars. Fourth, they should make readily available such items as skim or low-fat milk, margarine, low-fat salad dressings, and 100% whole-grain buns, so that **consumers** will find it easier to make healthful choices. Finally, for the health of all of us, these important **purveyors** of food should work with experts to provide optimal nutrition for the public.

VOCABULARY

prevalence: frequency or noticeability of something
disposable income: the part of a salary that can be spent after all the bills are paid
efficacious: a way of doing something that will produce a result
disclosing: giving information about a certain topic
consumers: the people who eat fast food
purveyors: the suppliers

DISCUSSION

1. What kind of fast food is available in your country? How would you rate this food in terms of nutritional value?
2. Do you think it is possible to produce fast food that is healthy?
3. What cultural differences or similarities exist between your country and the United States as reflected by the prevalence or scarcity of fast-food chains?

WRITTEN EXERCISE

1. The following is a revised version of the beginning of the first sentence in paragraph 2. Complete the sentence by making the other necessary changes. Then discuss which sentence is better.

   Americans are eating more fast foods because _____

   _____

   _____

2. Paragraph 3 is composed of two sentences. Combine them into one sentence.

_____

_____

3. In the following sentence, replace **in addition to** with **not only**, and make any other necessary changes.

First, in addition to disclosing the protein and vitamin contents of their foods, fast-food restaurants should provide information on the number of calories and the levels of important minerals and fats.

_____

_____

_____

═══════════ COMPOSITION TOPICS ═══════════

1. Write a composition describing the general health and fitness of people in your country. Include information about diet, exercise, illness, and attitudes about health.
2. Write a composition about the ideal lifestyle a person should have for optimal health.
3. Describe the medical system in your country, emphasizing its strong and weak points.

10

AMERICAN CULTURE II

- ⊟ Article use
- ⊟ Subject-verb agreement

DISCUSSION QUESTIONS

1. What United States customs have you experienced or heard about that are very different from customs in your culture? What are some customs that are the same?
2. When you meet someone for the first time, what do you say? How do you greet your friends? Your teacher or boss? What do you say or do when you leave?

OBJECTIVES

In this chapter, you will learn:

1. To use the definite and indefinite articles correctly
2. To understand when **not** to use an article
3. To use articles with proper nouns
4. To use articles in making generalizations
5. To use correct subject-verb agreement
6. To understand collective nouns

══════════════ PREVIEW ══════════════

DIRECTIONS: Read the following paragraph on appropriate greetings in the United States. All indefinite articles (a / an) have been omitted. See how much you know by inserting **a** or **an** wherever it is necessary.

1 What should you do when you meet American for the first time? Some people suggest that
2 you smile and say "Hi!" in informal situation or "How do you do?" in formal situation. Others
3 recommend firm handshake. Everyone will agree that kiss is not appropriate, even on the
4 cheek. It is common to make **small talk** when you first meet person. You can talk about the
5 weather, recent sporting event, or better yet, ask the other person question about his or her
6 life. In any case, don't remain silent when you meet people for the first time because if you do,
7 the American might think you are snob!

VOCABULARY

small talk: superficial conversation often about topics such as the weather

GRAMMAR CONSIDERATIONS: FOCUS

The following questions are based on the preview text and are designed to help you find out what you already know about the structures in this chapter. Some of the questions may be hard and some of them may be easy. Answer as many of the questions as you can. Work with a partner if your teacher tells you to do so.

1. Did you complete the preview section correctly? If you made any mistakes, record them here. Try to determine why you made each mistake.

_____

2. Based on the use of **a** and **an** in the text above, what are some of the rules for the use of the indefinite article (a / an)?

_____

GRAMMATICAL PATTERNS ONE

I. ARTICLE USE: AN OVERVIEW

Nouns in English are preceded by the articles **a / an** or **the** or by **no article** (∅). Note the examples below. This section will examine all three possibilities in detail.

THE INDEFINITE ARTICLE	**a / an**	▪ I bought **a** book yesterday.
THE DEFINITE ARTICLE	**the**	▪ **The** book I bought was very interesting
NO ARTICLE	∅	▪ It was about **culture shock.**

A. The Indefinite Article (a / an)

The indefinite article **a** or **an** is used only with count nouns that have not been specified.

	RULE	**EXAMPLE**
Noncount Nouns	▪ Never put **a** or **an** before a noncount noun.	Americans love **ice cream.**
Count Nouns	▪ Use **a** or **an** before an unspecified noun, i.e., one that has not previously been identified.	Most families own **a car.**

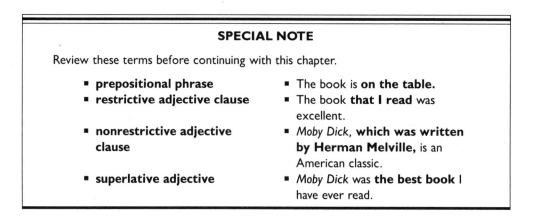

SPECIAL NOTE

Review these terms before continuing with this chapter.

▪ **prepositional phrase**	▪ The book is **on the table.**
▪ **restrictive adjective clause**	▪ The book **that I read** was excellent.
▪ **nonrestrictive adjective clause**	▪ *Moby Dick,* **which was written by Herman Melville,** is an American classic.
▪ **superlative adjective**	▪ *Moby Dick* was **the best book** I have ever read.

B. The Definite Article (the)

The definite article, **the,** can be used with both count and noncount nouns. Its use indicates that the speaker (or writer) and the listener (or reader) share a definite knowledge about the noun referred to. Note the ways in which this definite reference can be made.

	USE *THE* WHEN	**EXAMPLE**
Noncount Nouns	1. The noun has been qualified or limited by a prepositional phrase.[a] 2. The noun has been qualified by an adjective clause.[a]	▪ **The** milk *in the bottle* has soured. ▪ **The** wine *that I bought* is on the table.
Count Nouns	1. The noun has been qualified by a prepositional phrase or an adjective clause.[a] 2. The noun has been previously specified. 3. The noun refers to the class or the thing in general. 4. There is a superlative adjective + noun construction. 5. The noun is one of a kind.	▪ **The** car *in the lot* is not **the** car *that I picked out.* ▪ Mr. Jones bought a car yesterday. **The** car is a 1989 Cadillac. ▪ **The** Cadillac symbolizes success. ▪ **The most expensive** car I ever bought was a 1960 Corvette. ▪ **The earth** is round.

[a]There are a few exceptions to this rule. See section *E,* Some Exceptions to the Article Rules.

10.1   THE DEFINITE ARTICLE: *Education in the United States*

DIRECTIONS: Read the following sentences about the state of education in the United States. Then indicate why a definite article **(the)** precedes the italicized nouns. Refer to the chart above for a list of cases requiring definite article use.

EXAMPLE

The *personal computer* now plays an important role in secondary education in the United States. **The** precedes *personal computer* because it's a count noun and it refers to the computer in general.

1. The *high school diploma* used to be a valuable degree for getting a job in the United States at the beginning of the century. The *job* one got depended on a number of factors.

   _____

   _____

2. In today's world, the *job seeker* has a better chance of finding a good job by possessing a college degree.

   _____

3. The **attitude** that our grandparents had towards school was quite different from the *attitude* our children now have.

_____

4. It is very sad to many Americans that a country such as the United States—one of the *richest countries* in the *world*—does not place a high priority on the *education* of its young people.

_____

_____

5. Many parents are fighting against the *problems* of public schools—overcrowding, gang violence, apathy—and they are demanding that their children be given the *best possible education.*

_____

_____

C. No Article (∅)

There are cases in which **no article** is used before count or noncount nouns. Study the following chart for a list of these cases.

	NO ARTICLE PRECEDES	**EXAMPLE**
Noncount Nouns	1. Unspecified noncount nouns 2. Gerunds **(Verb-ing)** 3. References to social institutions 4. References to academic subjects of study	▪ **Success** is largely determined by wealth. ▪ **Making money** is important to many American women in their 30s. ▪ **Marriage** is increasing in the United States and so is **divorce.** ▪ My sister is studying **history.**
Count Nouns	5. Plural count nouns that refer to the class or thing in general 6. Locations that imply a specific activity 7. Titles or appointments	▪ **Cadillacs** are **symbols** of status. (See section D, Generalizations.) ▪ She drove to **work.** (See the special note on the next page.) ▪ She was appointed **chairperson.** ▪ George Bush was elected **president.**

SPECIAL NOTE

Pay careful attention to these cases:

I went
- to school.
- to church. **(to** + noun)
- to work.
- downtown. (noun)
- home.
- to the post office. (to + **the** + noun)
- to the bank.

10.2 FILL IN THE BLANKS: *Article Use*

DIRECTIONS: Fill in the blanks with **a / an, the,** or ∅, as appropriate.

Dear Chris,

I arrived at _____ airport in Charlottesville on time! _____ director of my school
was waiting for me with _____ sign. _____ sign said, "Welcome to Virginia,
Jean-Pierre!" I was _____ little embarrassed, but it was such _____ nice welcome.

After we got _____ suitcases, he drove me to _____ apartment that had been rented
for me. I can't believe how big _____ apartments in this city are. I have two bedrooms,
_____ kitchen, _____ bath, and _____ living room all to myself.

I wish I had _____ car, because _____ public transportation here is not very good. It
takes me about one hour to go to _____ school by bus. If I had _____ car, I could get there
in about 20 minutes. Charlottesville is _____ small city, so _____ traffic isn't heavy. And
_____ roads here are nice and wide.

_____ classes which I am taking are all excellent. I've gotten to know _____ other
foreign students who are also studying _____ business. Most of them are from Asian
countries, but there are _____ few from Europe.

Well, I had better "hit _____ books" as you Americans say. Please write me soon. I
miss _____ French food!

Love,

Jean Pierre

10.3   WRITTEN ACTIVITY: *A Letter Home*

DIRECTIONS: Write a letter to a friend or family member and tell him or her about your first week in a foreign country. If you have never lived in a foreign country, then write about a week that you spent in a different city. Pay careful attention to the use of articles.

10.4   WRITTEN ACTIVITY: *Reconstructing Headlines*

DIRECTIONS: The headlines in newspapers often delete punctuation, articles, and other words to save valuable space. Read the following historical headlines taken from the *Los Angeles Times* from 1940–1978 and insert appropriate punctuation, articles, and other words that will make the headline comprehensible and grammatical.

EXAMPLE

HEADLINES: LA BECOMES LARGEST US CITY TO ELECT BLACK MAYOR (May 30, 1973)

ANSWER: Los Angeles becomes the largest U.S. city to elect a black mayor.

1. GERMANS INVADE DENMARK; NORWAY AT WAR WITH NAZIS (April 9, 1940)

_____

2. TERRIBLE CONFLICT BREWING OVER GANDHI ASSASSINATION (January 31, 1948)

_____

3. BIG QUAKE ROCKS LA (July 21, 1952)

_____

4. SUPREME COURT OUTLAWS SEGREGATION IN SCHOOLS (May 18, 1954)

_____

5. FIRST CHILD IN LA GETS POLIO VACCINE (April 14, 1955)

_____

6. BROOKLYN DODGERS BUY LA ANGELS (February 22, 1957)

_____

7. ALASKA VOTED 49th STATE BY SENATE (July 1, 1958)

_____

8. PARIS GIVES ROUSING WELCOME TO KENNEDYS (June 1, 1961)

_____

9. KENNEDY ASSASSINATION TERMED ACT OF MAN 'ALIENATED' FROM REAL WORLD (September 28, 1964)

_____

10. EGYPT AND SYRIA ACCEPT CEASEFIRE (June 9, 1967)

_____

11. 9 OLYMPIC HOSTAGES DIE IN SHOOT-OUT (September 6, 1972)

_____

12. JONES ORDERED CULTISTS TO DRINK CYANIDE POTION (November 21, 1978)

_____

■ D. Making Generalizations

Below are four ways to make general statements about people or things in English. Note the difference in article and number use in each generalization and also the degree of formality.

COUNT NOUNS		
FORM	**USE**	**EXAMPLE**
1. THE + SINGULAR NOUN	■ Used for generalizations about plants, animals, ethnic groups, technical inventions, and with certain adjectives used as nouns (e.g., the rich)	■ **The computer** changed life in the United States during the 1980s. (technical inventions) ■ **The sloth** is a three-clawed animal found in Costa Rica. (animals) ■ The **rich** get richer and the **poor** get poorer. ■ The **crocus** is the first flower to bloom in spring.
2. THE + PLURAL NOUN	■ Used for generalizations about classes of people (ethnic groups, professional groups) and plural proper nouns	■ In business, **the Americans** are often direct in their refusals. **The Japanese** often find their bluntness disconcerting. ■ The **medical doctors** have a strong lobby. ■ The **American Indians** lost their land.

3. A / AN + SINGULAR NOUN	■ Can be used to make a generalization about **any** count noun	■ **A car** is a necessity in the city. ■ **A house** can be expensive in Washington, D.C.
4. PLURAL NOUN	■ Used for **any** count noun. This is less formal than the other constructions.	■ **Cars** are necessary in the city. ■ **Houses** can be expensive in Washington, D.C.
NONCOUNT NOUNS		
NOUN ONLY	■ **Never** use an article with **noncount** nouns when speaking about the nouns in general.	■ **Love** is a many splendored thing. ■ **Gold** is a precious metal. ■ **Death** and taxes are inevitable.

10.5 DISCUSS AND WRITE: *Making Generalizations*

DIRECTIONS: What kinds of generalizations can be made about the following ideas, people, and things? Choose two nouns from each of the following lists. In pairs or small groups, make some generalizations that you believe to be true. After you have shared your generalizations, write them down. **Show all the possibilities** for forming generalizations as described in the chart above.

Noncount nouns

                                            Count nouns

                              Living things   **Things**

Money   Man   Computer

Love   Woman   Fax machine

Life in the United States   Teacher   Microwave

Life in your country   Snake   Car

                                           Dentist

                                           Cactus

EXAMPLE

CUE: University student

ANSWER: A university student usually doesn't have much money.
                University students usually don't have much money.
                The university student usually doesn't have much money.

1. _____

   _____

2. _____

   _____

3. _____

_____

4. _____

_____

5. _____

_____

6. _____

_____

10.6   ARTICLE USAGE: *Proverbs in English*

DIRECTIONS: Each of the following sentences is a well-known proverb in English. Read each one and supply an appropriate article in the space provided **(the, a /an, ∅)**. Be ready to explain why you made the choice that you did.

1. _____ variety is _____ spice of _____ life.

2. You can't teach _____ old dog _____ new tricks.

3. _____ beauty is only skin deep.

4. _____ bird in _____ hand is worth two in _____ bush.

5. Every cloud has _____ silver lining.

6. _____ grass is always greener on _____ other side.

7. _____ practice makes perfect.

8. _____Rome wasn't built in _____ day.

9. _____money is _____ root of all _____ evil.

10. _____ money makes _____ world go round.

11. Write two proverbs from your culture here and be ready to talk about their meaning.

_____

_____

E. Some Exceptions to the Article Rules

Although you learned that count and noncount nouns qualified by an adjective clause or prepositional phrase are preceded by **the,** there are some exceptions to this rule. These are explained below.

COUNT NOUNS	
Compare: **(a)** I want to buy **a** suitcase *from Italy.* **(b)** Where is **the** suitcase *that you bought in Italy?*	▪ The meaning in (a) is "**any** suitcase from Italy," not a specific one, so **a** is used. ▪ In (b), both the speaker and listener **know** which suitcase is being referred to, so **the** is necessary.
Compare: **(a)** **A** car, *which can be quite expensive*, is indispensable to a foreign student in the United States. **(b)** **The** car *that my brother bought* doesn't have any air-conditioning.	▪ In (a), *car* is generic; it refers to all cars. It is followed by an adjective clause that does not specify which car. Use **a**. ▪ In (b), *car* has been limited by an adjective clause. You must use **the**.
NONCOUNT NOUNS	
Compare: **(a)** I love **cheese** *from Wisconsin.* **(b)** Where is **the cheese** *that you bought yesterday?* **(a)** **Hail**, *which is a combination of ice and snow*, can be quite dangerous. **(b)** **The hail** *that we get in my town* can be as big as golf balls.	▪ In (a), *cheese* is a generic noun meaning "any cheese from Wisconsin." ▪ In (b), the cheese has been specified. ▪ The noncount noun is generic followed by a nonrestrictive adjective clause.

10.7   FILL IN THE BLANKS: *Exceptions to Article Rules*

DIRECTIONS: Fill in the blanks with **a /an, the,** or **∅**, as appropriate.

1. I know _____ place where we can go for lunch.

2. This is _____ place which I told you about.

3. _____ pet, which can be quite a nuisance at times, can also be a joy to elderly people.

4. Most people don't like _____ steak which has been overcooked.

5. I gave _____ steak which I overcooked to the dog.

10.8   WRITTEN EXERCISE: *Articles*

DIRECTIONS: Fill in the blank with any noun that makes sense. You will have to decide whether to use **the, a / an** or **∅.**

EXAMPLE

CUE: _____ you gave me was beautiful.

ANSWER: The sweater you gave me was beautiful.

1. _____which bothers me most about a foreign language is the pronunciation.

2. _____ never makes me angry, but _____ sure does!

3. I really need _____; do you know where I can find it?

4. The area which intrigues me most in the United States is _____.

5. _____ is quite different in the United States, but _____ _____ is the same as in my country.

10.9   FILL IN THE BLANKS: *Articles*

DIRECTIONS: The following is a column by Andy Rooney on small talk. Fill in the blank with **a / an, the,** or **ɸ,** as appropriate. In some cases more than one answer may be correct.

Small Talk: Conversation or Giant Bore?

If there has ever been _____ book written about _____ small talk, and how to
                        1   2
conduct it, I've never seen it. During _____ holiday season is when we need _____ book
                                        3   4
like that _____ most. _____ cocktail party or dinner party can be _____ drag if people
          5   6   7
don't know how to small talk.

"How have you been?" isn't good enough. "How have you been?" leads inevitably to,
"Fine. And yourself?"

_____ person standing in front of you with _____ glass in his hand has hit _____
        8   9   10
ball back in your court and you're right where you started: In _____ conversational abyss.
                                                                11
You have to begin again.

_____ worst thing that can happen at _____ stand-up or sit-down party is to get stuck
12   13
with someone who doesn't want to talk to you and to whom you have no interest in talking.
Until someone else comes along and interrupts your tortured conversation, you have nothing to
do but continue with _____ idiotic pleasantries.
                     14
. . . One of _____ few ways to escape, when you're trapped one-on-one with someone
            15
at _____ party, is to say either, "Can I get you _____ drink?" or "I think I'll freshen this
   16   17
_____ little." You then disappear and hope that, before you return, _____ person has
18   19
found someone else to bore. This ploy is from _____ man's point of view. _____ woman
                                              20   21
can hardly break away by asking _____ man, "Can I get you another drink?" It is one of
                                22
_____ unfair things _____ women have to bear in _____ life.
23   24   25

One of _____ reasons _____ food is important at _____ party is not for its

26   27   28

nutritional value, but because it's _____ source of _____ small talk. If _____ food is

                   29   30   31

dull, _____ talk is often dull.

     32

II. ARTICLE USE WITH PROPER NOUNS

General Rules:

1. Use **the** before **CLASS + OF + NOUN.**
2. Use **the** before all **plural** proper nouns.

CATEGORY	NO ARTICLE	USE THE	EXCEPTIONS
LAND MASSES	**Planets** • Uranus, etc. **Continents** • South America, etc. **Countries** • France, etc. **Islands—singular** • Maui, etc. **Cities** • San Diego, etc. **Streets** • Fifth Avenue, etc.	 **Islands—plural** • the Virgin Islands, etc.	• the earth *the Netherlands* • The U.S, the USSR, • the Sudan • the Ivory Coast • the Hague • the Champs Elysees
REGIONS		• the south (of France) • the northwest, etc.	• southern France • New England
BODIES OF WATER	**Lakes** • Victoria Lake, etc. **Bays** • San Francisco Bay, etc.	**Lakes—plural** • the Great Lakes, etc. **The Bay of X** • the Bay of Biscayne, etc. **Rivers** • the Rhine River, etc. **Oceans** • the Atlantic Ocean, etc. **Canals** • the Erie Canal, etc.	

MOUNTAINS	▪ Mt. Everest, etc.	▪ the Matterhorn ▪ the Rocky Mountains	
DESERTS		▪ The Mojave Desert, etc.	
BUILDINGS/ INSTITUTIONS	**Universities (Name + University)** ▪ Harvard University, etc.	**Universities** (The University of X) ▪ The University of Texas, etc. **Museums** ▪ The Prado, etc. **Libraries** ▪ The Library of Congress, etc.	
DATES	▪ July 4, 1776, etc.	▪ the fourth of July, etc. **Decades** ▪ the 1980s, etc. ▪ the roaring 20s (era), etc.	
HOLIDAYS	▪ Christmas, etc.		

10.10 RAPID DRILL: *Article Use with Proper Nouns*

DIRECTIONS: Your teacher will give you a category. Provide **two examples** from this category, paying careful attention to article usage.

EXAMPLE

TEACHER: planets
STUDENT: the earth; Uranus

1. states
2. islands
3. bays
4. dates of national holidays
5. universities
6. lakes
7. countries
8. oceans
9. rivers
10. mountains

10.11   FILL IN THE BLANKS: *Articles* and *Proper Nouns*

DIRECTIONS: Refer to the chart on article use and supply **a / an, the,** or **∅,** as appropriate.

1. _____ United States

2. _____ Rochester Institute of Technology

3. _____ Rocky Mountains

4. _____ Alps

5. _____ Gulf of Mexico

6. _____ Metropolitan Museum of Modern Art

7. _____ 1980s

8. _____ Niagara Falls

9. _____ Seine River

10. _____ Los Angeles

11. _____ Mt. Holyoke College

12. _____ North America

13. _____ Hawaiian Islands

14. _____ J. Paul Getty Museum

15. _____ southern California

16. _____ Bay of Bengal

17. _____ Mississippi River

18. _____ Ivory Coast

19. _____ North Pole

20. _____ Antarctica

10.12   PAIRED ACTIVITY: *Articles* and *Proper Nouns*

DIRECTIONS: Many educators in the United States have lamented American schoolchildren's lack of knowledge of world geography and events. See if you can do better. Take turns asking your partner the following questions and write the answers in the space provided. Refer to the chart to verify correct article usage.

STUDENT A

1. What state, province, or country are you from? _____

2. On what day do Americans celebrate their independence from Britain? _____

_____

3. Which university in the United States has the best reputation? _____

   _____

4. What region of your country are you from? _____

5. What is the name of the mountain range in Colorado? _____

6. What oceans surround Indonesia? _____

7. What is the longest river in the United States? _____

8. In which region of the United States is California located? _____

9. During which decade were you born? Your mother? _____

10. I would like to see the painting of the Mona Lisa. Which museum must I go to?

    _____

STUDENT B

1. What is the name of the street you live on? _____

2. What is the highest mountain in the world? _____

3. Name two universities in the United States. _____

4. What is the name of the river that flows through Egypt? _____

5. What oceans surround Africa? _____

6. What region of the United States is Vermont located in? _____

7. What is the name of the most famous mountain in Japan? _____

8. What is the name of the street on which the U.S. Stock Exchange is located? _____

   _____

9. In what decade was President John F. Kennedy assassinated? _____

10. Which century did Adolph Hitler live in? _____

10.13   FILL IN THE BLANKS: *Article Review*

DIRECTIONS: Read the following column by Ellen Goodman and fill in the blanks with **a / an,** **the,** or **∅.** Refer to the charts that appear throughout the chapter.

... "Happy New Year" has become one of those meaningless generic greetings, _____
1
annual equivalent of _____ daily injunction to _____ niceness, as in "Have a nice day."
2   3
We know what has happened to _____ niceness in _____80s. What is happening to
4   5
_____ happiness?
6
_____ sentiment like "Don't Worry, Be Happy" may make it to _____ top of
7   8

_____ charts, but only because it's such _____ novel idea. As _____ goal, it never even
　　　9　　　　　　　　　　　　　　　　　　　10　　　　　　　　　　　11
makes _____ New Year's resolution list.
　　　　　12

Once upon _____ time, _____ pursuit of _____happiness was _____legiti-
　　　　　　　　13　　　　　　　　14　　　　　　　　15　　　　　　　　　16
mate, even _____ admired, American ideal. No less solid a citizen than John Hancock signed
　　　　　17
on to _____ happiness. Now _____ person who admits to this pursuit simply isn't regarded
　　　　18　　　　　　　　　　19
as serious.

. . . _____ happiness as _____ legitimate preoccupation is _____ victim of
　　　　　20　　　　　　　　　21　　　　　　　　　　　　　　　　22
_____ hostile takeover by _____ two other American pursuits: _____ fitness and
　　23　　　　　　　　　　　　24　　　　　　　　　　　　　　　　25
_____ competitiveness. This duo proved to be both leaner and meaner, more able to adapt to
　　26
_____ environment of _____ 80s and poised to take off during _____ 90s.
　　27　　　　　　　　　　28　　　　　　　　　　　　　　　　　　29
. . . If we are what we are supposed to eat, we are very serious indeed. We eat _____
　　　　　　　　　　　　　　　　　　　　　　　　　　　　　　　　　　　　　30
fiber to avoid _____ cancer and _____ oat bran to reduce _____ cholesterol. And if you
　　　　　　　　31　　　　　　　　　32　　　　　　　　　　33
think that there isn't _____ moral judgment in _____ new nutrition, read _____ ad of
　　　　　　　　　　　34　　　　　　　　　　35　　　　　　　　　　　36
_____ 80s: "Quaker Oats. It's _____ Right Thing to Do."
　　37　　　　　　　　　　　　38
As for _____ exercise, uptight is no longer _____ personality flaw. It's everybody's
　　　　　39　　　　　　　　　　　　　　　　　40
toning goal. _____ only sensuality praised under _____ Puritan ethic is _____ sweaty
　　　　　　　41　　　　　　　　　　　　　　42　　　　　　　　　43
pleasure of _____ good workout.
　　　　　　44
. . . Which brings us to _____ competitiveness. If you think that it's heavy lifting at
　　　　　　　　　　　　　　45
_____ gym, try _____ life down at _____ corporation. . . .Once _____ people
　　46　　　　　　　47　　　　　　　　　48　　　　　　　　　　　49
confessed to being _____ workaholics; now they brag about it. _____ old goal of _____
　　　　　　　　　　50　　　　　　　　　　　　　　　　　　　　51　　　　　　　　　52
four-day week has been replaced by boasts about _____ seven-day week.
　　　　　　　　　　　　　　　　　　　　　　53
. . . _____ problem is that _____ happiness isn't productive. _____ happiness
　　　　　54　　　　　　　　　　55　　　　　　　　　　　　　　　56
isn't aerobic. _____ happiness isn't driven. _____ happiness is about as hard-edged as
　　　　　　　57　　　　　　　　　　　　　58
_____ warm puppy.
　　59

═══ GRAMMATICAL PATTERNS TWO ═══

═══ PREVIEW ═══

DIRECTIONS: What do you know about tipping in the United States? Should you tip a waiter? How much? Read the following text on tipping customs in the United States to find out. Then answer the questions that follow.

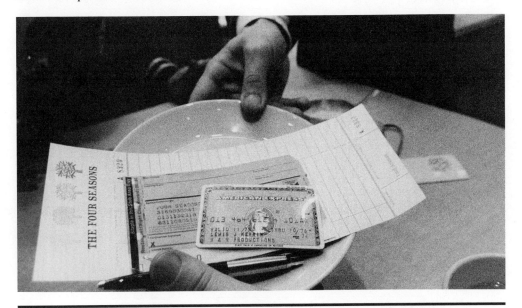

U.S. VISITORS TRIPPING ON OUR WAY OF TIPPING
by Sehyon Joh

1. A number of tourists visiting the U.S. face more than the language barrier when they visit New York or other large American cities. **The intricacies of tipping** have some of them baffled.

2. France, as well as many other European countries, has a "tip-included" policy which means the service is included in the bill. But if a customer is especially satisfied with the service, he or she might leave an extra franc or two on the table.

3. A tourism official tells the story of a French visitor who felt insulted when an American waiter followed him to the door, handed him the dollar he had left on the table as a tip and told him: "I think you need this dollar more than I do. Take it." The French visitor had assumed of course that the tip had already been included in the bill.

4. In many countries in Asia, there is basically no tipping, so **none of the waiters** expects to find a tip on the table after serving customers. In spite of these differences, foreign visitors learn quickly about U.S. tipping customs.

5. Just how much should a person tip? "**Fifteen percent** is acceptable and 20 percent is preferable," says John Turchiano, spokesman for the Hotel and Restaurant Employees Union Local 6. Lawrence Goldberg, an official at the Taxi Drivers and Allied Workers' Union said that for taxi drivers, **$25.00 a day** in tips is the average for a large city—about 25-30 percent of his income. When Goldberg was asked who the worst tippers were, he replied, "Those rich old ladies out shopping on Fifth Ave."

GRAMMAR CONSIDERATIONS: FOCUS

The following questions are based on the preview text and are designed to help you find out what you already know about the structures in this chapter. Some of the questions may be hard and some of them may be easy. Answer as many of the questions as you can. Work with a partner if your teacher tells you to do so.

1. Locate the following subjects in the preview text, underline them and write the verb in the space provided.

    "A number of tourists"_____(paragraph 1)

    "The intricacies of tipping"_____(paragraph 1)

    "France, as well as other European countries,"_____(paragraph 2)

    "None of the waiters"_____(paragraph 4)

    "Fifteen percent"_____(paragraph 5)

    "$25.00 a day"_____(paragraph 5)

2. Based on the above examples, fill in the blanks with **is** or **are**. Try to formulate a rule for subject-verb agreement for these cases.

    A. A number of Chinese visitors to the United States _____ surprised by the tipping customs here since tipping is prohibited in their country.

        RULE: _____

    B. $3.35 an hour _____ the average wage of a waiter in the U.S.

        RULE: _____

    C. Ten percent _____ not a sufficient tip for good service at an upscale restaurant.

        RULE: _____

    D. None of the workers in a fast food restaurant _____ given tips for service.

        RULE: _____

    E. A waiter, as well as a taxi driver and a hairstylist, _____ paid wages plus tips.

        RULE: _____

I. SUBJECT-VERB AGREEMENT

■ A. Some Special Cases

	EXAMPLE SENTENCE	**RULE/EXPLANATION**
A number of The number of	1. **A number of** foreign visitors **are** surprised by tipping customs. 2. **The number of** customers is 75.	▪ A plural verb always follows **a number of**, as in sentence 1. ▪ A singular verb always follows **the number of**, as in sentence 2.

Percents Fractions Amounts Distances	3. 20% **is** preferable. 4. Half **is** given to the busboy. 5. $3.35 **is the** minimum wage. 6. Five miles **is** an average distance for me to run.	▪ A singular verb follows **percentages, fractions, amounts,** and **distances** when they are not followed by an "of phrase."
Amounts + Of Phrases	7. Half of the tables **are** occupied. 8. The majority of the customers **are** happy. 9. A quarter of the cake **is** gone! 10. 21% of the population **is** poor. 11. 21% of the books **are** paperback.	▪ When an **of** phrase follows **percentages, distances, fractions,** and **amounts,** the verb agrees with the noun closest to the verb.
None	12. None of the workers **receives** a tip. 13. None of the workers **receive** a tip.	▪ Usually, a singular verb follows **none,** even if the noun following it is plural (12). ▪ In conversational English, a plural noun has become acceptable, as in (13).
Neither / nor Either / Or Not only / But also	14. Neither the host nor his guests **were** happy. 15. Neither the guests nor their host **was** happy. 16. Either John or his brothers **are** going to make dinner. 17. Not only the waiter but also the cook and busboy **work** for tips.	▪ The noun closest to the verb determines if that verb is singular or plural. ▪ This is true for the following two-part subject constructions: **either / or, not only / but also.**
As well as In addition to Together with	18. France, as well as other European countries, **has** a tip-included policy. 19. Waiters, in addition to others who work for tips, **are** usually generous tippers.	▪ The first noun determines if the verb is singular or plural. Other expressions (usually set off by commas) that follow this rule include: **in addition to, together with, not to mention.**

10.14 RAPID DRILL: *Subject-Verb Agreement*

DIRECTIONS: Complete the following sentences paying careful attention to subject-verb agreement.

1. Half of the English words I learn . . .
2. The majority of students in the class . . .
3. Neither my mother nor my father . . .
4. None of the Americans I know . . .
5. A million dollars . . .
6. Not only New York, but also other cities . . .
7. A number of leaders in the world . . .

8. Doctors, in addition to lawyers, . . .
9. 100% . . .
10. One quarter of my day . . .
11. Neither Italy nor other European countries . . .
12. A number of students in this class . . .
13. Michael Jackson, as well as other rock stars, . . .
14. The number of tests in this class . . .
15. Not only cigarette smoking, but also drinking and overeating . . .

10.15   WRITTEN EXERCISE: *Customs in Your Country*

DIRECTIONS: Write about four customs in your country that you think your teacher or classmates might not know about. These customs could be related to tipping, sharing food, birthdays, holidays, etc. Use the following expressions and pay careful attention to subject-verb agreement. Be ready to give an oral account of your written work.

1. A number of . . .
2. None of the . . .
3. Neither . . . nor . . .
4. . . . , in addition to . . .

B. Collective Nouns

A collective noun refers to a group of something. Examples of collective nouns include **audience, class, government, committee, family, flock, herd,** etc. Collective nouns may be followed by either singular or plural nouns. Note the difference in use.

EXAMPLE SENTENCE	EXPLANATION
1. The family **arrives** together at 7:00.	▪ When a **singular verb** is used with a collective noun, it emphasizes the group as a unit.
2. John just arrived and now the family **are** all here.	▪ When a **plural verb** is used with a collective noun, it emphasizes that the group members are acting individually.[a]
Exceptions: 3. The **police** carry guns in the U.S. 4. The **military** often retire at 45. 5. The **people** don't trust the news.	▪ These collective nouns are **always** plural.

[a]Collective nouns are more often plural in British English than American English (for example, The family are all in London).

10.16   COLLECTIVE NOUNS

DIRECTIONS: Circle the appropriate singular or plural verb, depending on the meaning of the sentence. Refer to the chart above to help you decide.

1. The committee is / are having a heated debate about the question of summer vacations.
2. The Bush family is / are spending the summer in Kennebunkport, Maine.
3. Meanwhile, the Smith family is / are taking separate vacations this year.
4. The government always keep / keeps in close contact with the president while he is on vacation.
5. People in the United States do / does not usually take vacations that are longer than four weeks.
6. The military is / are granted leaves or vacations, upon request.

10.17 PAIRED ACTIVITY: *Collective Nouns*

DIRECTIONS: Complete the following sentences and choose the appropriate verb. Then discuss your answers with a partner. See if your impressions are similar or different.

1. The police in the United States is / are _____

2. I think the military in the United States has /have _____

3. An audience at a rock concert is / are _____

4. An American family value / values _____

5. The government in the United States is / are _____

6. This class is / are _____

II. SPECIAL PROBLEMS WITH ARTICLE USAGE AND SUBJECT-VERB AGREEMENT

Pay special attention to these very common mistakes.

PROBLEM / INCORRECT FORM	EXPLANATION
1. MOST [INCORRECT: Most of Americans eat fast food.] CORRECT: **Most Americans** eat fast food. CORRECT: **Most of the Americans** eat fast food.	This problem can be corrected in these two ways.
2. GENERIC ABSTRACT NOUNS [INCORRECT: The money is very important to my host family.] CORRECT: Money is very important to my host family.	**Never** put **the** before a noncount noun when you are referring to that noun in general.
3. INDEFINITE ARTICLE [INCORRECT: She is teacher of English.] CORRECT: She is **a** teacher of English.	Students often forget to put **a / an** before a singular count noun.

4. COUNT / NONCOUNT NOUNS [INCORRECT: An adolescent needs many **advices**.] CORRECT: An adolescent needs a lot of **advice**. [INCORRECT: Do you have much ski **equipments**?] CORRECT: Do you have much **ski equipment**?	You must be very careful about the use of articles and quantifiers with noncount nouns.

■ 10.18 WRITTEN EXERCISE: *Error Analysis*

DIRECTIONS: Examine the following sentences for errors in article usage and count and noncount nouns. If you find an error, circle it and make your correction clearly above the error. Some sentences may not have any errors. If a sentence is already correct, do not change anything.

1. Confucianism influenced Korea greatly because it was a dominant ideology of Yi Dynsty.

2. So Korean has the characteristics of courtesy, desire for higher education, and quietness.

3. The swimming in the ocean requires more strength than the swimming in a pool.

4. Rick won a prize of a trip around the world, but he didn't accept the prize because it was sponsored by the weapons company.

5. The happiness that she is looking for can never be found during the life.

6. The traveling can be great experience for people because it provides exposure to other cultures.

7. In 1950s, the average American family consumed much more loaves of bread than they do today.

8. Many Americans think the divorce is increasing in California because most of families do not share time together.

9. The Earthquake Commission offers the following advices to people in high-risk areas: when an earthquake hits, stand under the door or the table.

10. If you ever visit the Great Lakes, be sure to go to Niagara Falls.

11. Louisa is planning the trip to southern part of France where she hopes to visit Roman ruins.

12. It is difficult for new parents to make decisions regarding the discipline.

13. Japanese has skillfulness.

14. Success in work in Japan is closely related with superior's evaluation rather than real ability.

15. In other words, vertical relationship is more important than horizontal one.

16. Most of Koreans have hot temperament.

17. When you ask the direction, the Japanese will be very kind and have patience to tell you what to do.

18. Neither John nor his brothers is planning on attending the play.

19. None of us likes to pay taxes.

20. The crowd are going wild over the new song by the Rolling Stones.

21. The majority of houses in this state is made of stucco.

COMPOSITION TOPICS

1. Foreign students often experience culture shock when they go to a foreign country. Describe an experience that you have had that illustrates the meaning of *culture shock.*

2. What do you know about food in the United States? Compare the type of food and also the ritual of sharing food in the United States with that of your culture.

THE SPIRIT OF AMERICA

☰ Passives

THE SPIRIT OF AMERICA   **(Life, Liberty and the Pursuit of Happiness)**

DISCUSSION QUESTIONS

1. What makes America so special? How would you describe the spirit of America, according to what you have read, heard or experienced?
2. Why have so many people from around the world immigrated to America?
3. How would you define "the American dream"?

OBJECTIVES

In this chapter you will learn:

1. To form the passive voice of English verbs in all tenses
2. To form and use the passive voice of modals, infinitives, and gerunds
3. To understand which English verbs have a passive voice
4. To understand when the passive voice should be used
5. To understand when the agent should be included in a passive sentence
6. To use passive verb forms as adjectives

══════ PREVIEW ══════

DIRECTIONS: Martin Luther King, Jr., was a black civil rights leader who fought for equality through peaceful resistance. Below is a famous speech delivered by Martin Luther King, Jr., in Washington, D.C., on August 28, 1963. Read the speech, referring to the vocabulary list when necessary.

I HAVE A DREAM
by Martin Luther King, Jr.

I say to you today, my friends, so even though we face the difficulties of today and tomorrow, I still have a dream. I have a dream that one day this nation will rise up and live out the true meaning of its creed, "We hold these truths to be self-evident, that all men are created equal." I have a dream that one day on the red hills of Georgia, sons of former slaves and the sons of former slave owners will be able to sit down together at the table of brotherhood. I have a dream that one day even the state of Mississippi, a state sweltering with the heat of injustice, sweltering with the heat of oppression, will be transformed into an oasis of freedom and justice. I have a dream that my four little children will one day live in a nation where they will not be judged by the color of their skin, but by the content of their character.

I have a dream today!

I have a dream, that one day down in Alabama—with its vicious racists, with its Governor having his lips dripping with the words of interposition and nullification—one day right there in Alabama, little black boys and black girls will be able to join hands with little white boys and white girls as sisters and brothers.

I have a dream today!

I have a dream that one day every valley shall be exalted, every hill and mountain shall be made low. The rough places will be plain and the crooked places will be made straight, "and the glory of the Lord shall be revealed, and all flesh shall see it together."

This is our hope.

VOCABULARY

rise up: stand
creed: a statement of the beliefs of a certain group of people
sweltering: giving off intense heat

oppression: the state of being kept down through unjust power or authority
transformed: changed from one state to another
oasis: anything which is a relief from difficulty or hardship
exalted: raised up
revealed: uncovered

CULTURAL NOTE / DISCUSSION

What do you know about Martin Luther King, Jr.? How does he symbolize the American spirit of independence, opportunity, and freedom?

GRAMMAR CONSIDERATIONS: FOCUS

The following questions are based on the preview text and are designed to help you find out what you already know about the structures in this chapter. Some of the questions may be hard and some of them may be easy. Answer as many of the questions as you can. Work with a partner if your teacher tells you to do so.

1. A passive verb in English is formed with a form of **be** and the **past participle** of the verb, for example, **is taught.** Underline the passive verbs in the speech. How many different tenses are used?
2. Based on the example from the text, what is the rule for forming the negative passive?
3. What is the purpose of using the passive form of the verbs in this speech? Who is the agent (performing the action) of those verbs? Why is the agent not mentioned?

═══════ GRAMMATICAL PATTERNS ONE ═══════

I. ACTIVE TO PASSIVE TRANSFORMATION

An English sentence can either be stated in active voice or passive voice. The diagram below demonstrates how the active to passive transformation is made.

SENTENCE IN ACTIVE VOICE

The average American	seeks	independence
subject	verb	object

There are three steps to making this active sentence passive:
1. Make the direct object of the active sentence the subject of the passive sentence.
   Independence _____

2. Make the verb passive: **be + past participle**
   Independence   **is sought** _____

3. If necessary, add **by** to the subject of the active sentence and make it the agent.

Independence   is sought   **by the average American.**

SENTENCE IN PASSIVE VOICE

Independence	is sought	by the average American.
subject	verb	agent

11.1 RAPID DRILL: *Active* to *Passive Transformation*

DIRECTIONS: Change each of the following active sentences to passive.

1. Whites forced blacks to sit in the back of school buses.
2. Martin Luther King, Jr., encouraged peaceful resistance.
3. Whites prevented blacks from eating at the same restaurants.
4. Whites discriminated against blacks in many other ways.
5. The constitution guarantees equality for all.
6. The constitution protects the rights of every American citizen.

II. PASSIVE VOICE IN DIFFERENT VERB TENSES

The chart below shows how the passive voice is formed in the various verb tenses. There is no passive form for present perfect progressive, simple future progressive, or past perfect progressive.

VERB TENSE	ACTIVE VERB	PASSIVE VERB
SIMPLE PRESENT **is / are + past participle**	The constitution **guarantees** equality for all.	Equality for all **is guaranteed** by the constitution.
PRESENT PROGRESSIVE **is / are + being + past participle**	Many leaders **are taking** steps to enforce the constitution.	Steps **are being taken** by many leaders to enforce the constitution.
PRESENT PERFECT **has / have + been + past participle**	We **have violated** the principles of the constitution in the past.	The principles of the constitution **have been violated** in the past.

SIMPLE PAST was / were + past participle	School segregation **violated** a constitutional right.	A constitutional right **was violated** by school segregation.
PAST PROGRESSIVE was / were + being + past participle	The Montgomery police **were violating** a constitutional right when they arrested a black woman on a bus.	A constitutional right **was being violated** by the Montgomery police when they arrested a black woman on a bus.
PAST PERFECT had + been + past participle	The government **had feared** a violent uprising.	A violent uprising **had been feared** by the government.
FUTURE will + be + past participle	We **will feel** the impact of the civil rights movement for years to come.	The impact of the civil rights movement **will be felt** for years to come.
FUTURE PERFECT will + have + been + past participle	By the time our children are grown, we **will have taught** them many lessons about civil rights.	By the time our children are grown, they **will have been taught** many lessons about civil rights.

11.2   RAPID DRILL: *Passive Voice in Different Verb Tenses*

DIRECTIONS: Change each active verb below to the passive.

EXAMPLE

CUE: catches
RESPONSE: is being caught

1. teaches
2. have written
3. was showing
4. will see
5. is eating

6. were striking
7. had spoken
8. will have performed
9. bring
10. are selling

11.3   WRITTEN EXERCISE: *Fill in the Blanks*

DIRECTIONS: In the passage below about Martin Luther King's life, fill in the blanks with the passive form of the verb in parentheses. Be sure that the verb is in the correct tense.

Martin Luther King, Jr., who _____ (born) in Atlanta, Georgia, on

January 15, 1929, _____ (recognize) today as having been one of

America's leading social reformers. His role as leader of the civil rights movement began in

1959 when a black woman in Montgomery, Alabama _____ (arrest) for refusing to give up to a white man her seat in the front of a bus. This incident served as the impetus for a bus boycott throughout Montgomery, which _____ (direct) by King. At the time, blacks _____ (discriminate) against severely all over the country, especially in the South, so they were ready for a fight. King's belief in nonviolent demonstrations, however, which (inspire) _____ by Ghandi, _____ widely _____ (adopt) by the civil rights movement. Although blacks _____ still _____ (discriminate) against to some degree at the present, Martin Luther King made significant gains in the struggle for greater equality. He will always _____ (remember) as the leader who peacefully convinced many Americans that the principles of the constitution _____ (not uphold). In 1964, he _____ (award) the Nobel Peace Prize, the first black to receive this award. In 1968, just as he was preparing to lead a nationwide campaign of the poor, Martin Luther King _____ (assassinate). His life _____ (commemorate) every January on Martin Luther King Day.

11.4   ORAL PRACTICE: *Freedom*

DIRECTIONS: Discuss the following topics as they relate to the history of your country. Use the passive voice in a variety of tenses.

EXAMPLE

FREEDOM: Freedom has not always been respected in this country. Many were and still are being persecuted for the color of their skin, their religious background, their political views, and their nationality.

1. Freedom of speech
2. Freedom of religion
3. Political opportunity
4. The right to vote
5. Equal rights (men and women–equal pay for equal work, etc.)

11.5   WRITTEN EXERCISE: *Civil Rights*

DIRECTIONS: Write a short paragraph about an important leader in your country who fought for civil rights for a group of people that were being oppressed or discriminated against. Use a variety of verb tenses to describe the events and actions that took place. If you have difficulty thinking of someone, write about a person from another country, for example, Bobby Kennedy, Nelson Mandela, and so forth.

III. VERBS THAT CAN BE PASSIVE

Not all English verbs can be both active and passive. The chart below provides guidelines about which verbs can be passive.

GENERALIZATION	EXAMPLE
1. Most transitive verbs can be active or passive: **take, bring, eat, teach, write, read, drive, etc.**	Ships **brought** immigrants across the ocean. (active) Many immigrants **were brought** across the ocean by ship. (passive)
2. Intransitive verbs cannot be passive: **be, seem, appear, sleep, rise, arrive, weigh** (when it is intransitive), **happen, occur, die**	The children **were been** sick by the food. [INCORRECT use of passive] Many **were arrived** in America with no money. [INCORRECT use of passive] Sasha **was weighed** only 90 pounds when she arrived. [INCORRECT use of passive]
3. **Have** cannot be passive.	These immigrants **had** many problems. (active) Many problems **were had** by these immigrants. [INCORRECT use of passive]
4. The verb **to be born** can only be used in the passive.	Her daughter **was born** in March. (CORRECT use of passive) She **born** her daughter in March. [INCORRECT use of active]

11.6   RAPID DRILL: *Verbs That Can Be Passive*

DIRECTIONS: If possible, change the active sentence to a passive sentence. Discuss the reasons why the change may or may not be possible.

1. Alicia lay down on the cot to rest during the trip.
2. The sun rises at 6:00 A.M. every day.
3. In the beginning, immigrants earned their salary through manual labor.
4. This country has a very diverse ethnic makeup.
5. Hispanics make up a large percentage of the immigrant population.
6. As Li was preparing to board, the officer weighed his baggage.
7. When the immigrants saw the Statue of Liberty, they knew they had arrived in America.
8. Something strange happened when Sachi spoke with an American for the first time.
9. Many people died during the trip due to the harsh conditions.
10. The highest wave of immigration occurred during this period.

IV. MODALS, INFINITIVES, AND GERUNDS IN THE PASSIVE VOICE

The following patterns are used for the passive voice of modals, infinitives, and gerunds.

MODALS

SIMPLE: **Modal + Be + Past Participle**
Immigrants **couldn't be convinced** that their lives would be more difficult in America.

PERFECT: **Modal + Have + Been + Past Participle**
Immigrants **must have been told** about the opportunities in America.

INFINITIVES

SIMPLE: **To + Be + Past Participle**
Many immigrants waited **to be processed** at Ellis Island.

PERFECT: **To + Have + Been + Past Participle**
Many immigrants felt lucky **to have been rescued** from their former lives.

GERUNDS

SIMPLE: **Being + Past Participle**
Some people hated **being packed** onto a ship like sardines.

PERFECT: **Having Been + Past Participle**
Many were grateful for **having been given** the opportunity to come to America.

11.7 RAPID DRILL: *Forming Passive Modals, Infinitives, and Gerunds*

DIRECTIONS: Change each of the active verb forms below to the passive.

EXAMPLE

can't drive   can't be driven

1. shouldn't take
2. want to carry
3. like teaching
4. could have refused
5. regret having accepted

6. denied promising
7. have to tell
8. hope to hire
9. hated reminding
10. must sell

11.8 WRITTEN EXERCISE: *Using Passive Modals, Infinitives, and Gerunds*

DIRECTIONS: The sentences below contain information about the immigrants to the United States who arrived in New York at Ellis Island in the late 1800s. Paraphrase each of the sentences, using a passive modal, gerund, or infinitive in your paraphrase. For some sentences, there will be more than one choice.

EXAMPLE

It was impossible for the government to accept all the immigrants.

All the immigrants <u>couldn't be accepted</u> by the government.

It was impossible for all the immigrants <u>to be accepted</u> by the government.

1. It was necessary to impose limitations on the number of immigrants.

   _____

2. When they arrived at Ellis Island, it was impossible to process them immediately.

   _____

3. They left their countries because they wanted freedom from hunger and poverty.

   _____

4. They really enjoyed it when the boat was taking them far from the problems of their native country.

   _____

5. Many of them didn't want to go through the examination and questioning at the port of entry because they feared rejection.

   _____

11.9   PAIRED WRITTEN EXERCISE: *A New Constitution*

DIRECTIONS: What is freedom? How much freedom should people have? Discuss these questions with your partner and decide on five principles that you would include in a constitution if you were writing it for your country. Write the five principles on the lines below. Each statement should include a passive modal.

EXAMPLE

People shouldn't be refused the right to choose and practice their religion.

A New Constitution

1. _____

2. _____

3. _____

4. _____

5. _____

GRAMMATICAL PATTERNS TWO

PREVIEW

DIRECTIONS: Read the following editorial that appeared in a local newspaper on July 5, the day after Independence Day in America.

HAPPY FOURTH OF JULY

1. Yesterday, on the Fourth of July, once again American independence was celebrated across the nation. Fireworks were **set off,** picnics were held in parks and on beaches, and parades were attended by young and old alike.

2. This is a holiday that has been celebrated by Americans every year for the last 200 years. We all **get caught up in** plans and activities so that we can **get the most out of** a day off from work, and if the holiday falls on a Friday or a Monday, the three day weekend is an opportunity to take off from the city to a favorite **getaway**.

3. However, as with many holidays, the purpose and origin of the holiday itself are often lost in the excitement and **preoccupation** of the celebration. In the heat of summer, the American memory should be taken back to the heat of a battle that was won by the spirit of independence, equality, and freedom. The American way of life should be characterized by that spirit, and that spirit should provide the **impetus** and inspiration to continue the fight to uphold these principles. As the hamburgers are **barbecued** and the baseball games won, each American should reflect on the independence that was gained by our country many years ago, and which is still being sought by many. This is the independence that many in our country and all over the world are still struggling to achieve—independence from poverty and hunger, independence from **repression**

and hatred; independence from the limitations that prevent human beings from living to their full potential.

VOCABULARY

set off: ignited and as a result exploded
get caught up in: get involved in
get the most out of: receive as much benefit as possible from something
getaway: a place to escape to
preoccupation: something that occupies all your time, energy, or thoughts
impetus: stimulus, incentive, impulse
barbecued: cooked outdoors over hot coals
repression: control that prevents natural development or expression

CULTURAL NOTE / DISCUSSION

Parades and picnics are the two most characteristic activities for the Fourth of July in America. Are these activities common for any holidays in your country? What is a typical parade in your country like? Describe a typical picnic.

GRAMMAR CONSIDERATIONS: FOCUS

The following questions are based on the preview text and are designed to help you find out what you already know about the structures in this chapter. Work with a partner if your teacher tells you to do so.

1. Why are the first two sentences in the preview written in the passive voice?
2. The first sentence in paragraph 3 has no agent. Who is the agent? Why is the agent omitted?
3. Underline the agent in the second sentence in paragraph 3. Is it possible to omit this agent? Why or why not?

I. WHEN TO USE THE PASSIVE

The passive voice in English is actually used much more infrequently than the active voice. It is used most commonly in formal written English. The chart below explains when it is appropriate to use the passive voice.

GENERALIZATION	EXAMPLE
1. TO EMPHASIZE THE RECEIVER OR RESULT OF THE ACTION	**Americans are taught** independence and self-sufficiency at an early age.
2. IF THE WRITER WANTS TO *PURPOSELY* OMIT THE AGENT BECAUSE THE AGENT IS UNNECESSARY	Coffee **is drunk** in America. (Obviously it is drunk by Americans.)

3. TO ACHIEVE OBJECTIVITY BY CONCEALING THE SOURCE OF INFORMATION	**It is often thought** that American families are not close because the children want to live independently.
4. TO PROVIDE INFORMATION ABOUT THE AGENT AFTER INFORMATION ABOUT THE TOPIC IS ALREADY KNOWN	**Baseball** is a very popular American sport. **It is played** all over the country.
5. TO AVOID CLUMSINESS, BAD STYLE, OR INAPPROPRIATENESS IN WRITING	[INCORRECT: American parents instill the value of independence in their children from an early age, which some psychologists **suggest** in this study that this may be why American families are not close.] CORRECT: American parents instill the value of independence in their children from an early age, which may be why American families are not close, as **was suggested** by psychologists in this study.

11.10 DISCRIMINATION EXERCISE: *Passive* vs. *Active*

DIRECTIONS: Each pair of sentences below contains an active sentence and a passive sentence. Discuss the distinction between the two sentences and the rationale for using one over the other.

EXAMPLE

a. American parents teach their children independence at an early age.
b. American children are taught independence at an early age.
In sentence **a,** the active voice is used to make it clear that it is parents who are teaching children independence, as opposed to teachers, society, etc.
In sentence **b,** the passive voice is used to emphasize the fact that independence is taught regardless of who may be the teacher.

1. a. In 1846 men, women, and children packed up and prepared for the journey west.
  b. In 1846 men, women, and children were packed up and prepared for the journey west.
2. a. "Every day was like a picnic," a girl remembered of her earliest weeks on the trail.
  b. It was said that for the young children every day was like a picnic during the earliest weeks on the trail.
3. a. Circumstances often left children with responsibilities. They were asked to drive ox teams, care for herds, and join in family decisions.
  b. Circumstances often left children with responsibilities. Their parents or other group members asked them to drive ox teams, care for herds, and join in family decisions.
4. a. These children faced hardships and responsibility that others never face until adulthood, which is why some psychologists suggest that they never really had a childhood.
  b. These children faced hardships and responsibility that others never face until adulthood, which is why, as suggested by some psychologists, they never really had a childhood.

11.11 WRITTEN EXERCISE: *Cowboys*

DIRECTIONS: The passage below, about cowboys, is written in the active voice. Decide which verbs should be written in the passive and make the changes in the text. Discuss your reason for making the change.

Being a cowboy was not as romantic a life as legend has made it out to be. Cowboys had many problems as they traveled across the country rounding up cattle so that they could sell the animals in a different location. For example, in 1866 herders drove approximately 200,000 longhorns north across Indian territory toward Missouri. First, the Indians demanded payment for the grass the cattle ate along the way. Then, a group of angry Missouri farmers stood in the path of the herd demanding that they turn back because disease-carrying ticks had infested the cattle. Sometimes the cowboys sent the cattle to a distant town by railroad in which case the cowboys had to prod the cattle up ramps with poles, a job that resulted in a lasting nickname— "cowpokes."

11.12 PAIRED PRACTICE: *National Holidays*

DIRECTIONS: Interview your partner about a national holiday such as Independence Day. Get as much information as possible about the history and traditions associated with the holiday. Write a short report on the holiday, using the passive whenever appropriate. Be prepared to present the information to the rest of the class if your teacher asks you to do so.

II. WHEN TO USE THE AGENT

As well as knowing when the passive voice is necessary, it is important to know when the agent should be used. The chart below provides guidelines on when to use the agent in a passive sentence.

DO NOT USE THE AGENT	EXAMPLE
1. THE AGENT WAS PREVIOUSLY MENTIONED.	**The president** gave a speech last night. Many questions about the immigration reform were answered.
2. THE AGENT IS UNKNOWN.	An anonymous letter was written to protest this action.
3. THE AGENT IS OBVIOUS.	The operation was performed at 3:00. (A surgeon performed the operation.)
4. THE SPEAKER OR WRITER WANTS TO CONCEAL THE AGENT.	A mistake was made when war was declared.
USE THE AGENT	**EXAMPLE**
1. TO IDENTIFY BY PROPER NAME THE PERSON RESPONSIBLE FOR A CERTAIN WORK	"This Land is Your Land" was written **by Woodie Guthrie.**
2. TO PROVIDE NEW INFORMATION BY USING AN INDEFINITE NOUN PHRASE	The shopping cart was invented **by a young entrepeneur.**
3. TO EMPHASIZE THE FACT THAT THE AGENT IS INANIMATE SINCE OMITTED AGENTS ARE USUALLY ANIMATE	America was founded **by a spirit of independence and freedom.**

11.13 RAPID DRILL: *Using the Agent*

DIRECTIONS: Each passive sentence below contains an agent. Discuss whether the agent is necessary and if possible omit the agent from the sentence.

EXAMPLE

Because "The Star Spangled Banner" is the national anthem of the United States, it is sung by Americans before major sporting events. (The agent is unnecessary because it is obvious.)

1. Many pioneers were killed by the cruel weather and harsh living conditions.
2. A gross error was made by the president when he declared war.
3. "Paul Revere's Ride" was written by Henry Wadsworth Longfellow.
4. The Navahos are a tribe of native Americans. They are known by people for their turquoise and silver jewelry.
5. Ranchers kept their cattle in pens until they were sold and shipped out by the ranchers.
6. Many of the Texas rangers were Mexican. Their feelings about the difficult cattle drives were expressed by them in trail songs.
7. Life on the trail was described by one young dedicated cowboy as an exciting but harrowing experience.

11.14   WRITTEN EXERCISE: *O.K.*

DIRECTIONS: Below is a short passage about the origin and use of the word *O.K.* Above the box is a list of agents that can be used for the passive sentences in the passage. For each passive sentence, choose an appropriate agent. Then decide whether the agent should be added, and if so, where it should be added. Be prepared to justify your decision.

a. by the public   **d.** by the average American   **g.** by Allen Walker Read
b. by reporters   **e.** by speakers of English   **h.** by travelers
c. by an amazing fact   **f.** by Americans

O.K.? O.K.!

1. Recently, international travelers who pay attention to the languages they encounter have been surprised. Conversations with the word "O.K." can be heard all over the world.

2. The word is used in the United States at least seven times per day. Therefore, the utterance "okay" is emitted into the American air more than 1.4 billion times every twenty-four hours. The word **O.K.** in English has replaced the expression **all right** or **alright**, which is still used, although far less frequently than it was one hundred years ago.

3. The most significant research into the history of **okay** has been done at Columbia University. **O.K.** was first seen in print in the Boston *Morning Post* of March 23, 1839. When the editor, Charles Gordon Greene, was interviewed, he said it stood for **all correct**, spelled **oll korrect**.

11.15   WRITTEN EXERCISE: *Collecting Data*

DIRECTIONS: Listen carefully to your teacher or other English speakers for the next few days and take notes as you listen for the word *O.K.* Report your findings to your partner or the class as a whole. Use the passive voice in a variety of tenses to describe each situation, and omit the agent when appropriate.

III. DIFFERENCES BETWEEN THE *BE* PASSIVE AND THE *GET* PASSIVE

Sometimes **get** can be used in place of **be** in passive constructions. The difference in meaning is demonstrated in the chart below.

DIFFERENCE	EXAMPLE
BE EXPRESSES A STATE	Many women **were convinced** that their lives could be better.
GET EXPRESSES A PROCESS (= BECOME)	Many women **got convinced** that their lives could be better.
BE IS FORMAL	Many women **were told** that their place was in the home.
GET IS INFORMAL	A lot of women **got told** that they had to stay home.

BE = NO INVOLVEMENT FROM THE SUBJECT	Most women **were hired** as secretaries. (They didn't have much choice in the matter.)
GET = SUBJECT HAS SOME INFLUENCE OVER THE RESULT	Most women **got hired** as secretaries. (This was **their** accomplishment.)
BE OFTEN TAKES AN AGENT **GET** RARELY TAKES AN AGENT	Many women **were told by men** that their place was in the home. Many women **got told** that they had to stay home.

11.16   WRITTEN EXERCISE: *Fill in the Blanks*

DIRECTIONS: In each pair of sentences, fill in the blank of one sentence with the correct form of **be** and the blank of the other sentence with the correct form of **get**. Be prepared to justify your choice.

EXAMPLE

a. Before the women's liberation movement, women <u>were</u> paid less than men.

b. After the women's liberation movement, women still <u>got</u> paid less than men for some jobs.

1. a. Some women _____ opposed to becoming involved with the movement.

   b. Some women _____ swept into the movement.

2. a. *The Feminine Mystique* _____ written by Betty Friedan, a feminist.

   b. Betty Friedan's book, *The Feminine Mystique* _____, published as a result of changing attitudes towards women.

3. a. Many women _____ promoted from office work because of the victories they had won.

   b. Many women _____ promoted to higher paying positions.

4. a. The effects of the women's liberation movement _____ felt by men all over the country.

   b. The message of the women's liberation movement _____ carried across the country.

11.17   PAIRED PRACTICE: *Family Life*

DIRECTIONS: Read the following short passage about the American family. With a partner, discuss characteristics about American family life and compare them with family traditions in your country. Use **be** and **get** with the passive whenever appropriate.

American family traditions are very different from family traditions in other countries around the world. American children are taught independence at an early age, so it is not uncommon for American teenagers to get hired at their first jobs when they're 16 years old. This strong independence can also be seen when young people reach the age of 18. At this age, they usually move out of their parents' house if they get accepted at a university or if they are offered a job. At a later age, it is not uncommon for families to be separated by long distances although this doesn't necessarily mean that a close relationship is not maintained.

SPECIAL NOTE

Notice the strong distinction in meaning between the passive formed by **be + past participle** to describe a **state** and the use of **get + past participle** to describe a **process.**

is married / get married	**is broken / get broken**
is hurt / get hurt	**is dressed / get dressed**

11.18   RAPID DRILL: *Oral Paraphrase*

DIRECTIONS: In each pair of sentences below, if the sentence describes a state, paraphrase it with **be + past participle** of the given verb. If the sentence describes a process, paraphrase it with **get + past participle** of the given verb.

EXAMPLE

MARRY
a. Susan and Bill took their vows yesterday.   They **got married**.
b. Susan and Bill live together.   They **are married**.

1. DRESS
   a. Sharon has clothes on.
   b. Sharon is putting her clothes on.
2. HURT
   a. Marc smashed his finger in the door.
   b. Marc has a bandage on his finger.
3. LOSE
   a. They can't find the street they are looking for.
   b. They took a wrong turn.

IV. PASSIVE VERBS THAT FUNCTION AS ADJECTIVES

There are some verbs that can function as adjectives when used in the passive voice. There are a few distinct categories of these verbs.

TYPE	ACTIVE VERB	PASSIVE VERB	PASSIVE VERB AS ADJECTIVE
STATIVE PASSIVE (e.g., **open, close, break**)	The teacher **closed** the window.	The window **was closed** by the teacher.	The window is **closed**. (The passive form of the verb describes a state.)
PARTICIPIAL ADJECTIVES OF FEELING OR MENTAL STATE (**surprise, amuse, bore**)	The new music called jazz **surprised** many Americans.	Many Americans **were surprised** by the new music called jazz.	They were **surprised**. Many **surprised** Americans listened to the new music called jazz.
IDIOMATIC USE OF PASSIVE FORM (**be + lost, gone, finished, done**)	no active counterpart	no passive counterpart	I am **lost**. New Orleans is **located** in Louisiana. Those times are **gone**.

SPECIAL NOTE

There is often confusion about the difference between the participial adjectives that are formed from a passive verb and those that are formed from an active verb, for example, **surprised-surprising**. Here are some ways to remember the distinction.

PASSIVE PARTICIPIAL ADJECTIVE
- The new music **surprised** many Americans. ACTIVE VERB
- Many Americans **were surprised** by the new music. PASSIVE VERB
- The **surprised** Americans listened to the new music. PASSIVE ADJECTIVE

The passive participial adjective:
1. has an **-ed** ending: surpris**ed**
2. can be used in a passive sentence: The Americans **were surprised.**
3. usually describes an animate noun: **Americans**

ACTIVE PARTICIPIAL ADJECTIVE
- The new music **surprised** many Americans. ACTIVE VERB
- The new music was **surprising**. ACTIVE ADJECTIVE

The active participial adjective:
1. has an **-ing** ending: surpris**ing**
2. can't be used in a passive sentence
3. usually describes an inanimate noun: **the new music**

11.19   RAPID DRILL: *Active* vs. *Passive Participial Adjectives*

DIRECTIONS: Below are some sentences about the origins of jazz. For each active sentence, make one sentence with a passive participial adjective and one sentence with an active participial adjective.

EXAMPLE

The music amazed the public.   **a.** The public was amazed.   **b.** The music was amazing.

1. The drumbeat in Congo Square excited the people who gathered there to dance.
2. Ragtime music astonished the Creole musicians who first heard it.
3. The use of improvisation baffled other musicians.
4. The new rhythms of jazz confused traditional musicians.
5. The intensity of the music frustrated listeners.
6. This music sometimes bored people who couldn't understand it.

11.20   PAIRED PRACTICE: *First Impressions*

DIRECTIONS: Discuss with your partner your first impressions of the United States or another country that you visited. If you've never been abroad, discuss your first impressions of a city you've traveled to in your country. You will make a statement using either the active or passive participial form of one of the following verbs. Your partner will ask a question for more information, using the other form of the same verb. Choose from these verbs: **surprise, shock, amaze, interest, amuse, frustrate.**

EXAMPLE

STUDENT 1:   When I visited France, I was very **surprised** at how friendly the French people were.
STUDENT 2:   Oh, really? Why was that friendliness so **surprising** to you?
STUDENT 1:   Because I had been told that the French were not friendly to Americans.

11.21   ORAL INTERVIEW: *American Specialties*

DIRECTIONS: Your teacher will assign you one of the following typical American foods. Interview an American to get the information listed at the top of page 257. If you are unable to interview an American, look for the information in the library.

FOODS

peanut butter	corn on the cob
watermelon	pancakes
coffee	banana split
hamburgers	french toast
pumpkin	corn on the cob

ORIGIN OF FOOD:
HOW IT IS PREPARED:
HOW / WHEN / WHERE IT IS EATEN OR DRUNK:
ANY ADDITIONAL CUSTOMS RELATED TO THIS FOOD:

11.22   WRITTEN FEEDBACK AND ORAL PRESENTATION

DIRECTIONS: Use the information you collected to write a paragraph that you will use as the basis for an oral presentation about the food you were assigned. Use the passive voice whenever possible and appropriate.

11.23   REVIEW EXERCISE

DIRECTIONS: Use what you have learned about the passive voice to fill in the blanks below.

PHILIP: Hey, Gina, I hear you're going to America soon.

GINA: Yes, I _____ (invite) to visit my relatives in Florida.

PHILIP: Oh really? _____ (tell) much about your family?

GINA: Well, I know that my grandfather's cousin _____ (send) to America before the outbreak of the war. He _____ (promise) a job in the butcher shop that another cousin owned at the time.

PHILIP: Boy, that must have been hard. _____ (prepare) for what was waiting for him? Did he know any English?

GINA: I don't think so, but apparently he _____ (bring up) in poverty, so he could only look forward to a better life.

V. SPECIAL PROBLEMS WITH THE PASSIVE

PROBLEM	EXPLANATION
1. INCORRECT FORM OF PAST PARTICIPLE [INCORRECT: Immigrants were **brung** across the ocean on ships.] CORRECT: Immigrants were **brought** across the ocean on ships.	The past participle form of irregular verbs must be memorized.
2. OMISSION OF ONE COMPONENT IN THE PASSIVE CONSTRUCTION [INCORRECT: If there is inequality, the constitution **not being upheld**.] CORRECT: If there is inequality, the constitution **is not being upheld**.	For certain tenses the verb **be** is used twice in a **passive** construction.

3. USE OF THE ACTIVE VOICE WHEN THE PASSIVE VOICE IS MORE APPROPRIATE [INCORRECT: American folk songs reflect the spirit of the people. **The writers wrote these songs** about every aspect of American life.] CORRECT: American folk songs reflect the spirit of the people. **These songs were written** about every aspect of American life.	In some situations, the passive voice is more appropriate than the active voice.
4. INCORRECT OMISSION OR INCLUSION OF THE AGENT [INCORRECT: The constitution was written.] CORRECT: The constitution was written **by the fifty-five delegates** to the constitutional convention. [INCORRECT: In May, 1787, fifty-five delegates arrived in Philadelphia to write the constitution. By the end of the summer, the constitution was written **by these delegates**.] CORRECT: In May, 1787, fifty-five delegates arrived in Philadelphia to write the constitution. By the end of the summer, the constitution was written.	It is important to know when the agent should be included or omitted.
USING THE PASSIVE IN VERB TENSES FOR WHICH IT SHOULD NOT BE USED [INCORRECT: I have been being taught English for many years.] CORRECT: I have been learning English for many years.	Do not use the passive voice in present or past perfect progressive, simple future progressive, or future perfect progressive.

■ 11.24 ERROR ANALYSIS

DIRECTIONS: Some of the sentences below contain errors in the use of the passive voice. If there is an error, correct it clearly above the sentence. Some of the sentences may be correct.

1. America was establish on the principles of liberty, equality, and justice for all.

2. These principles are of utmost importance to Americans, so countless battles have been fought by Americans when equal rights have been abused.

3. The constitution was written as a declaration of every American's commitment to these principles.

4. It is sometimes said that these are idealistic notions.

5. Visitors to America are sometimes surprising by the variety of ethnic groups that make up the population.

6. Many minority groups have helped by the persistence of civil rights leaders.

7. "The Star Spangled Banner," the national anthem of the United States, was wrote by Francis Scott Key.

8. Halloween is an American holiday that children particularly enjoy. Americans celebrate Halloween on October 31.

9. Any tourist who crosses the border has to checked for proper immigration documents.

10. Jazz was born in America and is now played all over the world.

COMPOSITION TOPICS

Use what you have learned in this chapter to write a well-developed essay about one of the following topics. Use the passive voice whenever appropriate.

1. Define the American dream giving examples of how that dream has been realized.
2. Describe the spirit of your country drawing on examples from the history, culture, and character of the people.
3. In your opinion, what human rights should be respected in any country? Give specific examples of how these rights can be upheld and how they are being disregarded.

12

DATING AND MARRIAGE

Modals

THE DATING SCENE
(If You're Single, It's A Must)

DISCUSSION QUESTIONS

1. Are you single? If so, do you want to get married someday? How is it possible to meet your future husband or wife? If you're already married, how did you meet your husband / wife?
2. What are the dating customs in your country?

OBJECTIVES

In this chapter, you will learn:

1. To use a variety of modals and their functions by reviewing

2. To use several new functions for the modals that you already know
3. To use the past forms of modals for a variety of functions
4. To use passive and progressive forms after modals
5. To understand question formation for modal constructions

PREVIEW

DIRECTIONS: Read the following telephone conversation between Jill, 28 years old, and Patty, 30 years old. Jill and Patty work together in a computer company and are very good friends.

 1 **JILL:** Hi, Patty, this is Jill.
 2 **PATTY:** Hi, Jill. How was the party?
 3 **JILL:** Oh, it was just great. You should've come.
 4 **PATTY:** I know, but I had to help my sister move. Did you meet anyone?
 5 **JILL:** Yeah, I met a couple of really nice guys. One of them **asked me out.** And listen to this! His friend wants to make it a **double date.** You should get a call from him tonight.
 6 **PATTY:** Oh come on, Jill, I haven't been on a **blind date** since high school. You must be kidding!
 7 **JILL:** You can't really call this a blind date. After all, I've seen him, and you know what good judgement I have **in this department.** You should see his eyes. They're your favorite color.
 8 **PATTY:** They aren't green! You can't be serious!
 9 **JILL:** And he likes to play tennis. I'd say it's **a match made in heaven.** You have to come. It's a must!
10 **PATTY:** I don't know. I've been so turned off by the whole dating scene since Gary **stood me up** last time.
11 **JILL:** Oh, Patty, **that's history.** Besides, this guy puts Gary to shame. You should really give him a chance. I can promise you won't regret it.
12 **PATTY:** O.K. I guess I'll **go for it.**
13 **JILL:** Great! Call me as soon as you hear from him.
14 **PATTY:** O.K. Bye.
15 **JILL:** Talk to you later.

VOCABULARY

to ask someone out: to ask someone to go on a date
to double date: to go out on a date with another couple
a blind date: a date with someone you've never met, usually arranged by a friend
in this department: in this matter (that we're discussing)
a match made in heaven: a couple who are perfectly suited to each other
to stand someone up: someone doesn't show up for a date
that's history: That is finished, over
to go for it: to attempt something that involves some risk or difficulty

CULTURAL NOTE / DISCUSSION

In the United States it is not unusual for men and women to wait until they are in their late 20s or early 30s to get married. This is often because people, especially women, are concerned about becoming established in their careers before they get married and think about having children. Therefore, there are many men and women in this age bracket who are single, have careers, and go out frequently on dates. We then say that they are part of the dating scene. Is there such a dating scene in your country? At what age do men and women get married in your country?

GRAMMAR CONSIDERATIONS: FOCUS

The following questions are based on the preview text and are designed to help you find out what you already know about the structures in this chapter. Some of the questions may be hard and some of them may be easy. Answer as many of the questions as you can. Work with a partner if your teacher tells you to do so.

A. Find an example in the dialogue of the following generalizations. Write the example in the space provided.

1. Jill uses *should* to tell Patty about something she expects to happen.

_____

2. Patty uses a form of *have to* to tell Jill about a commitment she made in the past.

_____

3. Patty uses *can't* to express disbelief.

_____

4. Jill uses *should* to describe something.

_____

B. Now, find the following sentences in the dialogue and come to an agreement with your partner about the function of each of the underlined modals. Make a generalization and write it in the space provided. Read the following example with your teacher.

EXAMPLE

You <u>should</u> really give him a chance. (line 11)
FUNCTION: <u>Should is used to give a suggestion</u>.

1. I <u>can</u> promise you won't regret it. (line 11)

   FUNCTION: _____

2. You <u>have to</u> come. (line 9)

   FUNCTION: _____

3. You <u>must</u> be kidding! (line 6)

   FUNCTION: _____

GRAMMATICAL PATTERNS ONE

I. MODAL FORMS

The following chart shows the forms that are possible with modals and their time reference.

FORM	EXAMPLE	TIME
MODAL + SIMPLE VERB	▪ I **can promise** you won't regret it. ▪ You **should get** a call from him tonight. ▪ I **had to help** my sister move.	Present Future Past
MODAL + PROGRESSIVE VERB	▪ You **must be kidding**. ▪ She **had to be kidding**.	Present Past
MODAL + PRESENT PERFECT VERBS	▪ You **should have come**.	Past[a]
MODAL + PRESENT PERFECT PROGRESSIVE VERB	▪ They **could have been dating**.	Past[a]

[a]Perfect modals **always** have a past time reference.

The context of the sentence will determine the time reference of the modal. Usually, time expressions are used to clarify the time reference. For example:

Karen has a big date tonight. She should wear something special.

Since the date is tonight, it can also be assumed it is tonight that Karen will wear something special.

II. THE USE OF MODALS

A. The Different Functions and Tenses of *Can / Could / Be Able To*

Can, could, and **be able to** are used for requests, offers, permission, ability, and possibility. As shown below, sometimes only the context will determine the distinction in these functions.

EXAMPLE	MEANING	FUNCTION
I **can't** read the letter.	▪ I am not **allowed** to read it because it's private.	PERMISSION
	▪ I am **unable to** read it because of your handwriting.	ABILITY
	▪ It's **impossible** for me to read it because I don't have time.	IMPOSSIBILITY
Can you help me?	▪ I am **asking** you to do this for me.	REQUEST
	▪ Is it **possible?** Do you have the time?	POSSIBILITY

SPECIAL NOTE

Notice the distinction between the function of **can, could,** and **be able to** in the following examples.

> I **could not** call him last night. (unsuccessful one-time action in the past)
> I **was able to** call him last night. (successful one-time action in the past)
> I **could** call him whenever I wanted to. (repeated action successful in the past)

12.1 ORAL PARAPHRASE: *State the Function*

DIRECTIONS: For each of the sentences below, paraphrase the various meanings that the sentence can have according to function.

EXAMPLE

We can't get married in my fiance's church.
The church will not give us permission because I am divorced. (PERMISSION)
The church doesn't have any openings on the day we planned to get married. (IMPOSSIBILITY)

1. I can't walk home from work.
2. Can you type this letter?
3. I couldn't pick up my package yesterday.
4. I can work for you tomorrow.
5. I was able to call my family from the post office last week.
6. I can't write this letter.
7. I can arrive at the church early.
8. When I was young, I could swim in the lake whenever I wanted to.

The chart below demonstrates how **can, could,** and **be able to** are often used with the same time reference. Note also that one form of the modal can be used for different time references.

TENSE	EXAMPLE	FUNCTION
PRESENT	I **can** play the piano.	Ability
	I **am not able** to give speeches.	Ability
	I **could** be in England right now.	Possibility
	(This is used in present unreal conditional sentences e.g., "I could be on the beach right now if I weren't so busy.")	
	I **can** take you home.	Offer
FUTURE	I **can** pick you up tomorrow at 4:00.	Possibility
	I **could** get married next year.	Possibility
	I **will be able** to attend my sister's wedding.	Possibility

| PAST | I **could** speak Spanish when I was very young. | Ability |
| | I **was able to** call him last night. | Possibility |

SPECIAL NOTE

CAN VS. COULD

As can be seen from the above examples, **can** and **could** are often used inter-changeably for the same function and tense. However, there is a slight distinction in meaning between these two modals in those cases. Look at the following examples:

I **can** arrive at the reception early to make additional arrangements.

I **could** arrive at the reception early to make additional arrangements.

Both of these examples express possibility in the future, but in the first example, the use of **can** expresses a slightly more *definite* possibility.

12.2   RAPID DRILL: *Can / Could / Be Able To*

DIRECTIONS: For each sentence below change the tense of the modal to the tense given at the end of the sentence. Then state what the function of the modal is. Sometimes there will be no change in the form of the modal despite the tense change.

EXAMPLE

I could arrive at the meeting early to help out. (past)

I wasn't able to arrive at the meeting early to help out.

1. I can sing a variety of international folk songs. (past)

2. I couldn't attend the meeting because I had a previous appointment. (future)

3. I wasn't able to take a vacation last year. (present)

4. I can drop him off at the party on my way home. (past)

5. I couldn't make any pie for dessert. (future)

6. I couldn't call him last week. (present)

B. Requests, Permission, and Offers

Notice in the chart below that nearly the same modals are used for these three functions. Discuss how the functions can be distinguished.

| POLITE REQUEST | Can / Could / May / Might | ▪ **Could** I get a price list, please? |
| | Can / Could / Would | ▪ **Would** you drop off the flowers tomorrow, please? |

PERMISSION	**May / Might / Can / Could** (Asking for permission) **May / Can / Can't / Could** (Giving / Refusing permission)	▪ **May** I ask for your only daughter's hand in marriage? ▪ You **can** attend the wedding reception even if you can't make it to the church.
OFFERS	**Can / Could** (Statement) **May / Can / Could** (Question)	▪ **I could** help you pick out your trousseau if you're having trouble making decisions. ▪ **May** I drive you home after the party?

12.3   ORAL PRACTICE: *Requests, Permission,* and *Offers*

DIRECTIONS: Using the cue provided, make a request or offer or grant or give permission.

EXAMPLE

CUE: You want to help send the wedding invitations.
RESPONSE: "I could help with the invitations."

1. You would like to bring a guest to your friend's wedding.
2. You don't want your daughter to stay out late.
3. You would like to pick your friend up on the way to a party.
4. You want to know if your teacher will let you miss class.
5. You would like to borrow a book about American weddings from your teacher.
6. You would like to help your friend move into a new apartment.
7. You want to know if your teacher will let you make up a test you missed.

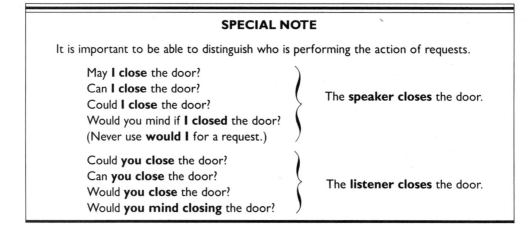

SPECIAL NOTE

It is important to be able to distinguish who is performing the action of requests.

May **I close** the door?
Can **I close** the door?
Could **I close** the door?
Would you mind if **I closed** the door?
(Never use **would I** for a request.)

     The **speaker closes** the door.

Could **you close** the door?
Can **you close** the door?
Would **you close** the door?
Would **you mind closing** the door?

     The **listener closes** the door.

12.4   RAPID DRILL: *Understanding Requests*

DIRECTIONS: For each request below, state what the result would be.

EXAMPLE

Would you mind lending me $1.00?
RESULT: The listener would give the speaker $1.00.

1. Can I borrow your book?
2. Could you turn the stereo down?
3. Would you mind if I smoked?
4. Would you light my cigarette?
5. Would you mind opening the window?

12.5   ORAL PRACTICE: *Making Requests*

DIRECTIONS: For each of the following situations, make two requests, one in which **you** want to perform the action and one in which you want **the listener** to perform the action. In most cases, it will be necessary to use a different verb for each request.

EXAMPLE

CUE: You want the phone number of the person you just met at a party.
RESPONSE: **Could I have** your phone number?
                   Would you mind giving me your phone number?

1. Your roommate has a beautiful book that you'd like to see.
2. You are going sightseeing and you'd like to borrow your friend's camera.
3. You would like to hear the end of the story that your teacher started telling at the end of the last class.
4. You'd like to talk on the phone sometime with the person you just met at a business lunch.
5. You need change for a dollar.
6. You need a ride to work / school tomorrow.

C. Expectation and Conclusion: Should / Ought to / Must

These two functions are similar because we have expectations or make conclusions based on previous information. However, notice the distinction in meaning as pointed out in the chart below.

EXPECTATION	should	▪ You **should** get a call from him tonight about the upcoming stag party.	Expresses what **will happen** in the future
	ought to	▪ The divorce rate **ought to** go down with the increased popularity of marriage counseling.	
CONCLUSION (Probability)	**must**	▪ These statistics **must** mean that most women prefer to establish a career first.	Expresses what **is true** at the present

12.6   WRITTEN EXERCISE: *Single Mother*

DIRECTIONS: Below are some sentences about a single working mother, Marj. After each sentence, there is one statement expressing <u>expectation</u> and one statement expressing <u>conclusion</u>. Decide whether the statement expresses expectation or conclusion and fill in one blank with **must** and the other with **should.**

EXAMPLE

CUE: Marj has been divorced with primary custody of her four-year old son, Nicholas, for two years.

RESPONSE: She <u>must be</u> be very busy. She <u>shouldn't</u> be so busy once her child starts school.

1. Marj works full-time at an advertising agency to support herself and her son.

    She _____ be getting a raise in the next six months, which will make life easier.

    She _____ be tired when she gets home at the end of the day.

2. She receives some child support from her ex-husband.

    She _____ appreciate having that extra support for Nicholas.

    She _____ be able to afford a private school for Nicholas next year.

3. Nicholas goes to stay with his father every other weekend.

    Nicholas _____ look forward to those visits since he is very close to his father.

    By next summer, Nicholas _____ be old enough to learn how to fish with his father.

4. Both Marj and her ex-husband contribute to an educational savings account for Nicholas.

    They _____ have $3,000 in the account by next summer.

    They _____ be very concerned·about being able to pay for Nicholas's education.

12.7   ORAL PRACTICE: *Expectation* and *Conclusion*

DIRECTIONS: Use **should, ought to,** or **must** depending on whether the question is asking you to make a conclusion or express an expectation.

EXAMPLE

QUESTION: Why do some people stay single?
ANSWER: They must not know anyone that they want to marry.

1. What will the next six months of your life be like?
2. Why is divorce so common now?
3. What will your city be like in ten years?
4. How can some people stay married to the same person for so many years?
5. How do you think it feels to give up a baby for adoption?
6. How will your English ability change by the end of this course?
7. Do you think there will be more women in the work force in the future?

PROBLEMS WITH *MUST* VS. *SHOULD*

DON'T USE *MUST* TO PREDICT THE FUTURE.

[INCORRECT:

- Lori and George have been dating for two years. They **must** get married.

Obligation, not conclusion

- They **must be going** to get married.]

Impossible form

CORRECT:

- They **must** love each other.

Conclusion

SHOULD CAN BE USED FOR *EXPECTATION* OR *SUGGESTION* WITH NO DIFFERENCE IN FORM.

- They **should** get married soon.

Expectation
(This is what we expect to happen.)
Suggestion
(This is what we think would be best.)

12.8   ORAL PRACTICE: *Should* vs. *Must*

DIRECTIONS: Comment on the following situations using **should** or **must** for expectation, suggestion, and conclusion.

EXAMPLE

SITUATION: Ted just got hired as a consultant to a large computer company after a six-month job search. This is a position that he has dreamed about for a long time.
CONCLUSION: Ted must be happy that he finally found a job.
SUGGESTION: He should be satisfied with the position.
EXPECTATION: He should receive a good salary for this position.

1. Coleen and Joe have four children. Joe has been unemployed for one year, and Coleen has been working as a nurse to support the family. Coleen and Joe just found out that they won $50,000 in the lottery.
2. Sharon is a university student who has done very poorly this semester. She still has a chance of passing if she does well on her final exams, so for the past week, she has been studying very hard.
3. Mohammed just arrived in the United States for a six-month intensive course of English language study. His wife and children were not able to come with him. He's hoping to improve his English and learn about American culture while he's here, but right now, he is very homesick.
4. Leo just returned to his country after spending six months in America. His English became very fluent while he was in America, and he made many American friends. He feels out of place back in his own country and is surprised to find that his friends don't understand him when he talks about his experiences.

D. Present and Past Habitual Activity

The top chart on page 270 shows the modals that are used to express present and past habits.

PRESENT HABITUAL ACTIVITY	be + used to + verb + -ing	Sharon **is used to taking** the bus.
PAST HABITUAL ACTIVITY	**used to**	Women **used to** stay at home with their children instead of having careers.
	would	They **would** sacrifice a career for their children.

12.9   RAPID DRILL: *Used to / Would*

DIRECTIONS: For each of the statements below about American marriage in the present, make a contrasting statement about what the past habit or custom was. Begin your statement with one of the following phrases: "In the past," or "Years ago."

EXAMPLE

CUE: Today many women don't get married until their late 20s or early 30s.

RESPONSE: In the past, women would get married in their early 20s.

1. Many couples choose to devote their lives to their careers and a variety of outside interests in place of having children.
2. If a married couple has children, they usually have only one or two.
3. Many women continue in their career after they have a child.
4. Because both the husband and wife are working, the child is taken to a day care center, or a babysitter comes to take care of the child.
5. Very often the extended family does not live in the same city, and the parents of a child can't depend on the child's grandparents or aunts and uncles for support.

12.10   WRITTEN EXERCISE: *American Dating Customs*

DIRECTIONS: The box below shows the difference in some American dating customs before and after the women's liberation movement. Write a paragraph contrasting the dating practices of yesterday and today. Use **would, used to,** and **be used to** whenever possible.

WHAT MEN DID BEFORE	WHAT WOMEN DO NOW
■ asked the woman out on a date	■ call the man for a date
■ opened car doors for women	■ open their own doors
■ paid the tab	■ pick up the tab or go dutch
■ lit a woman's cigarette	■ light their own cigarettes
■ made all the decisions about the date	■ take responsibility for the date

E. Description

This is a function that is most common in conversational English.

DESCRIPTION	should + verb of perception (see, hear, taste, smell)	You **should see** his eyes! They're your favorite color.

12.11   RAPID DRILL: *Using* Should *for Description*

DIRECTIONS: When your teacher or partner gives a cue below, use **should** to describe it.

EXAMPLE

CUE: You just returned from a trip to the Grand Canyon.
RESPONSE: You should see the Grand Canyon! It's amazing.

1. You just bought a brand new sports car.
2. You have been to a wonderful exhibit at the art gallery.
3. You really like the new CD that your favorite band or singer just released.
4. You're cooking soup and you think it's really good.
5. A friend of yours started wearing a new perfume that you think is very nice.

SPECIAL NOTE

Be careful not to confuse the use of **should** for suggestion, expectation, and conclusion.
Compare the following:
- From what I've heard about the price they paid, their wedding rings **should** be exquisite. (expectation)
- You **should** reconsider before you choose such an expensive wedding ring. (suggestion)
- You **should** see their wedding rings. They're beautiful! (description)

12.12   WRITTEN EXERCISE: *Functions of* Should

DIRECTIONS: Read the short passage below about divorce in the United States and ask your teacher any questions you may have about it. After you have read and understood the passage, discuss with your partner or the class as a group the issue of children in divorce and joint custody. As you discuss, use **should** to express expectation, conclusion, and description.

In a recently published report on divorce in the United States, statistics show that in the last ten years the divorce rate in the United States has increased significantly. Because of the increase in divorce, more attention is being paid to how divorce is affecting children and what arrangements are being made for custody of children when their parents get divorced. In the past, custody of the child in a divorce case was awarded to the mother. However, today many couples are trying joint custody, which means the child spends an equal amount of time with each parent. It is best if a couple can agree on a custody arrangement, but sometimes if the child is old enough, a parent will have the child testify in court in order to win the custody case.

F. Disbelief and Inappropriateness or Inaccuracy

These expressions are usually used in spoken English.

DISBELIEF	can't	<ul><li>You called your wedding off? You **can't** mean that!</li><li>I **can't believe** I ate the whole thing!</li></ul>
	must	<ul><li>She's going to be a single mother? You **must be** kidding!</li></ul>
INAPPROPRIATENESS OR INACCURACY	can't	<ul><li>You **can't** wear that dress! It's indecent.</li><li>You **can't** really call this a blind date. After all, I've seen her.</li></ul>

12.13   PAIRED PRACTICE: *Disbelief, Inappropriateness,* and *Inaccuracy*

DIRECTIONS: You and your partner have a friend who has decided to marry someone from another country. Take turns making the statements below about your friend. The other person should use **can't** or **must** to show that something is inappropriate or incorrect or to show disbelief and then give a suggestion related to that particular statement.

EXAMPLE

STUDENT A: Teresa is going to marry someone from another country!
STUDENT B: You must be kidding! She should think this over before she makes any rash decisions.

1. She's going to live in his country!
2. She's going to change her religion!
3. She's going to give up her career.
4. She'll only come back home to visit once a year!
5. She's going to be living in a very small village.

G. Suggestion / Recommendation / Advice

The chart below demonstrates how the modals used to give suggestions differ in strength.

WEAK	**might**[a]	You **might** make pizza.	Perhaps it's a good idea.
	could[a]	You **could** make bread.	I believe it's a good idea.
	should	You **should** make soup.	I believe it's the best idea.
	have to / must (conversational)	You **must** make pizza.	I very strongly believe it's the best idea.

STRONG	**had better**	You**'d better** make steak.	I am convinced that if you don't make steak, you'll be sorry.

[a]Pronunciation Hint: In order to express the above examples as suggestions, the following intonation pattern should be used:

You might make pizza.   NOT   I might make pizza.

You could make bread.   NOT   I could make bread.

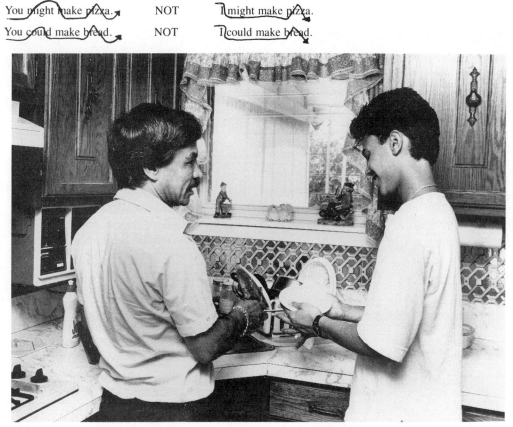

12.14   FILL IN THE BLANKS: *Marriage Counseling*

DIRECTIONS: In the dialogue below, a husband and wife are talking to their marriage counselor. For each suggestion given, fill in the blanks with the most appropriate modal from the chart beginning on page 272. There may be more than one correct answer.

WIFE: Rick just isn't willing to contribute at home. He thinks that because I'm the woman, I should do all the housework.

HUSBAND: Well, I'm at work all day. How can I do housework with a full-time job?

COUNSELOR: Yes, but Rick, don't forget that Cindy has a full-time job too. I don't know how

you feel about this, but you _____ share equally in the housework. Perhaps each

of you _____ have specific chores that you're responsible for.

HUSBAND: I don't know if that will work because even if I do some of the housework, I can't seem to do it right.

COUNSELOR: Cindy, if you want Rick to contribute more, you _____ trust him to do a good job.

WIFE: I realize that, but it's very difficult for me because he never does the kind of job that I would do.

COUNSELOR: That's because he's not you. You _____ start accepting him for what he

is, or he'll never trust you. You _____ appreciate the effort he makes and overlook the kind of job he's done.

12.15 ROLEPLAY: *Making Suggestions*

DIRECTIONS: Work in pairs. You and your partner have a brother, Rick, who is 32 years old and still single. You are very concerned about him because you know he really wants to get married. Use the above modals to make a variety of suggestions about how he can meet someone.

EXAMPLE

He might try joining a club.

12.16 EXERCISE: *Functions of Modals*

DIRECTIONS: Read the following cartoon and underline the modals. Discuss the function of each modal by paraphrasing the sentence in which it is used.

FOX TROT   by Bill Amend

Reprinted with permission of Universal Press Syndicate

H. Frustration or Annoyance

This function is used primarily in conversational English.

FRUSTRATION OR ANNOYANCE **HAS TO / HAD TO**[a]	
	• Of course, since we're having the reception outside, it **has to** rain! • They **had to** lower the tax deduction for married couples, didn't they?

MUST (question)	▪ **Must** the media print every detail about Charles's and Diana's married life?
WOULD	▪ You **would** show up at this party!
WOULD HAVE TO	▪ The teacher **would have to** announce my engagement to the class.

*If the proper intonation isn't used for this, the meaning can be interpreted as necessity. The falling intonation for tag questions is used and there is strong stress on the modal expression:

NECESSITY: They had to lower the tax deduction for married couples, didn't they?

ANNOYANCE: They had to lower the tax deduction for married couples, didn't they?

The teacher would have to announce my engagement to the class.

12.17 RAPID DRILL: *Expressing Frustration* or *Annoyance*

DIRECTIONS: When you studied progressive verbs, you learned that the progressive tense is used to express frustration or annoyance, for example, "You're always leaving the pots and pans in the sink." Below are a number of statements that a girlfriend used to express frustration to her boyfriend. Your partner or teacher will read the cue sentence, which will express frustration by using the progressive. Restate the sentence using **have to, must, would,** or **would have to.** If the past tense is used, make your restatement in the past tense.

EXAMPLE

CUE: You're forever standing me up.
RESPONSE: You have to stand me up, don't you?

1. You're always taking me to cheap restaurants.
2. You're forever talking about other women / men.
3. You're constantly reminding me about my weight.
4. You're continually talking about your accomplishments, but you show no interest in mine.
5. You're always asking me to make all the arrangements for our dates.
6. You're always asking me to drive.
7. You're forever showing up late for our dates.

12.18 ORAL PRACTICE: *Frustrating Situations*

DIRECTIONS: Express frustration or annoyance after your teacher or partner reads each of the situations below.

EXAMPLE

SITUATION: You receive a telephone call from a friend who says he is getting married. When he tells you the date of the wedding, you realize that you'll be out of the country.
FRUSTRATION: You had to schedule your wedding on a day I'm not going to be here, didn't you!

1. You just made arrangements to take your mother to a movie. Your boyfriend / girlfriend calls you up and asks you if you want to go out.

2. You are at a family wedding. You see your cousin walking toward you in the same outfit you have on.
3. You are sitting at the breakfast table with your family. You're looking in the newspaper for the announcement of your brother's wedding, which took place yesterday. You find it and discover that the newspaper has seriously misspelled your brother's name in the wedding announcement.
4. You're on the way to a wedding and you're 15 minutes late. You run out of gas.

I. Preference

Below are the expressions used to express preference.

MODAL	EXAMPLE	FORM
WOULD PREFER	**I'd prefer** to take the subway.	**prefer + to + verb**
WOULD RATHER	**I'd rather** make the decision at a later date.	**rather + verb**
WOULD JUST AS SOON	**I'd just as soon** get married in the university chapel.	**just as soon + verb**

12.19 PAIRED PRACTICE: *Preference*

DIRECTIONS: Take turns with your partner using the given cue and use one of the above forms to ask about a preference. Respond by stating your preference.

EXAMPLE

CUE: date someone from a different culture / date someone of a different religion
STUDENT A: Would you just as soon date someone from a different culture?
STUDENT B: I'd rather date someone of a different religion.

1. buy a new car / take a vacation
2. get married and have kids / be single
3. take a safari / go to a seaside resort
4. join a singles club / use a computer dating service
5. go to a disco / go to a movie

III. REVIEW

Below is a summary chart of modals according to their functions.

FUNCTION	MODAL	EXAMPLE
ABILITY	**can / be able to** (PRESENT) (PAST)	▪ Because of her artistic talent, she **can** design very well. ▪ He **was able** to dance years ago.

POSSIBILITY		
PRESENT	**can, be able to**	▪ The florist **can** deliver the bouquet early.
PAST	**was able to**	▪ Beth and Hiro **were able** to work out their cultural differences and got married.
FUTURE	**may / might**	▪ Carol **may** get married this summer if she decides she's ready to settle down.
	could / will be able to	▪ We **could** get married by next year.
	may / might	▪ We **may** go to Hawaii.
POLITE REQUEST	**can / could / may / might**	▪ **Could** I get a price list, please?
	would	▪ **Would** you drop off the flowers?
PERMISSION	**may / can / could**	▪ **May** I attend only the reception?
		▪ You **can** leave class early.
OFFERS	**may / can / could**	▪ I **could** help you prepare the food.
		▪ **May** I drive you home?
OBLIGATION		
PRESENT	**have to**	▪ Jim and Rose **have to** move.
	have got to	▪ We**'ve got to** decide by tomorrow.
	must	▪ You **must** have a blood test.
PAST	**had to**	▪ We **had to** wait for our test results.
SUGGESTION	**might**	▪ You **might** try another store.
	can / could	▪ We **could** have dinner.
	should	▪ You **should** give him a chance.
	ought to	▪ You **ought to** marry him.
	had better	▪ You**'d better** think very carefully.
	have to / must	▪ You **must** meet him!
EXPECTATION	**should**	▪ You **should** get a call from him soon.
	ought to	▪ The divorce rate **ought to** go down.
CONCLUSION	**must**	▪ The statistics **must** be right.
PRESENT / PAST HABITUAL ACTIVITY	**used to**	▪ Many women **are used** to balancing a career and a family at the same time. ▪ Women **used to** stay at home.
	would	▪ When she was young, she **would** dream of being a mother.
DESCRIPTION	**should** (+ see, hear, taste)	▪ You **should** see his eyes. They're your favorite color.
DISBELIEF	**can't**	▪ You **can't** mean that!
	must	▪ You **must** be kidding!

INAPPROPRIACY / INACCURACY	can't	• You **can't** wear that dress! It's indecent. • You **can't** really call this a blind date.
FRUSTRATION OR ANNOYANCE	have to must would / would have to	• You **had to** be late, didn't you? • **Must** the media exaggerate? • You **would** show up at this party!
PREFERENCE	would prefer would rather would just as soon	• **I'd prefer** to take the subway. • **I'd rather** make the decision later. • **I'd just as soon** get married now.

12.20 WRITTEN EXERCISE: *Situational Review*

DIRECTIONS: Read each situation and fill in the blanks in the statements that follow the situation with an appropriate modal.

EXAMPLE

Robin is waiting in the airport for Paul, her husband's brother, whom she has never met. She has only seen pictures of him. Suddenly she sees a man walking towards her.

a. This man looks different from the pictures, so she thinks, "That <u>can't</u> be Paul!"

b. The man is waving to her, so she thinks, "That <u>must</u> be Paul."

1. Randy and Maria are engaged to be married, and it is a week before their wedding. Randy has cold feet and wants to call the wedding off. Maria is talking to her best friend, Liz, about this.

   a. Maria is pleading with Liz for assistance and says, "You _____ help me!"

   b. Liz is shocked to hear the news and says, "He _____ be kidding!"

   c. Maria is so frustrated with the situation that she says, "He _____ get cold feet, didn't he?"

2. Sally and Dave are out on a date and have just had dinner. They are discussing their plans.

   a. Dave is really full and knows it is unhealthy to sit after eating so much. He says, "We

   _____ go sit in a movie after such a big meal!"

   b. Dave doesn't want to get up and leave yet, so he says, "_____ I buy you an after-dinner drink?"

   c. Sally feels very strongly that she needs to get some fresh air, so she says, "We

   _____ take a walk now."

3. Roxanne and Greg have made plans to go to Hawaii for their honeymoon. Greg's brothers are discussing the plans.

    a. The brothers think that the honeymoon will be great, so one of them says, "They

    _____ have a wonderful honeymoon in Hawaii.''

    b. One of the brothers thinks that the best recreation in Hawaii is water sports, so he says,

    "They _____ rent a boat.''

    c. One of the brothers thinks that it would be impolite for them to leave the reception early,

    so he says, "They _____ leave for the honeymoon until the reception is over.''

12.21 ORAL INTERVIEW

DIRECTIONS: Interview two or three English-speaking people between the ages of 20–35. Explain that you are a foreign student and that you are writing a report about dating and marriage customs.

1. How can a single person meet men / women in your country?
2. What are some rules about a first date in your country? (for example, dress, topics of conversation, behavior)
3. How are dating and marriage customs different today than they were in the past?

12.22 WRITTEN FEEDBACK

DIRECTIONS: Use modal constructions to report on your interview.

1. Write at least two sentences reporting the information you received about meeting men / women.
2. Write three sentences explaining rules about a first date.
3. Write one sentence explaining how dating and marriage customs are different today than they were in the past.

══════ GRAMMATICAL PATTERNS TWO ══════

══════════ PREVIEW ══════════

DIRECTIONS: Read the following letter that a young man wrote to the Dear Priscilla advice column in the newspaper.

Dear Priscilla,

1. I am 24 years old and single. For the past six months I've been dating Coleen, a girl that I met at work. I care very deeply for her and have even had thoughts of marriage, but now I'm sure there's no hope for that.

2. On our first date, Coleen told me that she's a very religious person. She also said that she's looking for a man who has the same religious convictions that she has. I know I should've told her the truth right then and there, but I could've lost the opportunity to get to know her better. You see, I'm an **atheist,** but I told her that I too am very deeply religious. All these months I've pretended to share her feelings about religion, and she must've believed me because we've become very close.

3. Last night we were at a movie and I made a sarcastic remark about the religious discussion two people were having. Coleen became furious. You should've heard her screaming at me! In my opinion, for such a religious person she shouldn't have been so hysterical. She might've tried to be more **levelheaded** about the whole issue. Anyway, I became furious too and told her the truth. I apologized and admitted I shouldn't have been pretending to be something I wasn't.

4. On one hand, I feel a bit relieved because I couldn't have pretended much longer. On the other hand, I really love Coleen and she should've called by now to make plans for tonight. Please help. . . .   Afraid That It's Over

VOCABULARY

atheist: a person who has no God or religion
levelheaded: rational and logical rather than irrational and impulsive

DISCUSSION

Is it important that two people who plan to marry share the same religious convictions? Can a relationship work if the man and woman have extremely different religious beliefs?

GRAMMAR CONSIDERATIONS: FOCUS

DIRECTIONS: Find four examples in the preceding letter of sentences containing modals and write them on the lines provided below. For each one, write what <u>really happened</u> and how the writer <u>feels about it</u>.

EXAMPLE

I know I should've told her the truth right then and there, but I could've lost the opportunity to get to know her better.

REALITY: He didn't tell her the truth, and he got to know her better.
FEELING: He regrets not telling the truth, but he's happy about getting the opportunity to know her better.

SENTENCE 1: _____

REALITY: _____

FEELING: _____

SENTENCE 2: _____

REALITY: _____

FEELING: _____

SENTENCE 3: _____

REALITY: _____

FEELING: _____

SENTENCE 4: _____

REALITY: _____

FEELING: _____

What generalization can you make about the meaning of these modal constructions?

_____

I. PERFECT MODALS

A. Perfect Modal Forms

Perfect modals are formed in the following way:

SIMPLE PERFECT Modal + have + past participle	I **should have told** her the truth.
PERFECT PROGRESSIVE Modal + have + been + verb - ing	I **shouldn't have been pretending** to be something I wasn't.

12.23 RECOGNITION EXERCISE: *Perfect Modal Forms*

DIRECTIONS: Underline all the perfect modals in the Dear Priscilla letter.

B. The Functions of Perfect Modals

In general, perfect modals are used to express **unfulfilled** or **unrealized** actions or events. They serve some of the same functions that have already been covered in this chapter, as demonstrated in the chart below.

MODAL	FUNCTION	EXAMPLE
COULD HAVE	possibility disbelief	▪ I **could've lost** the opportunity to get to know her better ▪ You **couldn't have** thought that I would accept such a foolish excuse! ▪ How **could** you **have thought** that I would accept such a foolish excuse? ▪ I **couldn't have** married her anyway because neither of us wanted to move to another country.
MAY / MIGHT HAVE	possibility (may or might) suggestion	▪ Your advisor **may have been able** to help you out with that application. ▪ She **might have tried** to be more levelheaded about the whole issue.

SHOULD HAVE / OUGHT TO HAVE	expectation	■ She **ought to have called** by now since it's 8:15 and she said she'd call by 8:00.
	regret or judgment about past action	■ I know I **should have told** her the truth right then and there. (But I didn't and I regret it.) ■ I **shouldn't have been pretending** to be something I wasn't. (I **did** pretend and I regret it.)
MUST HAVE	conclusion	■ She **must have believed** me because we've become very close.

SPECIAL NOTE

For the perfect form of **should,** notice this switch!

IF	THEN
■ If the past action is positive,	then the present statement is negative.
■ If the past action is negative,	then the present statement is positive.

12.24 ORAL DRILL: *Judgment* with *Should Have* and *Shouldn't Have*

DIRECTIONS: Below are some problems and the solutions that were made to the problems. Decide on a better solution for each problem and state it using **should have.**

1. John was very shy, so he never asked Maria out.
2. Jack didn't have enough money to pay for the dinner, so he left without paying.
3. Marge didn't know which date to accept for the dance, so she didn't go.
4. Bob didn't want to go out with Jill anymore, so he stood her up yesterday.
5. At the last minute, Annette decided that John wasn't the right person for her to marry, but it was the day of the wedding and everyone was in the church, so she married him anyway.
6. Kathy and Jim have been married for ten years and have a four-year-old son. They haven't been getting along for the past year and don't love each other anymore, but they decided to stay together for their son.

12.25 WRITTEN EXERCISE: *Problem-Solving*

DIRECTIONS: Read the passage at the top of page 283 with your partner and work together to complete the chart that follows the passage. First, state each problem of this situation in your own words. Then make a conclusion about each particular problem using **must have.** Finally, state how the problems **should have** been solved. Be ready to share your ideas orally with the class. There is an example at the beginning of each column.

Diane was married and pregnant with her first child. She had a full-time job as chief editor of a woman's magazine. She and her husband, Tim, discussed what her work schedule would be after she had the baby, but they couldn't come to an agreement. She had decided that she couldn't give up her career and she wanted to go back to work full time when the baby was six weeks old. Tim didn't agree with this; he thought she should stay home for the first year. He was willing to work long hours to provide the extra income for this. Diane was afraid that if she didn't go back to work right away, she would lose her position. John was worried that if Diane went back to work, the baby wouldn't get proper care.

PROBLEMS (REAL FACTS)	CONCLUSIONS	CRITICAL JUDGMENTS
1. Diane didn't want to give up her job.	1. She must have really enjoyed working at her job.	1. She should have returned to work when the baby was three months old.
2. _____ _____ .	2. _____ _____ .	2. _____ _____ .
3. _____ _____ .	3. _____ _____ .	3. _____ _____ .
4. _____ _____ .	4. _____ _____ .	4. _____ _____ .
5. _____ _____ .	5. _____ _____ .	5. _____ _____ .

12.26 READING AND DISCUSSION: *The "Baby M" Case*

DIRECTIONS: Read the following passage about a surrogate mother. Then, in pairs discuss the questions that follow the passage, using **must have** to make conclusions.

In 1984, Mary Beth Whitehead signed a $10,000 contract with Elizabeth and John Stern to be a surrogate mother for them because they were unable to have their own child. This meant that she would be artificially inseminated, carry their baby for nine months, deliver the baby, and give it up to them. After she delivered the baby, known as Baby M, Mary Beth had second thoughts and didn't want to give her up to the Sterns. She escaped with the baby, but she was found, and the case later went to court as a custody battle. The Sterns won custody of Baby M, and Mary Beth was given minimal visitation rights.

EXAMPLE

QUESTION: How do you think Elizabeth and John Stern felt when they found out they couldn't have a child of their own?

1. Why do you think Mary Beth Whitehead agreed to be a surrogate mother to begin with?
2. How do you think Mary Beth Whitehead felt after she delivered the baby?
3. What arguments do you think were used on both sides of the court case?
4. How do you think the Sterns felt when they won custody of Baby M?
5. How do you think Elizabeth Whitehead felt when the Sterns won custody of Baby M?
6. What are your opinions? Use **should have / shouldn't have.**

12.27   PAIRED PRACTICE: *Your Past*

DIRECTIONS: Use perfect modals to talk about your past with your partner. Express unrealized possibilities, regrets, disbelief, and untapped abilities. Try to use the following verbs along with any other verbs that you need: **work, do, spend, think, tell, buy, feel, teach.**

EXAMPLE

I should have worked at a part time job when I was in college, so that I wouldn't still be paying off student loans.

12.28   WRITTEN EXERCISE: *Arranged Marriages*

DIRECTIONS: For each situation below about the practice of arranged marriages, write sentences expressing the given functions. Use perfect modals. The first one is done for you as an example.

1. In some countries, there was no dating because arranged marriages were the custom.
   JUDGMENT: Parents should have allowed dating if that's what the children preferred.

   DISBELIEF: _____

   CONCLUSION: _____
2. In the past, a woman was expected to marry the man her family chose for her and devote her life to him.

   CONCLUSION: _____

   DESCRIPTION: _____

   IMPOSSIBILITY: _____
3. Since divorce was uncommon in those days, if either the husband or wife discovered that they were mismatched, they were forced to accept the situation.

   JUDGMENT: _____

   INABILITY: _____

II. PASSIVE AND PROGRESSIVE AFTER MODALS

As you saw in the chart at the beginning of the chapter, modals can be followed by progressive verb constructions with present or past time reference, as in the following examples.

MODAL + PROGRESSIVE

1. You **can't be taking** all those books with you!	PRESENT
2. The immigration office **should have been keeping** you informed about your visa.	PAST

MODAL + PASSIVE

3. Because of his outstanding achievement, he **should be awarded** the scholarship.	PRESENT
4. Contrary to the media reports, her life **couldn't have been saved.**	PAST

12.29 FILL IN THE BLANKS: *Progressive* and *Passive After Modals*

DIRECTIONS: Below are some sentences about teenage pregnancy. Fill in the blanks with a modal and the passive or progressive form of the verb in parentheses.

EXAMPLE

Teenage pregnancy is an issue that <u>should be discussed</u> (discuss) by teenagers, their parents, and their teachers.

1. Teenagers _____ (inform) about the dangers of promiscuity.

2. Such a high teenage pregnancy rate _____ _____ (avoid) through better education.

3. After some parents find out that their teenage daughters are pregnant, they realize that they _____ (educate) their daughters more carefully.

4. Some parents can't believe that this could happen to their daughters and they think that their daughters _____ (pressure) by their peers.

5. There is a lot of controversy about whether contraceptives should _____ _____ (distribute) to high school students at a school clinic.

6. Teenagers _____ (think) about the consequences of their actions.

12.30 WRITTEN EXERCISE: *Paraphrasing*

DIRECTIONS: Paraphrase each situation using a passive or progressive modal. The beginning of the paraphrase is provided.

EXAMPLE

It's impossible that Stan and Jill were communicating very well.

Stan and Jill *couldn't have been communicating very well.*

1. It was impossible to save their marriage.

Their marriage _____

2. I'm not sure if they were going steady when I met them, but it's possible.

They _____

3. Joe and Sarah didn't tell their parents they were getting married and I think that's wrong.

Their parents _____

4. They told everyone they were happy, but now we can only conclude that they were lying.

They _____

5. It's regretful that they weren't seeing a marriage counselor.

They _____

6. I can only conclude that they told their daughter, Kathy, about the separation.

Their daughter _____

12.31   WRITTEN EXERCISE: *Answering the Letter*

DIRECTIONS: Write an answer to the letter on pages 279–280. Use perfect modals in your answer.

III. SPECIAL PROBLEMS WITH MODALS

PROBLEM	EXPLANATION
USING THE WRONG VERB FORM AFTER A MODAL [INCORRECT: ■ We **must to do** our homework on time. ■ They **can getting** the food for the party. ■ I **could took** her out on a date. ■ We **should does** our homework on time.] CORRECT: ■ We **must do** our homework on time. ■ They **can get** the food for the party. ■ I **could take** her out on a date. ■ We **should do** our homework on time.	The present simple form of the verb follows a modal.
USING AN ENDING ON A MODAL [INCORRECT: ■ Bill **coulds earn** a higher salary as an accountant.] CORRECT: ■ Bill **could earn** a higher salary as an accountant.	Tense and person markers are never added to modals.

MIXING TWO MODALS TOGETHER [INCORRECT: ■ I **might can attend** the meeting.] CORRECT: ■ I **might attend** the meeting. OR ■ I **might be able to attend** the meeting.	Only one modal should be used at a time, except when a modal is used before **be able to.**
MAKING MODALS NEGATIVE WITH **DON'T** [INCORRECT: ■ We **don't can solve** this problem easily.] CORRECT: ■ We **can't solve** this problem easily.	Make a modal negative by adding **not** to the modal.
INCORRECT PARTICIPIAL FORM FOR PERFECT MODALS [INCORRECT: ■ I **could have went** out with him, but I didn't want to.] CORRECT: ■ I **could have gone** out with him, but I didn't want to.	The past participle form is used for perfect modals.

■ 12.32   ERROR ANALYSIS

DIRECTIONS: Find the error in each of the following sentences and correct it.

1. Karen thought that a computer dating service must to be a more reliable way of meeting eligible men.

2. When she first heard about the service, she didn't was able to decide if she wanted to sign up.

3. After she signed up, she had to deciding which man she wanted to contact.

4. She could have went out with ten different men.

5. She must is going to meet someone she likes eventually.

6. She cans refuse a date with any of these men if she wants to.

7. She had to gave a lot of information about herself when she filled out the application.

8. She should have wrote only the truth about herself, but she lied about her height.

9. She couldn't have meeting any men if she hadn't signed up for this service.

10. Caroline should might meet someone that she really likes through the computer dating service.

ANALYSIS OF AN AUTHENTIC TEXT

PREREADING QUESTIONS

Are astrological signs important to you? Do you want to make sure you marry someone with a compatible astrological sign? Is it important to get to know the family of your future husband / wife?

DIRECTIONS: Read the following excerpt from *Linda Goodman's Star Signs*. This description of the Cancer man (June 22–July 23) is addressed to the girlfriends of men born under this sign.

THE CANCER MAN

1. Let's hope you find his mother **congenial.** In fact, let's pray you do. It's fairly certain she'll pop up in his conversation frequently, in remarks like, "You use frozen pies and instant potatoes? My mother used to bake her own bread when I was a youngster." This **paragon** of virtue is quite likely to pop up just as often in person, when you least expect it. "Darling I have to cancel our date for the theater tonight. I'm driving mother out to the country for a few days." To put it mildly, the Cancer man may be **reluctant** to **dethrone** Mama and crown you as his new queen.
2. There are certain **traits,** however, that can even up the score in your relationship. For one, he'll be a pretty good chef himself. He may surprise you with his ability to whip up a gourmet meal.

VOCABULARY

Look up the following words in your dictionary if you're not sure of their meanings.

congenial
paragon
reluctant
dethrone
traits

COMPREHENSION QUESTIONS

1. How does the Cancer man feel about his mother?
2. How will a girlfriend of a Cancer man feel about his mother?

GRAMMATICAL ANALYSIS

DIRECTIONS: Decide which modals given in parentheses after each sentence can replace the underlined modal in the sentence without changing the meaning. Discuss how the meaning would change if the other modals were used.

1. My mother used to bake her own bread when she was a youngster. (would, had to, could)
2. Darling, I have to cancel our date for the theater tonight. (had to, must, should, might)
3. To put it mildly, the Cancer man may be reluctant to dethrone Mama. (must, can, should, had better)

4. There are certain traits, however, that <u>can</u> even up the score in your relationship. (may, could, should)

COMPOSITION TOPICS

In this chapter you have had the opportunity to find out about and discuss dating, marriage, and divorce. Now formulate your ideas in a well-organized and well-written composition. Choose a topic from those listed below.

1. Describe your match made in heaven. What personality traits should this person possess? What requirements does the person have to meet?

2. Compare the process of dating, engagement, and marriage in the United States with how it is done in your country. Are there certain rules, requirements, or customs that are followed?

3. Describe a relationship you had once that was not as successful as you would have liked. State what you could have or should have done differently.

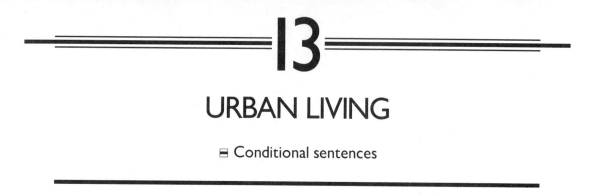

URBAN LIVING

▣ Conditional sentences

URBAN LIVING　　(Life in the big city)

DISCUSSION QUESTIONS

1. What American cities do you know about? If you could live in any American city, which one would you choose and why?
2. Do you know about any of the problems that exist in American cities? Are these problems similar to those in your country's cities?
3. What is being done in your country to solve these problems? If you had power and influence, how would you solve some of the urban problems in your country?

OBJECTIVES

In this chapter you will learn:

1. To use conditional sentences to express future, present unreal, and past unreal situations
2. To use conditional sentences to describe present and past habitual activity
3. To use mixed time reference in conditional sentences
4. To make inferences with conditional sentences
5. To use **wish** to express conditional meaning and to distinguish between **wish** and **hope**
6. To use several expressions that can replace *if* in conditional sentences

═══ PREVIEW ═══

DIRECTIONS: Read the following letter to the editor written by a resident of Los Angeles who is concerned about the problems that exist in that city.

IT'S A NICE PLACE TO VISIT BUT I WOULDN'T WANT TO LIVE HERE

Dear Editor:

1. I moved to Los Angeles 40 years ago from the East coast because it was being **lauded** as the closest thing to **paradise** in this country. For years, Los Angeles lived up to that description, but unfortunately that is no longer true. If someone had asked me 40 years ago, I never would have predicted that this city would change so much in such a short time. It seems that the leaders here should be doing more to put an end to the homelessness, gang violence, drug abuse, and severe smog that are plaguing our city. If there weren't such serious problems here in L.A. it would still be a desirable place to live, as it was in the past.

2. One of our leaders has the habit of claiming that homeless people have the problems they do because they're comfortable in that lifestyle. This is obviously just a **feeble excuse** for supporting what he feels are more worthwhile causes. Well, if he had paid more attention to this problem from the beginning of his administration, the number of "comfortable" homeless people on the streets wouldn't have risen so rapidly.

3. Drug abuse and the gang violence that results from it are making our streets unsafe and our schools a threat to our children's lives. If these problems were solved, we could send our children to school without worrying about whether they would make it home. Not long ago, if a child was caught smoking a cigarette on **school grounds**, severe punishment was enforced. Nowadays, children are caught selling or using drugs, and some of them carry weapons to arm themselves in wars against their **peers**.

4. Finally, we all know that the smog level in this city has reached dangerous proportions. If stricter **emission control** laws aren't enforced soon, the air that we breathe to keep us alive will eventually kill us.

5. I certainly hope that my concerns are shared by other people who came here for a higher standard of living and a more comfortable life but are finding their lives at risk instead.

A CONCERNED RESIDENT

VOCABULARY

lauded: praised

paradise: heaven, a perfect place

feeble excuse: a weak, unconvincing excuse

school grounds: the school building and immediate surrounding area designated as belonging to the school

peers: the people who share a similar rank, position, ability, and so forth

emission control: a limit on the amount of dangerous substance that can be let out into the air by cars, factories, and so forth

CULTURAL NOTE / DISCUSSION

Gang violence in American cities is becoming a serious problem. A gang is a group of youth usually of high school age and from one particular ethnic group. Gangs are usually involved in dealing drugs and, as a result, there is a high level of competition among different gangs. This very often leads to serious violence. Are there gangs in your country? What kinds of problems do these gangs cause?

GRAMMAR CONSIDERATIONS: FOCUS

The following questions are based on the preview text and are designed to help you find out what you already know about the structures in this chapter. Some of the questions may be hard and some of them may be easy. Answer as many of the questions as you can. Work with a partner if your teacher tells you to do so.

1. The following sentence from the preview describes a situation that is untrue or unreal in the present. In the space provided, write what the truth or reality of the situation is.
   If there weren't such serious problems in our city, it would still be a desirable place to live.

   REALITY: _____

2. Each of the following conditional sentences describes a situation that is untrue or unreal in the past. On the lines after each of the sentences, write what the truth or reality is.
   a. If he had paid more attention to this problem from the beginning of his administration, the number of "comfortable" homeless people on the streets wouldn't have risen so rapidly.

   REALITY: _____

   b. If someone had asked me 40 years ago, I never would have predicted that this city would change so much in such a short time.

   REALITY: _____

3. In the if- clauses of the following two sentences, notice that the present tense is used in sentence a, and the past tense is used in sentence b. Does sentence a describe a **present** situation? Does sentence b describe a **past** situation?
   a. If stricter emission control laws *aren't enforced* soon, the air that we breathe to keep us alive will eventually kill us.
   b. If these problems *were solved*, we could send our children to school without worrying about whether they would make it home.

GRAMMATICAL PATTERNS ONE

I. THE STRUCTURE OF THE CONDITIONAL SENTENCE

Most conditional sentences have a subordinate clause beginning with **if** and a main clause, which in most cases contains a modal and a main verb. As in other complex sentences, the order of the clauses is optional. Look at the following examples and notice the structure and punctuation of both sentences.

If I lived downtown, I could walk to work.
I could walk to work if I lived downtown.

If- Clause (Subordinate Clause)	Main Clause
If I lived downtown,	I could walk to work.

II. THE FUNCTION OF CONDITIONAL SENTENCES

The following chart summarizes the main types of conditional sentences and the function each of them serves.

TYPE	EXPLANATION	EXAMPLE
FUTURE	Depending upon the condition, something may happen in the future.	If we clean up our city, it will be a nicer place to live.
PRESENT UNREAL	Describes a situation that is not true or not real at the present time.	I wouldn't have to deal with these problems if I lived in the country.
PAST UNREAL	Describes a situation that was not true or real in the past.	If L.A. hadn't been so desirable years ago, I wouldn't have moved here.
PRESENT OR PAST HABITUAL ACTIVITY	Depending upon the condition, an activity was done habitually in the present or past.	If people moved here, it was for the beautiful weather and the wide open spaces.

A. Future Conditional

The following conditional patterns are used to express possibility or probability in the future. Notice that *will* is **not** used in the if- clause although the time reference is future.

VERB TENSE / MODALS IN IF- CLAUSE	VERB TENSE / MODALS IN MAIN CAUSE
SIMPLE PRESENT TENSE	FUTURE TENSE MODALS: MAY / MIGHT, CAN / COULD, SHOULD / OUGHT TO

• If stricter laws **aren't enforced**,	the air we breathe **will kill** us.
• If I **move** to Seattle,	I **should be prepared** for a lot of rain.
• If the downtown development **continues**,	we **could have** a really nice city.

13.1 RAPID DRILL: *Future Conditional*

DIRECTIONS: With a partner use the following cues to make statements about your future in the city you are presently living in.

1. If the population increases, . . .
2. If the cultural life improves, . . .
3. If more highways are built, . . .
4. If the crime rate goes up, . . .
5. If the immigrant population increases, . . .
6. If the public transportation system improves, . . .

SPECIAL NOTE

There are a few other ways of expressing future possibility with the conditional.

1. The following expressions added to the simple form of the verb in the **if**- clause emphasize lower probability in the future. Notice that this pattern is similar in structure to the future conditional pattern.

IF- CLAUSE	MAIN CLAUSE
If I **happen to move**,	I **might sell** my car.
If you **should happen to visit**,	you **could see** the new mall.

SHOULD
SHOULD HAPPEN TO } + SIMPLE
HAPPEN TO   VERB

FUTURE TENSE
MODALS: MAY / MIGHT, CAN / COULD, SHOULD / OUGHT TO

2. The following two patterns also express lower probability in the future. The pattern of these sentences is similar to the present unreal conditional pattern, which will be presented in the next section.

If I **were to sell** my car,	I **would have** some extra money.
(**were to** + simple verb)	(**would, might, could**)

The past tense can be used in the if- clause to emphasize lower probability.

If I **got** a new job,	I **could move** to another city.
If I **moved** to another city,	I **might** be happier.
(past tense)	(**would, might, could**)

Note that none of these patterns can be used in the negative except for the last one.

13.2   PAIRED ORAL PRACTICE: *Low Probability in the Future Conditional*

DIRECTIONS: A large American city is planning a benefit rock concert to raise funds for the homeless community. The concert will be held outdoors in the streets of a downtown neighborhood on a Saturday afternoon at 12:00. The planning committee is having a meeting to discuss the arrangements for the concert, and some of the committee members are asking questions about possible situations. Take turns with your partner asking and answering the questions. Use future conditional sentences and emphasize low probability.

EXAMPLE

QUESTION: What if it rains?

• ANSWER: If it should happen to rain, the concert will be postponed.

1. What if the city council objects to the idea?
2. What if we have a problem selling tickets?
3. What if some of the bands back out at the last minute?
4. What if we run out of food?
5. What if we need first aid?
6. What if the crowd gets out of control?

13.3   WRITTEN EXERCISE: *Fill in the Blanks*

DIRECTIONS: Below are some sentences about possible future situations. Fill in the blanks with a correct form of the verb given. Use any of the future conditional forms you have practiced.

1. If I _____ (win) the lottery next week, I _____

    _____ (take) a trip around the world.

2. I _____ (inform) my bank if I _____

    (change) my name.

3. If you _____ (shave) your head, many people _____

    _____ (look) at you strangely.

4. You _____ (have) a lot of diapers to change if you _____

    _____ (decide) to have a baby.

5. If an earthquake _____ (strike) tonight, you _____

    _____ (stand) under a doorway.

13.4   WRITTEN EXERCISE: *The Pollution Problem*

DIRECTIONS: Los Angeles is suffering serious environmental consequences from being a highly populated metropolitan area and the largest manufacturing center in the United States. In order to improve the situation, certain conditions must be met. For each problem stated below, write a future conditional sentence that expresses the possibility for solving the problem in the future. The first solution is provided for you.

1. PROBLEM: Paint pollution: Many polluting ingredients are released into the air by drying paint and solvents on houses, cars, aircraft, and other products.

   SOLUTION: If the polluting ingredients were to be taken out of the paint, there would be less harm to the environment.

2. PROBLEM: Millions of people commute to work in cars that emit pollutants into the environment.

   SOLUTION: _____

   _____

3. PROBLEM: Many polluting ingredients are being released by factories into the ocean, killing marine life and ultimately upsetting the balance of nature.

   SOLUTION: _____

   _____

4. PROBLEM: With the growing population in Los Angeles, there is an increasing amount of garbage that needs to be dumped.

   SOLUTION: _____

   _____

5. PROBLEM: The beautiful beaches are being littered with trash by inconsiderate sunbathers.

   SOLUTION: _____

   _____

B. Present Unreal Conditional

This conditional structure is probably the most difficult to master. It tends to be confusing because, although the time reference is present, the past tense of the verb is used in the if-clause. A good way to check your understanding of the unreal conditional is to state what is **real.** The chart below demonstrates how the reality can be stated, based on the unreal situation in the conditional sentence. Notice the following:

If	Then
Reality is positive.	Unreal conditional is negative.
Reality is negative.	Unreal conditional is positive.

VERB TENSE / MODALS IN *IF*- CLAUSE	VERB TENSE / MODALS IN MAIN CLAUSE
If there **weren't** such serious problems here, If I **wasn't** so busy, (informal spoken English) If I **didn't live** in a safe neighborhood, SIMPLE PAST **or** SIMPLE PAST CONTINUOUS **or** COULD + SIMPLE VERB	it **would** still be a desirable place to live. I **would** do volunteer work. I **might** feel less secure. WOULD (100% certainty) MIGHT, COULD (less certainty)

SPECIAL NOTE

If the verb **be** is used, **were** is the proper form regardless of the subject. However, in informal spoken American English, this form is becoming less common, and Americans often use **was.**

13.5 WRITTEN EXERCISE: *Gangs*

DIRECTIONS: The existence of gangs and gang violence is on the rise in the United States. Gang members usually come from the same ethnic group and are of high school age. Violence and drug dealing are common among gangs. For each of the following sentences about the existence of gangs and gang violence in U.S. cities, write a conditional sentence stating a present unreality based on the information given.

EXAMPLE

Some high school kids belong to gangs because it gives them a sense of identity.

If these kids had a stronger sense of identity, they wouldn't belong to gangs.

1. Some gangs are formed because ethnic groups want to protect their territory.

_____.

2. Gang members wear certain colors so that their fellow gang members can identify them.

_____.

3. Because many of the gangs are dealing drugs, life is very dangerous for them.

_____.

4. Since these kids can acquire dangerous weapons easily, gang warfare is very common.

_____.

5. Because these kids don't value human life, they are killing each other foolishly.

_____.

13.6   ORAL CHAIN DRILL: *If I Lived in Paris*

DIRECTIONS: One student will begin by completing the statement, "If I lived in Paris . . ."
The next student will begin a sentence with the new information the previous student provided
and will complete that statement. Continue in this manner so that each student can add some
information. For the next round, choose a new city.

EXAMPLE

STUDENT A: "If I lived in Paris, I would buy a lot of expensive perfume."
STUDENT B: "If I bought a lot of expensive perfume, I wouldn't have enough money to eat."

13.7   PAIRED ACTIVITY: *Your City*

DIRECTIONS: For each topic below, write a statement describing either a positive or negative
characteristic of your city. Then, discuss each topic with your partner using at least one present
unreal conditional sentence to qualify or clarify the statement you wrote.

EXAMPLE

TOPIC: Pollution
WRITTEN: The pollution level in my city is very low.
SPOKEN: "One very positive characteristic of my city is that the air is clean. The pollution
level is so low because my city is at a high altitude and there is very little industry there. If there
were more industry, I'm sure the air wouldn't be so clean."

1. TOPIC: Population

   STATEMENT: _____

2. TOPIC: Housing

   STATEMENT: _____

3. TOPIC: Culture / Entertainment

   STATEMENT: _____

4. TOPIC: Food

   STATEMENT: _____

5. TOPIC: Mass Transit

   STATEMENT: _____

C. Past Unreal Conditional

The forms in the following chart are used to describe unreal situations in the past. As with the
present unreal conditional, it is easier to understand the past unreal if the **reality** is clear.

VERB TENSE / MODALS IN THE *IF-* CLAUSE	VERB TENSE / MODALS IN THE MAIN CLAUSE
If someone **had asked** me thirty years ago, (Reality: Nobody asked me.) PAST PERFECT	I **would** never **have predicted** that this city would change so much. PERFECT MODALS: (WOULD, COULD, SHOULD, MAY, MIGHT) + HAVE + PAST PARTICIPLE
If social work agencies **had been receiving** more government assistance, (Reality: They weren't receiving assistance.) PAST PERFECT PROGRESSIVE	they **could have been doing** much more to help the homeless. PERFECT MODALS

Pronunciation Hint: In spoken English, **would have** is very often contracted in the following way:

I would have gone downtown this afternoon if I hadn't finished work so late.
I would've gone downtown this afternoon if I hadn't finished work so late.
I'd have gone downtown this afternoon if I hadn't finished work so late.
Ida gone downtown this afternoon if I hadn't finished work so late. (Not used with the negative.)

13.8   RAPID DRILL: *Past Unreal Situations*

DIRECTIONS: For each situation given below, make a statement expressing a past unreality.

EXAMPLE

CUE: Gary's flight to New York was at 7:00, so he had to get up very early.
RESPONSE: If Gary's flight hadn't been at 7:00, he wouldn't have had to get up so early.

1. He stayed up very late the previous night closing a business deal.
2. He overslept and missed his flight to New York.
3. There was an empty seat on the next flight, so he made his connecting flight in Chicago.
4. It was very late when he arrived in Chicago, so he couldn't call his friend who lives there.
5. He felt tired on the flight, so he fell asleep for a few hours.
6. He missed the in-flight movie because he was sleeping.
7. He had called his wife from Chicago, so she knew he was going to arrive late.
8. She couldn't pick him up at the airport because she was working.

13.9   PAIRED PRACTICE: *Stranger in a Strange Land*

DIRECTIONS: Tell your partner about an interesting, funny, unusual, etc. experience you had in a foreign city (any city other than your own). Your partner will then ask you questions about your story using past unreal conditional. You should answer the questions with the past unreal conditional.

EXAMPLE

STORY: When I was in Aswan, Egypt many years ago, it was very hot, and since my jeans had not finished drying, I put on a pair of shorts. I knew that it was not appropriate for a woman to wear shorts in public, but I just wanted to go from my hotel room down to the street to buy some fruit. I went out into the street in my shorts, and every person in the marketplace immediately turned to stare in horror at my legs. The people were hissing, whispering, and pointing, which made me feel very ashamed. I quickly ran back up to my hotel room to put my wet jeans on.

QUESTION: What would have happened if you hadn't left the marketplace?
ANSWER: Perhaps, if I hadn't left, someone would have told me to leave.
QUESTION: What would you have done if the people had only stared, but not hissed, whisperered, or pointed?
ANSWER: Maybe I would've bought my fruit quickly before running up to my room.

13.10   PAIRED ORAL ACTIVITY: *Living in a Commune*

DIRECTIONS: Read the following passage about communes. Then discuss in pairs what life would have been like for you if you had lived in a commune. Use conditional sentences to express unreality in the past.

---

1. In the 1960s, when idealistic young people grew tired of the problems of city living, many of them abandoned the city to create a utopian way of life in a commune. These were communities of people who escaped to areas far from cities or suburbs and started their own lives from scratch. They built their own houses, made their own clothes, grew their own food, and did their own baking.

2. They tried to live as a self-sufficient society. They shared all the tasks of daily life and held their property in common. Communes were based on a variety of popular beliefs such as neo-Buddhism, vegetarianism, and free love.

EXAMPLE

If I had lived in a commune in the 1960s, I would've baked my own bread.

D. Habits and Facts

The chart below demonstrates how conditional sentences are used to describe habitual activity and make statements of facts. Notice that in these sentences the verb tense in the **if-** clause corresponds to the verb tense in the main clause.

	VERB TENSE / MODALS IN *IF-* CLAUSE	**VERB TENSE / MODALS IN MAIN CLAUSE**
Habitual Activity	▪ (If) (when) people **decide** to move here, SIMPLE PRESENT ▪ If (when) a child **was caught** smoking, SIMPLE PAST	it **is** usually because of the weather. SIMPLE PRESENT severe punishment **was** enforced. SIMPLE PAST

Fact	If (when) too much exhaust **is emitted,** SIMPLE PRESENT	the smog level **rises.** SIMPLE PRESENT

NOTE: In these two types of conditional sentences, **when** or **whenever** can replace **if**: **When** people decide to move to this city, it is usually because of the weather.

13.11   RAPID DRILL: *Habitual Activity*

DIRECTIONS: Choose from the given cues below to formulate conditional sentences describing the habits of people in your city.

EXAMPLE

CUE: rent an apartment in the city

If people in my city rent an apartment in the city, they must pay very high prices.

1. have an appointment
2. ride the subway
3. go out for lunch
4. want to get some exercise
5. get out of the city
6. see a ballet / hear jazz / go to the theater, and so forth
7. have a picnic

13.12   WRITTEN EXERCISE: *City People*

DIRECTIONS: Write three sentences describing three more present habits of people in your city. For each sentence describing a present habit, write one sentence describing a contrasting habit of 50 years ago. Use **if, when,** or **whenever.**

EXAMPLE

a. If people in Long Island drive to work in the city, they take the freeway.
b. Fifty years ago, if people drove into the city they took country roads.

1. a. _____

   b. _____

2. a. _____

   b. _____

3. a. _____

   b. _____

13.13 PAIRED DRILL: *Scientific Facts*

DIRECTIONS: The most common context for conditional statements of fact is in the field of science. Student A should cover the Student B column; Student B should cover the Student A column. Student A will begin a conditional sentence using the information in the A column, Student B should find the information in the B column that completes the sentence.

EXAMPLE

A: oil is mixed with water   B: sits on the surface
STUDENT A: If oil is mixed with water, . . .   STUDENT B: . . . it sits on the surface

A	**B**
temperature drops below 0°C	it goes out
you throw something up	it turns to steam
you have two opposing forces	the result is water
water boils	they attract
a fire has no oxygen	it comes down
you combine two atoms of hydrogen with one atom of oxygen	water freezes

Now, think of at least two additional laws of science or nature and state them using the conditional.

1. _____

2. _____

13.14 WRITTEN EXERCISE: *Review*

DIRECTIONS: Restate each of the following sentences with a conditional sentence.

EXAMPLE

Because the crime rate in this city is so low, many people want to live here.
If the crime rate in this city weren't so low, many people wouldn't want to live here.

1. Washington, D. C. is a very exciting city because of its history as the capital city.

_____

2. Many people wanted to live in L.A. years ago because Hollywood was so exciting.

_____

3. Many residents of Boston go to Cape Cod during their holidays.

_____

4. The rich musical and cultural tradition draws people to New Orleans.

_____

5. In the past, many people went to San Francisco to visit and liked the city so much they returned to live there permanently.

_____

6. Thousands of people move to Seattle every year, which could mean overcrowding and pollution in the years to come.

_____

13.15 WRITTEN ASSIGNMENT: *Letter to the Editor*

DIRECTIONS: Write a letter to the editor of the local newspaper in your hometown or in the city where you are presently living. Discuss ways to improve the city, why certain problems exist, and what will happen if existing problems aren't solved. Use as many conditional sentences as possible in your letter, underline them and identify them.

GRAMMATICAL PATTERNS TWO

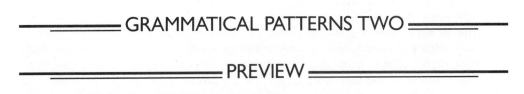

PREVIEW

PREREADING DISCUSSION QUESTIONS

What are the laws on the sale of guns in your country? Is it possible to acquire weapons illegally? Is there much crime as a result of weapons use? What kind of power does the police force in your city have? What is their primary function?

DIRECTIONS: Jack Warren, a radio talk show host, is interviewing Marianne Brown, the mayor of a large city in the United States about the drug and related crime problem in that city. Read the interview below with a partner.

---

1 WARREN: Mayor Brown, the statistics show that in the past year the number of **homicides** in your city has soared and that almost 50% of them were prompted by gang warfare or illegal drug dealing.

2 BROWN: Yes, I know, but had the voters approved the tax increase, we would be able to afford a larger police force. Right now, we're working with 1.68 officers per 1,200 residents. This means that our officers are unable to respond immediately to every call they get because they're so **swamped**.

3 WARREN: Are there any other explanations for these statistics, and if so, what are they?

4 BROWN: Well, Jack, even if we increase the police force, the killing will continue unless we restrict the sale of **vicious weapons**. Unfortunately, Assemblyman White's bill to control the spread of **assault rifles** wasn't passed last year. The situation will improve only if the bill is passed this year.

5 WARREN: Is there a chance of that happening?

6 BROWN: If the **polls** are correct, the bill should be passed. I think that people are finally beginning to realize that the constitutional right to bear arms does not include assault rifles. I really wish there had been more support for this idea last year. I'm sure we wouldn't be experiencing the present increase in homicides if we'd had that support.

7 WARREN: Well, Mayor Brown, I certainly hope that the bill does get passed so that you can make your city a safer place to live in.

8 BROWN: Thank you, Jack. I hope so, too. If I didn't have such an excellent city council, I wouldn't have been able to gain such extensive support for this campaign to begin with, so I'm sure that, as a team, we'll continue **to make headway**.

9 WARREN: Thank you for talking with us, Mayor Brown.

10 BROWN: Thank you, Jack.

VOCABULARY

homicides: a term to refer to murder or manslaughter
be swamped with: very busy
vicious weapons: terrible, dangerous weapons
assault rifles: a weapon designed for quick attack during war
poll: the instrument used for measuring public opinion
to make headway: to make progress in a difficult situation

GRAMMAR CONSIDERATIONS: FOCUS

In the three sentences on the next page, what is the time reference of the **if-** clause? What is the time reference of the result clause? What generalization could you make about the relationship between the **if-** clause and the main clause? How are these conditional sentences different from the types you've studied so far?

EXAMPLE

If the freeway system had been designed well, we wouldn't have the present traffic problems.

If the freeway system had been designed well	TIME REFERENCE: <u>Past</u>
we wouldn't have the present traffic problems	TIME REFERENCE: <u>Present</u>

GENERALIZATION: <u>A situation in the past affects the present.</u>

1. If the voters had approved the tax increase, we would be able to afford a larger police force.
2. I'm sure we wouldn't be experiencing the present increase in homicides if we'd had that support.
3. If I didn't have such an excellent city council, I wouldn't have been able to gain such extensive support for this campaign to begin with.

I. MIXED TIME REFERENCE IN CONDITIONAL SENTENCES

In addition to the conditional patterns covered in the previous section, there are cases when it is necessary to **mix** time reference to express the appropriate meaning. The chart below demonstrates how mixed time reference is used in conditional sentences.

NOTES	EXAMPLES

REAL PAST
AFFECTS FUTURE:
If an action or event already happened or has been happening, it may have some effect on what **will** happen in the future.
	1. ■ If you **studied,** you **will** pass.
	■ If you **didn't read** the text, you **will be** confused.
	  SIMPLE PAST FUTURE
	2. ■ If **you've paid attention, you will understand.**
	■ If **I've saved** enough money, I'll take a vacation.
	  PRES. PERFECT FUTURE
	3. ■ If **they've been studying,** they'll **get** good grades.
	■ If he's **been training,** he'll **win** the race.
	  PRES. PERFECT PROGRESSIVE FUTURE

UNREAL PRESENT
AFFECTS PAST:
An unreal situation or general truth in the present can be related to actions or events in the past.
	1. ■ If I **wrote** better, I **wouldn't have made** any mistakes.
	■ If I **had** a car, I **wouldn't have taken** the bus.
	■ If I **could sing,** I **would have performed** last night.
	  PAST WOULD / COULD + HAVE
	                          + PAST PARTICIPLE
	2. ■ If I **weren't taking** this class, **I couldn't have written** that essay.
	  PAST WOULD / COULD + HAVE
	  PROGRESSIVE + PAST PARTICIPLE

UNREAL PAST
AFFECTS PRESENT:
An unreal event or action in the past would affect what happens in the present.
	1. ■ If I **hadn't moved** here, I **would be living** in Rome.
	■ If I **had grown up** in Paris, I **would speak** French.
	  PAST WOULD / COULD / SHOULD /
	  PERFECT OUGHT TO + PRESENT or
	                    PRESENT PROGRESSIVE VERB

13.16 WRITTEN EXERCISE: *Fill in the Blanks*

DIRECTIONS: The sentences below are about a street fair that was organized by the merchants and residents of one area of a city in upstate New York. Fill in the blanks by using the correct forms of the given verbs. Add any necessary modals. If there is more than one possible answer, discuss the difference in time reference.

1. If there (be) (not) _____ so many enthusiastic residents who support

     the street fair, we (have) (not) _____ such a successful turnout.

2. If it (rain) _____ yesterday, we _____ (have)

     the street fair today.

3. If you (enjoy) _____ the fair yesterday, you (want) _____

     _____ to come back for next year's fair.

4. If I (go) _____ to the fair, I (tell) _____ you

     about it now.

5. If I (live) _____ closer to the center of town, I (walk) _____

     _____ to the fair yesterday.

6. If I (be / not) _____ so broke, I (spend) more money on crafts at the

     fair.

13.17   PAIRED ORAL ACTIVITY: *Hollywood—Yesterday and Today*

DIRECTIONS: Below is a chart describing what Hollywood was like before it became the center of film production and some of the changes that took place after that happened. Discuss with a partner what Hollywood might be like today if these changes had not taken place.

EXAMPLE

If film companies hadn't constructed production studios everywhere, Hollywood would still be a small village.

BEFORE	CHANGES
<ul><li>small village</li><li>wide treelined streets</li><li>two or three restaurants</li><li>smalltown atmosphere</li><li>one traffic cop</li><li>residential area</li></ul>	<ul><li>Film companies constructed production studios everywhere.</li><li>New people swarmed into the village looking for opportunities in the film business.</li><li>Many movie stars built extravagant homes.</li><li>Supermarkets, banks, and parking lots were built.</li></ul>

13.18   WRITTEN ASSIGNMENT: *Past and Present in Your City*

DIRECTIONS: Write a paragraph about your city describing how it used to be and how it has changed. Use mixed time reference to create sentences like the ones about Hollywood.

EXAMPLE

If my city hadn't grown so quickly over the past five years, we wouldn't be seeing so many new housing developments going up.

II. INVERTED WORD ORDER

Sometimes to emphasize low probability in a conditional sentence, the *if* is omitted, and inverted word order is used. This can occur in the three types of conditional sentences as can be seen in the examples below.

NOTES	EXAMPLE
FUTURE **Should** and **were** are placed at the beginning of the sentence to replace **if**. (This form is used to further emphasize low probability.)	<ul><li>If you **should** discover that you run short of funds, you can take out a loan. NEW SENTENCE:</li><li>**Should** you discover that you run short of funds, you can take out a loan.</li><li>If you **were to** move to another city, you could work for the branch office of this bank. NEW SENTENCE:</li><li>**Were** you to move to another city, you could work for the branch office of this bank.</li></ul>

PRESENT UNREAL When the verb **be (were)** is used in the **if-** clause, it is moved to the beginning of the sentence. (This form is used to emphasize the unreality of the situation.)	▪ If you **were** in a different city right now, you wouldn't be enjoying yourself so much. NEW SENTENCE: ▪ **Were** you in a different city right now, you wouldn't be enjoying yourself so much.
PAST UNREAL **Had** is moved to the beginning of the sentence to replace **if**. (This form is used to emphasize the unreality of the situation.)	▪ If someone **had asked** me 30 years ago, I would never have predicted that this city would change so much in such a short time. NEW SENTENCE **Had** someone **asked** me 30 years ago, I would never have predicted that this city would change so much in such a short time.

13.19 PAIRED PRACTICE: *Inverted Word Order*

DIRECTIONS: You work for a travel agency in a country other than your own. Your client is going to your country to visit the capital city. Based on each of the situations below, use conditional sentences with inverted word order to advise your client. Take turns with your partner playing the roles of agent and client.

EXAMPLE

CUE: Your client thinks a friend will be traveling with him / her, but there is a chance of traveling alone, so your client wants information about tour groups.
RESPONSE: Were you to travel alone, we could sign you up with a tour group.

1. Your client doesn't think s / he will have a car but would like some advice on places to visit if s / he does.
2. Your client doesn't know if the friend s / he will be traveling with is interested in the history of the city, but would like some suggestions in order to be prepared.
3. The client lost his / her passport and has to apply for a new one.
4. The client doesn't think there will be enough time but wants to know what other city would be worth visiting.
5. The client isn't yet sure when this trip will take place. Discuss special events / attractions that the client would see during different seasons.
6. The client just missed the 30-day advance purchase discount by two days.
7. The client is no longer a college student so s / he doesn't qualify for a student discount.
8. The client isn't a member of the international travel group, which would also provide some discounts.
9. The client is complaining about his / her last trip, which was booked through a different travel agency.

III. *WISH* AND *HOPE*

Since **wish** is often used to refer to unreal situations, it is related to some of the conditional forms already covered in this chapter. There is often confusion between **wish** and **hope** because they are similar in meaning. **Wish** usually expresses a feeling of regret about an event whose outcome is known or expected. **Hope** usually expresses a feeling about an event whose outcome is unknown. Notice the difference in verb tenses and meaning in the following chart.

TIME REFERENCE	EXAMPLE	NOTES
PRESENT WISH	▪ I **wish** I **were** in Hawaii. (I am not in Hawaii, and I regret it.) ▪ I **wish** the sun **was shining.** (The sun is not shining, and I regret it.) ▪ I **wish** I **had** a bicycle. (I don't have a bicycle, and I regret it.) ▪ I wish I **could sing.** (I can't sing.)	▪ Main verb is simple past, past progressive, or **could.** ▪ As with the present unreal conditional, **was** is acceptable in spoken English.
HOPE	▪ I **hope** Jim **is enjoying** Tokyo. (I don't know whether he is or not.)	▪ Usually present progressive is used after **hope** to refer to a present situation.
PAST WISH	▪ I **wish** there **had been** more support for this bill last year. (There wasn't support, and I regret it.) ▪ I **wish** I **could have attended** the meeting, but I was busy. (I couldn't attend, and I regret it.)	▪ Past perfect tenses of the verb or **could have + participle** is used for past time reference after **wish.**
HOPE	▪ I **hope** Jack **didn't forget** the mail. (I don't know whether he forgot it.) ▪ I **hope** you **weren't sleeping** when I called. (I don't know whether you were sleeping.)	▪ Simple past, past progressive, present perfect, or present perfect progressive tenses are used after **hope** for past time reference.
FUTURE WISH	▪ I **wish** the voters **would** realize that assault weapons are different from recreational weapons. (They don't realize this now, but I would like them to realize it in the future.) ▪ I **wish** it **would rain** tonight. (Most likely, it won't rain.)	▪ Use **would** to express a **wish** about the future. ▪ A wish about the future is very close in meaning to a hope about the future, except that the probability is much lower when it's a wish.
HOPE	▪ I **hope** it **rains** tonight. (There is a good chance that it will rain.) ▪ I **hope** we'll **receive** our salary soon.	▪ Use simple present or future tense to express **hope** about the future.

13.20   ORAL PRACTICE: *Wish List*

DIRECTIONS: Think about your favorite restaurant. Wouldn't you like to be there right now? Make a wish list about this restaurant using **wish** and **hope,** and share it with your partner or other classmates.

EXAMPLE

I wish I were at Cafe Roma in San Francisco right now. I wish I were relaxing at one of their outdoor tables, waiting to order. I wish I were waiting for my plate of pasta to be served to me. I wish I could have a big basket of their warm, fresh Italian bread. I wish I had ordered cappucino for dessert the last time I was there. I hope I can go back there soon. I hope they haven't changed the menu.

13.21   EXERCISE: *Switching Lanes*

DIRECTIONS: Read the cartoon below and ask your teacher about any vocabulary you don't understand. Discuss the situation of the driver in each lane, using conditional statements and statements with **wish** and **hope.**

EXAMPLE

If I weren't in this lane, I wouldn't be moving so slowly.

Reprinted with permission of the New York Times Syndications Sales Corporation.

13.22   WRITTEN EXERCISE: *Foreign Students in U.S. Cities*

DIRECTIONS: Below is some information about the experiences of some foreign students in U.S. cities. For each sentence given, (a) write a corresponding conditional sentence; (b) write a sentence using **wish;** (c) write a sentence using **hope.**

EXAMPLE

Chikako was driving 80 mph on the freeway and got a speeding ticket.

CONDITIONAL: If she hadn't been driving 80 mph on the freeway, she wouldn't have gotten a speeding ticket.

WISH: Chikako wishes she hadn't been driving so fast.

HOPE: She hopes she doesn't get caught speeding again.

1. Serge visited the new downtown shopping mall and spent too much money.

   CONDITIONAL: _____

   WISH: _____

   HOPE: _____

2. Xin was walking in the city, and a homeless person asked her for some money.

   CONDITIONAL: _____

   WISH: _____

   HOPE: _____

3. Because the public transportation system in this city is so poor, Lorenzo has to drive everywhere.

   CONDITIONAL: _____

   WISH: _____

   HOPE: _____

4. Carlos won't be able to see the Empire State Building when he is in New York because he probably won't have time.

   CONDITIONAL: _____

   WISH: _____

   HOPE: _____

5. Maria asked a stranger for directions to the train station. She got lost because the stranger gave her the wrong directions.

   CONDITIONAL: _____

   WISH: _____

   HOPE: _____

IV. MAKING INFERENCES

Conditional sentences are used to make inferences. An inference is a conclusion based on previous knowledge or information, as shown in the box below. Notice that almost any combination of tenses is possible in this type of conditional sentence, depending on the meaning being expressed. Very often the modals **should, must, have to,** or **ought to** are used in the main clause to emphasize expectation or conclusion based on the previous information.

INFERENCE	PREVIOUS INFORMATION
■ If the polls **are correct,** the bill **will be passed.**	■ The polls show that people are in support of the bill.
■ If the statistics **are correct,** the number of homeless in this city **has tripled** in the last five years.	■ The statistics say that the number of homeless has tripled in the last five years.
■ If the smog level **was** that high last week, there **must have been** a heat wave.	■ The smog level is usually that high only when there is a heat wave.

13.23   RECOGNITION EXERCISE: *Previous Information in Inferences*

DIRECTIONS: When you use a conditional sentence to make an inference, there is previous information upon which you are basing the inference. For each inference below, identify the previous information.

EXAMPLE

If Americans want to see good theater, they usually visit New York.
PREVIOUS INFORMATION: New York has some of the best theater in the United States.

1. If Jim decided to move to Key West, he must like the beach.

   MISSING INFORMATION: _____

2. If Carol has been living in New Orleans for the last five years, she should be hearing some good music.

   MISSING INFORMATION: _____

3. If you have a job on Wall Street, you must work well under stress.

   MISSING INFORMATION: _____

4. If David moved from Dallas to L.A., he should be having better success as a musician.

   MISSING INFORMATION: _____

5. If you live in Seattle, you must not mind rain.

   MISSING INFORMATION: _____

13.24 PAIRED ORAL PRACTICE: *Making Inferences*

DIRECTIONS: Work with a partner. Take turns reading each of the situations below, and use a conditional sentence to make an inference about each one.

EXAMPLE

SITUATION: You have heard from many sources that Carnival in Rio De Janeiro is very exciting. You're not sure, but you think that a friend of yours, Sam, is going to Rio this year for Carnival.

INFERENCE: If Sam is going to Rio for Carnival, he's going to have a great time.

1. The streets in your neighborhood always flood when there is a rainstorm. You've been visiting a friend in another city for two days and have heard reports of a serious rainstorm in your city. What is happening to the streets?

   _____

   _____

2. There was a van Gogh exhibit in Chicago last week. You think that your friend Chris, who loves van Gogh, was in Chicago last week. What did Chris do?

   _____

   _____

3. You have devised a model plan for urban development that you believe can improve every major city in the United States. You have effectively implemented this plan in New York. You are, therefore, convinced that it will work in other cities as well. How can you persuade the city council?

   _____

   _____

4. You've heard that Chicago is an exciting city to live in. You think that Kevin, a former colleague, is now working there. How do you think he feels about where he lives?

   _____

   _____

5. Ruth was offered a job as director of Housing and Urban Development. However, she wanted an annual salary of $50,000. You just heard that she took the job. What salary do you think was agreed upon?

   _____

   _____

13.25 PAIRED ORAL ACTIVITY: *Cities of the World*

DIRECTIONS: Below is a chart with information about four major cities in the world. Use the information to discuss the questions that follow the chart. Use conditional sentences to make inferences based on the information given.

	NEW YORK	TOKYO	RIO DE JANEIRO	LONDON
TIME	12:00 P.M.	2:00 A.M.	2:00 P.M.	5:00 P.M.
WEATHER Nov.–Feb. March–May June–August Sept.–October	very cold, snow mild, frequent rain hot, humid cool, occasional rain	cold, dry mild, sunny, dry hot, humid cool, frequent rain	very hot mild, occasional rain very cold warm, humid	very cold, rainy mild, frequent rain hot, humid cool, frequent rain
SERIOUS PROBLEM	crime	pollution	overcrowding	litter

1. What time will it be in the second city, based on the time given for the first city?
   New York: 6:00 P.M. / Tokyo: ?
   Tokyo: 7:00 A.M. / Rio de Janeiro: ?
   Rio de Janeiro: 3:00 P.M. / London: ?
2. Discuss what kind of clothes you expect people to be wearing based on the given month.
   New York: December
   Tokyo: October
   Rio de Janeiro: January
3. Discuss the problem each person must deal with because of the city that person lives in.

EXAMPLE

Gary lives in Tokyo and has allergies.
INFERENCE: If Gary lives in Tokyo, he must be having problems with his allergies.

   a. Chantal comes from a small town in the French countryside and now lives in Rio de Janeiro.
   b. Marcia is a fanatic about cleanliness and is now living in London.
   c. Chikako is living alone for the first time in New York.

V. REPLACING *IF*

The following words and phrases are used to replace **if** in conditional sentences.

WORD / PHRASE	EXAMPLE	MEANING
only if	■ I would move out of the city **only if** I could live close enough to attend cultural events.	ON THE EXCLUSIVE CONDITION THAT . . .

provided that	• **Provided that** I live in a quiet neighborhood, I enjoy city life.	ON THE CONDITION THAT...
even if whether . . . or not (in spoken English) whether (in written English)	• **Even if** I could live close enough to attend cultural events, I wouldn't move out of London. • **Whether** you live downtown **or not,** the air pollution will affect you. or • **Whether** you live downtown or uptown, the air pollution will affect you.	REGARDLESS (the condition has no importance)
    unless	• **Unless** I'm lucky enough to find a cheap apartment, New York will be too expensive for me. • Tokyo life will not suit you **unless** you like crowds.	IF . . . NOT or EXCEPT ON CONDITION THAT . . .
in case suppose / supposing	• **In case** your car breaks down, you can take the subway to work. • **Suppose** your car breaks down, how will you get to work?	IF THIS SHOULD / WERE TO HAPPEN (low probability)

13.26 WRITTEN EXERCISE: *Long-Distance Marriage*

DIRECTIONS: Read the following passage and complete the sentences that follow, based on the information in the passage and your own ideas.

LONG-DISTANCE MARRIAGE

Bill and Marilyn are married and have no kids. Bill is a stockbroker on Wall Street in New York City, and Marilyn is an assistant production manager at a major movie studio in Los Angeles, CA. Because of their professions, they have to live in two different cities and are unable to spend much time together. They talk on the telephone several times during the week and take turns flying to see each other on the weekends. They are able to live happily this way because they are very dedicated to their jobs and they never grow tired or bored with each other.

1. This arrangement will continue to work for Bill and Marilyn **unless** _____

_____ .

2. Bill and Marilyn can have a happy marriage **provided that** _____

_____ .

3. They talk to each other on the telephone several times during the week **even though** _____

_____ .

4. Bill would move to Los Angeles **only if** _____

_____ .

5. In case _____ ,

Bill and Marilyn will have to change their present situation and live in the same city.

6. Whether this seems like an ideal living situation for a marriage, _____

_____ .

7. Suppose _____ ,

what will Bill and Marilyn do? _____

8. Even if _____ ,

Bill and Marilyn will continue to see each other on the weekends.

13.27   ORAL PRACTICE: *Replacing* If

DIRECTIONS: Work with a partner and discuss the plans that you have for the next six months of your life. Use the expressions from the above chart to replace *if* in conditional sentences.

EXAMPLE

Provided that I have enough money, I will study English in America for six months.

VI. SHORTENED FORMS

Very often, shortened forms of conditional constructions are used after yes / no questions. Look at the following example of a yes / no question and the shortened forms of the conditional that follow.

Are you going to be riding the bus to work every day?

AFFIRMATIVE: **If so,** you should buy a pass.

If you **are** going to be riding the bus to work every day, you should buy a pass.

NEGATIVE: **If not,** you don't need a pass.

If you **aren't** going to be riding the bus to work every day, you don't need a pass.

■ 13.28   PAIRED PRACTICE: *Shortened Forms of Conditionals*

DIRECTIONS: Ask your partner the given question and add on a shortened form of the conditional. Use affirmative and negative forms.

EXAMPLE

Are you a native of this city? If not, where are you from?

1. Do you like big cities?
2. Have you ever been to New York?
3. Do you have a map of this city?
4. Have you ever ridden the buses in this city?
5. Did you live in an apartment when you were growing up?

■ **13.29 CONDITIONAL REVIEW**

DIRECTIONS: Fill in the blanks with the correct form of the verb.

1. If I _____ about it more carefully, I never would have left my
   hometown.
   a. thought
   b. had thought
   c. were thinking

2. I would go to Bangkok if I _____ enough money.
   a. would have
   b. have
   c. had

3. If you should happen to visit me in Jakarta, I _____ show you around
   the city.
   a. will
   b. would
   c. would have

4. I wish I _____ Tibilisi when I was in Russia.
   a. would have visited
   b. visited
   c. had visited

5. I wouldn't have made as many friends during my stay in America if I
   _____ a shy person.
   a. were
   b. had been
   c. would be

6. I _____ I can visit Beijing someday.
   a. wish
   b. hope

7. If you _____ two sticks together, you can start a fire.
   a. rub
   b. would rub
   c. are rubbing

VII. SPECIAL PROBLEMS WITH CONDITIONAL SENTENCES

PROBLEM	EXPLANATION
REVERSED ORDER OF CONDITION AND RESULT [INCORRECT: If L. A. didn't attract so many prospective movie stars, it wouldn't be the center of film production.] CORRECT: If L. A. weren't the center of film production, it wouldn't attract so many film stars.	The **condition** is placed in the **if-** clause, and the **result** is placed in the main clause.

OMISSION OF **WOULD** OR OTHER MODAL [INCORRECT: If I **were** in my country right now, I **had** a job.] CORRECT: If I **were** in my country right now, I **would have** a job.	A modal is often used in the main clause of a conditional sentence.
USE OF **WOULD** IN **IF-** CLAUSE [INCORRECT: If I **would** be living in a different city, I would be happier.] CORRECT: If I **were** living in a different city, I would be happier.	**Will** and **Would** are not used in the **if-** clause of conditional sentences.
INCORRECT VERB TENSE [INCORRECT: If I **wasn't** sick yesterday, I wouldn't have missed the concert.] CORRECT: If I **hadn't been** sick yesterday, I wouldn't have missed the concert.	A certain verb tense is required depending on the time reference.

■ 13.30 ERROR ANALYSIS

DIRECTIONS: Find the error in each of the sentences below, and correct it.

1. If I hadn't moved to a city with such a high smog level, I didn't develop such serious sinus problems.

2. If there is better mass transit in L. A., there wouldn't be such terrible smog.

3. If I lived in Tokyo, Japanese would be my native language.

4. The ozone layer deteriorates if too much carbon monoxide would be allowed to enter the atmosphere.

5. If you had a car, you're required to have a smog check done regularly.

6. If I have more money, I could attend more cultural events.

7. If there wouldn't be so many skyscrapers downtown, I would feel better about taking walks down there.

8. If you are putting two opposite forces together, they are attracting.

9. If I will be going to Atlanta on Saturday, I will drive.

10. If I didn't speak English, I wouldn't have been born in the United States.

ANALYSIS OF AN AUTHENTIC TEXT

DIRECTIONS: Read the following article by Ellen Goodman about the differences between urban and rural life.

COUNTRY MUSIC
by Ellen Goodman

1. "Is it quiet up there?" My friend asks this question **wistfully**. She has called long distance, from her city to my countryside, from her desk to my cottage.

2. "Yes," I answer her. There is no urban **clatter** here. No jarring cosmopolitan Muzak of subway and construction, rock and rush-hour voices. We are protected. The water that surrounds this island absorbs the **din** of the other world. Yes, it is quiet up here. ·

3. Slowly, I sift through the hundred sounds that form this rural chorus. A honeybee shopping the rose hips in front of the porch, a **vole** rustling through the bushes, a hawk piping its song above me. If I concentrate, I imagine that I can even make out different voices of the wind moving through **alder, bayberry, or birch**.

4. . . . I do not live my urban life at such a frequency. Like most city people, I have been trained to listen each day only to the squeakiest wheel, the most insistent, hardest-rock level of audio demands.

5. . . . Some of my friends by now have senses so damaged by the urban **cacophony** that they **squirm** when they are left alone with the crickets. They cannot adjust to country music. And yet it seems to me that it is only when we leave behind the alarms and bells and buzzes and sirens, all these external demands, that the quietest sound of all comes into range: our inner voice.

6. George Eliot once wrote, "If we had keen vision and feeling of all ordinary human life, it would be like hearing the grass grow and the squirrel's heart beat and we should die of that **roar** which lies on the other side of silence." How overwhelming to literally hear the life story of everyone we meet. But I think more often of the **roar** that keeps us from silence, the **roar** of daily life that makes it "impossible to hear myself think."

VOCABULARY

cacophony, clatter, din, roar: words that describe the "noise" of the city
wistfully: the feeling of longing or yearning for something that can't be had
vole: a type of rodent that is similar to a mouse
squirm: the snakelike movement made when in an uncomfortable or painful situation
alder, bayberry, birch: types of trees

COMPREHENSION QUESTIONS

1. Why does the author's friend ask the first question wistfully?
2. How is "city music" different from "country music"?
3. Why does the author prefer "country music"?

WRITTEN EXERCISE

A. DIRECTIONS: Use conditional sentences to paraphrase (write in your own words) the following sentences from the text.

1. Some of my friends by now have senses so damaged by the urban cacophony that they squirm when they are left alone with the crickets. (Paragraph 5)

_____

2. And yet it seems to me that it is only when we leave behind the alarms and bells and buzzes and sirens, all these external demands, that the quietest sound of all comes into range: our inner voice. (Paragraph 5)

_____

3. How overwhelming to literally hear the life story of everyone we meet.

_____

B. DIRECTIONS: Write three conditional sentences that would express the feelings of the author's friend about living in the city vs. living in the country.

1. _____

2. _____

3. _____

COMPOSITION TOPICS

Use what you have learned in this chapter about conditional sentences to write a composition about one of the following topics.

1. If you could live in any city in the world, which city would you choose? What would your life be like in that city?

2. How would your life have been different if you had been born in another part of the world? Choose another city or country and discuss how your life would have been different if you had grown up there.

3. If you could design an ideal city, what would it be like?

AGE IS A STATE OF MIND

⊟ Gerunds and infinitives

Reprinted with special permission of North American Syndicate, Inc.

AGE IS A STATE OF MIND
(You're As Young As You Feel)

DISCUSSION QUESTIONS

1. How do you feel about getting old? Do you agree with the expression "age is a state of mind"? At what age will you be old?
2. How do you imagine yourself at 60 or 70? What kind of life do you hope to be living?
3. What do people in your country do to look and feel younger?

OBJECTIVES

In this chapter, you will learn:

1. To use an infinitive or a gerund as subject of a sentence
2. To use an infinitive or a gerund as the direct object of certain verbs
3. To use a gerund as the object of a preposition
4. To use an infinitive or a gerund as complement of the verb **to be**
5. To use an infinitive as the complement of certain adjectives
6. To use the past, passive, and past passive forms of infinitives and gerunds
7. To use infinitive phrases as replacements for adverb, adjective, and noun clauses

═══ PREVIEW ═══

DIRECTIONS: Read the following letter from a 16-year-old boy written to his grandmother on her one-hundredth birthday.

Dear Grandma,

1. Happy Birthday!! It's hard for me to believe that you're 100 years old today. Congratulations on becoming a **centenarian**.

2. I'm really proud to have a 100-year-old grandmother who refuses to let age get in the way of life. You have such an active, rewarding life that it seems wrong to even call you old. You still have your garden and your birds, and you always know what's happening in the world. I especially think it's **cool** that you still have parties with your friends to have fun. I hope to be an active, fun-loving **senior citizen** like you when I reach your age. Some of my friends say it's difficult to think about old age because it depresses them. They imagine that anyone over the age of 60 must live in a **nursing home**, helpless and lonely. I always tell them about you and that my goal is to be just like you when I'm 100, and that's not depressing at all.

3. For many people, aging can be difficult, and they are really afraid of old age. Their mistake is thinking that at a certain age they will be too old to be happy. Like you, my philosophy is that we only have one life to life, so every day must **count**.

4. I'm so glad Mom always encouraged me to come and stay with you every summer when I was little because I learned so much from you about gardening and taking care of the birds. And I always liked watching the news with you in the evenings because you had such strong opinions about everything. I really learned a lot during those summers.

5. Well, Grandma, I just wanted to let you know that you're the most special lady I know. To be honest, you seem just as **young at heart** as many of the 16-year-old girls I know. To have your energy and spirit for life is a gift. Happy Birthday! And many, many more!

Love,

Derek

VOCABULARY

centenarian: a person who has reached the age of 100

cool: a slang expression, especially popular among young people, which is used to express approval of something

senior citizen: an elderly person

nursing home: a place where sick or handicapped elderly people, who are incapable of living on their own, are given medical care and supervision

count: have value, be important

young at heart: to have a young attitude regardless of your age

CULTURAL NOTE / DISCUSSION

It is very common in the United States to place an elderly relative in a nursing home if the person is unable to live independently without care or supervision. Despite the fact that the family of this elderly person may have the necessary accommodations and financial resources to provide care in their own home, the American value of independence often motivates the family to have the person cared for in a nursing home. How are the elderly cared for in your country? Are many elderly people placed in homes for the elderly or nursing homes?

GRAMMAR CONSIDERATIONS: FOCUS

The following questions are based on the preview text and are designed to help you find out what you already know about the structures in this chapter. Some of the questions may be hard and some of them may be easy. Answer as many of the questions as you can. Work with a partner if your teacher tells you to do so.

1. a. In this example from the preview, which of the following verbs could take the place of **hope?** (want, appreciate, enjoy, promise, refuse) Write them on the line below the example: I **hope** to be an active, fun-loving senior citizen .

Did you use a rule to choose the verbs?

If you replace **hope** with one of the verbs you did **not** write on the line, what other change will you have to make?

b. What is the difference between the **boldfaced** constructions in the following two examples from the preview?

I **hope to be** an active, fun-loving senior citizen when I reach your age.

I'm really **proud to have** a 100 year old grandmother.

Can you think of any words to replace **proud** in the example above?

2. If you wanted to make **it** the subject of the sentence below, what words would **it** replace?
   To have your energy and spirit for life is a gift.
   Could **having** replace **to have** in this sentence?

3. Why is the gerund from of **discover** used in the following sentence from the passage?
   We are very interested in discovering what kind of lifestyle and particularly what kind of
   personality determines longevity.
   Could you use an infinitive in place of the gerund?

GRAMMATICAL PATTERNS ONE

I. INFINITIVES

An infinitive consists of **to + verb** and takes the place of a noun. An infinitive can have a variety of functions in a sentence.

A. Infinitive As Subject of the Sentence

The box below explains how an infinitive can be used as the subject of a sentence.

GRAMMATICAL FUNCTION	NOTES
SUBJECT OF THE SENTENCE ■ **To age** gracefully is difficult. ■ **It** is difficult **to age** gracefully.	■ Using **it** as the subject of the sentence is much more common than using an infinitive. ■ The infinitive subject is more formal.

14.1 ORAL PRACTICE: *Infinitive Subjects*

DIRECTIONS: Below are some stereotypical ideas about getting old. State whether you agree or disagree with each statement, and in your response, instead of using an infinitive subject, use **it** as the subject. Provide a reason for your opinion.

EXAMPLE

CUE: **To be** old is depressing.
RESPONSE: I disagree that **it** is depressing **to be** old. There are many happy senior citizens who live full, active lives.

1. To live an active life if you're over 75 is impossible.
2. To get old is terrible.
3. To live in a retirement community must be boring.
4. To date when you're over the age of 60 is uncommon.
5. To travel when you're old is dangerous.
6. To learn a new language is impossible if you're over 50.

B. Infinitive As Direct Object

There are certain verbs that are followed by infinitives. Some of them are listed in the chart below along with some helpful hints for memorization. See the chapter appendix for a more complete list.

VERBS	EXAMPLE	NOTES
TYPE A VERBS MUST BE FOLLOWED BY AN INFINITIVE:		
agree, arrange, decide, deserve, hope, intend, need, learn, promise, plan, prepare, refuse, seem, tend, etc.	▪ She **arranged** to care for her grandmother. (She will care for her in the future.) ▪ I **expect** to receive a letter today. (I don't know whether I will actually receive it.) ▪ Carol **intends** to change her job. (Whether in fact she will change is unknown.) ▪ She **pretended** to be my sister. (In reality, this is impossible.)	The **verb + infinitive** construction *often* refers to **hypothetical, future, unknown, incomplete,** or **impossible** events although this is not always the case.
TYPE A VERBS FOLLOWED BY A (PRO)NOUN + INFINITIVE:		
advise, allow, cause, convince, encourage, force, get, hire, invite, order, permit, warn, etc.	▪ The teacher **advised** *us* to study verbs. ▪ The doctor **convinced** *me* to eat less. ▪ The policeman **forced** *them* to pay a fine. ▪ I **hired** *an agent* to sell my house. ▪ The court **ordered** *the man* **not** to speak. ▪ Customers **are allowed** to park there. ▪ I **was encouraged** to buy a new house. ▪ The cashier **was hired** to work nights. ▪ The students **were permitted** to leave.	▪ Notice that these verbs usually indicate a speech act. ▪ If the construction is made negative, **not** is inserted between the pronoun and the infinitive. ▪ If these verbs are used in the passive, the pronoun is omitted.
TYPE A VERBS THAT MAY BE FOLLOWED BY A (PRO)NOUN + INFINITIVE:		
ask, beg, choose, dare, expect, need, promise, want, would like	▪ We **begged** to see a movie. (Result: **We** see a movie.) ▪ We **begged** *them* to see a movie. (Result: **They** see a movie.)	There is a difference in meaning if the pronoun is omitted.

14.2 WRITTEN EXERCISE: *Sentence Completion*

DIRECTIONS: A seventeenth-century poet, George Herbert, said, "And now in old age, I bud again." Think about how you would like to bud again in old age and complete the following sentences by adding an infinitive and additional ideas.

EXAMPLE

CUE: I need _____

RESPONSE: I need <u>to stay active as long as I am able</u>.

1. I hope _____.

2. I expect _____.

3. I intend _____.

4. I plan _____.

5. I refuse _____.

6. I will arrange _____.

7. I must prepare _____.

8. I refuse _____.

14.3   ORAL PRACTICE: *Verbs Followed By a (Pro)noun + Infinitive*

DIRECTIONS: Based on the cue provided, take turns with your partner asking and answering questions. Use the **verb + pronoun + infinitive** construction.

EXAMPLE

CUE: friend / invite
QUESTION: Has a friend ever invited you to do something dangerous?
ANSWER: Yes, one time a friend invited me to go skydiving.

1. parents / advise
2. teacher / ask
3. friend / convince
4. government / encourage
5. policeman / order
6. doctor / warn

14.4   WRITTEN PRACTICE: *Anti-Aging Advice*

DIRECTIONS: Below is some advice that a doctor gave a group of people at a lecture on anti-aging. On the lines provided below the lecture, use the **verb + (pro)noun + infinitive** construction to restate what he told them.

EXAMPLE

"Avoid caffeine and you will lessen the risk of heart problems." (He warned them to avoid caffeine.)

. . . Summing up, in the fight to hold on to your precious youth, there are many steps that you can take to win the battle. First of all, you should take Vitamins A, C, and E so that body tissue is not so quickly damaged. By slowing down that process, you will increase your body's ability to function. Also, live in a quiet environment so that you won't suffer such drastic hearing loss. One of the most heartbreaking effects of old age is losing the ability to communicate. In addition, if you want to slow down the loss of vision, you'd better use brighter and more focused lighting when you read. Very important, don't forget to maintain a calcium-rich diet so that you can prevent osteoporosis. If you are able to keep your bones strong, you will prevent painful breaks and fractures. Please limit your calorie intake, and your life span will increase significantly. It has been found that people who maintain their optimal weight live longer. Don't smoke! You're automatically cutting your time short if you do. You can exercise well into your eighties, and you will be a healthier 80-year-old as a result. Finally, most important, please keep a positive mental attitude, and I guarantee you'll live longer.

1. _____

2. _____

3. _____

4. _____

5. _____

6. _____

7. _____

8. _____

SPECIAL NOTE

The passive voice emphasizes the action expressed in the verb rather than the performer of the action. The pronoun is therefore omitted if the passive voice is used.

14.5   RAPID DRILL: *Omitting the (Pro)noun After the Passive*

DIRECTIONS: Change each of the above statements that you wrote from active voice to passive voice to emphasize the content of the lecture.

14.6   RECOGNITION EXERCISE: *Verbs That May Be Followed by a (Pro)noun + Infinitive*

DIRECTIONS: For each of the following sentences, state *who* would be carrying out the action of the infinitive that is underlined.

EXAMPLE

CUE: Paul wants his wife to learn English.

RESPONSE: Paul's wife will learn English.

1. Children expect their grandparents to spoil them.
2. My teacher wants to write an autobiography.
3. Sally begged her mother to stop smoking.
4. Jamie asked his grandfather to buy him a bicycle.
5. My boss chose to give a speech at the company banquet.

■ II. INFINITIVE AS COMPLEMENT OF AN ADJECTIVE

An infinitive can be used as the complement of an adjective, which means that the infinitive **adds to** or **completes** the idea expressed in the adjective. The chart below lists some of the adjectives that can be followed by an infinitive complement. See the appendix at the end of the chapter for a more complete listing.

BE + ADJECTIVE + INFINITIVE		
ADJECTIVE	**EXAMPLE**	**NOTES**
afraid **content** **disappointed** **happy** **eager** **glad** **pleased** **proud** **sad**	I am **afraid** to tell him that I lost my visa. She would be **content** to sit in front of the T.V. We were **disappointed** to hear he was sick. I'm very **happy** to be here with you. The students are **eager** to improve their grammar. I'm sure that you're **glad** to be returning home. I'm **pleased** to announce the winner of the car. They were **proud** to be selected as ambassadors. My father was **sad** to see me leave.	▪ When these adjectives are used, the subject of the sentence is living (animate). ▪ Notice that these adjectives express feelings.

BE + ADJECTIVE + (FOR + (PRO)NOUN) + INFINITIVE		
boring **disappointing** **exciting** **easy** **safe** **interesting**	It is **boring** (for me) to listen to his stories. It **was disappointing** to hear the test results. It was **exciting** to receive a letter from China. It was **easy** to find your house. When I was young, it was **safe** to walk at night. It was **interesting** to find out more about Jim. [INCORRECT: I am **interesting** to find out more about Jim.]	▪ When these adjectives are used, the subject of the sentence must be **it.** A common error is made by using a live subject with an adjective that ends in **-ing** in this construction. (See the chapter on passives for more explanation.)

BE + ADJECTIVE + ENOUGH + INFINITIVE	
EXAMPLE	**MEANING**
▪ She's 16. She's **old enough** to drive in the United States. ▪ He's 14. He's **not old enough** to drive in the United States.	▪ She is the **minimum age** necessary in order to drive. ▪ She has **not yet reached the minimum age** necessary in order to drive.

BE + TOO + ADJECTIVE + INFINITIVE	
▪ She's 101. She's **too old to drive.** ▪ She's 65. She's **not too old to drive.**	▪ She is **over the maximum age** for driving. ▪ She has **not yet reached the maximum age** for driving.

14.7   WRITTEN PARAPHRASE: *Sentence Completion*

DIRECTIONS: Below are some thoughts of a woman as she reflects on growing old. After each statement, write how she feels by paraphrasing what she said. Use the adjectives from the preceding chart.

EXAMPLE

"When I realized that I was growing old, I experienced a kind of death of self."
She was sad to realize that she was growing old.

1. "I have seen friends who are intelligent, personable, and creative give in to their lined faces, which they daily confront in the mirror."

_____ .

2. "I am not this old woman in the mirror, but the inner young girl with dreams yet to fill."

_____ .

3. "Even though I am no longer young, I can become a writer."

_____ .

4. "I felt a great sense of relief when I discovered that it wasn't too late to explore my creative talents."

_____ .

14.8   ORAL PRACTICE: *Infinitive as Adjective Complement*

DIRECTIONS: Discuss an elderly person, such as a grandparent, whom you have known and liked all your life. Use adjectives from the chart to describe the person.

EXAMPLE

I have always been proud to have such a fun-loving, active grandmother.

14.9   RAPID DRILL: *Too / Enough* and *Infinitives*

DIRECTIONS: Change the following sentences so that you are using **too** or **enough** and an **infinitive.** For each sentence make a positive and a negative statement.

EXAMPLE

Nathan can't start preschool yet, because he's only two years old.

POSITIVE: Nathan is not old enough to start preschool.

NEGATIVE: Nathan is too young to start preschool.

1. Rafael can't compete in the Olympics because he's 45 years old.
2. Susan can't buy beer in California because she's only 17 years old.
3. Cherie is 78 years old and still gets jobs playing the piano.
4. Richard will be able to vote in the 1992 U.S. presidential election because he'll be 18 years old.
5. If necessary, Dan could be drafted because he's 18 years old.
6. Mary is 38 and she's pregnant.
7. Sangadji can't study English in this intensive program because he's only 12 years old.
8. Cindy is 40 years old, and she would never date a 23-year-old man.

III. GERUNDS

A gerund consists of **verb + -ing** and also takes the place of a noun. Like infinitives, gerunds can serve a variety of functions in a sentence.

A. Gerund As Subject of the Sentence

Below are examples of how a gerund can be the subject of the sentence.

FUNCTION	EXAMPLE	NOTES
SUBJECT OF THE SENTENCE	<ul><li>**Aging** can be difficult for some people.</li><li>**Creative writing** is one of my grandmother's talents.</li><li>**His not appreciating her help** surprised me. (The fact that he did not appreciate her help surprised me.)</li><li>**Listening to her** was difficult.</li><li>It was difficult **listening to her.**</li></ul>	<ul><li>Gerund subjects are more common than infinitive subjects.</li><li>The gerund can be part of a noun phrase.</li><li>A possessive (pro)noun before a gerund phrase can take the place of a noun clause.</li><li>As with infinitives, it is possible to replace the gerund subject with **it** when it is followed by the verb **be** and an adjective.</li></ul>

14.10   RAPID DRILL: *Gerund Subjects*

DIRECTIONS: Although Derek's grandmother is 100 years old, she is fairly active. In each pair of sentences below, there is a statement about her activity and a statement describing the effect of the activity. Combine the pairs of sentences into one sentence with a gerund subject.

EXAMPLE

She gardens every day. This makes her feel useful.
Gardening makes her feel useful.

1. She has parties with her friends. This makes her feel young.
2. She takes long walks. This helps her to stay in shape.
3. She participates in a theater group and plays the piano on weekends. These activities add to her income.
4. She writes letters to friends in other countries. This keeps her in touch with the world.
5. She visits her grandchildren and plays with them. This is exciting for her.
6. She watches the news on T.V. every day. This keeps her up to date with current events.

14.11   WRITTEN PRACTICE: *Possessives in Gerund Phrases as Subject*

DIRECTIONS: Answer all of the following questions with a subject containing a possessive (pro)noun in a gerund phrase. Use a noun, pronoun, or the name of the person.

EXAMPLE

QUESTION: What impresses you about one of your grandparents?
RESPONSE: My grandfather's playing golf at the age of 80 impresses me.

1. What surprises you about a friend that you have?

   _____

2. What is something that your teacher does that helps you to learn?

   _____

3. What is something that your boyfriend / girlfriend / husband / wife does that annoys you?

   _____

4. What is something that a child does that amuses you?

   _____

5. What is something that your government does that makes you angry?

   _____

14.12   PAIRED ORAL PRACTICE: *Famous Sayings*

DIRECTIONS: Working in pairs, Student A should look only at the section below labeled Student A. Student B should look at the section labeled Student B. Student A has several explanations for famous sayings that contain infinitives or gerunds as subject of the sentence. Student B has the list of famous sayings. When Student A reads the explanation, Student B should try to find the famous saying that matches the explanation. Once you have made the match, discuss whether you agree with the saying.

EXAMPLE

EXPLANATION: I would rather suffer from a relationship that is over than not have had that relationship at all.
SAYING: It is better to have loved and lost than never to have loved at all.

STUDENT A: EXPLANATIONS

1. It is perfectly natural to make a mistake, but it requires special effort and understanding to accept an apology for a mistake.
2. The best way to acquire skills or knowledge is through experience.
3. The more I find out about something, the better I will be able to comprehend it.
4. It's difficult to accept a theory without any physical evidence.

STUDENT B: SAYINGS

a. Seeing is believing.
b. To err is human, to forgive—divine.
c. To know is to understand.
d. Learning is doing.

◼ B. Gerund As Direct Object

A gerund can also serve as a direct object after certain verbs. The chart below lists some of these verbs and helpful hints for memorization. See the chapter appendix for a more complete list.

VERBS	EXAMPLE	NOTES
TYPE B VERBS MUST BE FOLLOWED BY A GERUND:		
admit, advise, anticipate, avoid, appreciate, deny, defend, dislike, enjoy, finish, mind, recall, recommend, recollect, regret, resent, risk, suggest, tolerate, understand	▪ He **admitted** lying about his age. (He lied in the past.) ▪ The students **denied** cheating on the test. (The cheating is a completed action.) ▪ I've **finished** writing the report. (The writing has been completed.) ▪ Bob **recommends my** going to the theater. (The pronoun emphasizes that I will go.) ▪ My boss **resents** Jim's arriving late for work. (I arrive late and he doesn't like it.)	▪ A **verb + gerund** construction often refers to a **real, past, known, complete,** experience or event. ▪ A possessive (pro)noun is sometimes added before the gerund to indicate who is carrying out the action of the gerund.

14.13   WRITTEN PARAPHRASE: *Retirement Communities*

DIRECTIONS: Following is some information about retirement communities. Read the passage. Then in the space provided below the passage, rewrite it using gerunds as direct objects after verbs. The first one is done for you as an example.

Many senior citizens do not feel bad if they have to live in a retirement community. At one retirement community in Ohio, residents feel good about their living situation because they can come and go as they like. They can live on their own in apartments, cottages, or duplexes that are furnished with their personal belongings. About 40 percent of them drive their own cars because they don't want to be dependent on others for transportation. When Charles Dilgard, the community's chief executive, came to the community 20 years ago, he thought the residents didn't have a sense of independence. He remembers that they were being given too much love and care. At the time, Dilgard said that the residents should have more autonomy. Dilgard also said the residents should be provided with more facilities.

Many senior citizens enjoy living in retirement communities.

_____

_____

_____

_____

_____

_____

_____

_____

_____

_____

14.14   RAPID DRILL: *Possessives Before Gerunds*

DIRECTIONS: Change the given sentence to a sentence containing a **verb + possessive + gerund** construction.

EXAMPLE

John wanted to give his report after the deadline, and the teacher accepted this.
The teacher accepted John's giving his report after the deadline.

1. My daughter, Carol, anticipated that I would take her to a movie.
2. She appreciated it when I invited her.
3. She suggested that we go to see a murder mystery.
4. I didn't invite her boyfriend, Steve. Her boyfriend resented this.
5. My daughter understood why Steve was upset.
6. Perhaps he couldn't appreciate the fact that a mother would want to spend some time alone with her daughter.

14.15   WRITTEN EXERCISE: *Paraphrase*

DIRECTIONS: For each situation described in the cue, write a sentence by using the verb provided in parentheses, a (pro)noun, and a gerund. Use a noun, pronoun, or a person's name. Sometimes you will have to use the negative form of the verb.

EXAMPLE

1. You are on your way to the airport to pick up your mother, and you think that she will arrive late.

   (anticipate) I anticipate my mother's arriving late.

2. Your office mate never cleans up his desk, and you don't like it.

   (dislike) _____

3. A friend always lies to you, and you are really upset.

   (forgive) _____

4. You've been having a sleeping problem, and your mother said that you should see a doctor.

   (recommend) _____

5. Your father always gives you lectures, and you are angry.

   (appreciate) _____

6. Your grandmother wants to live alone, and you don't think that it's a good idea.

   (advise) _____

7. Your company decided to prohibit smoking in the building, and you are a smoker.

   (resent) _____

14.16   WRITTEN EXERCISE: *Infinitive* or *Gerund As Direct Object?*

DIRECTIONS: A plastic surgeon in Miami, Florida, has placed the following advertisement in the local newspaper, hoping to attract elderly people to his clinic for plastic surgery. Fill in the blanks with either the **infinitive** or **gerund** form of the verb in parentheses.

HOW ABOUT A FACE LIFT?

Do you need _____ (get rid of) some of those unwanted wrinkles on

your face? Do you dislike _____ (find) new wrinkles every day? I bet you

would appreciate _____ (say) goodbye to those unnecessary age lines

forever! If you intend _____ (fight) the look of old age, I recommend

_____ (pay) me a visit for a face lift. We can arrange _____

_____ (make) you look 20 years younger in a few short hours. I promise _____

_____ (return) your youthful appearance to you. I strongly suggest _____

_____ (take) advantage of this opportunity now. I dare you _____

_____ (look) younger than you are! You won't regret _____

(place) your faith in my proven skills.

CALL FOR AN APPOINTMENT TODAY!

C. Gerund As Object of a Preposition

Any time a verb follows a preposition, the verb must be in gerund form. The chart below lists some common idiomatic expressions with prepositions that are always followed by gerunds.

EXPRESSION	EXAMPLE	NOTES
TO **look forward to** **be used to**[a] **be accustomed to** **feel up to**	▪ I am **looking forward to** getting a raise. ▪ My grandmother **is used to** living alone. ▪ I'm **not accustomed to** sleeping late. ▪ I don't **feel up to** playing basketball today.	▪ Because these expressions end in **to** they can be confused with **verb +** **infinitive** constructions.
ABOUT **think about** **talk about** **complain about** **worry about** **be surprised about**	▪ I'm **thinking about** moving to London. ▪ We're **talking about** going on strike. ▪ She **complained about** getting sick. ▪ I'm **worried about** paying my bills. ▪ Lenny's **surprised about** getting fired.	▪ If a verb is used in the progressive, the sentence will contain two **-ing** verb forms.

FOR **thank someone for** **make an excuse for** **make up for**	• I **thanked the nurse for** helping me. • I **made an excuse for** being sarcastic. • My date **made up for** being late by buying me roses.	• Notice that the gerund construction with the idiom **make up for** is followed by the preposition **by** + **gerund.**
IN / ON **be interested in** **take part in** **plan on** **count on**	• I'm **interested in** improving my French. • We **took part in** helping the poor. • You should **plan on** leaving at 6:00. • You can **count on** my being early.	
OF **be afraid of** **be tired of** **be proud of** **approve of**	• Are you **afraid of** getting bored? • She's **tired of** explaining the directions. • Jan's **proud of** having so many friends. • We don't **approve of** cheating.	
WITH **be satisfied with** **be fed up with** **put up with** **be preoccupied with**	• I'll be **satisfied with** getting a raise. • They're **fed up with** being broke. • I won't **put up with** your misbehaving. • She's **preoccupied with** dieting.	

*See the modals chapter for more information on **be used to.**

14.17   WRITTEN EXERCISE: *The Fountain of Youth*

DIRECTIONS: Try to imagine what it would be like if we all could drink from a fountain of youth so that we would never age. Using one expression from each group in the chart beginning on page 335, write six advantages of drinking from the fountain of youth. If you can think of any disadvantages, add those.

EXAMPLE

People wouldn't **be preoccupied with** getting old and losing their youthful appearance.

1. _____

2. _____

3. _____

4. _____

5. _____

6. _____

GRAMMATICAL PATTERNS TWO

PREVIEW

DIRECTIONS: Read the following report that describes the characteristics of centenarians.

CENTENARIANS: THE SECRETS OF SUCCESSFUL AGING

1. There are an estimated 25,000 centenarians in the United States, and their numbers are rapidly increasing. To better understand what promotes **longevity,** the lives of centenarians and their personal characteristics need to be closely examined. We are very interested in discovering what kind of lifestyle and particularly what kind of personality determines longevity.

2. Although we may anticipate being told that there are **uniform traits** among centenarians, this is not true. It was originally thought that centenarians must be calm, **serene,** Type B personalities, with stress-free lives. However, there are centenarians who thrive on living **fast-paced, high tension** lives. As far as physical characteristics are concerned, very few claim to have been **obese** at any time in their lives. Many admit to having been social drinkers throughout their lives, and many like to drink coffee. Centenarians have a wide range of nutritional habits—some are vegetarians, but most eat meat. Most of them eat just about everything.

3. There are a few shared traits among centenarians, one of them being a **genetic propensity** toward long life; most centenarians have long-living **forebears.** They also share a sense of **altruism.** Most feel fortunate to have been blessed with **prosperity** and good health and have given help to people who aren't as fortunate. Most centenarians also have a basic love of life. They know how to treasure each day and they enjoy the simple pleasures of life. Centenarians can be party-givers, gardeners, or intellectuals. Many appreciate never having been robbed of their appetite for learning, so they are the kind of people who look for people, experiences, and opportunities that will teach them something. Many of them spend a lot of time reading to satisfy this appetite for learning. You won't find many centenarians who are soft or **slack.** They set high standards and make themselves follow through even if it requires a lot of effort.

VOCABULARY

longevity: living to an old age
uniform traits: the same characteristics
serene: calm, peaceful
fast-paced: moving quickly
high-tension: full of tension
obese: extremely fat
genetic propensity: a quality which is inherited through genes
forebears: ancestors
altruism: the quality of giving to other people
prosperity: wealth, abundance
slack: inactive, lazy

GRAMMAR CONSIDERATIONS: FOCUS

The following questions are based on the preview text and are designed to help you find out what you already know about the structures in this chapter. Work with a partner if your teacher tells you to do so.

1. In the preview text find two examples of infinitives in the past tense. Write them on the line below. How was the past tense of these infinitives formed?

_____

2. In the following sentence from the preview, is it possible to use a gerund after **like**? Why or why not?

> Many admit to having been social drinkers throughout their lives,
> and many like to drink coffee.

3. What question is answered by the infinitive phrase in the following sentence from the preview? Write the question on the line that follows the sentence.

> Many of them spend a lot of time reading to satisfy their appetite for learning.

_____

I. TYPE C VERBS: FOLLOWED BY AN INFINITIVE OR GERUND

There are some verbs that can take either infinitives or gerunds as direct objects with little or no difference in meaning, as is shown in the chart below.

TYPE C VERBS ARE FOLLOWED BY EITHER AN INFINITIVE OR A GERUND:		
WITH NO DIFFERENCE IN MEANING—		
VERB	**EXAMPLE**	**MEANING**
attempt	Tomorrow I will **attempt to surf**.	Tomorrow I will **attempt surfing**.
begin	I **began to study** two years ago.	I **began studying** two years ago.
continue	I will **continue to study**.	I will **continue studying**.
hate	I **hate to sleep** late in the morning.	I **hate sleeping** late in the morning.
like / love	He **loves to receive** her letters.	He **loves receiving** her letters.
prefer	She **prefers to take** the bus.	She **prefers taking** the bus.
start	Tomorrow I will **start to work**.	Tomorrow I will **start working**.
OR WITH A DIFFERENCE IN MEANING—		
try + infinitive + gerund	▪ Many elderly people try to stay active. ▪ My grandmother has **tried taking** long walks for her heart problems.	▪ Make an attempt/make an effort ▪ Experiment to find out if a new method works

regret		
+ infinitive	▪ I **regret to admit** that I'm over the hill. (usually used with **say, tell, inform, admit**)	▪ Feel sorry about saying something negative
+ gerund	▪ I **regret losing** all my old photographs.	▪ Feel sorry about something that has already happened
remember		
+ infinitive	▪ I always **remember to mail** my bills on time.	▪ The remembering occurs before the action.
+ gerund	▪ I **remember** always **mailing** my bills late when I was young.	▪ The remembering occurs after the action.
forget		
+ infinitive	▪ My son never **forgets to call** on my birthday.	▪ The result of forgetting is that the action doesn't take place.
+ gerund	▪ I'll **never forget calling** my son when he was in Europe. (usually used with **never**)	▪ An action is not forgotten after it takes place.
stop		
+ infinitive	▪ I always **stop to buy** the newspaper on my way home.	▪ Stop for the purpose of accomplishing a task
+ gerund	▪ I **stopped buying** the newspaper when my eyes went bad.	▪ Interrupt an action in progress.

14.18 RECOGNITION EXERCISE: *What Happened First?*

DIRECTIONS: For each sentence below, identify which action of the two that are underlined happens first.

EXAMPLE

I always stop to look in that shop on the way home.
FIRST: **stop** SECOND: **look**

1. I must remember to write a letter tonight.

   FIRST: _____ SECOND: _____

2. Sharon stopped smoking five years ago.

   FIRST: _____ SECOND: _____

3. I'll never forget visiting my great aunt in Italy.

   FIRST: _____ SECOND: _____

4. Would you <u>stop</u> at the store <u>to pick up</u> some milk on your way home?

     FIRST: _____ SECOND: _____

5. Don't you <u>regret dropping</u> out of high school?

     FIRST: _____ SECOND:_____

6. I <u>remember hating</u> physical education classes when I was in high school.

     FIRST: _____ SECOND:_____

7. I didn't <u>forget to call</u> my grandparents on their fiftieth wedding anniversary.

     FIRST: _____ SECOND: _____

8. I <u>regret to admit</u> that I've never been out of this country.

     FIRST: _____ SECOND: _____

■ 14.19   WRITTEN EXERCISE: *Fill in the Blanks*

DIRECTIONS: Fill in the blanks in the passage below with the correct infinitive or gerund form of the verb provided.

Although Caroline Towers is 93 years old, her memory is sharp as a whistle. She never forgets

_____ (call) her grandchildren on their birthdays, and she always stops

_____ (buy) them presents when she goes to visit them.

She   likes   _____   (do)   this   because   she   remembers

_____ (get) presents from her grandmother when she was a little girl. She

tries _____ (remember) their favorite colors and their special interests.

Her sons and daughter always tell her to stop (buy) _____ presents for

the grandchildren because they are afraid the children will become spoiled. However, Caroline

can't regret _____ (show) her grandchildren that they are special to her.

14.20   WRITTEN EXERCISE: *Review of Troublesome Verbs*

DIRECTIONS: At the end of each of the following sentences, there is a verb in parentheses. Write one sentence using the **verb + gerund** construction and one sentence with the **verb + infinitive** construction.

EXAMPLE

Robert smokes a pack of cigarettes a day. (stop)

INFINITIVE: Robert stops to buy cigarettes every day on his way home from work.

GERUND: Robert would like to stop smoking, but he can't.

1. Gail doesn't want any more wrinkles on her face. (try)

   INFINITIVE: _____

   GERUND: _____

2. Although Cynthia is 85, she has many friends all over the world whom she still keeps in touch with. (forget)

   INFINITIVE: _____

   GERUND: _____

3. Dan is 74 years old and has never been married. (regret)

   INFINITIVE: _____

   GERUND: _____

4. My grandfather has taken his dog for a walk in the forest every day for the last 10 years. (remember)

   INFINITIVE: _____

   GERUND: _____

II. INFINITIVES AND GERUNDS AS COMPLEMENTS

Infinitives and gerunds can function as complements of the verb **be** and other linking verbs as shown in the chart below.

COMPLEMENT	EXAMPLE	NOTES
INFINITIVE	▪ My goal **is to live** an active life. ▪ He **appears to be** younger than he is. ▪ The children **seem to like** the book. My **hope is to retire** when I'm fifty. ▪ My **dream** is **to become** a doctor.	▪ Occurs after **be, seems, appears** ▪ Often used with nouns that express **incomplete, future, impossible** actions or events such as **hope, dream, goal**

| GERUND | <ul><li>Because she is bedridden, the **solution** is **finding** a private nurse.</li><li>The **result** of the successful interview was **getting** the job.</li><li>The **key** to staying young is **maintaining** an active life.</li><li>What I'm really **looking forward to** is **reading** all the books I haven't read.</li><li>What I appreciate about this school is **meeting** people from other countries.</li></ul> | <ul><li>Occurs only after **be**</li><li>Often used with nouns that express **past, complete, known,** or **fulfilled** actions or events such as **result, solution, secret, key.**</li><li>Used in combination with verbs normally followed by gerunds when they occur in a noun clause as subject of the sentence</li><li>This pattern is less common than using a gerund subject.</li></ul> |

14.21   ORAL PRACTICE: *The Stages of Life*

DIRECTIONS: Your teacher will assign you a role: child, adolescent, or adult. Complete each of the following statements with an infinitive or gerund complement according to the stage of life you are in.

1. My primary goal in life is _____ .

2. My dream has always been _____ .

3. What I really enjoy about this age is _____ .

4. I seem _____ ,

    but _____ .

5. The key to being happy is _____ .

6. What I am anticipating with great excitement is _____ .

7. The solution to all my problems would be _____ .

8. The worst part about being this age is _____ .

14.22   WRITTEN EXERCISE: *Infinitive* and *Gerund Complements*

DIRECTIONS: Read the following passage by Ann Guidici Fettner and Pamela Weintraub about longevity research—the study of aging and how to avoid it. Then, with an infinitive or gerund complement, complete each statement about the research in the space provided. The first one is completed as an example.

1. Scientists in the forefront of longevity research are studying chemical changes that occur in the body over time. They are convinced that information about these changes will provide increased comprehension of the problems related to aging, which may result in an aging cure.
2. The thymosins (a family of hormones) play a key role in keeping people healthy, so scientists are investigating how they work. If we can give the elderly enough thymosin to keep the T cell

level high, we should be able to enhance immunity throughout old age. One type of T cell is the *killer* cell, which attacks foreign organisms and cancer cells directly. Major progress was made when scientists discovered that thymosins prime the levels of brain hormones involved in reproduction, growth, and development. In five to ten years people will take these thymosins daily to maintain a whole complement of characteristics associated with youth. Scientists realized that daily intake of thymosins could push the average person's vigorous years upward of eighty or ninety simply by boosting the immune system. Scientists know that other substances may also prove to be potent antiaging agents, but they must find them.

1. One way to find an aging cure is <u>to understand the problems related to aging</u>.

2. The goal of scientists is _____

     _____ .

3. The solution to weakened immunity in old age is _____

     _____ .

4. The job of the *killer* cell is _____

     _____ .

5. A major breakthrough in the research was _____

     _____ .

6. Something we can look forward to is _____

     _____ .

7. A positive result of the research was _____

     _____ .

8. One difficulty for scientists is _____

     _____ .

III. INFINITIVES AS REDUCED CLAUSES

Infinitive phrases are used to replace adverb, adjective, and noun clauses. When this happens, the infinitive phrase is answering a specific question and serving a particular function. The chart below provides examples of each of these types of clauses reduced to infinitive phrases along with their corresponding questions and functions.

ADVERB PHRASE / CLAUSE	FUNCTION	INFINITIVE PHRASE
▪ Many centenarians spend a lot of time reading **because they want to satisfy their appetite for learning**. ▪ Many centenarians take long walks **so that they can stay in shape**.	WHY? / FOR WHAT PURPOSE?	▪ Many centenarians spend a lot of time reading **to satisfy their appetite for learning**. ▪ Many centenarians take long walks **to stay in shape**.[a]

ADJECTIVE CLAUSE		INFINITIVE PHRASE
▪ I have many letters **that I must write**. ▪ This is the person **whom you should see**. ▪ The library is the place **where you can find information about your topic**.	ACCOMPLISH A TASK / SUGGESTION	▪ I have many letters **to write**. ▪ This is the person **to see**. ▪ The library is the place **to find information about your topic**.
NOUN CLAUSE		**INFINITIVE PHRASE**
▪ Centenarians know **how they can treasure each day**. ▪ My doctor told me when **I should exercise**. ▪ He finally decided **where he should spend his vacation**.	ABILITY SUGGESTION	▪ Centenarians know **how to treasure each day**. ▪ My doctor told me **when to exercise**. ▪ He finally decided **where to spend his vacation**.

*a*This is commonly referred to as the *infinitive of purpose*.

14.23 RAPID DRILL: *Replacing Clauses with Infinitive Phrases*

DIRECTIONS: Replace the clause in each of the sentences below with an infinitive phrase.

EXAMPLE

I have to take certain steps if I want to stay young-looking.
I have to take certain steps to stay young-looking.

1. My neighbor is the person who can teach you about sailing.
2. I need a face lift so that I can change the shape of my eyes, which make me look sad and droopy.
3. Richard's boss was teaching him how he could use the computer.
4. Mr. Sanborn is the teacher whom you should consult about university placement.
5. If I want to fight the inevitability of aging for a few years, I must have cosmetic surgery done.
6. I have a lot of work that I must complete by Monday.
7. This is the way in which you should write a business letter.
8. There are many beautiful sights that you should see in this city.
9. "Senior Living" is the place where you should live if you want spacious independent accommodations.

14.24 PAIRED PRACTICE: *Answering Questions*

DIRECTIONS: Ask your partner a question based on the cue provided. Your partner should respond using an infinitive phrase.

EXAMPLE

CUE: how / stay young   QUESTION: How can I stay young?
RESPONSE: Staying young at heart is the best way to stay young.

1. where / good Italian food
2. why / learn English
3. how / get into a good university
4. who / talk to about visa problems
5. where / find good prices on clothes

14.25   ORAL INTERVIEW: *Cosmetic Surgery*

DIRECTIONS: Interview two or three Americans or other English speakers about cosmetic surgery. Ask the following questions.

1. Would you ever consider cosmetic surgery such as a face lift, or liposuction? Why or why not?
2. Why do so many famous people, such as movie stars, have cosmetic surgery?
3. Why do ordinary people agree to such surgery?
4. Why do you think people want to hang on to their youthful appearance?

14.26   WRITTEN FEEDBACK

DIRECTIONS: Based on the information you collected from your interview, complete the following sentences with infinitive phrases.

1. Many famous people, such as movie stars, have cosmetic surgery done _____

    _____ .

2. Many ordinary people have cosmetic surgery done _____

    _____ .

3. People want to hang on to their youthful appearance _____

    _____ .

14.27   PAIRED PRACTICE: *Oral Report*

DIRECTIONS: Based on the information already discussed in this chapter and what you have read, prepare an oral report with your partner on the techniques people use to prevent aging. Write at least 10 sentences for the report, and when you present it to the class, divide the sentences up so that each of you is giving half the report. Use infinitive phrases whenever possible to replace either an adverb, adjective, or noun clause.

IV. PAST AND PASSIVE INFINITIVES AND GERUNDS

It is possible to use gerunds and infinitives for the functions already covered in this chapter in the past tense or in the passive voice. The following chart demonstrates these possibilities.

NOTES	EXAMPLE	PAST / PASSIVE FORMS
1. PAST GERUND • With the past gerund form, there is an emphasis on the *completion* of the action. • Some verb + gerund constructions *cannot* be followed by a past gerund. **(suggest, recommend, consider, risk)**	• I **denied taking** the money. • I **denied having taken** the money. (Both of these sentences have past time reference.) [INCORRECT: He **suggested having gone** to that movie.]	**having + past participle**
2. PAST INFINITIVE • Distinguishes between present and past or future time reference.	• Centenarians feel lucky **to be living** long lives. (Present) • Centenarians feel lucky **to have lived** long lives. (Past) • She **appears to have won** the race. (Past) • I **hope to have finished** by Friday. (Future)	**to + have + past participle**
3. PRESENT - PASSIVE GERUND • The passive forms emphasize the action or event expressed in the verb.	• We anticipate **being told** that there are uniform traits among centenarians.	**being + past participle**
4. PRESENT - PASSIVE INFINITIVE	• Centenarians need **to be** closely **examined.**	**to + be + past participle**
5. PAST - PASSIVE GERUND	• They appreciate never **having been robbed** of their appetite for learning.	**having + been + past participle**
6. PAST - PASSIVE INFINITIVE	• Most centenarians feel fortunate **to have been blessed** with prosperity and good health.	**to + have + been + past participle**

14.28   RECOGNITION EXERCISE: *Past* and *Passive Infinitives* and *Gerunds*

DIRECTIONS: For each sentence, determine the time reference of the sentence.

EXAMPLE

I appreciate finally being given a chance to meet a centenarian. (Present)

1. I dislike reaching the age of 40.
2. My teacher seems to have enjoyed her vacation.
3. I would prefer to have been given a retirement plan at work.
4. Susan recommends teaching at that school.
5. My brother is relieved to have finished his thesis.
6. The lecture will be about finding a job.
7. Most centenarians admit to helping other people.
8. My grandmother is pleased to have delivered the good news about increased retirement pay.

14.29   ORAL PRACTICE: *Older Is Wiser*

DIRECTIONS: Describe an experience from your past that made you wiser or taught you a lesson. Use a variety of past and passive forms.

14.30   WRITTEN EXERCISE: *Past* and *Present Infinitives* and *Gerunds*

DIRECTIONS: Below is a passage about a 97-year-old man who has been hawking newspapers (peddling in the street) in San Francisco for 40 years. Fill in the blanks with past and passive forms of the verbs given in parentheses.

Harold Douglas claims _____ (start) hawking newspapers on street

corners before there were automatic streetlights. He is proud _____

(know) as the oldest hawker in San Francisco. He happily mentions _____

_____ (greet) yesterday by dozens of people who shook his hand as he stood on his

street corner. He refuses _____ (stay) in the house all day staring out the

window at nothing. He appreciates _____ (permit) to sell newspapers

every day on the street corner. He regrets _____ (suffer) from a severe

case of pneumonia this past winter, which kept him from his job. He is happy _____

_____ (raise) as a hard worker. He has never liked sitting around.

V. CAUSATIVE VERBS: *Let, Make, Help, Get*

It is important to know which of these verbs take an infinitive as direct object and their meaning.

VERB AND RULE	EXAMPLE	MEANING
DON'T USE *TO*		
MAKE + (PRO)NOUN + SIMPLE FORM OF VERB OR ADJECTIVE	▪ My teacher **makes me write** an essay every week. ▪ Taking tests **makes me nervous.** ▪ Watching T.V. **makes me sleepy.**	▪ Require, force ▪ Cause a physical or emotional reaction

HAVE + (PRO)NOUN + SIMPLE FORM OF VERB **or** + NOUN / PRONOUN + PARTICIPLE (PASSIVE)	▪ Kathy **has her kids clean** their rooms on Saturdays. ▪ Kathy **has her house cleaned** every Saturday.	▪ Delegate work or responsibility to someone ▪ Work or responsibility is taken from you.
LET + (PRO)NOUN + SIMPLE FORM OF VERB	▪ The IRS won't **let me withdraw** money from my retirement account without a penalty.	▪ Allow, enable
USE *TO*		
GET + (PRO)NOUN + INFINITIVE **or** + NOUN + PARTICIPLE (PASSIVE)	▪ We should **get my grandmother to go out** dancing with us. ▪ I **get my suits dry cleaned** every two weeks.	▪ Coerce, persuade ▪ Delegate work or responsibility
***TO* IS OPTIONAL**		
HELP + (PRO)NOUN + SIMPLE FORM OF VERB	▪ Staying busy **helps my father forget** about his age. ▪ Writing **helps me to express** myself.	▪ Provide assistance in making something happen

14.31 ORAL PRACTICE: *Causative Verbs*

DIRECTIONS: Use causative verbs from the preceding chart to answer the following questions your teacher or partner asks you.

1. Are you easily persuaded? Give some examples.
2. If you had a teenage son or daughter, what kinds of rules would you have?
3. In your job or at home, what kind of work do you delegate to other people?
4. What kinds of things does your English teacher require?
5. When you're studying a second language, how can you best remember vocabulary?

14.32 WRITTEN EXERCISE: *Fill in the Blanks*

DIRECTIONS: Fill in the blank with the appropriate causative verb, a noun or pronoun if necessary, and the correct form of the verb in parentheses.

When the police officer saw me speeding, he _____ (pull over) to the

side of the road. I couldn't remember where the car registration was, so my wife

_____ (find) it. I wanted to tell the officer why I was driving so fast, but

he wouldn't _____ (explain). Finally, I _____
(listen) by saying that my wife was about to give birth. He jumped into action and

_____ his assistant _____ (call) an ambulance.

VI. SPECIAL PROBLEMS WITH GERUNDS AND INFINITIVES

PROBLEM	EXPLANATION
For + Gerund or **For + Infinitive** to express purpose: [INCORRECT: I would turn around on the street just **for having** a look at him.] CORRECT: I would turn around on the street just **to have** a look at him. [INCORRECT: John studied his notes **for to prepare** for the test.] CORRECT: John studied his notes **to prepare** for his test.	Use the infinitive form to express purpose. Don't use the gerund after **for** unless you're explaining the use of something.
Incorrect form after certain verbs: [INCORRECT: The mechanic **recommended to change** the oil.] CORRECT: The mechanic **recommended changing** the oil.	Certain verbs must be followed by gerunds, and certain verbs must be followed by infinitives.
Enough before the adjective or **much** after **too:** [INCORRECT: He's **enough old** to drive a car.] CORRECT: He's **old enough** to drive a car. [INCORRECT: He's **too much old** to run marathons.] CORRECT: He's **too old** to run marathons.	**Enough** follows the adjective. **Too** is followed directly by the adjective.

■ 14.33   ERROR ANALYSIS

DIRECTIONS: Find the errors with the use of gerunds and infinitives in the following sentences and correct them.

1. The teacher suggested to read the newspaper so that I could improve my English.
2. Some elderly people belong to clubs just for having an opportunity for social contact.
3. Martin is enough educated to get a better job in his profession.
4. It is difficult to imagining what my life would be like if I were 100 years old.
5. The doctor convinced to eat more calcium-rich foods for stronger bones.
6. The mother promised taking the children to the country for the weekend.

7. The spectators were exciting to see their team winning the game.
8. Her brother didn't help her move shocked me.
9. After many months of hard labor, the workers finished to build the apartment complex.
10. The ground was too much wet to play golf.
11. The police officer pulled over the driver for giving him a speeding ticket.
12. I'm used to leave work every day at 5:00.
13. The nursing home residents appreciated we sang folk songs for them.
14. The child always stops buying candy on the way home from school.
15. After the movie, we considered having gone to get some ice cream.
16. These library books need being returned in three weeks.
17. The court made the woman to pay a fine for driving without a license.
18. The foreign dignitaries were interested to meet with the president.
19. After a very persuasive speech, the salesperson got him buy the cologne.
20. My hope is living a long, healthy, happy life.

ANALYSIS OF AN AUTHENTIC TEXT

DIRECTIONS: Read the following article about aging, referring to the vocabulary on page 351.

IN THE BATTLE AGAINST AGING, WE FORSAKE GRACE FOR A LARGER ARSENAL OF WEAPONS
by Ellen Goodman

"I don't intend to grow old gracefully. I intend to fight it every step of the way."

What am I to make of this message? The Census Bureau just announced that the average age of Americans is now a **notch** over 32 years old. The first of the 75 million baby-boomers have passed 40. Their midlife is marked by the emergence of all sorts of products to help them fight it every step of the way.

There are more than the usual number of **unguents** and **elixirs** that promise to rub the age out of our skins and preserve our energy. There are more than the usual products to cover gray hair and fill in the face lines. There are more than the usual **admonitions** to leg-lift a path to eternally youthful thighs.

Men who could accept their baldness or risk the **ridicule** of a toupee now have the chance of growing hair again. Women and men who had to accept their **crow's feet** or risk the knife to retrieve their younger, tauter skin can now chemically iron their skin.

In modest ways, aging has begun to look like a personal choice. How far are you willing to go to stay the same?

Clearly the money is in youth products. There is no way to sell self-acceptance. There may be a profit in the natural look but not in nature.

As we are offered this expanding **array** of weapons, we increase our defense budget. And with each item, with each choice, how much harder it becomes to negotiate a peaceful coexistence with our own age.

How much harder it becomes to age gracefully.

VOCABULARY

notch: a little bit
unguents: creams, oils
elixirs: preparations designed to prolong life
admonitions: warnings
ridicule: mocking, laughing
crow's feet: the wrinkles at the outer edge of the eye
array: selection

DISCUSSION QUESTIONS

1. Discuss some of the methods used to fight the aging process and their purpose. How effective do you think these methods are?
2. Do you agree that there is no way to sell self-acceptance? Do you think that by looking and feeling younger, self-acceptance improves?
3. What does the author mean by the difference between the natural "look" and nature?

═══════ COMPOSITION TOPICS ═══════

Use what you have learned in this chapter about gerunds and infinitives to write a well-organized essay on one of the following topics.

1. Describe the attitude in your country toward aging. What aspects of lifestyle, opportunities, and services for the elderly reflect this attitude?
2. Describe the three stages of your life: childhood, adolescence, and adulthood.
3. Would you like to drink from the fountain of youth? Why or why not?

APPENDIX

TYPE A VERBS MUST BE FOLLOWED BY AN INFINITIVE:

VERBS	EXAMPLE
1. afford	We **can't afford** to buy a house.
2. agree	The courts **agreed** to suspend the sentence.
3. appear	The child **appeared** to be sick.
4. arrange	She **arranged** to care for her grandmother.
5. ask	She **is asking** to go on the trip with us.
6. beg	He **begged** to have ice cream with his pie.
7. (not) care	I **don't care** to spend my vacation away from home.
8. claim	He **claims** to have spent only $5.00 for that book.
9. consent	The lawyer **consented** to defend her.
10. decide	I **decided** to transfer to another school.
11. deserve	She **deserves** to receive the outstanding citizen award.
12. expect	We **expect** to get a loan from the bank.
13. fail	She **failed** to complete the project on time.
14. hesitate	**Don't hesitate** to ask questions if you don't understand.
15. hope	I **hope** to receive a scholarship for that school.
16. intend	Do you **intend** to stay in this city for long?
17. learn	They **learned** to play soccer when they were growing up.
18. manage	Somehow he **managed** to get all of his clothes into his suitcase.
19. mean	I **didn't mean** to step on your foot.
20. need	We **need** to discuss this problem before it becomes serious.
21. offer	A friend **offered** to take me home after work.
22. plan	She **plans** to go to graduate school.
23. prepare	The pilot **is preparing** to land the plane.
24. pretend	She **pretended** to be shocked at the news.
25. promise	They **promised** to return the shovel when they were done.
26. refuse	The manager **refuses** to give us our money back.
27. seem	The students **seem** to like their new books.
28. struggle	He must **struggle** to write letters when he's on vacation.
29. swear	I **swear** to keep our secret while I'm away.
30. threaten	The city council **is threatening** to ration water.
31. wait	The children **are waiting** to get on the bus.
32. wish	I **don't wish** to discuss this issue any further.

TYPE A VERBS FOLLOWED BY A (PRO)NOUN + INFINITIVE:

1. advise	The teacher **advised** *us* to study verbs.
2. allow	She didn't **allow** *me* to leave class early.
3. ask	The cashier **asked** *me* to date the check.
4. cause	The heat **caused** *her* to pass out.
5. challenge	The history book **challenges** *us* to remember many dates.

6. **convince**	The doctor **convinced** *me* to eat less.
7. **dare**	My friends **dared** *me* to jump off the cliff.
8. **encourage**	His coach **encouraged** *him* to train every day.
9. **forbid**	The school **forbids** *us* to have more than three absences.
10. **force**	The police officer **forced** *them* to pay a fine.
11. **get**	They **got** *the police officer* to drop the charges.
12. **hire**	I **hired** *an agent* to sell my house.
13. **instruct**	The teacher **instructed** *us* to open our books.
14. **invite**	I **invited** *my boss* to have lunch with me.
15. **order**	The guards **ordered** *the protesters* to leave.
16. **permit**	His father **permitted** *him* to drive when he was 16.
17. **persuade**	Her mother **persuaded** *her* to apply to graduate school.
18. **remind**	Please **remind** *me* to buy some stamps.
19. **require**	The law **requires** *us* to take a blood test before marriage.
20. **teach**	My piano instructor **is teaching** *me* to use the pedal.
21. **tell**	The clerk **told** *me* to pay at the cash register.
22. **urge**	My accountant **urged** *me* to file my income taxes early.
23. **warn**	My doctor **warned** *me* to quit smoking.

TYPE A VERBS THAT MAY BE FOLLOWED BY A (PRO)NOUN + INFINITIVE:

1. **ask**	The cashier **asked** to see some identification.
	The cashier **asked** *me* to show some identification.
2. **beg**	We **begged** to see a movie.
	We **begged** *the teacher* to show us a movie.
3. **choose**	She **chose** to lead the discussion.
	She **chose** *me* to lead the discussion.
4. **dare**	How **could** you **dare** to jump off the cliff?
	My friends **dared** *me* to jump off the cliff.
5. **expect**	I **expected** to pass with a very good grade.
	My father **expected** *me* to pass with a very good grade.
6. **need**	I **need** to help my sister with a problem.
	I **need** *you* to help me with this problem.
7. **want**	She doesn't **want** to make the wrong decision.
	She doesn't **want** *them* to make the wrong decision.
8. **would like**	I **would like** to know the answer.
	I **would like** *them* to know the answer.

TYPE B VERBS MUST BE FOLLOWED BY A GERUND:

1. **admit**	He **admitted** lying about his age.
2. **anticipate**	The director **anticipated** being in the meeting for an hour.
3. **appreciate**	He **appreciated** hearing the good news about his vacation.
4. **avoid**	I **avoid** eating chocolate.
5. **complete**	We **completed** arranging the table just as the guests arrived.
6. **consider**	**Have** you ever **considered** traveling around the world?
7. **delay**	The students **delayed** returning to class after the break.

8.	**deny**	The child **denied** taking the money.
9.	**discuss**	They **have discussed** moving to another city.
10.	**dislike**	I **dislike** getting up early in the morning.
11.	**enjoy**	He **enjoys** shopping for antiques.
12.	**escape**	We barely **escaped** having an accident during the snowstorm.
13.	**finish**	I've **finished** writing the report.
14.	**can't help**	I **can't help** thinking about this problem.
15.	**keep**	If it **keeps** raining, we'll have to cancel our plans.
16.	**mention**	They **mentioned** going out to eat.
17.	**mind**	I **don't mind** taking the bus home.
18.	**miss**	We **miss** taking walks in the park.
19.	**postpone**	Let's **postpone** getting together until you recover.
20.	**practice**	Perhaps you **should practice** giving your speech beforehand.
21.	**quit**	I **quit** attending the meetings because I didn't have time.
22.	**recall**	I **don't recall** giving anyone this information.
23.	**recollect**	She **couldn't recollect** leaving her keys in the office.
24.	**recommend**	Bob **recommends** my going to the theater.
25.	**resent**	My boss **resents** my arriving late for work.
26.	**resist**	We **must resist** allowing our opponent to overtake us.
27.	**risk**	You **will risk** losing your job if you continue to be careless.
28.	**suggest**	Someone **suggested** taking a drive into the country.
29.	**tolerate**	I **can't tolerate** smoking in my house.
30.	**understand**	Her father **couldn't understand** her wanting to travel so far.

TYPE C VERBS ARE FOLLOWED BY EITHER AN INFINITIVE OR A GERUND: WITH NO DIFFERENCE IN MEANING—

1.	**begin**	Yesterday I **began to read** a new novel.
		Yesterday I **began reading** a new novel.
2.	**can't bear**	I **can't bear to see** homeless people on the street.
		I **can't bear seeing** homeless people on the street.
3.	**can't stand**	My grandmother **can't stand to hear** my loud music.
		My grandmother **can't stand hearing** my loud music.
4.	**continue**	If you **continue to smoke** you may get sick.
		If you **continue smoking** you may get sick.
5.	**hate**	Some children **hate to eat** vegetables.
		Some children **hate eating** vegetables.
6.	**like**	Jan **likes to be** on time.
		Jan **likes being** on time.
7.	**love**	Marc **loves to play** tennis.
		Marc **loves playing** tennis.
8.	**prefer**	I **prefer to walk** if I can.
		I **prefer walking** if I can.
9.	**start**	She **started to study** English in high school.
		She **started studying** English in high school.

OR WITH A DIFFERENCE IN MEANING—

1. **forget**	I always **forget to lock** my bicycle.
	I'll never **forget going** to Disneyland when I was a child.
2. **regret**	I **regret to tell** you that our company can't hire you.
	He **regretted going** to the interview in shorts.
3. **remember**	You **should remember to mail** your application by May 15.
	I'll always **remember flying** to Florida when I was three years old.
4. **stop**	I **must stop to buy** some milk on my way home from work.
	I **will stop smoking** tomorrow.
5. **try**	My mother **will try to find** a new job next month.
	She **will try sending** her resume to a few companies first.

15

THE FUTURE IS IN OUR HANDS

⊟ Comparative structures

THE FUTURE IS IN OUR HANDS   **Bigger Is Not Better**

DISCUSSION QUESTIONS

1. How do you think life will change in the next 10–20 years as we approach the twenty-first century?
2. What important technological advances have you seen in your lifetime? Have any of these had a negative impact on society or the environment?
3. What kind of dangers do we face on this planet as we progress into the future? What can you do personally to lessen these dangers?
4. Why is it important for people all over the world to think and act as a "world community"?

OBJECTIVES

In this chapter, you will learn:

1. To understand the rules for the comparative and superlative forms of adjectives and adverbs
2. To understand the sentence patterns used for making comparisons
3. To use superlative constructions
4. To use equal comparative constructions
5. To use conditional comparative constructions
6. To use comparative words or expressions to express a progressive change of state

═══ PREVIEW ═══

DIRECTIONS: The following article discusses the necessity of returning to a simple lifestyle in order to save the earth. Read the article, referring to the vocabulary list below when necessary.

VOLUNTARY SIMPLICITY
by Duane Elgin

1. Quietly and without **fanfare,** people from all **walks of life** in the United States have been experimenting with a lifestyle called voluntary simplicity. This approach, which stresses **frugal** consumption, spiritual growth, and environmental respect, encourages people to pursue lives that are outwardly simple and inwardly rich.

2. Why? Because the earth has **finite** nonrenewable resources, increasing environmental pollution, and an economic system that promotes an uneven distribution of goods. As economist E. F. Schumacher pointed out, "We must live simply that others may simply live." . . . Some strategies for practicing voluntary simplicity on a personal level include using products that are **durable,** energy efficient, and nonpolluting; recycling metal, glass, and paper products; using public transit, **car pools,** and smaller cars; eating lower on the food chain (fewer processed foods, more simple, healthy foods appropriate for sustaining life on a small planet); becoming more self-reliant; and pursuing work that contributes to the well-being of the world.

3. . . . In short, we must change our everyday habits of consumption. The material possessions that we strive for so **arduously** must lose the intensity of their appeal. **Mainstream** culture under the **sway** of voluntary simplicity would encourage people to live in smaller homes that combine functional simplicity and beauty. The person who was previously envied for having an expensive car and the latest in fashion might be criticized for tasteless **ostentation,** totally inappropriate in a world of great human need.

4. This does not mean that people should completely turn away from the material things of life. Rather, it means that people must increasingly sense that the totality of life is not well served by the endless **accumulation** of luxuries and nonessentials.

5. I believe that if we consciously simplify our lives, finding a satisfying balance between the material and spiritual aspects of existence will be much easier. It is a personal decision and personal responsibility. Each one of us must act to restore the balance. But the cumulative result of our individual actions can transform our nation and the world.

VOCABULARY

fanfare: a display that is usually noisy and showy

walks of life: representing different professions, age groups, social status, educational background, etc.

frugal: thrifty, economical

finite: something defined by limits or an end

durable: long-lasting despite frequent use

car pools: two or more people sharing rides to work or school

arduously: with much energy, strenuously

mainstream: belonging to the largest representative group of a culture or society

sway: persuasion, conviction

ostentation: a showy display of wealth

accumulation: collection, gathering, storing up

CULTURAL NOTE / DISCUSSION

Material possessions, especially cars, have traditionally been highly regarded in American culture. People work very hard all their lives to accumulate as many material possessions as possible. Therefore, the practice of voluntary simplicity will be very difficult to undertake for the average American. Does your culture have the same high regard for material possessions? Would the concept of voluntary simplicity be easily accepted in your culture? What are some specific ways it could be practiced in your country?

GRAMMAR CONSIDERATIONS: FOCUS

The following questions are based on the preview text and are designed to help you find out what you already know about the structures in this chapter. Some of the questions may be hard and some of them may be easy. Answer as many of the questions as you can. Work with a partner if your teacher tells you to do so.

1. Find four adjectives in paragraph 2 that are used to express comparison between present lifestyle and that of voluntary simplicity. Write them below. How are these forms different? What rule can you make about the formation of comparative adjectives?

   _____   _____

   _____   _____

2. In the following sentence from paragraph 3, how would you change the first boldfaced phrase to correspond in form to the second one? What rule can you make about these forms?

   The person who was previously envied for having **an expensive** car and **the latest** in fashion

   might be criticized for tasteless ostentation, totally inappropriate in a world of great human

   need.

GRAMMATICAL PATTERNS ONE

I. REVIEW OF COMPARATIVE FORMS

A. Comparative Forms of Adjectives

The chart below states the rules for the comparative and superlative forms of adjectives.

RULE	FORMS		
	ADJECTIVE	**COMPARATIVE**	**SUPERLATIVE**
ONE-SYLLABLE ADJECTIVES Add **-er** and **-est** to the adjective.	big small	bigger smaller	the biggest the smallest
TWO-SYLLABLE ADJECTIVES **1.** If a two-syllable adjective ends in **y, -ple,** or **-ble,** use **-er** and **-est.** If the adjective ends in **y,** change the **y** to **i** and add **-er** or **-est.**	easy simple humble	easier simpler humbler	the easiest the simplest humblest
2. Use either **-er** and **-est** or **more** and **most**[a] if the adjective ends in **-ly, -ow, -er,** or **-some.**	friendly	friendlier / more friendly yellower / more yellow handsomer / more handsome	the friendliest / the most friendly the yellowest / the most yellow the handsomest / the most handsome
3. Some words without suffixes can use **-er** and **-est** or **more** and **most.** **4.** For other two-syllable adjectives use **more** and **most.**	quiet stupid wasteful	quieter / more quiet stupider more wasteful	the quietest / the most quiet the stupidest the most wasteful
ADJECTIVES WITH MORE THAN TWO SYLLABLES If the adjective has more than two syllables use **more** and **most.**	beautiful	more beautiful	the most beautiful
IRREGULAR FORMS There are a few adjectives whose comparative and superlative forms are completely different words.	good bad little far	better worse less farther	the best the worst the least the farthest

[a]**Less** and **the least** can be substituted for **more** and **the most.**

15.1 PAIRED PRACTICE: *Comparative Forms of Adjectives*

DIRECTIONS: As you discuss the following issues related to voluntary simplicity, take turns with your partner, using the adjective in parentheses to ask for a comparison of the two items provided. As you respond, explain your reasons for your choice.

EXAMPLE

CUE: carpooling / taking the bus (energy-efficient)
STUDENT A: Which is more energy-efficient, carpooling or taking the bus?
STUDENT B: Carpooling is more energy-efficient.

1. paper / plastic (bad)
2. potato chips / banana (wholesome)
3. air conditioner / fan (extravagant)
4. airport / train station (quiet)
5. cans / bottles (good)
6. shower / bath (wasteful)
7. fast food / a home-cooked meal (nutritious)
8. recycling paper / throwing paper in the garbage (costly to the environment)

B. Comparative Forms of Adverbs

The chart below states the rules for comparative and superlative forms of adverbs.

ADVERBS			
TWO-SYLLABLE ADVERBS **More** and **most** are used to form comparative and superlative forms of two-syllable adverbs.	**quickly** **often** **seldom**	**more quickly** **more often** **more seldom**	**the most quickly** **the most often** **the most seldom**
ONE-SYLLABLE ADVERBS There are a few one-syllable adverbs whose comparative and superlative are formed by adding **-er** and **-est.**	**fast** **hard**	**faster** **harder**	**the fastest** **the hardest**
IRREGULAR FORMS There are a few adverbs whose comparative and superlative forms are completely different words.	**little** **well** **badly** **far**	**less** **better** **worse** **farther**	**the least** **the best** **the worst** **the farthest**

15.2 WRITTEN PRACTICE: *A Better Future*

DIRECTIONS: For each pair of sentences below, one of the blanks should be filled in with the comparative form of the **adjective** given before the sentence, and the other blank should be filled in with the comparative form of the **adverb.**

EXAMPLE

SAFE: a. The air will be <u>safer</u> if the present pollution levels drop.

      b. We will be living <u>more safely</u> if we reduce the present pollution levels.

1. PEACEFUL

   a. We must work _____ towards solutions of global problems.

   b. The world will be _____ if nations continue to work together.

2. SIMPLE

   a. People should try to live _____ lives.

   b. We must live _____ so that others may simply live.

3. CONVENIENT

   a. Shopping will be _____ with the help of computers.

   b. We will be able to shop _____ with the help of computers.

4. GOOD

   a. With a mass transit system that is designed _____, we will be less dependent on cars.

   b. With _____ mass transit, we will be less dependent on cars.

5. QUIET

   a. Long before all of the many conveniences of the present, life was much

      _____.

   b. People used to live _____ before all of the many present-day conveniences.

15.3 PAIRED PRACTICE: *Getting to Know You*

DIRECTIONS: Circle one of the numbers on the scale to rate yourself on each pair of questions. Then compare and discuss your characteristics with those of your partner's. Use the comparative forms of adjectives and adverbs when you discuss your differences. Be prepared to report to the class if your teacher asks you.

EXAMPLE

QUESTION: How **competent** are you in English? How **well** do you speak the language?

0	1	2	3	4	5	STUDENT A
0	1	2	3	4	5	STUDENT B

COMPARISON: She is **more competent** in English. She speaks the language **better**.

1. How friendly are you? Do you make friends easily?

     0   1   2   3   4   5

2. How **conscientious** are you about the environment? Do you recycle **carefully**?

| 0 | 1 | 2 | 3 | 4 | 5 |

3. How **ambitious** are you? Do you work **hard**?

| 0 | 1 | 2 | 3 | 4 | 5 |

4. How **funny** are you? Can you make people laugh **easily**?

| 0 | 1 | 2 | 3 | 4 | 5 |

5. How **adventurous** are you? How **far** away from home have you traveled?

| 0 | 1 | 2 | 3 | 4 | 5 |

II. COMPARATIVE PATTERNS

A. The Basic Comparative Pattern

A comparative sentence has the following basic pattern:

| X | + | VERB | + | COMP. | + THAN + | Y |
| People in America | | live | | more extravagantly | than | many other people. |

The comparative pattern that you are most familiar with is formed on the basis of adjectives and adverbs. However, it is also possible to make a comparison on the basis of nouns and verbs, as is shown in the following examples:

BASIS FOR COMPARISON	EXAMPLE
ADJECTIVE	My car is **more expensive** than your car.
ADVERB	My car runs **more efficiently** than your car.
NOUNS	My car uses **more gas** than your car.
VERBS	My car **costs more** than your car.

SPECIAL NOTE

X and **Y** in the comparative pattern can be any form that a noun can take: noun phrase, gerund phrase, and noun clause. For example:

Plastic bags are more harmful than **paper bags.**

Riding a bicycle is much less damaging to the environment than **driving a car.**

The **Y** is often a reduced clause as in the following example:

You are more accepting of technological advances than **I (am).**

In informal spoken English, the subject pronoun **I** in the sentence above would become the object pronoun **me.**

You are more accepting of technological advances than **me.**

15.4 RAPID DRILL: *Comparative Patterns*

DIRECTIONS: Use the information below to make comparisons about Lisa and Maria and their concern about the environment. Use more than one pattern for each comparison.

EXAMPLE

LISA:
has written over 100 letters to her congress-woman about environmental protection.

MARIA:
has never written a letter about environmental protection

Lisa has written **more letters** than Maria has.
Lisa **is more concerned** about environmental protection.

MARIA	LISA
1. doesn't care about the environment	has a strong sense of responsibility
2. throws newspapers in the garbage	recycles her newspapers diligently
3. her car emits a lot of harmful fumes	her car has an efficient smog control system
4. takes 20-minute showers	is careful about the length of her showers
5. uses her car air conditioner when it's hot	never uses her car air conditioner
6. drives everywhere	tries hard to avoid driving her car

SPECIAL NOTE

It is not always necessary to state the second half of the comparison if a comparative statement is being made about an understood topic. For example, in a lecture about global warming you could hear the following comparative statement: **We will experience warmer temperatures and higher water levels.** It is understood that the comparison is between the present and the future.

15.5 WRITTEN PRACTICE: *A High-Tech World*

DIRECTIONS: The sentences below describe some recent advances in technology that have changed our lives. For each one, write two comparative sentences of different types from the chart above. The sentences should state the effect of the technological advances. The second half of the comparative pattern can be omitted since it is understood that the past is being compared with the present.

EXAMPLE

Portable phones have become common.

ADJECTIVE: We can be more mobile while we talk on the phone.

ADVERB: People can use the phone more frequently since they don't have to interrupt their activity in order to talk.

NOUN: Talking on the telephone is a less time-consuming activity since we can work and talk at the same time.

VERB: Because of the availability of portable phones, people talk on the telephone more.

1. Camcorders are used by families to record special events and the growth of their children.

_____

_____

2. Fax machines have become a popular medium for the quick transmission of information.

_____

_____

3. Personal computers have become a common addition to the household.

_____

_____

B. Substitutions, Omissions, and Additions in the Comparative Pattern

In order to avoid unnecessary repetition when making a comparison, the phrase in the second part of the comparative pattern is often substituted or omitted. The chart below shows several substitutions, omissions, and additions that can be made.

	SUBSTITUTION / OMISSION / ADDITION	**NOTES**
My van is better than	**your van.** **yours.**	▪ Substitute a possessive adjective + noun with a possessive pronoun.
This van is faster than	**that van.** **that one.** **the other van.** **the other one.** **the other.**	▪ Substitute **that** + singular noun with **that one.** ▪ Substitute **the other** + singular noun with **the other one** or **the other.**
These vans are better than	**those vans.** **those.** **the other vans.** **the other ones.** **the other two, three, four,** etc. **the others.**	▪ Omit the plural noun after **these** and **those.** ▪ Substitute **the other** + plural noun with **the other ones; the other two, three,** etc.; or **the others.**

These vans are better than	**the vans** I saw. **the ones** I saw. **those** I saw.	▪ Substitute **the** + plural noun (before an adjective clause) with **the ones,** or **those.**
This information is better than	**the information** that I have. **that** which I have.	▪ Substitute **the** + noncount noun (before an adjective clause) with **that.**
My car has better smog control than yours. My car has better smog control than yours **has.** Wayne likes air conditioning more than Jim. (Wayne likes air conditioning more than he likes Jim.) Wayne likes air conditioning more than Jim **does.** (Wayne likes air conditioning more than Jim likes it.)		▪ Add an auxiliary to the end of the sentence. ▪ Sometimes the auxiliary is necessary to avoid ambiguity. Notice the two possible meanings of the sentence on the left.

15.6 RAPID DRILL: *Substitutions, Omissions, and Additions*

DIRECTIONS: In each of the following sentences, make a substitution or omission for the idea that is repeated in the second half of the comparative pattern.

EXAMPLE

CUE: This water filter is better than **the water filter** you have.
RESPONSE: This water filter is better than **the one** you have.

1. The city council's solution to the landfill problem is more sensible than the solution proposed by private businesses.
2. The contamination from this oil spill was much worse than the contamination that resulted from the previous spill.
3. The problems we have had with water shortage this summer are less severe than the problems that we had last summer.
4. My recycling efforts have been more productive than her recycling efforts.
5. The loss presented by closing unsafe nuclear power plants is far less than the loss that can result from keeping them open.

15.7 ORAL PRACTICE: *Sentence Completion*

DIRECTIONS: Complete the following sentences with a comparative pattern using substitutions, omissions, and additions from the chart beginning on page 364.

EXAMPLE

CUE: This school . . .
RESPONSE: This school is much bigger than the one I attended before.

1. Verb tenses in English . . .
2. Your watch . . .
3. The problems we face in the future . . .

4. The education you get in a private school . . .
5. The salary that I make . . .
6. This language learning experience . . .
7. The present political system in my country . . .
8. The friends that I have now . . .

15.8   PAIRED ORAL PRACTICE: *The Cordless Phone*

DIRECTIONS: Take turns with your partner asking and answering questions about the three cordless phones described in the chart below. Use comparative patterns with substitutions, omissions, and additions.

EXAMPLE

QUESTION: How does the Nova compare to the Sonika and the Echo in price?
ANSWER: The Nova is more expensive than the other two.

	SONIKA	**ECHO**	**NOVA**
Price	$30.00	$75.00	$150.00
Reception	▪ always some static ▪ can be used 100 feet from home	▪ occasional static ▪ can be used 500 feet from home	▪ never static ▪ can be used 1 mile from home
Recharge	▪ can stay off for 15 minutes before recharging	▪ can stay off for an hour before recharging	▪ can stay off up to 5 hours before recharging
Special Features	▪ push button	▪ push button, redial, call waiting	▪ push button, redial, call waiting, goes underwater

III. FUNCTIONS OF THE COMPARATIVE

So far, you have studied how to compare one characteristic in two different people, places, or things, for example, John's life is **simpler** than Mary's life. The chart below demonstrates two more possible types of comparison.

FUNCTION OF COMPARISON	BASIS FOR COMPARISON	EXAMPLE
▪ Compare two characteristics in two different people, places, or things.	ADJECTIVE	▪ A computer is **more efficient** than a fax machine is economical.
	ADVERB	▪ A **computer records** information more quickly than a **fax machine sends** it.

	NOUN	▪ John has more **daughters** than **Mary** has **sons**.
	VERB	▪ **John sings** better than **Mary plays.**
▪ Compare two characteristics in one person, place, or thing.	ADJECTIVE	▪ John is more **ambitious** than he is **aggressive**.
	ADVERB	▪ John **thinks more quickly** than he **talks**.
	NOUN	▪ John has **more ideas** than he has **time** to implement them.
	VERB	▪ John **gives** more than he **takes**.

15.9 PAIRED ORAL PRACTICE: *Socially Responsible Investment*

DIRECTIONS: The chart below contains information about a few companies where you could invest your money. The information in the chart is related to how socially responsible the company is on the basis of different criteria. The rating scale is 1–5, which means that if the company receives a 1, it is very socially responsible about that particular issue and if it receives a 5, it is probably going to be blacklisted. Use the different types of comparatives from the preceding chart to compare the degree of social responsibility of the three companies on a variety of issues. At the end of the discussion, decide which company you would invest your money with.

EXAMPLE

City Bank does more to protect the environment than Alcon Corporation.
City Bank cares more about the environment than it does about health care.
RT Systems invests more money in affordable housing than City Bank does in environmental protection.

CRITERIA	ALCON CORP. (Develops Software)	RT SYSTEMS (Telecommunications)	CITY BANK (Large Commercial Bank)
ENVIRONMENTAL PROTECTION	5 Stopped using all chemicals that harm the ozone and recycles all paper	3 Recycles paper but still uses some harmful chemicals	3 Stopped using all harmful chemicals but doesn't recycle paper
AFFORDABLE HOUSING	4 Made major investments in affordable housing development	1 Has investments only in commercial property development	3 Has made one investment in affordable housing project, but also has commercial development

ANIMAL RIGHTS	4 Makes annual contribution to animal-protection organization	2 Owns major stock in tuna company that kills dolphins	2 Invests in ivory taken from elephants who must die for the ivory
FAIR LABOR PRACTICE	2 Doesn't offer the same benefits to male and female employees	1 Expects employees to work extra hours without pay	4 Offers bonuses for extra work and has the same benefits package for male and female employees

IV. SUPERLATIVE CONSTRUCTIONS

In the chart below are some commonly used superlative constructions. Notice that a few of them use comparative structures to express a superlative meaning.

PATTERN	EXAMPLE
1. THE (ADJ. + -ER) OF THE TWO (NOUN) 2. THE (ADJ. + -EST) OF THE THREE, FOUR, FIVE, ETC. (NOUN) These two patterns are used to **emphasize the particular person, place, or thing** possessing the characteristic to a superlative degree rather than the characteristic itself.	▪ Alcon is the **more responsible of the two** companies. ▪ RT Systems is the **most responsible of the three companies**.
3. (ADJ + -ER) THAN EVER 4. THE (ADJ. + -EST) EVER 5. (ADJ. + -ER) THAN ANY OTHER	▪ Alcon is being **more responsible than** it's **ever** been before. ▪ Alcon is being the **most responsible** it's **ever** been. ▪ Alcon is **more responsible than any other** company I've investigated.
6. THE (ADJ. + -EST) OF ALL	▪ This company is **the most responsible of all**.
7. THE ADJ + EST)[a] 8. THE (ADJ. + -EST) EVER[a]	▪ You're **the greatest!** ▪ This was **the best** dinner **ever!** (This was the best dinner I have ever eaten.)

[a]These two patterns are used in colloquial spoken English, usually for the purpose of praising someone or something.

15.10 PAIRED ORAL PRACTICE: *Superlative Constructions*

DIRECTIONS: Using the cue provided, take turns with your partner to ask each other a question. You should answer the question using one of the superlative constructions from the preceding chart.

EXAMPLE

telephone / telegraph / fax machine (efficient)
QUESTION: Which machine is the most efficient?
ANSWER: A fax machine is the most efficient of the three.

1. solar energy / nuclear energy (safe)
2. world peace / one world language / world television system (probable)
3. communities on the moon / communities under water (exciting)
4. the air today / the air in the past (polluted)
5. nuclear war / global warming / earthquakes (threat)
6. a cure for cancer / a cure for AIDS / a solution for famine (probable)

15.11 ORAL PRACTICE: *The Best Ever*

DIRECTIONS: Choose from the topics that follow, and then describe your experiences using the superlative constructions from the chart on page 368.

1. Describe three or four friends of yours on the basis of the following characteristics: reliable, interesting, smart, lazy, etc.
2. Describe three movies of one type that you've seen.
3. Compare two cars you've driven.
4. Discuss jobs that you've had or schools that you've attended.
5. Describe beautiful sights you've seen, for example, Niagara Falls, The Great Pyrimad, The Grand Canyon, etc.
6. Describe three trips you've taken.
7. Describe two gifts you've received.
8. Discuss accidents or illnesses that you've had.

GRAMMATICAL PATTERNS TWO

PREVIEW

DIRECTIONS: Below is a newspaper article written at the end of 1989, looking back on the passing decade—the 80s—and forecasting what is to come in the next decade—the 90s. Read the article, checking below for any unfamiliar vocabulary.

---

1. As the 1980s come to a close, it is important to stop and reflect for a moment on the changes that the decade has brought, and, at the same time, to look at the upcoming decade to see what is **in store** for us. The more perceptive we are, especially about the technological advances and environmental changes that we have experienced in the past decade, the better prepared we will be to progress into the next decade.

2. In the 1980s we saw more and more that man cannot continue to **wreak havoc** on the natural world without producing long-lasting, irreversible damage. We discovered in the 80s that the gases that industry and the automobile have continually **emitted** into the air are ultimately causing the temperature of the planet to rise by blocking the escape of heat into the atmosphere. This **greenhouse effect** is as frightening as the hole scientists found in the ozone layer. Also a result of synthetic chemicals, such a hole deprives us of the necessary protection from the dangerous ultraviolet light of the sun. There were other disasters similar to these two, which will hopefully force us to **take stock of** how handicapped a planet we are leaving our children. There was the deadly gas leak from a **pesticide** plant in Bhopal, India; a devastating oil spill from a ripped tanker in Alaska; and, of course, the radioactive cloud that swept Europe after an accident at the Chernobyl nuclear power plant. Looking into the 90s, unless we act, our planet will become increasingly threatened, with greenhouse gases raising temperatures, turning temperate places into tropical ones, and drying up the corn belt.

3. Contrary to expectations, as a result of the technological and scientific advances in the 80s, life often became more confusing than simple. It became possible for women to **conceive babies for childless couples,** but later they found themselves in **custody battles** because they couldn't bear to give up the child. **Embryos** were frozen for safekeeping, but more custody battles arose when the parents of such embryos decided to divorce. However, life did become simpler and more exciting in many ways as more machines and **gadgets** such as portable phones, camcorders, fax machines, and computers helped to cut down on time and energy spent in everyday activities, and made information more **accessible**.

4. Some **futurists** predict that in the 90s, humans will live on the moon and will learn how to build and **launch planets**. We may also see a world television system, pizza delivery in space, and a natural form of sugar that doesn't have any calories. Cars will be as safe for the environment as they are for passengers since they'll be solar powered to prevent pollution and computer powered to prevent accidents.

VOCABULARY

in store: to be expected in the future
wreak havoc: cause a lot of destruction
emitted: sent out into the air, especially when referring to gas or odors

greenhouse effect: too much carbon dioxide rises and heats up the atmosphere causing global temperatures to rise

take stock of: make an assessment or conclusion about something

pesticide: chemicals usually used on crops of growing fruits and vegetables to prevent insects from eating them

conceive babies for childless couples: (surrogate mothers) some women have received money to be artificially inseminated, carry, and deliver a baby for a couple who can't have children

custody battles: a fight that parents undertake to have the legal right to a child

embryos: the form of human life up to the third month after conception

gadgets: little machines or devices that have a very specific purpose

accessible: available

futurists: people who predict the changes that will come in the future

launch planets: design a planet here on earth and send it into space

DISCUSSION

What are some of the predictions made in the article? Which do you agree with? What other predictions would you make about the future?

GRAMMAR CONSIDERATIONS: FOCUS

DIRECTIONS: Look at the article in the preview to find examples of the following generalizations. Write the examples on the lines provided.

1. The author compares the greenhouse effect and the hole in the ozone layer. Find that sentence in paragraph 2. What structure is used? What is the relationship between the two? Can you find a similar structure in paragraph 4?

2. In the first sentence of paragraph 1 what words does the author use to emphasize the step-by-step change? Can you find a word in the last sentence of paragraph 2 that is used for the same emphasis?

_____

3. The second sentence in paragraph 2 uses a comparative pattern to express a conditional relationship. Rewrite the sentence, beginning with **if**.

If_____

_____

4. Underline the words in the following sentence that are used to make a comparison. Can you think of any other words that could replace these words? What is the opposite of these words?

There were other disasters similar to these two, which will hopefully force us to take stock of how handicapped a planet we are leaving our children.

_____

I. USING *AS . . . AS* FOR EQUAL COMPARATIVE CONSTRUCTIONS

When a comparison is based on two equal qualities or characteristics, the following patterns are used.

BASIS FOR COMPARISON	EQUAL RELATIONSHIP (SAME)	UNEQUAL RELATIONSHIP (NOT THE SAME)
ADJECTIVE AS + ADJ. + AS AS + ADJ. + NOUN + AS	▪ John is **as tall as** Mary. ▪ John is **as tall a person as** Mary.	▪ John is **not as tall as** Mary. (Mary is taller than John.) ▪ John is **not as tall a person as** Mary.
ADVERB AS + ADV. + AS	▪ John runs **as fast as** Mary.	▪ John does **not run as fast as** Mary. (Mary runs faster than John.)
NOUNS AS + MUCH / MANY / LITTLE / FEW **VERBS** AS + MUCH / LITTLE + AS	▪ John makes **as much money as** Mary. ▪ John works **as much as** Mary.	▪ John does **not make as much money as** Mary. (Mary makes more money than John.) ▪ John does **not work as much as** Mary. (Mary works more than John.)

15.12   RAPID DRILL: *As . . . As*

DIRECTIONS: Compare life in the future with life in the present, using **as . . . as** and the cues below. Make either a positive or negative statement.

EXAMPLE

people / work / hard
People will work as hard as they do now.

1. be / international conflict
2. computers / necessary
3. cars / damaging to the environment
4. people / travel
5. English language / popular
6. Americans / compete / agressively
7. young people / like computer games
8. pollution / problem

15.13   EXERCISE: *The End is Coming*

DIRECTIONS: Read the cartoon below and complete the following.

1. Replace **sooner** with the following words: **fast, quick, slow.**
2. Change the sentence in the cartoon to the negative.

© 1989 United Feature Syndicate, Inc.

12-30 BRAD ANDERSON

Reprinted by permission of United Media.

"It's coming sooner than I expected..."

SPECIAL NOTE

Sometimes **so...as** is used in this construction when the two items being compared are unequal. For example: This computer is not **so efficient as** the other one.

15.14 WRITTEN PARAPHRASE: *The Earthling and the Extraterrestrial*

DIRECTIONS: It is the year 2030. An extraterrestrial has been saved from a spaceship that landed on earth. Below are some sentences making comparisons about the extraterrestrial and an earthling. Paraphrase each pair of sentences by using the **as...as** comparative pattern.

EXAMPLE

The earthling is six feet tall. The extraterrestrial is seven feet tall.
The earthling is not as tall as the extraterrestrial.

1. The extraterrestrial's planet has four seasons. Earth has four seasons.

   _____

2. The earthling is a little anxious to help the extraterrestrial return home. The earthling is very eager to learn about the extraterrestrial's planet.

   _____

3. The earthling sleeps about eight hours every night. The extraterrestrial only sleeps four hours.

   _____

4. The extraterrestrial is hungry every three hours. The earthling is hungry every three hours.

   _____

5. The earthling has only one solution for the greenhouse effect on earth. The extraterrestrial has a few solutions for the greenhouse effect on earth.

_____

6. There is a very advanced recycling system on the extraterrestrial's planet. Earth has a primitive recycling system.

_____

15.15   PAIRED PRACTICE: _How Equal Are We?_

DIRECTIONS: Interview your partner about the state of technology in his / her country. Then write five statements using the **as . . . as** pattern to express the equality or inequality of your two countries. After you have written the statements, discuss the advantages and disadvantages of the technological innovation. Here are some suggestions for topics.

Phone system   Electronic equipment
Computer use   Transportation
Household appliances   Space exploration

EXAMPLE

Portable phones aren't as popular in my country as they are in my partner's country.

1. _____

2. _____

3. _____

4. _____

II. CONDITIONAL COMPARATIVE CONSTRUCTIONS

The comparative pattern below is used to express a conditional relationship between the two things being compared. Notice how the meaning of the comparative sentence corresponds to that of the conditional sentence.

PATTERN	THE + (COMPARATIVE) + SUBJ. + VERB + OBJ. / COMPLEMENT, THE + (COMPARATIVE) + SUBJ. + VERB
EXAMPLE	The more relaxed John is, the more productive he is.
CONDITIONAL	If John is relaxed, he is productive.
EXAMPLE	The more carefully I take an exam, the better chance I have of passing.
CONDITIONAL	If I take an exam carefully, I have a better chance of passing.

15.16 WRITTEN EXERCISE: *Conditional Comparative Constructions*

DIRECTIONS: Read the following conditional sentences and change each to a comparative construction.

1. If we release more chloroflourocarbons into the atmosphere, the hole in the ozone layer will get bigger.

   _____

2. If we wait longer to actively recycle waste, our landfill problems will get worse.

   _____

3. If we are less careful about industrial waste, our waters will become more polluted.

   _____

4. If we make more intelligent decisions about our future, our future will be better.

   _____

5. If we think more responsibly, we will act more cautiously.

   _____

15.17 ORAL PRACTICE: *Your Future*

DIRECTIONS: Take turns with your partner choosing from the statements below to discuss what you would like for the future of your children. When one student makes a statement, the partner should ask, "Why?" The student who made the statement should explain with a conditional comparative sentence.

EXAMPLE

STUDENT A: I want my children to read a lot.
STUDENT B: Why?
STUDENT A: Because the more they read, the more knowledgeable they'll be.

1. I hope they (make a lot of friends, earn a lot of money, find a lot of opportunities, have a lot of experiences, speak many languages, see many countries).
2. I want them to (live peacefully, act cautiously, make decisions wisely).
3. I want them to be (ambitious, self-confident, creative, honest, healthy).
4. I don't want them to (get bad grades in school, get into trouble, have bad luck, lie to me).
5. I don't want them to be (lazy, dishonest, unsuccessful, sick).

15.18 ORAL INTERVIEW: *The Future of Your Country*

DIRECTIONS: Interview an English-speaking person about the future of the country you are presently living in. Ask for three ways the country can be improved in the future. For each statement your respondent makes, ask for a reason why that will make the country better. Record your responses below.

EXAMPLE

STATEMENT:　People in my country should be less wasteful.
REASON:　There will be a more even distribution of goods.

1. STATEMENT: _____

　　　REASON: _____

2. STATEMENT: _____

　　　REASON _____

3. STATEMENT: _____

　　　REASON: _____

15.19　WRITTEN RESPONSE

DIRECTIONS: Write a conditional comparative sentence for each statement and reason you were given by your respondent in the interview.

EXAMPLE

(based on example above)
The less wasteful people are, the more even the distribution of goods will be.

1. _____

2. _____

3. _____

III. EXPRESSING A PROGRESSIVE CHANGE OF STATE

The following chart lists some words and expressions that are used to express a progressive change of state, which is very closely related to the comparative.

WORD / EXPRESSION	EXAMPLE
REPETITION OF THE COMPARATIVE **more and more** **bigger and bigger**	**More and more** countries are realizing that we are all part of one world community.
ADVERBS **increasingly** **progressively**	We are becoming **increasingly** aware of the ways we can work together as a world community.

VERBS	
increase (= becoming more) **decrease** (= become less) **worsen** (= become worse) **improve** (= become better) **lessen** (= become less)	The need to work together is **increasing.**
ADJECTIVES -ing forms of the above verbs	There is an **increasing** need to work together as a world community to prevent destruction of the planet.

See the chapter on progressive verb tenses for more information.

15.20 RAPID DRILL: *Oral Paraphrase*

DIRECTIONS: Paraphrase each statement below with one of the words or expressions from the preceding chart to express a progressive change of state.

1. The pollution is getting worse.
2. Prices are getting higher every day.
3. Our chances for saving our planet are quickly going down.
4. People are becoming more involved in positive action to save the environment.
5. The acid rain problem is becoming very dangerous.
6. There are many more viruses because of the bacteria in the air.
7. There is a need for greater community involvement in the recycling program.

15.21 WRITTEN PARAPHRASE: *Progressive Change of State*

DIRECTIONS: Below are some suggestions for implementing the concept of voluntary simplicity, the plan for simplifying our lives in the future. Paraphrase each suggestion by using a word or expression from the preceding chart to express a progressive change of state.

EXAMPLE

There must be moderation of the overall level of consumption in developed nations.
There must be a decreasing amount of consumption in developed nations.

1. There should be more extensive use of electronic communication as a substitute for indiscriminate expensive physical travel.

   _____

2. We should see a mounting consumer revolution as people boycott companies whose policies are unethical with regard to the environment.

   _____

3. There should be massive investments in cleaning up the environment.

   _____

4. We should force a decline in agribusiness, with its heavy reliance on petrochemicals, coupled with a rebirth of family farming using organic modes of food production.

_____

5. We should create a redefinition of the good life—an overall lowering of material expectations, with an increase in appreciation of the nonmaterial aspects of life.

_____

IV. OTHER WORDS USED IN COMPARATIVE CONSTRUCTIONS

The following words and expressions are often used to express comparative relationships.

WORD EXPRESSION	EXAMPLE	NOTES
SIMILAR TO, LIKE, DIFFERENT FROM, THE SAME AS	My T.V. is **similar to** his.	▪ used with the verb **be**
SIMILAR, DIFFERENT, THE SAME, ALIKE	Mike and Susan have **similar** stereos. Their stereos are **similar.**	▪ used as an adjective
LIKE, COMPARED TO	**Like** your computer, mine has an internal hard disk drive.	▪ used as a preposition before a noun that is being compared
THE DIFFERENCE BETWEEN	What is **the difference between** these two radios? The **difference between** the two radios is the price.	▪ often used in a question asking for a comparison ▪ when used in a statement is followed by a noun phrase and the verb **be**
WHILE, WHEREAS	**While** your computer is compatible with two other computers, mine is compatible with none.	▪ used as a subordinating conjunction
DIFFER (FROM) COMPARE (TO)	How does this microwave **differ from** that one? How do the two **differ?**	▪ verbs used to make a comparison

15.22 FILL IN THE BLANKS: _Comparative Expressions_

DIRECTIONS: The dialogue below takes place in a robot store in the year 2010. Fill in the blanks with an appropriate expression from the chart above.

SALESPERSON: May I help you?

CUSTOMER: Yes, I'm looking for a robot to do my housework, _____

the one my friend has.

SALESPERSON: I see; well, could you give me a little more information? Each robot we carry is

_____ .

CUSTOMER: The one my friend has looks _____ the one over there

holding the broom and dustpan. Oh yes, and it has the same name, Robo-Clean. I'm sure

they're _____ .

SALESPERSON: Well, I don't know if you've seen any others, but _____

Robo-Clean, this one over here, Mr. Domestic, does windows, and it whistles while it

works.

CUSTOMER: Oh, really? How does Mr. Domestic _____ Robo-Clean in

thoroughness?

SALESPERSON: That's a very good question! _____ Mr. Domestic will

get the dust out of every corner in your house, Robo-Clean will sweep the dust under the

rug.

15.23 WRITTEN EXERCISE: *Similarities and Differences*

DIRECTIONS: For each pair of electronic devices below, write one sentence stating the similarity and one sentence stating the difference between the two devices.

EXAMPLE

TELEPHONE / FAX MACHINE

SIMILARITY: A telephone and a fax machine are alike since they both use telephone cables to operate and the operator of either needs to input a telephone number.

DIFFERENCE: A fax machine is different from a telephone in that it transmits the written word whereas a telephone transmits the human voice.

1. AUDIO TAPE RECORDER / VIDEOCASSETTE RECORDER

    SIMILARITY: _____

    DIFFERENCE: _____

2. 35 MM CAMERA / CAMCORDER

    SIMILARITY: _____

    DIFFERENCE: _____

3. RECORD / COMPACT DISC

    SIMILARITY: _____

    DIFFERENCE: _____

4. HAND-HELD PERSONAL ORGANIZERS / COMPUTERS

    SIMILARITY: _____

    DIFFERENCE: _____

15.24 ORAL PRACTICE

DIRECTIONS: Imagine what a house of the future will look like and compare it to the houses of today. Discuss the design of the house, kitchen appliances, entertainment equipment, methods of cleaning, etc. Take into consideration changes in the house that will protect the environment as well as make our lives simpler. Use the comparative expressions from the chart on page 379.

EXAMPLE

Compared to the house of today, a future house will be designed to be energy efficient with many windows and skylights to let in the light and heat of the sun.

V. SPECIAL PROBLEMS WITH THE COMPARATIVE

PROBLEM	EXPLANATION
USING A DOUBLE COMPARATIVE [INCORRECT: Computers are **more better** than typewriters.] CORRECT: Computers are **better** than typewriters.	Don't add **more** to an adjective or adverb that is already in its comparative or superlative form.
REPLACING THAN [INCORRECT: The 90s will be better **from** the 80s.] CORRECT: The 90s will be better **than** the 80s.	Use **than** in the comparative pattern.
ATTACHING A REGULAR ENDING TO AN IRREGULAR FORM [INCORRECT: The pollution here **is badder** than in my city.] CORRECT: The pollution here is **worse** than in my city.	Use the correct irregular forms instead of a regular ending.
USING **MORE** FOR AN ADJECTIVE THAT REQUIRES AN **-ER** or **-EST** ENDING [INCORRECT: We will have **more big** problems in the future.] CORRECT: We will have **bigger** problems in the future.	Don't use **more** if you can use the **-er** and **-est** endings.
PLACING **MORE** AFTER THE ADJECTIVE OR ADVERB [INCORRECT: Janet is intelligent **more** than Pete.] CORRECT: Janet is **more** intelligent than Pete.	Place **more** before the adjective or adverb.

■ 15.25 ERROR ANALYSIS: *Comparative Structures*

DIRECTIONS: Find any error in the use of comparative constructions in the following sentences. Correct the errors clearly above the sentences.

1. Pollution control is more better now than it was 10 years ago.

2. This machine is alike a machine I saw in a science fiction movie 10 years ago.

3. This city has the worstest recycling program I've ever seen.

4. The simpler our lives become the planet will survive longer.

5. In the future, houses will be functional more than they are now.

6. People are becoming involved in saving the environment quicker than we had ever hoped.

7. The cars of the future will not look the same than the ones we drive today.

8. The day when we see smog-free cities is more far in the future than we think.

9. Nuclear energy poses a much bigger threat from solar energy does.

10. Hopefully, the acid rain problem won't get more worse in the future.

11. The technological progress in this country is the same the other countries.

═══════ ANALYSIS OF AN AUTHENTIC TEXT ═══════

A UNION FOR PEACE AND SURVIVAL
by Dawna Nolan

1. Earth. One small planet in a seemingly infinite universe. Ever since the first photos of our earth as it looks from space captured the imaginations of people around the world, the reality of living in a global village has seemed much more immediate.

2. And since the time when Canadian educator Marshal McLuhan first **coined the term**, the concept of all of humanity belonging to a *global village* has become more of a technological reality as well. Scientific advances from jet travel to nuclear weaponry to telecommunications have lessened the distances between peoples making us speedily aware of, and affected by, events in the far corners of the earth.

3. . . . There are many organized groups working for peace, human rights, and the environment who also provide the means for differences to be resolved and similarities shared. An innovative, valuable tool for them is a global computer network called PeaceNet. This computer-based communication system helps groups such as Greenpeace, Global Link, the Christic Institute, and many others to communicate and cooperate more effectively and efficiently.

4. One of these groups, Beyond War, based in Palo Alto, California, is built on **the premise** that war is obsolete in the nuclear age. Its many educational projects are designed to raise public awareness of the value of **conflict resolution.** The annual Beyond War Awards is one such project, and this year's theme is Building Our Common Future.

5. **Grassroots groups** have also been active in promoting global peace and survival. For example, the Boise Peace **Quilt** Project was begun in 1981 by two Idaho women who wished to make a concrete statement in support of world peace. They and 40 other people made a quilt and sent it to the Soviet Union as a **gesture** of friendship. Since then, the endeavor has involved **scores** of men, women, and children and has produced more than a dozen quilts.

6. One of the quilts, the National Peace Quilt, is a vibrant red, white, and blue, and is made up of one square for each of the 50 states. The intent is to have every U.S. senator spend one night sleeping under this quilt. Said Senator Spark Matsunaga of Hawaii, "I swear I woke with the biggest smile my face has ever worn. I realized the power of the human spirit, represented by thousands of women and children from the 50 states who have united to create an inspirational symbol for the political leaders of this great nation to direct it towards unseen greatness, if not plain survival."

VOCABULARY

coined the term: to make a word or expression familiar to people when it was previously unknown or unfamilar

the premise: the understanding

conflict resolution: a systematic method of solving problems peacefully

grassroots groups: average people who work together to promote change

quilt: a large bed covering made up of small individual squares of material; each square can have a picture or symbol sewn into it

gesture: symbol

scores: a large number of

COMPREHENSION QUESTIONS

1. What do we mean by the concept of *global village*?
2. What is the benefit of the global computer network, PeaceNet?

GRAMMATICAL ANALYSIS

1. Senator Matsunuga said that he woke with the biggest smile his face has ever worn. What did he mean? What is another way he could have described the way he felt when he woke in the morning?
2. Paragraph 1 ends with the words "much more immediate." How could you finish the comparative pattern? (. . . much more immediate than . . . ?)
3. Write three sentences using comparative structures to describe the effect that this quilt project must have had on the people involved.

_____

_____

_____

══════ COMPOSITION TOPICS ══════

In this chapter you have mastered the use of a variety of comparative constructions. Use what you have learned to write a composition about one of the following topics.

1. Compare life in your country when you were growing up with life in the present. Focus especially on technological advances and environmental changes.
2. In the preceding text, Dawna Nolan mentions that the work of one group is based on the premise that war is obsolete. What is necessary in order to make war obsolete? How must we change our behavior individually and globally?
3. Write an essay with your own recommendations for what the average person can do to improve the future of our children.

INDEX